TOO BIG TO JAIL

TOO BIG TO JAIL

How Prosecutors Compromise with Corporations

BRANDON L. GARRETT

The Belknap Press of
Harvard University Press
Cambridge, Massachusetts
London, England
2014

First Printing

Library of Congress Cataloging-in-Publication Data
Garrett, Brandon, author.
Too big to jail : how prosecutors compromise with corporations / Brandon L. Garrett.
pages cm
Includes bibliographical references and index.
ISBN 978-0-674-36831-6 (hardcover : alk. paper)
1. Corporation law—United States—Criminal provisions.   2. Tort liability of
corporations—United States.   3. Corporate governance—Law and legislation—United
States.   4. Corporations—Corrupt practices—United States.   5. Criminal liability of
juristic persons—United States.   6. Prosecution—United States.   I. Title.
KF1301.A2G37 2014
345.73'0268—dc23   2014013351

To Kerry

CONTENTS

Abbreviations ix

1. United States vs. Goliath 1
2. The Company in the Courtroom 19
3. What Happens to a Prosecution Deferred? 45
4. The Ostriches 81
5. The Victims 117
6. The Carrot and the Stick 147
7. Enter the Monitors 172
8. The Constitutional Rights of Corporations 196
9. Foreign Corporate Criminals 218
10. The Future of Corporate Prosecutions 250

Appendix 291
Notes 307
Acknowledgments 357
Index 361

ABBREVIATIONS

ABA	American Bar Association
CEO	Chief Executive Officer
CFO	Chief Financial Officer
CFTC	Commodities Futures Trading Commission
DOJ	Department of Justice
DPA	Deferred prosecution agreement
ENRD	Environment and Natural Resources Division
EPA	Environmental Protection Agency
FBI	Federal Bureau of Investigation
FCPA	Foreign Corrupt Practices Act
FDA	Food and Drug Administration
FDCA	Food, Drug, and Cosmetics Act
FIRREA	Financial Institutions Reform, Recovery, and Enforcement Act
GAO	General Accountability Office
HHS-OIG	Department of Health and Human Services Office of Inspector General
IRS	Internal Revenue Service
LIBOR	London InterBank Offered Rate
NPA	Non-prosecution agreement
OCC	Office of the Comptroller of the Currency
OSHA	Occupational Safety and Health Administration
SEC	Securities and Exchange Commission

TOO BIG TO JAIL

⮕ 1 ⮕

United States vs. Goliath

"I know what this is about. I have been expecting you."[1]

It was not until 2006 that The Banker finally got the knock on his door. Six police officers and a prosecutor were standing there with an arrest warrant.

He later recalled, "I was a true Siemens man, for sure. I was known as the keeper of the slush fund. We all knew what we were doing was illegal." The Banker was in charge of just some of the multinational bribery operations at Siemens Aktiengesellschaft, a German multinational firm, ranked in the top 50 of the Fortune Global 500 list of the world's largest corporations. It has more than 400,000 employees in 190 countries and makes everything from trains to electrical power plants to home coffeemakers. Among its many activities was paying more than a billion dollars in bribes around the world to secure lucrative business from foreign governments. Now Siemens would be prosecuted, and not just in Germany but also in the United States.

This book is the first to take a close look at what happens when a company is prosecuted in the United States. A corporate prosecution is like a battle between David and Goliath. One would normally assume that federal prosecutors play the role of Goliath. They wield incredible power, with the ability to hold a corporation liable for a crime by even a single employee and the benefit of expansive federal criminal laws. It is hard to think of federal prosecutors as the little guy in any fight. Yet they may play the role of David when up against the largest and most powerful corporations in the world.

Some companies are not just "too big to fail" but also "too big to jail": they are considered to be so valuable to the economy that prosecutors may not hold them accountable for their crimes. The expression "too big to jail" has mostly been used to refer to failures to prosecute Wall Street banks. A dismayed reaction to the lack of prosecutions after the last financial crisis is understandable, but to see why corporations may escape prosecution, it is important to understand exactly how a company can be prosecuted for a crime and the many practical challenges involved. The very idea that a corporation can be prosecuted for an employee's crime seems odd on its face, and even among criminal lawyers, the topic of corporate crime had long been obscure. Over the past decade, corporate crime exploded in importance—not only because of greater public interest in accountability but also because prosecutors transformed their approach to targeting corporations.

In this book, I present data collected from more than a decade of cases to show what really happens when prosecutors pursue corporate criminals. I examine the terms of the deals that prosecutors now negotiate with companies, how prosecutors fine companies to punish them, the changes companies must make to prevent future crimes, and whether prosecutors pursue individual employees. The current approach to corporate prosecutions raises "too big to jail" concerns that extend beyond Wall Street banks to the cases brought against a wide range of companies. I argue that prosecutors fail to effectively punish the most serious corporate crimes. Still more troubling is that not enough is known about how to hold complex organizations accountable; prosecutors exacerbate that problem by settling corporate prosecutions without much transparency. My main goal in exploring the hidden world of corporate prosecutions is to encourage more public attention to the problem of punishing corporate crime. To go deeper inside the decision making of prosecutors and companies, in each chapter not only do I present data describing the larger patterns in corporate prosecutions and non-prosecutions, but I also tell the stories of how particular companies such as Siemens fared. The Siemens story is an important one to begin with: the case broke all records for the biggest prosecution for foreign bribery.

How were the Siemens bribes paid? The Banker did not pay them himself. True to his nickname, he instead "organized the cash" by transferring funds from anonymous bank accounts in Switzerland and Lichtenstein or using dummy corporations to hide where the money was coming from and where it was going. He explained how he carried the cash undetected: "For a million euros, you don't need a big suitcase because the bills aren't very big. A briefcase is enough—200,000 euros isn't so much that you couldn't carry it in your coat pocket."[2] In the countries where Siemens was pursuing lucrative government contracts—whether it was Greece, Nigeria, Argentina, or Bangladesh—executives hired "consultants" to help them "win" the government contracts. The consultants received a fee and personally delivered the bribes to government officials.

Siemens paid bribes around the world—more than a billion dollars from 2002 to 2007. The Banker's division dealt with telecommunications and had a bribery budget of $40–50 million a year. He recalled how the telecom unit was kept "alive" by bribes and how other major divisions at Siemens operated this way. Bribery was pervasive and "common knowledge."

Bribing foreign government officials is a crime in Germany, the United States, and many other countries. In 2008, prosecutors in Germany charged The Banker with corruption, leading to a conviction, two years' probation, and a $170,000 fine.[3] He received leniency on account of his cooperation with the authorities. When he later spoke to journalists, he expressed disappointment that Siemens treated him like an "outsider" and gave him a "kick in the pants" while people at the top were not held accountable. "I would never have thought I'd go to jail for my company," he later said. "Sure, we joked about it, but we thought if our actions ever came to light, we'd all go together and there would be enough people to play a game of cards."[4]

The controversy surrounding this global bribery scheme would eventually bring in prosecutors around the world, notably those in the United States. They would wield a powerful new approach to targeting corporations, one I explore throughout this book. In the Siemens case, was The Banker right that underlings would be the only ones held accountable, or would the storm reach the summit—the top executives or the company itself?

No Soul to Be Damned, No Body to Kick

How exactly are corporations convicted of a crime? The word *corporation* comes from *corpus*, the Latin word for "body." A corporation may be a body, but it is a collective body that can act only through its employees. As the British lord chancellor Edward Thurlow reportedly remarked in the late eighteenth century, corporations have "no soul to be damned, no body to kick."[5] Corporate persons obviously cannot be imprisoned. However, companies can face potentially severe and even lethal consequences, even if in theory they can be "immortal." They can be forced to pay debilitating fines or suffer harm to their reputation. When convicted they can lose the government licenses that make doing business possible; for example, a company can be suspended or even barred from entering into contracts with the federal government.

The federal rule for corporate criminal liability is powerful and long-standing. In its 1909 decision in *New York Central & Hudson River Railroad v. United States*, the Supreme Court held that a corporation could be consti-tutionally prosecuted for a federal crime under a broad rule.[6] The rule is simple: an organization can be convicted based on the criminal conduct of a single employee. That standard comes from a rule called the master-servant rule or respondeat superior—"let the master answer" in Latin—which makes the master responsible for the servant's acts. Under that rule, an em-ployer was responsible for an employee's wrongs if those wrongs were com-mitted in the scope of employment and at least in part to benefit the em-ployer. As the Court suggested in *New York Central*, the master or corporation may be in the best position to make sure employees are properly supervised to prevent lawbreaking. The Court emphasized "the interest of public pol-icy," since giving companies "immunity" from criminal prosecution would make it hard to "effectually" prevent "abuses."[7] Rather than spend time on theoretical questions about when and whether corporations should consti-tute legal persons, I focus on whether corporate prosecutions are actually effective in preventing crime. Many have debated corporate personhood, in-cluding in response to the Court's ruling in *Citizens United v. Federal Election Commission* (2010) that the First Amendment protects corporations against regulation of election spending.[8] To understand corporate prosecutions, though, what matters is not *Citizens United* but rather the strict master-servant rule from the less well-known *New York Central* case.

Today, a corporation is a "person" under federal law, as are other types of business organizations. The very first section of the U.S. Code, with defini-tions that apply to all federal laws, including those dealing with crimes, de-fines a person to include "corporations, companies, associations, firms, part-nerships, societies, and joint stock companies, as well as individuals."[9] As a result, federal prosecutions may be brought against any type of organization. The *U.S. Sentencing Commission Guidelines Manual* uses the word *organiza-tion* because the guidelines cover criminal sentences for all kinds of companies, including partnerships not formally incorporated by a state. Prosecutors convict giant multinational corporations such as Siemens, large domestic public corporations with millions of shareholders, and mom-and-pop companies with just a few owners or only one owner.

In theory, a corporation can be prosecuted for just about any crime that an individual can be prosecuted for (except for crimes with heightened intent, such as homicide). In practice, corporations are prosecuted for crimes likely to take place in a business setting, such as accounting fraud, banking fraud, environmental violations, foreign bribery, money laundering, price fixing, securities fraud, and wire fraud. Important corporate prosecutions are chiefly brought by federal prosecutors, in contrast to prosecutions of smaller-scale corporate crimes or prosecutions of individuals, which are overwhelmingly brought at the local level.[10]

Data on Corporate Prosecutions

Over the past decade, there has been an increase in the size and importance of federal prosecutions of corporations, though not in the number of cases brought. One of my goals in writing this book was to uncover and present data explaining how corporations are actually prosecuted. As Figure 1.1 illustrates, the data that I have gathered show a large spike in corporate criminal fines over the past few years.

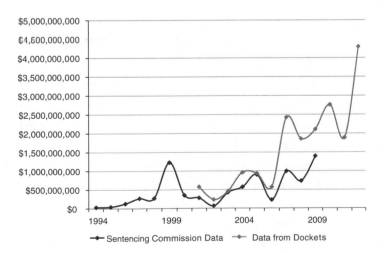

Figure 1.1 Total Criminal Fines for Organizations, 1994–2012

In the past, given the modest sentences for companies, it was often not worth the effort to prosecute them.[11] Corporate fines grew after 1991, when the U.S. Sentencing Commission, a group convened by Congress to write rules for sentencing federal criminals, adopted the first sentencing guidelines specifically designed for corporations. More resources were also devoted to corporate prosecutions in response to Enron and other corporate scandals that shook the United States in the early 2000s, prompting the Department of Justice to form an Enron Task Force and later a Corporate Fraud Task Force (now called the Financial Fraud Enforcement Task Force).[12] Figure 1.1 shows total fines for the approximately 3,500 companies convicted from 1994 to 2009. It includes data from the Sentencing Commission for the earlier period, but from 2001 to 2012 the more dramatic rise in fines is shown in the data that I collected by hand from more than 2,250 court dockets and corporate prosecution agreements.

To understand what has really changed, we need to look behind the aggregate data displayed in Figure 1.1. The bulk of those corporate fines were actually paid in a small number of blockbuster cases, such as the Siemens case. For example, the large spike in 2009 is because the pharmaceutical giant Pfizer paid a then-record fine of nearly $1.2 billion. That single fine made up about half of the total for that year. Other massive antitrust cases, foreign bribery cases, and illegal pharmaceutical sales cases involve fines in the hundreds of millions. There is still more about corporate prosecutions that those totals do not capture. The criminal fines are only a fraction of the costs imposed on companies. For example, as part of criminal settlements, companies were required to pay billions more to victims of fraud. Also not reflected in the fines are structural reforms that prosecutors require companies to adopt to prevent future crimes.

What is clear from the reported activity of prosecutors is that over the past decade they have embraced a new approach: deferred prosecution agreements. Prosecutors enter agreements that allow the company to avoid a conviction but which impose fines, aim to reshape corporate governance, and bring independent monitors into the boardroom. The rise of such deferred prosecution agreements, and non-prosecution agreements, in which no criminal case is even filed, means that the official Sentencing Commission statistics on corporate convictions, as shown in Figure 1.1, fail to capture many of the most important cases. Corporate fines are up, but the big story of the twenty-first century is not corporate fines or convictions but prosecutors changing the ways that corporations are managed. Prosecutors now try to rehabilitate a company by helping it to put systems in place to detect and prevent crime among its employees and, more broadly, to foster a culture of ethics and integrity inside the company. This represents an ambitious new approach to governance in which federal prosecutors help reshape the policies and culture of entire institutions, much as federal judges oversaw school desegregation and prison reform in the heyday of the civil rights era in the 1960s and 1970s.

What initially attracted me to studying these corporate agreements with prosecutors was that, as a former civil rights lawyer, I was surprised to see prosecutors taking on for themselves the hard work of changing institutions. I have spent years researching wrongful convictions and DNA exonerations in individual criminal cases, in which errors may implicate larger problems in our criminal justice system. I turned my attention to the very different world of corporate prosecutions because a single prosecution of a company such as Siemens can have enormous repercussions in the U.S. and the global economy, particularly since other industry actors will be watching and nervous about whether they might be next. I quickly learned, however, that there is not much information out there about when or how corporations are prosecuted.

There is no official registry for corporate offenders, nor is there an official list of deferred prosecution and non-prosecution agreements by federal prosecutors. I decided to create these resources. Over the years, with invaluable help from the UVA Law Library, I created a database with information on every federal deferred prosecution or non-prosecution agreement with a company. In one place or another, this information was publicly available, but I wanted to put it together in order to learn who these firms were, what they did, what they were convicted of, and how they were punished.

There have been more than 250 such prosecution agreements entered over the past decade. I made this database available online as a public resource, and it remains the most authoritative and complete source.[13] I then amassed a second and much larger archive of more than 2,000 federal corporate convictions, mostly guilty pleas by corporations, and placed these data online as well.[14] These data have real limitations; although prosecutors pound their chests when bringing the largest corporations to justice, in many other cases no charges are brought. We have no way to know how often prosecutors decline to pursue charges against corporations—they do not usually make those decisions public—except when they enter non-prosecution agreements. We do not know how often corporations commit crimes, as the government does not keep data on corporate crime, which is hard to detect and to define.

More than 250 federal prosecutions since 2001 have involved large public corporations. These are the biggest criminal defendants imaginable. Prosecutors have taken on the likes of AIG, Bristol-Myers Squibb, BP, Google, HealthSouth, JPMorgan, KPMG, Merrill Lynch, Monsanto, and Pfizer. Such Fortune 500 firms can and do mobilize astonishing resources in their defense. The Siemens case illustrates the titanic scale of the power plays at work in federal corporate prosecutions, making them unlike anything else in criminal justice.

Convicting Siemens

The story of the prosecution of one of the world's biggest corporations began in one of the world's smallest countries—the principality of Lichtenstein. In early 2003, a bank in Lichtenstein owned by the royal family was having auditors review its records. The bank auditors noticed something strange: millions of euros were bouncing around between Panama, Lichtenstein, and the British Virgin Islands. The bank secrecy laws in Lichtenstein, like those in Switzerland, make banks an attractive place for some people to keep money. Auditors were on the lookout for unusual transactions that might be the work of terrorists or other criminals trying to take advantage of this secrecy to engage in money laundering. They noticed odd transactions between offshore companies, including large sums going into an account of an offshore firm called Martha Overseas Corp. That company was incorporated in Panama, but it was controlled by an executive of Siemens working in Greece—and the money going into the account was coming from another offshore company, one based in the British Virgin Islands and controlled by another executive of Siemens.

The bank informed Siemens of this problem in 2004 and began to block these money transfers. They also notified bank regulators in Germany and Switzerland, who in turn contacted regulators in Austria and Italy. Two years later, German police appeared on The Banker's doorstep in Munich and seized documents from more than thirty Siemens offices.[15]

The case of Siemens (and three of its subsidiaries in Argentina, Venezuela, and Bangladesh) became a truly global prosecution. Siemens had paid more than $1.4 billion in bribes between 2002 and 2007 to government officials in sixty-five countries in Asia, Africa, Europe, the Middle East, and South America. All sorts of major public works projects were implicated. The focus of the U.S. case against Siemens was kickbacks paid under the U.N. oil-for-food program in Iraq, in which Siemens paid $1.7 million in return for forty-two contracts with $80 million in revenue and over $38 million in profits.[16]

At first glance, the Siemens scandal might seem to be a problem for German prosecutors, not American ones. After all, why would bribes paid to foreign officials by a German company, already under investigation in Germany, trouble U.S. prosecutors? But many companies, Siemens included, do business in the United States. Bribe transactions may pass through U.S. wires. Even more important, Siemens is a public corporation with stock listed on the New York Stock Exchange (NYSE), giving U.S. prosecutors jurisdiction. The U.S. Department of Justice (DOJ) and the U.S. Securities and Exchange Commission (SEC), which regulates companies with publicly listed stock, both have authority over a firm such as Siemens.

It would be U.S. prosecutors who seized the lead in this multinational case and collected the lion's share of the fines. The DOJ and the SEC began to investigate upon hearing of the raids; both handle matters related to foreign bribery. When a company such as Siemens has ties in the United States, it falls under a law called the Foreign Corrupt Practices Act (FCPA). The FCPA makes it a violation to bribe foreign officials, to keep inaccurate books and records, or to have inadequate internal procedures to prevent bribe payments. This criminal law was enacted in 1977 in the wake of the Watergate scandal and revelations that corporations regularly bribed government officials. The SEC discovered in the mid-1970s that hundreds of U.S. companies had spent millions of dollars from slush funds for illegal bribery overseas.[17] The head of enforcement at the SEC at the time recalled wondering, "How does Gulf Oil record a transaction of a $50,000 cash payment? I wanted to know, what account did they charge? Do they have an account called 'Bribery'?"

The idea of a bribery account was not far off the mark in the Siemens case. Prosecutors discovered that Siemens kept "cash desks" in its offices—literally desks filled with cash—where employees could withdraw large sums to write off as "useful expenditures," which were understood to be bribes. The SEC called the bribery "unprecedented in scale and geographic reach." The DOJ called it "corruption on an absolutely stunning scale."[18]

For decades, FCPA prosecutions were very rare, but in the past decade they accelerated. Federal prosecutors have generally become more aggressive regarding foreign corporate prosecutions, but one reason FCPA prosecutions became more common was a late 1990s expansion of the statute in response to an international treaty to combat corruption. That treaty was signed by many of the major first-world countries, including Germany, which banned foreign bribery itself for the first time upon signing. Perhaps U.S. prosecutors felt more comfortable prosecuting a German corporation for something that was now also illegal in Germany and of concern to its prosecutors. Indeed, in the Siemens case, the DOJ and SEC collaborated closely with the Munich Public Prosecutor's Office.

In response to the threat of a federal prosecution, Siemens's board launched a massive internal investigation, spending more than $500 million investigating the case. Siemens also hired attorneys at a New York law firm, who billed an additional $800 million. The attorneys then brought on board accountants who reviewed 40 million bank documents and 127 million accounting records, billing $100 million more just on information technology to analyze all of that data.[19] The investigators uncovered $100 million in bribes to Argentine officials, perhaps well spent, since Siemens secured a $1 billion contract to create national identity cards. They found $5 million in bribes for mobile phone contracts in Bangladesh. The list went on and on. They reviewed transactions in more than sixty-five countries and uncovered over $1 billion in bribes not found by European regulators.[20]

Why would a company such as Siemens want to investigate its own wrongdoing? It does not help a murder suspect to confess his guilt to one crime and then go on to admit to dozens of others. That might even be a good way to get the death penalty. Yet Siemens not only confessed but also spent hundreds of millions hiring top-notch lawyers to uncover its own crimes—and rather than seal its fate, somehow this all helped the firm.

Like the vast majority of criminal defendants big or small, corporate or human, Siemens eventually pleaded guilty. Each year just a handful of corporations have trials, just as few individual defendants have them. The Siemens plea bargain was entered in the U.S. District Court for the District of

Columbia and included $450 million in fines paid to the DOJ, $350 million to the SEC, and $800 million to the Munich Public Prosecutor's Office.[21]

Paying a record $1.6 billion in fines for activities it helped to discover may sound like a raw deal. But like any other criminal defendant, Siemens bargained to avoid a "trial penalty." At a trial, the fines could have been far greater; the plea agreement cited a sentencing guidelines fine range of $1.35 billion to $2.7 billion. Consider too the gains that Siemens received from paying bribes over the years; Siemens may have profited many times over from bribes used to secure lucrative government contracts around the globe.

The cooperation may have paid off in other ways beyond a lower fine. Siemens pleaded guilty only to violations of FCPA accounting requirements and not to payment of illegal bribes, which also is prohibited by the FCPA (and which Siemens admitted it had done on a grand scale). In so doing, Siemens apparently avoided being suspended or barred from U.S. government contracting, which would have had a huge impact on its long-term business—perhaps far more harmful than any fine.[22]

But the plea agreement went further than simple punishment. Siemens had to rehabilitate itself through a range of structural reforms. The company agreed to undertake compliance obligations, including a new ethics program specially designed to detect and prevent foreign bribery and other corruption. Siemens also agreed to commit "no further crimes" and to cooperate with the U.S. government in ongoing investigations, particularly of its own employees.

Most significant, Siemens agreed to submit to a continuous audit by a corporate monitor, who would for four years have power to review documents, speak to employees, supervise compliance efforts, and make recommendations about how Siemens would improve its corporate governance to prevent corrupt payments. The monitor selected, Dr. Theo Waigel, was extremely prominent; he had been a German minister of finance and was the first non-American monitor appointed in a federal prosecution. The selection of a German monitor to oversee compliance at a German firm represented a new kind of cross-national collaborative prosecution. Siemens also hired a separate independent U.S. counsel to help monitor FCPA compliance.

The prosecutions led to the resignation of Siemen's CEO at the time, who wrote a memoir titled *Summit Storms* denying knowledge of the corruption schemes.[23] There were also additional convictions. Siemens Argentina,

Siemens Bangladesh, and Siemens Venezuela all pleaded guilty and agreed to pay $500,000 fines.[24] Munich prosecutors convicted two former Siemens employees in addition to The Banker.[25] U.S. prosecutors announced grand jury indictments of six additional former executives at Siemens. Siemens was the cooperator—the corporate informant, if you will—blowing the whistle on its former employees. In return, the prosecutors lauded Siemens's "outstanding" help.

The Banker's fears were thus realized. He was right that individual low-level employees like him would get prosecuted as scapegoats while those at the top would go free. But perhaps the prosecution would lead to significant changes in how Siemens operates. The former CEO may never have been implicated, but the company did have a chance to transform itself.

In the French novelist Honoré Balzac's novel *Le Père Goriot*, a jaded Parisian advises a young student that honesty "will get you nowhere." "The secret of great fortunes, when there's no obvious explanation for them, is always some forgotten crime—forgotten, mind you, because it's been properly handled."[26] Today, just as in 1830s Paris, great business crimes can go undetected and unpunished. In the wake of the last financial crisis, many people have asked if prosecutors are doing enough to bring corporations to justice. Prosecutors have been using a new strategy for fighting business crime, seeking to target not only greedy people but also corporations themselves. The new approach represents a real break from the past, and it is as fascinating as it is understudied. Each chapter of this book poses a different question to explore a different aspect of how corporations are now prosecuted.

How is a corporation prosecuted? The corporate trial of the century, the 2002 trial of the Big Five accounting firm Arthur Andersen, was the rare case that shows what happens when a corporation takes its case before a jury. Andersen was prosecuted for its obstruction of efforts to investigate its role in the collapse of Enron. The sheer scale of the document destruction by Andersen was remarkable—trucks were carting off documents to be shredded around the clock—but did employees intend to break the law? Andersen tried its case in the media, mobilizing protesters, a public relations campaign, and squadrons of top lawyers. Federal prosecutors brought the case as a showpiece to demonstrate their new seriousness about corporate crime. At the eleventh hour, Andersen rejected the deal prosecutors offered and took the case to the jury. This was a serious gamble: if Andersen was convicted, it would be barred from doing certified accounting for public companies. The case ended in twin disasters for the company and for prosecutors: a conviction that destroyed the firm yet was thrown out on appeal by the U.S. Supreme Court.

How do prosecutors negotiate with corporations? Prosecutors compromise. Regrouping and licking their wounds after the Andersen case, federal prosecutors developed a new, subtler form of jujitsu: the deferred prosecution. The approach had humble origins in a plan to give lenient treatment to first-time drug offenders in Brooklyn back in the 1930s—file a case, defer it or put it on hold to give the defendant a chance to stay clean, and if he does, have the judge dismiss it. The later prosecution of KPMG, a major accounting firm like Andersen, ended very differently from that of its former competitor. KPMG avoided a grand jury indictment and a conviction by signing a deferred prosecution agreement. The agreement saw KPMG pay large fines, close down part of its business, and hire a monitor to supervise a new compliance program. This is an example of the most striking change in the past decade: many of the largest firms now receive deferred prosecution agreements or non-prosecution agreements. Well over half (148 of 255, or 58 percent) of the firms receiving such agreements between 2001 and 2012 were public firms or their subsidiaries. These agreements ostensibly reward efforts by corporations to implement reforms on their own, but often it is not clear what reforms are demanded or whether they actually work.

Who goes to jail? Usually no one. In about two-thirds of the cases involving deferred prosecution or non-prosecution agreements and public corporations, the company was punished but no employees were prosecuted. This is surprising, because a corporation is like no other snitch. KPMG did not just sign an agreement—it also agreed to turn over information to prosecutors, fire employees involved, and refuse to pay their attorneys' fees. Employees are in a terrible bind—they can be fired for not cooperating in an investigation of what went wrong, and their employer may also turn them in, along with their documents and emails, to get a good deal from prosecutors. A judge threw out prosecutions of former KPMG employees, finding prosecutors had pressured KPMG to take action against them. Just as in the Siemens case, few employees were ultimately convicted. A handful of notable cases involve convictions of CEOs and high-level officials, but not many. It can be very hard to hold employees accountable in complex cases where many people took part in decisions—but that makes it all the more crucial for prosecutors to really hold the company accountable.

What role do victims play in corporate prosecutions? Victims cannot easily participate in corporate criminal cases. The victims of the tragic and preventable explosion at the Texas City refinery in 2005 tried to make their voices heard and convince the judge to make sure BP never acted so recklessly again. They failed. Other victims had modest successes. Companies can pay large sums in restitution to victims—a few cases involve multimillion-dollar restitution funds—but most do not. In addition, some corporations do community service—not by cleaning up litter or whitewashing graffiti but by contributing money to causes such as the environment, affordable health care, or investor awareness. With the persistence of cases in which judges ignore victims' objections to lenient corporate settlements, one lesson of the BP incident is that we need better ways for judges to consider the public interest in corporate prosecutions.

How is a corporation punished? Not by relying on strict and narrow sentencing guidelines, as with individuals, but by using more flexible guidelines that may give the biggest fish the best deals. Fewer major public corporations are convicted each year; they usually get leniency. Yet many mom-and-pop corporations plead guilty each year, and their names illustrate how far from the Fortune 500 they can be: Andy's Orchids, Joe's Cajun Seafood, Little Rhody Beagle Club, and Ohio Fresh Eggs. Many are unable to pay a fine, and a few are put out of business—the corporate "death penalty." In contrast, large firms often receive deferred prosecution agreements and pay lower fines, if any: 47 percent of those getting deferred prosecution or non-prosecution agreements paid no fine at all. Almost every time prosecutors explained how a fine was calculated, it was at the very bottom, or quite a bit below the bottom, of the range suggested in the sentencing guidelines. If prosecutors are not adequately rehabilitating firms, then they should impose the full criminal fines that the law demands.

Who oversees corporate prosecution agreements? A new kind of person—the corporate monitor—can play a crucial part in overseeing the process of trying to rehabilitate a prosecuted company. Monitors have sweeping powers and represent a new role in criminal justice. The monitor appointed to supervise reforms at Bristol-Myers Squibb did more than oversee compliance—he asked the board to fire the CEO and investigated entirely new violations. Although 25 percent of the deferred prosecution and non-prosecution agreements provide for monitors (65 of 255 agreements), this raises the question of why 75 percent do *not*. And none of the work that monitors do is made public. Nor is selection of these high-paid monitors transparent, leading to controversy over allegations of favoritism and cronyism. A substantial number of agreements (31 percent) do not even speak to implementing a compliance program. One wonders again how seriously prosecutors are taking corporate reforms.

What criminal procedure rights do corporations have? Corporations have many of the same constitutional criminal procedure rights as individuals. How often are those rights used in criminal cases? Not often. But one corporation went to trial and had a conviction reversed. Lindsay Manufacturing was exonerated and had a trial conviction dismissed after "flagrant" prosecutorial misconduct came to light. Lawyers specializing in white-collar crime and corporate defense form a growing and prominent part of practice at the nation's top law firms, and we may see much more constitutional litigation by corporations seeking still more lenient results in criminal cases.

How are foreign corporations prosecuted? Foreign corporations are increasingly important targets and pay far larger fines on average: $35 million compared with $4.7 million for domestic firms. One example is the prosecution of a multinational defense contractor, BAE, based in the United Kingdom. U.K. authorities had long declined to prosecute it for extensive bribery, but the United States eventually took action, resulting in a prosecution agreement. Although few foreign countries hold corporations strictly criminally liable, they must now reckon with the unparalleled reach of U.S. prosecutors. Indeed, in response to the BAE case, the U.K. passed a new Bribery Act much like the FCPA. Corporate prosecutions have gone global.

Are corporate prosecutions effectively preventing crime? Corporate prosecutions can be made stronger, as I detail in Chapter 10. However, there are fundamental questions that cannot be answered, as prosecutors target corporations in a way that is strikingly opaque. What is the corporate crime rate? Not only is there little in the way of data, but also defining what constitutes a crime can be difficult. How many companies go unpunished? Are some corporate crimes uncovered but not investigated or charged? While I present data describing outcomes in corporate prosecutions, these data still cannot tell us everything we would want to know about how well prosecutors exercise their discretion, which largely remains a black box.

Given that corporations have "no soul to be damned, no body to kick," a number of scholars have argued over the years that corporations should not be prosecuted at all. They contend that since only individuals can be held morally accountable for crimes, prosecuting a corporation is as nonsensical as prosecuting a stone. Critics also point out that the company can be fined in a civil case brought by an agency such as the SEC, which may be more experienced with industry practices and regulations and better able to supervise structural reforms. In my view, criminal punishment of the most serious corporate violators is justified, because the corporation itself may promote a culture of lawbreaking that can be remedied only at the corporate level. And corporations do not fear civil cases the way they fear prosecutions—for good reason. Criminal prosecutions bring with them far more serious consequences, including potentially debilitating fines, harm to reputation, and collateral consequences such as suspension and debarment.

Most corporate violations are not handled criminally, and the decision to bring a corporate criminal case should not be reached lightly. But society's ideas about what should be criminally punished can and should evolve. Congress has not been shy about defining new business-related crimes. Over the past decade, holding corporations criminally accountable has become more firmly ingrained in prosecution practice, in sentencing, and perhaps also in our culture. Companies such as Siemens probably did not think much about the FCPA a decade ago; now they know a serious breach can mean prosecution. Ten or fifteen years ago people might not have asked after a financial crisis why no big banks were prosecuted. Now it is a common belief that the company itself should sometimes be held accountable.

Still, there are good reasons to worry whether the right corporations are being prosecuted and whether the punishments fit the crimes. Prosecutors say that they target the most serious corporate violators. Yet the fines are typically greatly reduced in exchange for little oversight. If one justification for prosecuting a company in the first place is egregiously bad compliance, then one wonders why so little is typically done to deter or correct it. Are these prosecutions really helping to reform corporate criminals? Which compliance programs actually work? We simply do not know. While there are no silver-bullet solutions to these vexing problems, there are concrete ways to improve matters, including by insisting on more stringent fines, imposing ongoing judicial review, monitoring, and mandating transparency.

Corporate prosecutions upend our assumptions about a criminal justice system whose playing field is tilted in favor of the prosecution. It is admirable that prosecutors have taken on the role of David in prosecuting the largest corporations—but if they miss their shot at Goliath, the most serious corporate crimes will be committed with impunity. The surge in large-scale corporate cases shows how federal prosecutors have creatively tried to prevent corporate malfeasance at home and overseas, but real changes in corporate culture require sustained oversight of management, strong regulators, and sound rules and laws. Congress enacts new criminal laws intended to bolster regulations, but it is perennially unwilling to provide adequate resources to many agencies to carry out enforcement of those regulations. That is why prosecutors can fill an important gap—and when they do prosecute a corporation, they can wield the most powerful tools. A broader political movement toward greater corporate accountability more generally, with stronger regulations and enforcement, could make prosecutions far less necessary. But if we take as a given the larger dynamics of our economic and political system, modest changes could improve the role criminal cases play in the larger drama.

Corporate criminal prosecutions serve a distinct purpose—to punish serious violations and grossly deficient compliance—and this purpose is not served if companies obtain kid-glove non-prosecution deals in exchange for cosmetic reforms. Corporate convictions should be the norm, and in special cases in which prosecutors defer prosecution, they should impose deterrent fines and stringent compliance requirements. A judge should carefully supervise all corporate agreements to ensure their effective implementation.

Sentencing guidelines and judicial practices could be reconsidered, but prosecutors themselves can revitalize the area by adopting a new set of guidelines to strengthen the punishment reserved for the most serious corporate criminals.

Although I propose reforms, my main goal in this book is to describe the hidden world of corporate prosecutions. Corporate crime deserves more public attention. What is particularly chilling about the problem is that corporate complexity may not only enable crime on a vast scale but also make such crimes difficult to detect, prevent, and prosecute. We need to know much more. When we ask if some companies are being treated as "too big to jail," it is not enough to ask whether the largest firms are so important to the economy that they are treated as immune from prosecution. We also need to ask whether individuals are held accountable. We need to evaluate whether the corporate prosecutions that are brought are working. We need to look beyond the press releases announcing eye-catching fines and ask whether adequate criminal punishment is imposed and whether structural reforms are working.

The Banker feared that although Siemens was punished, most others would not face the same consequences. He may have been right to worry. After all, not only do prosecutors regularly offer leniency, but we do not know how many corporate crimes go undetected or unprosecuted. As The Banker put it: "The Eleventh Commandment is: 'Don't get caught.'"[27]

2

The Company in the Courtroom

"I obstructed justice," admitted David Duncan, a former senior managing partner for Arthur Andersen, as he testified in federal court on May 13, 2002.

Andersen was one of the five largest accounting firms in the world, and Duncan had led a large team doing accounting work for the Enron Corporation both in Houston, where Enron was based, and around the globe.[1] An energy, commodities, and services company, Enron had ambitious ventures in electricity, natural gas, communications, and even water. It had been named "America's Most Innovative Company" by *Fortune* for several years running and was one of the largest corporations in the country.

With the formalities out of the way, the prosecutor asked, "Did there come a time in the fall of 2001 that you committed a crime?"

"Yes."

"What did you do?"

"I instructed people on the engagement team to follow the document retention policy, which I knew would result in the destruction of documents," Duncan answered.[2]

About a month before this trial, Duncan had pleaded guilty to obstruction of justice. He faced a maximum of ten years in prison, but he had yet to be sentenced and was free on bail.[3] If he cooperated, prosecutors could offer him a shorter sentence. At this trial, Duncan was providing that cooperation, but not by testifying against any of his former co-workers, Enron CEO Kenneth Lay, or anyone else at Enron. Instead, he was testifying against his former employer. The criminal defendant was Arthur Andersen itself, the firm where he had worked for twenty years—and which was now on trial for its life.[4]

On day six of the trial, Duncan took the stand. He began by recalling his life just a few months before as a different time, when he "did well" as a partner at Andersen. Partners were paid based on a "grading system," and with all of his Enron business, he scored in the top 10 percent.[5] He was even asked to serve on the CEO's advisory council in late 2001, shortly before Andersen fell apart. Duncan had been fired just four months previously, in January 2002, because Andersen concluded that he had played an improper role in destroying documents. Now the tables were turned, and he was the government's star witness in a long and complicated trial. If Duncan had committed a crime, Andersen could be liable for it, so it would be Andersen arguing he had not done so.

Andersen and Enron

Arthur Andersen was a real person, one who founded his eponymous accounting firm in 1913. He was a paragon of business ethics, with the motto "Think straight, talk straight." Andersen was known to turn down potential clients, no matter how much they would pay, if they used flawed accounting methods. More than a founder and namesake, he would come to embody the firm's reputation for integrity. The modern Andersen was one of the "Big Five" accounting firms, with offices around the world and the largest of corporate clients. Andersen, called simply "the Firm" by employees, was headquartered in Chicago, Illinois, and had almost 30,000 employees in the United States and a total of more than 85,000 worldwide. Andersen was known for emphasis on training new hires on its culture, standards, and procedures—the nickname for an employee was "Android."[6] But the culture was changing as partners focusing on consulting work took on more power within the company. In the late 1980s the firm created Andersen Consulting, which began to earn more of Arthur Andersen's revenue.[7] By the late 1990s, Andersen Consulting was at odds with the auditing side of the firm, and in 1997 it broke off. With its auditing business slowing and the loss of the consulting business, there was increasing pressure to keep clients and raise revenues.[8]

A bright spot in the late 1990s was the growing Enron engagement team, as the group doing Enron work was called. At the trial, Duncan said Enron was a "very big" client. How big? It generated somewhere between $50 to $55 million in fees each year, an amount that rose annually, reaching $58 million in 2000. Under Duncan's leadership, about a hundred employees worked full-time on Enron matters, including on-site at Enron's offices. Their approach was unusual, since Andersen did not only audits of Enron's financial statements but also "integrated audits," which gave opinions on Enron's compliance and internal controls. They hoped this would be a model for consulting work with other corporate clients.[9]

Ultimately, the close relationship between Enron and Andersen became a liability rather than an asset. On August 14, 2001, Jeffrey Skilling, Enron's CEO, suddenly resigned, as it became clear that Enron's supposedly vast assets were a house of cards. The value of Enron's stock was falling, and an Enron accountant who used to work for Andersen warned of a "wave of accounting scandals."[10] That whistle-blower told Enron CEO Kenneth Lay that there was a serious problem with the way Enron reported its finances. This development had to be taken seriously by Andersen as well, since the firm had been reviewing Enron's books for years. On August 28, the *Wall Street Journal* reported on possible misconduct at Enron, and the SEC announced an informal inquiry.[11] Andersen began its own internal investigation and realized that, among other problems, there had been an outright error. This led Enron to admit that its earnings were $1.2 billion lower than reported—a major announcement known as a "restatement." A restatement can damage the reputation of a company, and under securities laws, shareholders can sue for being misled by inaccurate financial statements. Indeed, lawsuits were imminent.

Enron had reported profits that did not exist and kept losses off its balance sheet using complex entities. One was called Chewco, a shell corporation named after Chewbacca, the big furry sidekick from the movie *Star Wars*. As a shell, Chewco did not do its own business or have employees or operations. Instead it was used to hide losses occurring in another Enron company, named Joint Energy Development Investment Limited, or JEDI, after the set of *Star Wars* characters. Despite the whimsical names of these shell companies, their consequences were serious.

In October 2001, Enron issued an earnings report suggesting that these were one-time-only problems. Duncan responded with a memo stating that this was misleading and that Enron should correct its report. Andersen decided to ignore Duncan's advice. At the time, one of Andersen's lawyers in the main Chicago office, Nancy Temple, wrote an email to an outside lawyer suggesting edits to tone down Duncan's memo so that it would not look as though Andersen "had a responsibility to follow up." She also asked that her name be deleted from the memo, along with any "reference to consultation with the legal group."[12] Those edits came back to haunt Andersen.

Andersen was already on thin ice as a recidivist. The U.S. Securities and Exchange Commission (SEC), which regulates public corporations, had just settled civil charges against Andersen with a record fine of $7 million and a permanent injunction requiring that Andersen never violate securities laws again. In that case, auditors who raised concerns about the accounting processes used by a major client, Waste Management, were told by supervisors to do nothing. Years later, Waste Management restated $1.7 billion in earnings, which was then the largest such correction in history (Rite Aid has since seized the title).[13] If Andersen was found to have violated the SEC decree by breaking securities laws, then the SEC could prevent Andersen from doing any future work for public corporations. That would mean the end of Andersen, since doing work for public corporations was its lifeblood. There were more reasons aside from Enron that made such SEC action seem like a real possibility, since the SEC had also begun to inquire into accounting irregularities at other Andersen clients, including Boston Chicken, Global Crossing, Sunbeam, and WorldCom.

Types of Companies

A criminal prosecution may affect different types of companies quite differently. Although a company may be prosecuted in federal court, all companies are recognized and created under state law. In the United States, about 2 million corporations are created each year by filing incorporation papers with a state and paying a filing fee. Delaware has long been known as the leading state for incorporations because of its reputation for being convenient and legally favorable. There are 50,000 more corporate persons registered in the state than human residents.[14] One key reason to form corporations is the concept of "limited liability," which means that if the corporation goes under, the owners are not liable for its debts. The same concept applies to the aptly named limited liability company (or LLC), the most popular type of business entity today.

Some of the most significant criminal prosecutions are of the biggest public corporations; about 5,000 are listed on major American stock exchanges.[15] A prosecution of a public company may hurt the company's share price and therefore harm the vast number of people who own the stock. While those shareholders are the owners, they normally have no reason to know about the crimes. The shareholders do not run the company; they elect a board of directors, which hires management, such as the CEO, to run day-to-day operations. Most of the millions of corporations in the United States are privately owned, and a prosecution of a private company mostly affects the owners. Some are family businesses and very small. Some are shell companies, like Chewco, that do not have any actual operations. While there are legitimate reasons to use a shell, such as nature conservation groups using a dummy company to buy land to preserve, they can also be used for nefarious reasons, including tax evasion, money laundering, and fraud.

Arthur Andersen, LLP was a limited liability partnership, a less common type of company that is owned by its partners, a term for co-owners who work together. Professional firms such as law firms and accounting firms are often LLPs. A prosecution of such a partnership raises special issues. If Arthur Andersen went under, the partners could lose both their jobs and their stake in the company, the amount of money they had paid in once they were made a partner. The partners would not, however, be responsible for all of the debts or liabilities that Andersen incurred, including as a result of lawsuits by victims of Enron who blamed Andersen.

Federal law makes corporations and other types of organizations liable for criminal acts. Of course, federal laws also regulate companies in all sorts of other ways. Public corporations like Enron must accurately report detailed information to the SEC, which regulates the stock markets. A private partnership like Arthur Andersen does not need to report financials to the SEC, but it was an auditing firm, and its accountants had the job of making sure that firms like Enron kept their books in order. It was responsible to the SEC for the accuracy of its client's financials. Under SEC rules, the agency could prohibit (disbar) convicted professionals, including accountants, from doing work for public corporations.[16] Andersen would lose its major customers if disbarred and would likely "die" by going bankrupt or ceasing operations.

Andersen's Crisis Response Team

To save the firm from the dire fate that might befall it if convicted, Andersen's partners set up a crisis response team with lawyers, accountants, managers, and others. The team met almost daily and began to respond to document requests from the SEC and send out messages to employees that document retention—and document destruction—would be an issue. Ironically, the very team assembled to respond to its legal problems would only create more of them for Andersen.

From the very beginning the lawyers likely knew that the SEC would get involved. On October 12, Nancy Temple, the attorney in Andersen's Chicago office, added a new label in their internal tracking system for "Government/regulatory investigation." That was important, because it indicated that she understood this problem would involve government scrutiny.

That same day, Temple sent out an email asking that the entire Enron engagement team be reminded of the "documentation and retention" policy at Arthur Andersen. This policy stated that "confidentiality and proper management of client engagement information is critical." Not every document can be saved, and corporate employees are not required to be pack rats. Andersen handled vast quantities of confidential information and quite properly had detailed policies in place to be sure that extra documents would not be circulated and unnecessary documents would be routinely destroyed. The policy was detailed and mundane, basically saying that each project should have a single, central file, and unnecessary documents should be discarded. The policy also made clear that if litigation was threatened, everything relevant should be saved and that an SEC investigation was reason to postpone the destruction of documents.

Temple's email was open to interpretation. Was it intended to simply restate the obvious—that Andersen, like any company, had a documentation and retention policy—or was the message designed to encourage document destruction? Perhaps Andersen's employees needed no email reminder. Two days before, at a training meeting, one of the partners said that everyone should comply with the policy, and if documentation was "destroyed in the course of [the] normal policy and litigation is filed the next day, that's great."

On October 16, 2001, Enron announced the billion-dollar accounting error. The next day, the SEC formally announced its inquiry into Enron with a "letter of investigation" sent to Andersen.[17] This was serious. One high-ranking Andersen partner circulated an email saying, "The problems are just beginning and we will be in the cross hairs. The marketplace is going to keep the pressure on this and is going to force the SEC to be tough."[18] On October 23, in a call with Enron investors, Lay admitted there would be lawsuits in addition to the SEC inquiry.[19]

That same day, David Duncan called an urgent meeting of Andersen management and partners. In the week that followed, massive quantities of Enron-related documents were sent to the shredders. On October 25 alone, 2,380 pounds were shredded. While a big accounting office would have plenty of confidential documents to shred, the normal amount was only 70–90 pounds per day.[20] Tens of thousands of emails were deleted as well. The shredding continued through early November, when the SEC sent a formal subpoena asking Andersen for Enron-related documents.

Failed Negotiations

The trial of Arthur Andersen did not have to happen. The firm announced its full cooperation with investigators in an op-ed in the *Wall Street Journal* written by Andersen's managing partner and CEO, Joe Berardino. He promised to acknowledge any mistakes and offered to help push for broader reforms.[21] In December, Enron filed the biggest corporate bankruptcy in U.S. history, and in January 2002, the DOJ confirmed that federal prosecutors had begun investigating Andersen. Prosecutors were not charging Arthur Andersen with giving criminally dishonest advice to Enron, although maybe they could have if the documents had still been there showing what advice Andersen gave. Instead, the case focused on Andersen's decision to shred them.

Arthur Andersen was charged with a count of obstruction of justice. Title 18 of the United States Code contains many of the core federal crimes, including obstruction of justice, which covers the withholding or destroying of evidence. The section of the code under which Andersen was charged makes it a crime to "knowingly, intentionally and corruptly persuade[]" others to withhold documents or alter documents for use in "official proceedings," including "regulatory and criminal proceedings and investigations."[22] It takes two to obstruct justice under that particular statute (although there are other statutes, which did not apply to Andersen's situation, in which a second person is not required).[23] A convict can be fined, imprisoned for up to ten years, or both. Obviously, the firm could not be imprisoned, but its employees could, and the firm faced fines and other sanctions.

Even at this point, Andersen could have avoided a trial. The vast majority of criminal defendants never get a trial, instead settling their cases by accepting a plea bargain and admitting their guilt. The same is true for corporate defendants. The U.S. Sentencing Commission publishes data on federal sentencing, and by its accounting, only a handful of the roughly 200 companies convicted each year take their chances with a criminal trial.[24]

On January 15, 2002, Andersen fired Duncan and suspended three others who had done Enron work. Andersen clearly wanted to give the impression it was cleaning house and ready to cooperate. Andersen also released emails regarding the role of Nancy Temple on the legal team. The U.S. House of Representatives held hearings, and representatives asked questions about Temple's October 12 email mentioning the document retention policy. Temple was also asked about altering the memo that Duncan had prepared.[25] At the hearings, Duncan pleaded the Fifth and did not testify. One congressman asked: "Is Mr. Duncan being made a scapegoat here this morning?"[26]

Prosecutors were offering Andersen an exit strategy: the firm could avoid an indictment and a conviction by signing an agreement with prosecutors. Under this agreement, which would remain in effect for three years, Andersen would admit wrongdoing but would not plead guilty, and it would cooperate in the investigation of the wrongdoing. Andersen apparently sought some assurance that the SEC would not take further action to bar it from doing work for public corporations, but the SEC was undecided.[27] In addition, state regulators could bar Andersen from doing accounting work; state prosecutors were beginning to investigate Andersen, and federal prosecutors could not stop them.[28]

Andersen decided to go to trial rather than sign a deferred prosecution agreement.[29] The firm took an aggressive approach, calling the prosecution "a gross abuse of governmental power." So on March 7, in the Southern District of Texas federal courthouse, Andersen was indicted by the grand jury for obstruction of justice. Andersen would ultimately spend $50 million on its legal defense, according to one report, and may have spent more.[30]

Meanwhile, Andersen's CEO, who had denied that there was any order from the top to destroy documents, resigned on March 26. And in April 2002, David Duncan pleaded guilty to obstruction of justice.

The Trial Begins

The trial would take place in the federal courthouse in Houston, only seven blocks from where Enron's world headquarters stood. As is typical in federal criminal cases, the prosecutors gave the defense very little information before the trial began. At the time of jury selection, prosecutors had not given the defense a list of the witnesses they planned to call.[31] Nevertheless, the defense was not completely in the dark. After all, they may have had the best access to Andersen's documents and emails—those that had not been disposed of. Indeed, the defense estimated that there were 78 *billion* pages of documents related to Andersen's work with Enron from 1997 to 2001.[32] This was nothing like a typical criminal case, which may contain a few dozen pages of police reports, interview notes, or crime lab test results.

How would jurors be selected in a case where the defendant was a corporation? In addition to typical questions about whether potential jurors or their family members had been convicted of a crime or whether any were practicing attorneys, the jurors were asked if they or their family members were accountants or employees of Enron. The prosecutors told prospective jurors that this was not a typical defendant—this was a partnership, a type of company that doesn't "act with pencils or books or desks. They act through their people. Because at the end of a day, a legal entity is a collection of people." A prosecutor asked whether the jurors could handle the fact that "a partnership can be found guilty through the actions of . . . very few or only even one of its employees." The prosecutor asked the potential jurors, "Is there anyone who [thinks] that doesn't sound like very fair that a partnership that has thousands of people can be convicted based just on the crimes of a few bad apples? Is there anyone who thinks that that sounds somewhat unfair? Anyone?"[33]

Once selected, the judge reminded the jurors, "No *Newsweek*, no *Time*, no news-coverage kind of magazines or newspapers . . . Do whatever it is to get away from any media coverage."[34] This was such a big case that the media could be covering it anywhere: "It could be in the Lifestyle section, as well as the business page or the front page and it could be during some kind of interview with someone and Katie Couric could be doing a human interest on somebody."[35] The judge put it bluntly: "I don't want you watching any news on TV, listening to any news or any talk radio on the radio and reading any newspapers."[36] The judge also warned the jurors the case could last as long as a month; they should be prepared for a big commitment.

Andersen sought to put on a human face both inside and outside the courtroom. Maybe the jurors would listen to the judge's warnings and stay away from news media, but Andersen felt that the public mattered as well. A major corporation has media access that no ordinary criminal defendant has. Andersen took out full-page newspaper ads and detailed the government's "legal errors" on the company website. Employees stood in protest at the courthouse on the day of the indictment wearing shirts with the slogan "I am Arthur Andersen," which they also chanted, and signs such as "I didn't shred, my kid needs to be fed."

This strategy was not new, and corporations often try to convey that they have a human size. AT&T is well known for having advertised nationwide beginning over a century ago how it was a "friend and neighbor," using images of real employees such as telephone operators.[37] Companies use ads to show how they are like a family or even how their customers can become part of the family. Everything about a corporation, from its logo and slogan to advertisements, mission statements, and websites, may try to convey that the corporation has a culture, is a community, and cares about its employees and customers.

In an individual criminal case, the defendant wants to convey that he or she is a sympathetic person. In a corporate criminal case, the defendant wants to do the same, and perhaps also try to mobilize public pressure and influence to prevent a prosecution in the first place. Such pressure would not help Andersen, however. President George W. Bush quickly sought to distance his administration from the scandal despite (or possibly because of) ties he had had with Kenneth Lay and Enron while in Texas. Before the trial, President

Bush declared his "outrage" and ordered all federal agencies to review their contracts with Arthur Andersen (amounting to $60 million a year).[38]

The government began the trial by telling the jury that "Arthur Anderson is a huge accounting partnership. They are a billion dollar firm. They have offices all over the world."[39] Prosecutors told a story blaming the culture and practices of management: a small "management team" came together to respond to this crisis, and knowing that the SEC responds slowly, they tried to take advantage of this to cover their tracks. Duncan had already pleaded guilty to obstruction of justice, prosecutors said, and "that alone will be sufficient" for a conviction. Nancy Temple had sent the email about document retention minutes after writing about how regulators would be involved in the matter. Andersen's partners were "smart, experienced, and cautious" people who would never admit they were trying to obstruct justice, but "they knew that the law was coming," and their words and actions would show that the massive document destruction was intended "to quietly help their firm."[40]

In contrast, the lead defense lawyer told the jury: "Who is Arthur Andersen? Arthur Andersen is its employees."[41] The lawyer, not prone to understatement, began by telling the jury, "You're going to hear evidence about what I believe the evidence will show you is one of the greatest tragedies in the criminal justice history of this country." Prosecutors were unfairly blaming this "proud firm of 28,000 employees in this country" for the "horrible consequences" of Enron's misdeeds.[42] Andersen's lawyer told the jurors he wanted them to "help us go on a search" for whoever had engaged in obstruction of justice. Among those 28,000 employees and 1,700 partners, who was the bad apple? "You know, the little routine 'Where is Waldo?'" the lawyer added.[43] "Where is Waldo? Who are they?"

The lawyer's final words in his opening statement to the jury were: "When it's all over, you still won't know where Waldo is and you still will not have found a corrupt persuader, you will just have a destroyed company."[44]

The defense strategy was to argue that Andersen employees may have been in utter disarray as it became clear what a perilous state their client Enron was in, but there was no concerted plan to conceal evidence. Pinning blame on a particular "Waldo" might be hard for prosecutors. The key witnesses were Andersen employees or former ones, perhaps still sympathetic to their firm. And smoking-gun documents may have been shredded.

The Prosecution and the Defense

The prosecution began by emphasizing that Andersen employees had known the SEC would soon come knocking. The first witness was an SEC official who said he could not recall another Big Five accounting firm destroying documents right before getting an SEC subpoena.[45] The prosecutors focused on Nancy Temple's October 12, 2001, email to another member of the crisis response group:

> It might be useful to consider reminding the engagement team
> of our documentation and retention policy. It will be helpful to
> make sure that we have complied with the policy. Let me know
> if you have any questions.

Right around that date there was an enormous surge in deliveries to the courier service Andersen used at its Houston office to pick up documents for shredding. Most weeks showed less than 500 pounds delivered for shredding, but that week there was an enormous spike to almost 2,500 pounds.[46] Similar document destruction occurred at offices in Portland, Chicago, and even London.

The "no more shredding" notice went out only after formal SEC document requests were served on November 8, 2001.[47] The next morning when Duncan arrived at work, he saw the subpoena from the SEC. When Duncan's assistant heard about the SEC requests, she double-checked with him about shredding; she recalled at trial that "he bit my head off and said, 'No! We're not supposed to be shredding anymore. Who's asking you to shred?'" He told her to make sure employees "know they're not supposed to be shredding anymore. Now!"[48] She sent an email to the Enron engagement team with the subject line "No More Shredding," which went on to state: "Per Dave—No more shredding. . . . We have been officially served for our documents."[49]

To commit a federal crime, Duncan had to do more than destroy documents on his own, which he admitted doing. He needed to have "corruptly" and "knowingly" persuaded someone else to destroy documents, and he must have done this to keep the documents from being used in official proceedings—such as an SEC investigation. Was David Duncan the corrupt persuader?

At trial, Duncan recalled that Enron was considered a "high risk" client.[50] Duncan was asked about October 12, 2001, the day Nancy Temple sent the email to the other top legal team member about reminding employees of the usefulness of the documentation and retention policy.[51] That reminder was repeated over and over by others.

Duncan talked about the "unusual" big meeting of managers and partners later in the month, on October 23, where Duncan addressed the entire group. Duncan could not recall another time when managers were convened just to hear a reminder about the document retention policy. He also said that he had learned on October 19, 2001, that the SEC was beginning an inquiry, and he then called a meeting to discuss what to do.[52] When the prosecution asked, "Did anyone ever say anything about whether the policy called for any destruction of documents?" he answered, "No. I believe that was generally understood." Copies of the policy were made available at the meeting, and it was after that meeting that the highest volume of shredding occurred.[53] Duncan also admitted that he personally destroyed documents, expected others to do the same, and saw them doing so.[54] He said Nancy Temple had told him that extraneous documents are often used against companies in litigation, but he added that at the time he had thought it wasn't a crime to destroy documents unless the SEC had issued a subpoena legally demanding them.[55]

The next day, Andersen's lawyer cross-examined Duncan. The defense's goal, as the lawyer put it to the judge, was to explore the "state of mind" of the government's "corrupt persuader."[56] In January 2002, when Andersen fired Duncan and suspended others on the Enron team, Duncan initially agreed to be jointly defended by Andersen's lawyers. But later he withdrew, switched sides, and agreed to cooperate with prosecutors.[57] Andersen had explained Duncan was fired because he had called the "urgent meeting" on October 23 and seemed to be behind the document destruction. Andersen had maintained that the rest of the firm should not be faulted, as the destruction was "undertaken without any consultation with others in the firm and at a time when the engagement team should have had serious questions about their actions."[58] Now that it was on trial, though, Andersen was arguing that neither Duncan nor anyone else was at fault.

Duncan admitted that not until he was fired had he looked into whether the document destruction he had done was illegal.[59] He did "a lot of soul searching."[60] Even though Duncan was cooperating with the government, he was not exactly a whistle-blower. After all, he did not think Andersen was at fault for all of Enron's accounting improprieties. He said some were concealed from Andersen, while others, such as the $1.2 billion restatement, were good-faith errors or "did not have clear black and white answers" under accounting standards.[61] Andersen's lawyer implied that Duncan had somehow talked himself into, or had been talked into, believing that he committed a crime.[62] The defense brought in twenty-one boxes of documents to show how many documents were *not* destroyed.[63]

The cross-examination stretched over two days, and at one point, the judge commented, "You're asking him the same question over and over again. . . . I feel like a dead horse."[64]

Once the defense finished its questioning, the government returned to ask Duncan one last time, "Did you plead guilty because you are guilty?"

"Yes," he answered.[65]

The star witness for the prosecution was at times confused and reluctant, and Andersen's lawyer rhetorically asked the press, "How can he be a corrupt persuader?"[66] The defense argued that David Duncan had been "persuaded that he committed a crime" and had pleaded guilty only under pressure from prosecutors.[67] Nor did Duncan think he had done anything wrong in terms of his actual work for Enron: "I do not believe I committed accounting fraud," he said.[68] He cooperated with the government, but he did not admit much, nor did he point fingers at others.

The prosecution had another candidate for a corrupt persuader: Nancy Temple, the lawyer on Andersen's crisis response team. While Duncan asserted his Fifth Amendment privilege against self-incrimination at hearings before a U.S. House of Representatives committee, Temple had chosen to testify. At trial, it was the reverse, as Temple asserted the Fifth Amendment and never took the stand. But maybe that meant prosecutors could attack an empty chair and blame someone who could not respond in person.

The prosecution had a paper trail. Temple's first computer entry on October 12, 2001, noted a potential government or regulatory investigation.[69] Her handwritten notes suggested she was concerned about the possibility of an SEC inquiry. Also helpful for the prosecutors was a written record from a second partner (who took the Fifth as well and did not testify) saying he would use the phrase "document retention policy" as a euphemism when he wanted to talk about destroying documents.

Did the jurors follow it all? It was reported after the trial that two jurors fell asleep during its first two weeks. Andersen's defense team had every reason to try to make the evidence seem as complicated, boring, and technical as possible. The strategy almost worked.

The main goal of the defense was to show there was no Waldo: no one at Andersen had had criminal intent, and employees had not been trying to hide evidence from the SEC. The defense asked employees what they thought about the document retention policy. Some said they thought it just meant that files needed to be orderly.[70] The person to whom Temple sent the email said that the email was in response to a question about not having seen the policy before and that nothing was destroyed in response.[71] Duncan's assistant testified she had had no intent to do anything wrong and that Duncan had never said anything about the SEC. It was simply that the Enron documents had been neglected, meaning the files were a "mess" and needed to be straightened up.[72]

Others testified that Duncan "had the classic deer-in-the-headlights syndrome" and simply "didn't understand the ramifications" of his actions.[73] And though Duncan said he had committed a crime, the defense argued that the crime required persuading others to obstruct justice, and Duncan could not have been the one to illegally convince others to obstruct justice, since he had not been listened to or had simply been negligent rather than "corrupt."

After six long weeks, the case was coming to a close. What would the jury do? Would they see Andersen's employees as loyal to a fault or see Enron as the "real villain" and Andersen as a victim?[74] This decision would hinge on the standard for when a corporate person can be convicted of a crime by an employee, and on this score, prosecutors had a remarkable weapon—the federal standard for corporate criminal liability.

The Old and Exploded Doctrine

More than a century ago, the Supreme Court recognized in *New York Central & Hudson River Railroad* that corporations may be held strictly accountable for a crime by an employee.[75] At the time, railroads defined American industry, perhaps in the way Enron symbolized the high-tech and energy boom and bust of the 1990s. The New York Central & Hudson River Railroad and two employees were indicted for charging a sugar company less than the published shipping rate. This violated the Elkins Act, a federal law that sought to prevent side deals and favoritism by railroads. Documents showed that the rebates had been given, so no one disagreed about those facts.

Instead, the railroad argued that the Elkins Act violated the Constitution when it made the corporation criminally liable for the acts of its employees. The railroad argued that to "punish the corporation is in reality to punish the innocent stockholders, and to deprive them of their property without opportunity to be heard, consequently without due process of law." While all criminal defendants are presumed innocent until proven guilty, the corporation could not by definition be guilty, since "no action of the board of directors could legally authorize a crime," and the shareholders had not done anything wrong either.

In response, the Supreme Court noted that corporations had long been prosecuted for crimes. English authorities such as William Blackstone may have said a corporation "cannot commit treason, or felony, or other crime in its corporate capacity," but as historian Paul Halliday has written, there was a long history of corporations—often municipal corporations—being held accountable by having their charter revoked by the English Crown. In the most famous incident, the City of London was dissolved (as a corporation), with its rights later restored by Parliament.[76] The concept was that corporations existed as creations of the state. A corporation is "invisible, immortal, and rests only in intendment and consideration of the law," as Sir Edward Coke put it.[77] On the flip side, as Blackstone noted, if the corporation "has broken the condition upon which it is incorporated," then "the incorporation is void."[78]

The American colonies had direct experience with the uncertain rights and responsibilities of corporations. In one of the most dramatic incidents, King James II sought to revoke Connecticut's corporate charter, sending a governor and soldiers to obtain it. According to the quite wonderful but perhaps embellished accounts, the Connecticut General Assembly received the new governor in their chambers with the charter document before them in a mahogany box. The legislators debated at length the correct approach, pontificating until nightfall, when suddenly all of the candles were mysteriously blown out. When the candles were relit, the charter was gone. A man had run off with the charter and placed it in the hollow of a massive oak tree, now Connecticut's state tree and ever since called the "Charter Oak."

After the Founding, states increasingly granted charters to corporations to provide transportation and other services. Courts held corporations liable for creating public nuisances—what we might call environmental violations.[79] Courts also increasingly held corporations liable in civil cases; the New York Court of Appeals explained in 1860 that failure to hold them accountable for injuries would turn them "into most mischievous monsters."[80] Beginning in the nineteenth century, more courts began to hold corporations liable for crimes.[81] Where states drew the line, and where most states still draw it, is barring prosecution of a company for violent and intentional crimes such as assault, battery, and homicide.

As a result, the railroad case was easy for the Supreme Court. The decision was unanimous, with the Court noting that these employees were authorized to set rates for the railroad—they were "clothed with authority" by the railroad corporation" and so were "bound to respect" federal law. As the Court put it, quoting a well-known criminal law treatise from the time, "If, for example, the invisible, intangible essence or air which we term a corporation can level mountains, fill up valleys, lay down iron tracks, and run railroad cars on them, it can intend to do it, and can act therein as well viciously as virtuously." Corporations in the Gilded Age were reshaping America; that is why there was "every reason in public policy" to hold the corporations liable for crimes. Regulating railroads simply would not be effective if only the employees were prosecuted, since these acts were, after all, for the "benefit of the corporations of which the individuals were but the instruments." The Court could not "shut its eyes to the fact that the great majority of business transactions in modern times are conducted through these bodies." To give a company "immunity from all punishment because of the old and exploded doctrine that a corporation cannot commit a crime" would take away practically "the only means" to prevent "abuses" by corporations.

The federal courts approved the same rule for other federal crimes. In 1918, Judge Learned Hand wrote that "there is no distinction in essence between the civil and the criminal liability of corporations, based upon the element of intent or wrongful purpose."[82] Some states adopt a narrower standard for when a corporation can be criminally liable, and many use the Model Penal Code and its requirement that conduct by an employee be permitted or tolerated by management.[83] But the federal standard remains broad—broader than standards for corporate liability elsewhere in the world. The corporation is liable when any employee commits a crime so long as the employee was acting within the scope of employment and for the corporation's benefit.

The Sweep of Federal Criminal Law

Not only is the standard for holding corporations liable broad, but so are the underlying federal crimes. Consider the obstruction-of-justice statute at issue in the Andersen case. The statute applies to anyone who "knowingly" and "corruptly" induces others to conceal information from any pending official investigation. Other bread-and-butter crimes use words such as *willfully*. The required level of criminal intent is often low.

There are also many, many thousands of federal criminal laws. In fact, no one knows exactly how many; a retired Justice Department official given the unfortunate job of trying to count them all in the 1980s stated, "You [could] have died and resurrected three times" and still have no answer.[84] Some of the laws are obscure and minor, such as the one making it a crime to misuse the image of Smokey the Bear. And it depends how you count them, as some provisions have phrases that judges have interpreted as creating separate crimes.[85] When an administrative agency is established to regulate, say, securities or food and drugs, Congress also often makes it a crime to willfully violate any regulation the agency enacts; over time, the regulations may come to number in the hundreds or thousands.[86] On the other hand, most obscure laws are rarely used. Corporations are mostly convicted of fraud, environmental offenses, antitrust activity, food and drug violations, and a few other crimes.

Some federal criminal laws were product of corporate scandals. Securities fraud statutes grew out of the Great Depression and the enactment of the 1933 and 1934 Securities Acts. The statutes of the Racketeer Influenced and Corrupt Organizations (RICO) Act came about as the result of 1960s revelations of the corrupting influence of organized crime. The Foreign Corrupt Practices Act (FCPA) grew out of the Watergate Special Prosecution Force, which found that corporations had slush funds dedicated to illegal campaign donations in the United States and bribes overseas.[87] The 1980s brought still more scandals, including the savings and loan failures, insider trading cases, and government contracting abuses, with new criminal statutes passed in response to each, including the Money Laundering Prosecution Improvements Act of 1988, the Major Fraud Act of 1988, and the Antitrust Amendments Act of 1990. In the aftermath of Enron and Andersen, Congress passed the Sarbanes-Oxley Act and made a series of changes to criminal laws. The global financial crisis produced the Dodd-Frank Act, with provisions to encourage whistle-blowers to come forward. Federal criminal law continues to adapt and respond to white-collar crime.

The Andersen Case Concludes

The approach of federal law to corporate crime was expressed in the broad jury instructions in the Andersen case. The judge told the jury: "The Defendant in this case is a partnership rather than an individual. Under the law, a partnership is a person and may be liable for violating the criminal laws." However, such an entity is only "legally bound by the acts and statements its agents do or make within the scope of their employment."[88] So long as the agent was dealing with a matter that was "generally entrusted" to the agent or "in line" with his or her duties, the corporation is on the hook. Even if the employee was violating company policy, the company can be convicted. The judge explained:

> In order for a partnership agent to be acting within the scope of his or her employment, the agent must be acting with the intent, at least in part, to benefit the partnership. It is not necessary, however, for the Government to prove that the agent's sole or even primary motive was to benefit the partnership. Furthermore, the Government need not prove that the partnership was actually benefited by the agent's actions.[89]

Just one criminal agent was enough. And there was no question that the relevant employees were acting within the scope of their jobs. What did it mean, though, to corruptly persuade others to obstruct justice?

This key jury instruction was complicated—maybe too complicated—because it grew out of a fight between the lawyers. The jurors were instructed that the purpose of the action must have been "in part, to subvert, undermine, or impede the fact-finding ability of an official proceeding."[90] The judge told the jury, "It is not necessary for the Government to prove that an official proceeding was pending or even about to be initiated at the time the obstructive conduct occurred." Both sides argued at length with the judge about the crucial question of what employees of Andersen must have been doing when they destroyed documents.[91] The prosecutors asked for the phrase "subvert, undermine, or impede" to be included in the instruction. The defense argued this was vague. The word *impede*, they claimed, "can be anything." Prosecutors countered that employees must have been impeding an official inquiry.[92] The defense wanted to include the word *dishonestly*, to highlight that well-meaning actions were not enough to convict. In fact, the standard jury instruction in the Fifth Circuit defined *corruptly* as "knowingly and dishonestly, with the specific intent to subvert or undermine the integrity" of proceedings. The defense lawyer argued the judge was going "where the courts have not gone before"—a *Star Trek* reference, the lawyer added.[93]

In the end, the judge gave the jury an instruction without the word *dishonestly*, instead using the phrase "subvert, undermine, or impede." The instruction did not say anything about a specific intent to destroy documents to be used in a particular official proceeding. The judge reminded the jury that "the fact that David Duncan pleaded guilty is not evidence of the guilt of Andersen, but you may consider it in evaluating David Duncan's testimony."[94] The judge also reminded the jury not to think anything of the fact that Temple and several others "were unavailable to testify," nor of the fact that some people were not charged as defendants.[95] Would the jury properly understand those instructions and be able to sort through the huge body of evidence?

With the jury having heard the judge's instructions, both sides presented their closing arguments—their chance to leave a final impression and try to make the sprawling case simple and clear. The prosecution placed the chief blame not with David Duncan but with Nancy Temple and the legal team, arguing, "Arthur Andersen's legal department was the driving force behind this." They emphasized that the Andersen partners and lawyers were acting intentionally. "Andersen knew the drill. They knew the stakes with the SEC," the prosecutor said. "They knew that Enron was déjà vu all over again with Waste Management and Sunbeam," two of the previous cases involving Andersen and accounting investigations.[96] The Andersen lawyers would have been "insane" not to be worrying about being sued by the SEC. Why else would they send out messages about the importance of following the document retention policy—to simply make sure everyone's files were not messy? The prosecutor emphasized, "You don't worry about mopping the floor when the building's on fire."[97]

The defense responded with outrage. The lead defense lawyer almost had to be restrained by federal marshals when he refused to stop objecting during the prosecutor's closing arguments (he announced, "May the record reflect that the marshals have just asked me to sit down").[98] Maybe that was intended to show the depth of emotion the lawyer felt for the corporation that was on trial. During his own arguments, the lawyer said: "They had no evidence that anybody did this for an improper purpose. . . . Did it look suspicious? You bet."[99] But the entire case was "the most incredible tragedy and rush to judgment," where everybody "assumed this company was guilty."[100] Even early on in the trial, he had complained to the judge, "I do not believe we're receiving a fair trial."[101] With his time running out, the lawyer emphasized that it would be "wrong" to have "ruined" such a large firm and this trial was the "only chance we have ever had to recapture the legacy and reputation of Arthur Andersen."[102] To the end, the defense sought to portray the company as a human victim. Perhaps this was like a death penalty case—an appeal to mercy was needed, since the defendant would not survive a conviction.

The prosecution had the last word in rebuttal (although the defense repeatedly interjected, behavior the judge called "absolutely outrageous"). If Andersen was a person, it was no different from a common criminal. No criminal can "go into a crime scene" and say, "Because the police might be coming, let's get rid of the gun." Everyone must be "accountable under the law," even "a Big Five accounting firm."[103]

The jury deliberated for ten days. It included three women and nine men, most of whom were black or Latino. They were initially split evenly, six to six, but as they continued to deliberate for days, more changed their votes to convict.[104] During that time, they sent questions to the judge asking to see things or for clarifications. They asked for the jury instructions, for office supplies, and to read all of David Duncan's testimony again.[105] The jurors also asked to see a dictionary. The judge said they could not have one, telling them, "If you have a word you would like to find, please indicate that word."[106] The jury then sent a note on the seventh day, with three jurors apparently still voting to acquit: "We are not able to reach a unanimous decision." The judge gave the jury an instruction colloquially called a dynamite instruction (because it can blow apart deadlocked jurors), telling them to deliberate more to see if they could come to a verdict. As time passed, the defense asked for a mistrial, but the judge responded, "We're here. Let's let the jury deliberate and see what happens."[107]

The jury then asked a good question: "If each of us believes that one Andersen agent acted knowingly and with corrupt intent, is it [required] for all of us to believe it was the same agent?"[108] This question went to the heart of the case: who was the corrupt persuader—and could there be more than one? The government had proposed language suggesting that maybe more than one employee could add up to a corrupt persuader, but eventually withdrew it.[109] The defense argued, "The only issue for 12 people to unanimously agree on, from our perspective, was obviously the possibility of Duncan or Temple."[110] The defense wanted the jury given more instructions that it had to be one specific person, and the judge said, "I understand your position, but I am not going to send back another note. I'm not going to send back another instruction."[111]

After deliberating for ten days, sequestered in a hotel, the jury voted to convict on June 15, 2002. Apparently there had been a lone holdout juror who was initially not convinced there was a single person who corruptly persuaded, but the holdout seemed to have concluded that, based on the October 16 email, Temple was the "corrupt persuader." That juror spoke to reporters after the trial, calling the email the "smoking gun."[112] David Duncan's testimony admitting his guilt was apparently not the deciding factor, at least not for the holdout juror.

Now Andersen faced up to five years' probation and a $500,000 fine. One prosecutor spoke of how the case sent a message: "Don't destroy the evidence." The lead prosecutor commented, "We are not finished with Arthur Andersen." Andersen had been badly damaged even before the verdict, having laid off 7,000 employees, sold many of its practices in the United States, and lost a quarter of its clients.[113] Under SEC rules, once it was convicted Andersen had to give up doing accounting work for public companies. Andersen notified the SEC that it would stop auditing public corporations by August 31, 2002, and on that day Andersen gave up its licenses.[114] Its St. Louis office sold off the contents of its three floors at a public auction; apparently the designer Herman Miller chairs were the first to go. (Former Andersen employees were allowed to go to a special pre-sale, perhaps to buy their own office furniture.)[115] Many partners and employees had left for other accounting firms, while thousands more employees who had had nothing to do with Enron were now out of work.

Reversal and Aftermath

The case slowly made its way to the U.S. Supreme Court on appeal. The Fifth Circuit Court of Appeals unanimously affirmed the conviction, calling it "clear at every step" that "the SEC was the feared opponent and initiator of a proceeding and not some other shadowy opponent."[116] Then the Supreme Court took up the case. Among those filing a friend-of-the-court brief on Andersen's behalf was the U.S. Chamber of Commerce, "the world's largest business federation," which wrote in opposition to the "potential criminalization" of document retention policies, saying that it could "paralyze" businesses.[117] It also criticized prosecutors for prosecuting the "corporate structure" rather than individual people.

When the Supreme Court held oral arguments, the justices seemed suspicious of the conduct at Andersen. Justice Antonin Scalia noted, "We all know that what are euphemistically termed 'record-retention programs' are, in fact, record-destruction programs."[118] Justice Anthony Kennedy added, "Well, that's like in—the old—the rule in the Army, 'Make two copies of everything you throw out.'" (That line earned laughter from the spectators.) But there were also incredulous questions about the broad way the government was interpreting the obstruction-of-justice statute. Justice Sandra Day O'Connor pointed out that although Duncan had pleaded guilty, it was lawful and "perfectly okay" for him to destroy documents on his own. The question was whether he had corruptly persuaded anyone else to destroy documents.

In May 2005, the justices unanimously voted to reverse the conviction. The problem, they said, was one of state of mind. The statute required that someone must "knowingly" and "corruptly" persuade. Neither side at trial had focused on connecting the words *knowingly* and *corruptly*, but the justices suggested that the two words together required the prosecutors to show a more specific bad intent to keep evidence from officials. The jury was told that "even if [the] petitioner honestly and sincerely believed its conduct was lawful," it could convict. The justices were troubled that the jury instruction

did not really use the word *corruptly*, instead including language about actions that "subvert, undermine, or impede" a proceeding. That instruction
did not clearly tell the jury that they had to find that there had been a direct,
"knowing and dishonest" intent to specifically convince a person to destroy
documents relevant to a particular official proceeding. That said, judges are
still divided on exactly what the word *corruptly* means in the statute, since
the Court never said what was the right way to explain it to the jury.[119]
Meanwhile, the jury foreman told the press that he thought "the Supreme
Court has made a grave error."[120]

The defense lawyers celebrated: "It's an incredible triumph for the judicial
system in America to do this even though the company has been destroyed
and the employees are scattered to the winds."[121] This outcome suggests a
twin problem. Corporate convictions can have terrible collateral effects on
innocent people: employees, shareholders, and the public. Yet failing to prosecute the firm may let it continue to violate the law with impunity. Andersen
had been repeatedly targeted in civil enforcement actions, and it was on notice long before the Enron case existed.

Federal prosecutors were widely called responsible for destroying Andersen, though they do not really deserve that blame or credit—not fully, at
least.[122] Andersen had already been on the edge, rapidly shedding employees
and clients, and the SEC and other prosecutors and regulators were waiting
in the wings. If you are already dying, maybe you do not mind risking the
death penalty a trial might bring. Still, prosecutors were right that in order
to bring more prosecutions against large corporations, they would need a
strategy. As one judge has put it, when prosecutions can be "a matter of life
and death to many companies," prosecutors may be the ones who hold "the
proverbial gun to [the corporation's] head."[123] Yet many corporations are
convicted each year without suffering Andersen's fate. The reputation of an
accounting firm may be greatly affected by fraud allegations, but how about
those with diverse sets of clients and customers, such as Siemens? Does
someone deciding which coffeemaker to buy care about bribes in a mass
transit project in Argentina? If regulators decide not to suspend or debar a
firm, then the collateral consequences of a conviction may be small.

Enron and Arthur Andersen were just two of the corporations that collapsed as the dot-com bubble burst, an event that uncovered still more major
corporate scandals. No less than 10 percent of publicly listed companies re-

stated their earnings.[124] Federal Reserve chairman Alan Greenspan spoke of how "an infectious greed seemed to grip much of our business community."[125] In response, Congress enacted new legislation, known as the Sarbanes-Oxley Act, which included new crimes, corporate disclosure requirements, new oversight for accountants, regulation of corporate audit committees to reduce conflicts of interest, and additional enforcement resources.[126]

Congress also changed the criminal laws, enacting a broader version of the obstruction-of-justice law that Arthur Andersen was prosecuted under.[127] The fraud statute saw an increase in penalties, particularly in major financial cases.[128] Congress created two new crimes, conspiracy to commit a securities offense[129] and retaliating against whistle-blowers.[130] Congress asked the U.S. Sentencing Commission to consider more severe sentences, given "the growing incidence of serious fraud offenses" and the need to "deter, prevent, and punish such offenses."[131] The commission took the hint and enhanced punishments for a range of white-collar offenses, including crimes involving millions of dollars in losses to victims and obstruction of justice.[132] More recently, Congress enacted the Dodd-Frank legislation in 2010, providing the SEC with additional enforcement resources and adding rewards for whistle-blowers reporting major corporate crimes.[133]

Do tougher laws really discourage corporate crime? The newest white-collar crimes have rarely been enforced. Companies have found ways to adapt to the new rules, as I will describe, and only a handful suffered the fate of Andersen. Law professors David A. Skeel and William J. Stuntz have argued that such get-tough legislation, while moralistic in tone, is deeply immoral in practice because it is "both rarely and idiosyncratically" enforced.[134] One question is whether a few unlucky individuals—celebrities such as Martha Stewart or truly notorious white-collar criminals such as Bernard Madoff—receive the brunt of enforcement while the vast majority of corporations and executives get off scot-free. Some, including law professor Vikramaditya Khanna, view seemingly tough corporate crime legislation as a good thing for corporations: it allows Congress to appear to be responding to public outcry without creating new forms of regulation, civil liability, or liability for corporate managers themselves.[135] Prosecutors have limited resources—how much do corporations have to fear from them, compared with, say, the SEC, which can issue rules that apply across the board?

Although officials were talking about a new get-tough corporate prosecution approach, the September 11, 2001, attacks drew federal resources toward national security and away from financial fraud investigations. As a consequence, the Andersen case resulted in a new approach toward corporate prosecutions, which is the subject of this book. In the next chapter, I describe how prosecutors would increasingly emphasize the goal of rehabilitating corporate criminals rather than convicting them, with a focus on settling cases and requiring structural reforms.

To this day, a shell of Arthur Andersen remains. It never declared bankruptcy, and it still operates a conference center outside Chicago. As its ranks melted away, many partners and employees went on to successful careers at other accounting firms. The consulting wing of the company, which split off before the trial, is a major multinational corporation called Accenture, having discarded the tainted Andersen name. What is left of Andersen is still defending itself in court, not from prosecutors but from the last remaining lawsuits by shareholders and other private individuals who claim that Andersen's shoddy auditing harmed Enron and other companies. The DOJ could have prosecuted Andersen again after the Supreme Court reversed the conviction—and maybe it would have won again with corrected jury instructions—but there was obviously no point. As an anonymous DOJ official said at the time, "Why would you charge a company that's already defunct?"[136]

❧ 3 ❧

What Happens to a Prosecution Deferred?

According to Google, "Don't be evil," its famous unofficial motto, is about "much more than" treating customers well.[1] Within the company, Google explains that "trust" and "mutual respect" among workers are keys to success, as is maintaining "the highest possible standards of ethical business conduct." When Google signed a non-prosecution agreement in Rhode Island in 2011, forfeiting $500 million for accepting illegal Canadian pharmaceutical advertisements, did that mean Google had violated its motto and done something "evil"? When prosecutors began investigating, Google promptly adopted new practices to require screening and certification of online pharmacies.[2] Prosecutors also required Google to hire an independent company to screen ads and report to the Food and Drug Administration. Did prosecutors improve the moral character of Google by holding it accountable? That was the goal: to reshape a company's culture. After the Arthur Andersen case, prosecutors emphasized a different approach by offering companies deals to avoid a criminal indictment or conviction. The biggest early test of the approach came in the case of another major accounting firm: KPMG.

Standing before a U.S. Senate subcommittee in 2003, the partner who headed KPMG's Personal Financial Planning practice explained how the company had done nothing wrong. Tax shelters marketed by KPMG were "aggressive" and "complex and technical," but they were also "consistent with the laws in place at the time" and subjected to "rigorous" review.[3]

At around the same time that Arthur Andersen was under scrutiny, the Internal Revenue Service (IRS) announced that KPMG was being investigated for marketing tax shelters to wealthy individuals resulting in billions of dollars in lost taxes. KPMG was not alone in this business, as law firms, major banks, and other accounting firms set up these tax shelters for their clients. A Senate committee began an investigation and conducted hearings in November 2003. Under sharp questioning from Senator Carl Levin, the KPMG partner denied that the tax shelters were designed primarily to help customers avoid paying taxes.

"Is it not the case that these were designed and marketed primarily as tax reduction strategies?" asked Senator Levin.

"Senator, I would not agree with that characterization," the partner responded.

Levin said, "All right. Now, let's look at what other parties involved in transactions said about that issue." He then cross-examined the witness like a lawyer at a trial, reading out loud documents the Senate had obtained showing that an investment advisory firm had asked KPMG to "achieve the desired tax results."

"You don't see anything in there about investment, do you?" asked Levin.

"Senator, my testimony is that these were investment strategies that were presented to individual taxpayers that had tax attributes that those investors found attractive."

Senator Levin kept asking whether there was "any doubt" that these tax shelters were designed to reduce a person's taxes.

The partner began, "Senator, I don't know how to change my answer to—"

"Well, try an honest answer," Senator Levin interjected.

What emerged was that KPMG not only stood to profit from these tax shelters but also was being paid a percentage of clients' tax savings. When asked about this, the partner said that was true only "in a very indirect way."[4]

Two months after the Senate hearings, KPMG announced that the partner who had given the opening statement and was in charge of the unit selling the shelters would be placed on leave. Another senior partner in charge of tax planning would be retiring—not because of any wrongdoing, but because of "ongoing consideration" of its tax practices.[5] Much later, KPMG admitted in a statement to prosecutors that its employees provided "false," "misleading," and "evasive" testimony before the Senate.[6]

Perhaps KPMG was a "good" corporation trying to disavow the acts of a few employees. Can a corporation actually be "good," "bad," or even "evil"? I was surprised to see the view prosecutors have adopted toward corporations. I would have expected those who bring criminals to justice to adopt a strict, hard-nosed approach toward holding companies accountable for crimes. After all, organizations of all kinds are defined as "persons" in federal laws, and prosecutors can take advantage of the unforgiving federal rule holding a company strictly accountable for a crime by an employee.

Instead, federal prosecutors began to treat corporations in a nuanced and "soft" way. By 2003, the overriding goal of corporate prosecutions was to try to rehabilitate a firm's culture, not to punish. At the time of the Enron and Andersen investigations, President George W. Bush called for a "new culture" with a "sense of corporate responsibility."[7] Shortly thereafter, as fraud scandals spread to Adelphia, WorldCom, HealthSouth, and other major companies, a deputy attorney general spoke about corporate culture as a "web of attitudes and practices that tends to replicate and perpetuate itself," and how prosecutors can "change corporate cultures that foster criminal conduct."[8] New policies for corporate prosecutions would follow.

Rehabilitation is neglected in our criminal justice system, as our overpopulated prisons are designed mainly to punish, not to make convicts better people. Yet corporate prosecutions are a dramatic exception. Prosecutors say a central goal is to rehabilitate corporations, to try to help make them better and more ethical. When deferred prosecution and non-prosecution agreements first became common, I thought they could be a promising development. The agreements might structurally reform entire corporations, holding wrongdoers responsible and preventing future crimes. However, the more I have examined how prosecutors have actually implemented the new approach, the more troubled I have become. Prosecutors allow many large companies to avoid an indictment or a conviction, largely freeing them from judicial oversight. From 2001 through 2012, 58 percent of the companies receiving deferred prosecution or non-prosecution agreements were publicly listed on a U.S. stock exchange (148 of 255), while only about 6 percent of those convicted *without* such an agreement were public (125 of more than 2,000 firms).

Prosecutors have entered deferred prosecution or non-prosecution agreements with a long list of household names: AIG, America Online, Barclays, Boeing, Bristol-Myers Squibb, CVS Pharmacy, General Electric, GlaxoSmith-Kline, HealthSouth, JPMorgan, Johnson & Johnson, Merrill Lynch & Co.,

Monsanto, and Sears. But it is not always clear what prosecutors get in exchange for offering leniency to some of the world's largest companies. The terms of these agreements often lack any rigorous structural reforms. Most did require the creation of some kind of compliance program (63 percent, or 160 of 255 agreements), but only a quarter called for independent monitors to supervise compliance, and fewer required evaluating the effectiveness of compliance. More typically, prosecutors ask the company to hire new compliance employees (35 percent, or 88 of 255 agreements), but almost one-third did not mention implementing a compliance program at all (31 percent, or 78 of 255 agreements). The agreements were short-lived, lasting for an average of just over two years. It is doubtful that a large company's culture can be reformed in so little time. Despite the genuine ambition of the new approach, reading the terms of these agreements tells us something quite unsettling about how large corporate prosecutions are actually resolved.

The Fourth One Left Standing

After Arthur Andersen's fall, the Big Five accounting firms that audit the largest corporations in the United States were down to the Big Four. The fall of Enron and a burst of corporate fraud scandals prompted further investigation into questionable accounting practices.[9] While the Senate was conducting its investigation, the IRS issued summonses to one of the Big Four, KPMG. KPMG did not fully comply. Now the question loomed: Would KPMG go the way of Andersen? Would we now have just a Big Three? This looked possible; prosecutors soon filed "the largest criminal tax case ever" against KPMG.[10]

KPMG International is a global network of accounting firms with origins in three different accounting firms, one founded by Piet Klynveld in Amsterdam in 1917, one founded by William Barclay Peat in London, and one founded by James Marwick in New York City in 1897. These came together in the 1980s, with the G in the name coming from Dr. Reinhard Goerdeler, an accountant who helped merge the firms.[11] KPMG International is registered in Switzerland and provides tax and accounting services all over the world, while KPMG LLP, the U.S. branch, is a partnership incorporated in Delaware.

The Big Four operate on a far larger scale than accounting firms that do work for individuals and small businesses, and they can take on accounting for major public corporations. In the Andersen case, Enron charged forward with risky financial and accounting practices, some of which Andersen may have ratified. But in the KPMG case and other tax shelter cases that would follow, it was the reverse, with tax advisors, accountants, and lawyers coming up with the schemes themselves.

What was KPMG like as a workplace? It is hard to tell from the outside, but KPMG has been ranked highly for its environment. Its website says that the company promotes "a culture of trust and collaboration, flexibility and diversity," and highlights how "clients talk about our high level of professional ethics, our loyalty and our approachability."[12] Its motto, "Cutting through complexity," which presumably refers to solving business problems and not to avoiding tax laws, is not as catchy as Google's "Don't be evil."[13] The culture at KPMG had not been traditionally aggressive; the firm did not try to "sell" its services, preferring to offer them in a more genteel way to major corporations and multimillionaire clients.

For a group of tax partners, that restrained culture changed in the late 1990s. This was a time of a great economic growth, and newly wealthy individuals turned to the major accounting firms, law firms, and tax advisors to shield income from federal taxes. Tax evasion is not just failing to pay all of one's own taxes—it is involvement in a scheme to avoid paying taxes. The employees at KPMG, alongside other accountants, lawyers, and banks, designed a series of complex tax shelters and marketed them to wealthy individual clients. KPMG did not just provide tax advice; it actively began selling tax shelter "products." The target customer had $20 million in capital gains each year, easily enough to justify paying to shelter the funds.

The tax shelters were complicated and confusingly named, going by acronyms such as FLIPS, OPIS, and BLIPS. The main idea was simple, though—to create miniature companies for wealthy clients to invest in, allowing them to deduct their investments or paper losses while taking very little real risk or actual losses.

Take BLIPS, or Bond Link Issued Premium Structure. This scheme proposed the creation of an artificial loss in order to shelter income from taxes. Doing so required another firm, known as the "promoter." One promoter of BLIPS was a company, Presidio Advisory Services, founded by two former

KPMG employees. The taxpayer would pay a percentage of the taxes he or she sought to avoid to a shell company. The shell company then got a much bigger loan from a bank—Deutsche Bank was one of the banks and would later be prosecuted—with interest payments over several years so large that the client would appear to be facing a loss.[14] Yet the bank's money would never be at risk, as careful conditions placed on the loan ensured that it would basically remain in the bank's own vaults. The supposed business investments of the shell company were very small and made only with the taxpayer's money, not with the loan from the bank. The shell company would make small investments in foreign currency—perhaps the Hong Kong dollar or Argentinean peso—but these were done only briefly, as a "fig leaf."[15] One of the employees at Presidio later testified that it would take an "unbelievable miracle" for the shell company to actually make money on its investments: "Given that BLIPS only lasts 60 days, there is no chance to profit."[16] When the shell company was dissolved, often on the sixtieth day, all the partners received their money back.[17] The taxpayer would claim the millions of dollars of interest due on the huge loan as a "loss," trying to take advantage of a quirk in partnership tax law. Meanwhile, the bank, the lawyers, KPMG, and the "promoter" would all get a fee. Everyone won, except the government.

The other shelters were just as complicated or more so. The FLIPS and OPIS shelters involved entities set up—where else?—offshore in the Cayman Islands. As one of the KPMG partners later candidly put it, these shelters "stood out more like a sore thumb," as "no one in his right mind would pay such an exorbitant price" for that option.[18] Another shelter, the SOS shelter, was popular within the firm, and fourteen KPMG partners used it themselves.[19] These shelters were among KPMG's top revenue producers until they were shut down. BLIPS was approved by KPMG for sale in 1999 and sold to 186 people before the IRS listed it as potentially abusive in 2000. But in just one year, BLIPS earned $53 million in revenue and generated billions of dollars in tax losses.[20]

What was the attitude within the firm toward these shelters? We know something about the culture at KPMG during this time from internal emails later obtained by the Senate committee that investigated the matter. Its report described a "corporate culture" that placed "ongoing pressure" on the tax professionals at the company to sell these shelters.[21] Initially, people at KPMG went back and forth about whether the various shelters were legal, ultimately giving an opinion that it was "more likely than not" they were allowed. High-level partners at both its Tax Department and its Washington, D.C., office were involved. Internal documents indicated that they felt some of the regulations were vague, and even if they were caught, the fines would be a fraction of their profits: "no greater than $14,000 per $100,000 in KPMG fees."

One former KPMG partner testified at the Senate hearings in 2003 that he was "never comfortable" that the BLIPS shelter would actually create a "reasonable opportunity to make a reasonable pre-tax profit." He had expressed his discomfort in an email, saying that if there really was no potential for profit, then "our opinion is worthless." He described how he was "disappointed with the decision" to let this tax shelter go forward, but because there were "a lot of smart partners with significant experience" who approved it, "there was really nothing left for me to say."[22]

Emails showed major disagreements within KPMG. One KPMG employee emailed that "the whole thing stinks" and that "I believe we are filing misleading, and perhaps false, returns by taking this reporting position."[23] The discussions at KPMG could at times be crass; one employee declared, "I do believe the time has come to shit and get off the pot," only to receive a reply from the second-in-command at the tax services practice: "I believe the expression is shit OR get off the pot, and I vote for shit."[24]

Other KPMG partners testified there was a "rigorous debate" and "disparate views" but that they ultimately approved the shelters. One testified that "money was not a consideration" and that they had engaged in "intensive meetings" and review over several months in 1999 before deciding to go forward.[25] To be on the safe side, KPMG also required customers to sign a letter attesting that they had reviewed the shelters themselves. However, KPMG did not register the shelters with the IRS. The IRS had a procedure for someone organizing a shelter to notify the agency, describe the transaction, and learn if the shelter posed potential problems. KPMG's lawyers noted that by not registering the shelters, they risked prosecution, but registering the shelters might make them harder to sell, and they would "not be able to compete" with other tax advisors.[26]

The internal emails indicated they were not so conservative in their marketing. One read: "We are dealing with ruthless execution, hand-to-hand combat, blocking and tackling. Whatever the mixed metaphor, let's just do it." The Senate Report concluded that KPMG turned its tax professionals into salespeople, "pressuring" them to "meet revenue targets, using telemarketing to find clients, using confidential client tax data to identify potential buyers, [and] targeting its own audit clients for sales pitches."[27] Senator Levin described the typical phone call like this:

> "We know you made a lot of income. Do you want to pay less taxes on that income?" And the people who are supposed to pay taxes will say, "Well, is it legal? Is it proper?" They say, "Yes, we got a legal opinion saying it's proper."

KPMG created an entire telemarketing center to try to sell tax shelters to multimillionaires. Emails also shed light on the culture in the group: "SELL, SELL, SELL!!" Another warned the partners, "Look at the last partner scorecard. Unlike golf, a low number is not a good thing. . . . A lot of us need to put more revenue on the board."[28]

Unlike typical accountants, KPMG was not paid by the hour, did not charge a flat fee, and was not compensated based on the returns from these supposed investments. Instead, KPMG, the banks, and other participants in creating the shelters were paid a percentage of the taxes avoided—usually 5–7 percent (KPMG's share was usually about 1 percent).[29] Yet many states make it illegal to pay a percentage fee to accountants.[30]

Enter the IRS

In March 2000, two more tax partners at KPMG advised that these shelters were "frivolous" and would "lose" in court, but the leadership at KPMG's tax practice decided to continue selling them.[31] The IRS became concerned that the shelters were not real investments with "economic substance," and in August 2000 it issued a notice stating that shelters without real economic substance were in its opinion not allowed and penalties could result from their use.[32] No court had ever ruled the tax shelters illegal, nor had the IRS issued a regulation declaring them illegal, as doing so would take time, given the cumbersome process involved. To more quickly respond to creative new tax shelters it views as problematic, the IRS can issue a notice to "list" the practice as illegal in its view. Congress later changed the IRS Code, and regulations were adopted making BLIPS illegal.[33]

Administrative agencies such as the IRS have broad authority to conduct investigations, including sweeping powers to subpoena or request documents, call witnesses, and even require a witness to submit a statement under oath. The Supreme Court famously said an agency "has a power of inquisition" and "can investigate merely on suspicion that the law is being violated, or even just because it wants assurance that it is not."[34] Dating back to 1864, the IRS has had the power to issue a summons to a taxpayer suspected of filing an incorrect return, and the IRS can now inquire into "any offense connected with the administration or enforcement of the internal revenue laws."[35]

When the IRS issued its summons, KPMG provided hundreds of boxes of documents, but it withheld as privileged important documents regarding some of the shelters. In 2002, the IRS asked a judge to order KPMG to provide those documents; the judge concluded KPMG had "misrepresent[ed]" these "tax shelter marketing activities" as privileged when they were clearly not.[36] KPMG later admitted it had falsely claimed to have given the IRS all the documents requested.[37] The IRS asked KPMG for the names of their tax shelter clients, and also asked for names from two of the other Big Four accounting firms: Ernst & Young and PricewaterhouseCoopers (as well as another accounting firm, BDO Seidman).

At the same time, the Senate began its own investigation, and KPMG failed to hand over requested documents related to the SOS shelter and use of shelters by its own partners.[38] At hearings in November 2003, Senator Levin not only sharply questioned witnesses but also demanded an end to the practices: "The engine of deception and greed needs to be turned off, dismantled, and consigned to the junkyard where it belongs." Meanwhile, the IRS estimated tax losses of $33 billion from these listed tax shelters—and another $52 billion from other questionable tax shelters.[39]

What would the IRS do? Most agencies are hands-off until a problem comes to their attention, since they do not have the resources to investigate most companies or even do much spot-checking. The IRS processes millions of tax returns each year from companies and hundreds of millions of tax returns from individuals, the most complicated of which may be very hard to understand. IRS enforcement budgets have shrunk; the agency has lost thousands of employees, and it can do few audits of big companies.[40] An agency such as the IRS can create detailed standards for companies to follow and then encourage reporting and self-regulation by promising serious consequences for those that do not comply. As SEC chairman and later U.S. Supreme Court Justice William O. Douglas put it, "Self-discipline is always more welcome than discipline imposed from above."[41] That is why agencies increasingly emphasize transparency—disclosing accurate information to regulators and the public—so that misconduct does not occur in the first place, or is disclosed if it does happen. If an agency learns a company has violated regulations or laws, it has several options. It may give the company a warning and an opportunity to correct the problem. Or it may decide to pursue civil remedies such as fines or orders to cease illegal activity (injunctions), either before its own administrative judges or in more formal proceedings before a federal judge.

However, if the agency thinks a person or corporation is being defiant or has violated the rules in an egregious way, it may decide that the case should be criminal. Agencies have different procedures and practices to make this decision, and no agency refers very many cases for criminal investigation. The IRS has a "strong preference" for prosecuting individuals and not companies for tax fraud.[42] Yet the KPMG case was seen as worthy of prosecution, and by December 2003 the IRS had referred the case to its criminal investigators.

Following the U.S. Senate hearings, the IRS referred the case to the U.S. attorney for the Southern District of New York to consider a possible prosecution.[43] Meanwhile, the IRS gave taxpayers who used these shelters about six weeks to come forward and pay the taxes they owed, with no penalty— but if they did not pay, they would face "more severe consequences later."[44] The IRS ended up settling with about 1,200 individual taxpayers and recovering $3.7 billion in unpaid taxes from those who came forward as part of the settlement initiative.[45]

The Brooklyn Plan

How would prosecutors approach KPMG now that they had been called into action? In 2002, President George W. Bush created the Corporate

Fraud Task Force, consisting of prosecutors to coordinate investigation and prosecution of companies (in 2009 it was rebadged as the Financial Fraud Enforcement Task Force).[46] The task force was centered at the Department of Justice's offices in Washington, D.C., although it worked with the various U.S. attorneys' offices around the country, regulators such as the SEC and IRS, and some state prosecutors. A new strategy emerged, using a procedure that traced its origins back to, of all things, a 1930s plan to deal with first-time juvenile offenders in Brooklyn, New York.[47] The so-called Brooklyn Plan began with a prosecutor's idea to file a case in court but defer a prosecution, a procedure known as diversion. If the juvenile stayed out of trouble for a year or so, the charges would be dropped. Diversion programs, now used around the country, aim to channel low-level offenders out of the system, give them a chance, and focus on the more serious offenders. The new approach suggested that corporations were more like juveniles—not entirely innocent, but mainly in need of guidance, rehabilitation, and supervision.

The modern corporate culture revolution dates back to 1991 and the implementation of the U.S. Sentencing Guidelines, which emphasize rewarding a company for efforts to "promote an organizational culture that encourages ethical conduct and a commitment to compliance with the law."[48] Before then, compliance programs were important only in a few industries where regulations required them, along with some voluntary initiatives, such as those in the defense industry after the military procurement scandals of the 1980s.[49] Now compliance programs are pervasive across the U.S. economy. There are entire professional organizations of people who specialize in compliance work. Companies often have dedicated ethics and compliance officers, separate from their legal department or general counsel, who oversee this work.[50]

Shortly before the IRS sent the KPMG case to the U.S. attorney, the Department of Justice had put a new theory of corporate prosecutions into writing, one that focused on corporate culture and compliance. There had been a few corporate deferred prosecution agreements before. The first that I have found was in 1992, with Salomon Brothers, and there were a dozen such agreements overall in the 1990s. In 1999, under Deputy Attorney General Eric Holder, the DOJ issued its first memo providing guidelines for corporate prosecutions.[51] The deferred prosecution approach was more firmly set out in 2003 in a set of revised DOJ guidelines. These principles for the prosecution of organizations, contained in the *U.S. Attorneys' Manual*, used by federal prosecutors, were popularly called the "Thompson Memo" after Larry Thompson, the deputy attorney general who revised them.[52] While DOJ has revised the guidelines several more times (the McNulty Memo released in 2006 contained revisions by then-deputy attorney general Paul J. McNulty, and the Filip Memo released in 2008 contained revisions by then-deputy attorney general Mark R. Filip), the principles still maintain the same basic approach.

At the heart of the approach are nine factors to consider when deciding to prosecute a company. It begins with factors you would think would matter most to prosecutors: (1) the seriousness of the offense, (2) the pervasiveness of wrongdoing within the corporation, and (3) the firm's history of similar conduct. The next three factors turn to cooperation and compliance: (4) the firm's timely and voluntary disclosure of wrongdoing, (5) the firm's compliance program, and (6) any remedial actions, such as firing wrongdoers and cooperating with prosecutors. The last three factors discuss whether a criminal prosecution is a good idea given (7) the harm a prosecution would cause, including to shareholders, (8) the adequacy of prosecutions of individuals, and (9) whether it would be enough to impose civil or regulatory remedies. Lawyers hang on each word in the guidelines to argue that their client should receive leniency.

Without receiving real leniency in exchange for self-reporting and compliance, corporations would have little incentive to disclose their crimes or adopt compliance measures that might uncover still more crimes, as law professor and economist Jennifer Arlen has explored in her work.[53] The new approach encouraged prosecutors to defer prosecution in order to permit a company to improve its compliance program and to cooperate. The DOJ said this would make prosecutors "a force for positive change of corporate culture, alter corporate behavior, and prevent, discover, and punish white collar crime."[54] These agreements, as one prosecutor put it early on, provide "a way to get better results more quickly . . . We're getting the sort of significant reforms you might not even get following a trial and conviction."[55] The new approach would produce very different negotiations with corporate targets, ones where the goal is to come to a deal that can rehabilitate the culture of the corporation. But those guidelines say nothing about how to actually accomplish that goal.

The Study of Corporate Culture

Can prosecutors on the outside promote sound compliance inside a company? There are different ways of categorizing corporate cultures, or subcultures. We all know that working for one employer can be very different from working at another, even if they are similar companies in the same industry. In a classic treatment, Terrence Deal and Allan Kennedy talk about a "work-hard, play-hard culture," a "tough-guy macho" culture, a "process culture," and a risk-taking "bet-the-company" culture.[56] Procedures and codes of ethics may also help define culture, as may supervision and discipline of employees. There are competing assessment tools: one well-known example designed by Kim S. Cameron and Robert E. Quinn uses the "Competing Values Framework" based on employee surveys, and describes the culture of a firm in four dimensions: whether it is hierarchical or flexible and "ad hoc," and whether it is internally focused, with a "clan" culture, or 4 outwardly or market/results focused.[57] Cameron and Quinn acknowledge that some companies may be more effective with one type or another. None of those cultures necessarily tolerates poor ethics or criminal conduct, nor do prosecutors use any such tools to try to assess a company's culture.

If there is a problem with a company's culture, how do managers change it?[58] Some scholars who study corporate crime, such as Brent Fisse and John Braithwaite, suggest the use of internal controls and procedures.[59] Others suggest that compliance procedures and codes of ethics may send a message that what is valued is just following rules, rather than doing the right thing for its own sake. As one scholar puts it, "There are no quick and easy techniques for building a new organizational culture."[60] There is an enormous literature on trying to change an organization, written by people who study business, corporate governance, management, organizational theory, and sociology. None suggest that such work is easy. Efforts to improve compliance may need to go beyond rewriting the rules to an ongoing process affecting how employees think and behave. Compliance may be most difficult to implement where the legal rules are not crystal clear, as with much of federal criminal law.[61] That said, prosecutors are not trying to change everything about a company's culture—just its compliance with criminal law.

Negotiating with Prosecutors

The negotiations between KPMG and federal prosecutors began at the highest levels, with executives meeting directly with the U.S. Attorney. Those meetings do not occur in a typical criminal case, and normally such negotiations would remain secret until a deferred prosecution agreement was reached. The KPMG case was different. A team of six or more prosecutors participated in negotiations, as did the U.S. attorney himself. There were far more lawyers on the KPMG side, along with a welter of lawyers from different firms hired by former KPMG employees. Twenty-two million pages of documents in the case and details about how the negotiations occurred would later be aired before Judge Lewis Kaplan in the Southern District of New York.

KPMG hired new lawyers "to come up with a new cooperative approach," with a team led by a former prosecutor who had previously represented Enron and other major clients. He promised prosecutors that KPMG would now be "as cooperative as possible." Many meetings followed, and the U.S. attorney told KPMG's lawyer that its cooperation was lacking: "Let me put it this way. I've seen a lot better from big companies."[62]

KPMG then appealed to the U.S. attorney's superiors in Washington, D.C. In effect, the company was trying to go over the heads of the prosecutors working on the case, even the U.S. attorney, to argue for more lenient treatment. This is unheard of in run-of-the-mill criminal cases, but it is not at all unusual in major corporate prosecutions. Large companies hire lawyers with access, and KPMG secured a meeting with the deputy attorney general to plead its case and argue that it was in "full compliance" with the new corporate prosecution guidelines.[63]

Meanwhile, the clock was ticking on the prosecution. A grand jury convened, and it is rare for one not to indict. After an indictment, the criminal process would move quickly toward a trial. At the eleventh hour, Arthur Andersen had rejected a deal and gone on to trial, but KPMG made a different decision. Perhaps the meeting in Washington, D.C., had paid off and KPMG's lawyers had been able to emphasize their extraordinary efforts to cooperate.[64] On August 29, 2005, the DOJ and the IRS announced that the criminal prosecution of KPMG would not go forward, though prosecution of individual employees would proceed. KPMG itself would get a deferred prosecution agreement.

Recall the nine factors in the DOJ's principles for prosecuting organizations. Why did KPMG avoid an indictment? On the first factor, seriousness of the offense, and the second factor, the pervasiveness of wrongdoing, KPMG may not have come off well. Perhaps on the third factor, the firm's history of similar conduct, KPMG scored better. But on the fourth factor, KPMG could not cite timely and voluntary disclosure of wrongdoing; it had even kept documents from the IRS and the U.S. Senate. Perhaps it could cite factor five, a compliance program, but whatever that program was, it did not prevent aggressive marketing of these tax shelters. KPMG could cite its remedial actions, such as firing wrongdoers and cooperating with prosecutors, and it could emphasize the harm a prosecution would cause by pointing to the fate of Andersen. On factor eight, KPMG could say prosecuting employees would be adequate, and on factor nine, it could pay civil fines.

Attorney General Alberto Gonzales gave a speech at a press conference announcing the agreement. That alone suggests this was an extremely high-profile settlement. At the press conference, the attorney general highlighted "the reality that the conviction of an organization can affect innocent workers and others associated with the organization, and can even have an impact on the national economy."[65] KPMG sounded too big to fail—and to jail.

While the "too big to jail" concern is real, I want to emphasize here that prosecutors are absolutely right to try to avoid collateral consequences of a corporate conviction. The KPMG case is an important illustration of that. Particularly after Arthur Andersen's collapse, there were few big accounting firms left. Convicting and destroying KPMG might have weakened the accounting industry, which audits corporations to prevent and detect corporate fraud. Prosecutors settled the case in a way designed to avoid those negative consequences. Rather than merely label the settlement as a suspect "too big to jail" deal, we should focus on the substance of the agreement and whether it effectively held KPMG accountable.

As it turned out, there would be no conviction for KPMG, nor any indictment before a grand jury. Grand juries are specialized, with a simple function: whether to issue an indictment accusing a defendant of a crime. They decide if there is enough evidence to bring the charges, whether the court has jurisdiction, and whether the charges are in fact a crime. A grand jury is not purely a formality, as sometimes it does not return an indictment (although prosecutors can convene another one). It also provides prosecutors with a chance to obtain documents and call witnesses. Its proceedings are secret, but the government may rely on the same material to bring other criminal or civil cases.[66] Moreover, the indictment itself can be a blow to a company's reputation. Deferred prosecutions avoid all of those consequences of grand jury proceedings.

Would the judge allow a prosecution to be put off? The judge perhaps could have told prosecutors that the deal was unfair, too lenient, or inappropriate given the purposes of a criminal prosecution. However, the judge apparently ratified the deal without any changes to the terms on August 29, 2005, after a hearing at which KPMG entered a plea of not guilty.[67] This was not surprising; no federal judge before or since has rejected a deferred prosecution agreement.

A Corporate Confession

Of the more than three hundred agreements I have read, the one with KPMG is among the most intrusive. It begins with a detailed admission of wrongdoing under the heading "Acceptance of Responsibility for Violation of Law." It stated that KPMG "assisted high net worth United States citizens to evade United States individual income taxes on billions of dollars in capital gain and ordinary income by developing, promoting and implementing unregistered and fraudulent tax shelters."[68] KPMG admitted that a "number of KPMG tax partners engaged in conduct that was unlawful and fraudulent." An additional ten-page, single-spaced statement of facts described the conduct and called it "deliberately approved and perpetrated at the highest levels" at KPMG.

Why ask the corporation to confess its sins? Like individuals when they plead guilty, a company may be asked to admit guilt in detail, and be given a lighter sentence under the sentencing guidelines based on "affirmative acceptance of responsibility."[69] Usually prosecutors ask firms entering deferred prosecution or non-prosecution agreements to admit their wrongdoing and accept responsibility. Of the agreements obtained, 89 percent included an acceptance of responsibility or admissions (206 of 232 agreements).[70] Regulators, in contrast, do not always demand a confession. The SEC had a long-standing policy allowing a firm to "neither admit nor deny" wrongdoing when settling a civil case, which became controversial. A federal judge rejected a civil settlement with Citibank that did not include an admission of wrongdoing, saying it was neither "fair" nor in the "public interest."[71] A series of other federal judges raised similar questions, and the SEC now says it will typically avoid such language.[72]

Federal prosecutors have said they always "require a complete admission of wrongdoing." Appearing before Congress in 2013, a DOJ official explained that no matter what kind of agreement there is between prosecutors and a company, "the company must fully acknowledge its criminal wrongdoing and may not retract that."[73] That is not entirely true. Just over 10 percent of deferred prosecution and non-prosecution agreements did not include an acceptance of responsibility or admission of guilt. In those cases, there was rarely any explanation why the company was not required to admit anything. Many of those agreements date back to the early 2000s, and the practice may have changed. But still more troubling is that in about one-fifth of the cases, admissions were not made in any detail.

The vast majority of agreements did include a statement of facts (80 percent, or 186 of 232 agreements obtained). Most of those statements included detailed admissions, as in the KPMG case. But some companies were able to keep what happened out of the public eye.[74] Roger Williams Medical Center admitted only that the government had "sufficient evidence" to prove offenses.[75] Similarly, in the Barclays Bank non-prosecution agreement in 2012, the bank signed an agreement with a detailed description of conduct in which employees manipulated submissions to key benchmark interest rates. Barclays admitted, accepted, and acknowledged responsibility for that conduct, but nowhere in the agreement did Barclays admit to or accept responsibility for having committed any particular crime.[76]

When a corporation confesses, it has to do so through its employees. Deferred prosecution and non-prosecution agreements are signed by the corporation's lawyers or officers to show they entered into the agreement voluntarily. Sometimes there is documentation of a resolution in which the corporate board approved the deal; in the Ingersoll-Rand deferred prosecution agreement, the CEO signed a certificate stating that he was "duly authorized by Ingersoll to execute this Agreement on behalf of Ingersoll and all the subsidiaries named herein." He added that the agreement was voluntary and "no one has threatened or forced me, or to my knowledge any person . . . in any way to enter into this agreement."[77]

Companies also agree to never contradict or deny their public confession. The agreement entered with Pfizer said it "expressly and unequivocally" admitted that it committed the crimes charged and "will not make any public statement contradicting anything" in the charges.[78] One company has been criticized for violating such provisions. In 2013, after entering a deferred prosecution agreement, Standard Chartered Bank referred to its violations as "clerical errors." This resulted in a meeting between prosecutors and the top executives of the bank and a public retraction of that statement.[79]

In any future criminal proceedings, the corporation could be bound by its confession. In any future civil case, the company would not be able to contradict its statements. The scope of these admissions is a complex subject, and they are very carefully crafted for a reason, given potential ramifications in future litigation. More work should be done to examine their scope; currently there is no uniform policy or practice for admissions in corporate prosecutions.

These agreements typically state that cooperation is one of the main reasons the company received leniency and that the company is obligated to cooperate even after the agreement is over. KPMG's agreement was "permanent" in that it required continuing cooperation with the Department of Justice, including in any prosecutions of its employees.

The New Regime

A wave of agreements with prosecutors followed the adoption of this strategy focusing on changing corporate culture. Almost two-thirds were publicly listed on U.S. stock exchanges (58 percent, or 148 of 255) and others, such as KPMG, were private but very large. Many were among the largest corporations in the United States or the world. Of those receiving deferred prosecution agreements, 22 percent were on the Fortune 500 and 20 percent were on the Fortune Global 500 for foreign corporations (some of those were subsidiaries of Fortune 500 firms). Still more, or 31 percent, were either a Fortune 500 or Global 500 firm in the year they entered into the deal with prosecutors.[80] The highest-ranking firms include Chevron (fourth on the Fortune 500 and seventh on the Global 500 at the time), Boeing (twenty-sixth), and AIG, which was ninth on the list in 2006—it had gone up in the rankings since its prosecution in 2004, when it was tenth on the Fortune 500.

There were only a handful of deferred prosecution or non-prosecution agreements like this before 2001; I have located fourteen of them. The traditional approach was to either prosecute or not, possibly offering leniency in exchange for cooperation. Even if a prosecution goes forward, there can still be a deal. Corporations plead guilty, and a plea agreement can include similar terms, such as requirements that a company hire a monitor and improve compliance. A deferred prosecution or non-prosecution agreement is even more lenient, though, because it does not involve the judge to the same degree, and avoids both an indictment and a criminal conviction.

In most deferred prosecution or non-prosecution agreements between federal authorities and corporations, prosecutors provide the reasons they decided not to prosecute. Often there is a paragraph or a section describing such "relevant considerations." A typical explanation noted "significant remediation" and how the company "voluntarily and timely disclosed" the misconduct as part of its "extraordinary" cooperation.[81] These descriptions are quite brief and often do not explain how forthcoming the company actually was or the circumstances of the reporting and cooperation. Even if a company "timely disclosed" its misconduct, was it an unprompted self-report, or did the company come forward only after a whistle-blower or competitor had already tipped off the authorities? One would want conscientious self-reporting to be well rewarded. The descriptions in these agreements, however, do not usually offer any basis for assessing whether prosecutors truly reward prompt self-reporting, valuable cooperation, or other factors.

In some cases, collateral consequences were cited as reasons for offering an alternative to prosecution. In the Beazer Homes mortgage fraud case, prosecutors cited the fear that harsher criminal penalties would "jeopardize the solvency" of the firm and threaten the jobs of 15,000 employees and contractors who had nothing to do with the wrongdoing.[82] Very few firms were defunct or facing insolvency, however.[83] Instead, promises to cooperate and rehabilitate can be enough to avoid a conviction.

No data were kept on deferred prosecution or non-prosecution agreements. The U.S. Sentencing Commission keeps data on cases in which a defendant is sentenced, but these non-prosecution deals involve no formal sentence. A deferred prosecution is filed with the court and remains on the judge's docket until the term is completed and the case is dismissed. A non-prosecution is never filed with a judge at all; such an agreement states that prosecutors will not file if the corporation complies.[84] Since prosecutors themselves did not themselves track these agreements until recently, some are likely missing from public records, including at least twenty-seven agreements entered since 2001. We do not know why those particular agreements are missing; so far litigation by my students, who have pursued Freedom of Information Act requests, has uncovered one such agreement, and it was not at all clear why that agreement had ever been kept from the public in the first place.[85] Such secrecy is troubling; a central goal in prosecuting a corporation is to send a message to industry that violations will not be tolerated. In fact, DOJ officials were questioned sharply in the Senate in 2011 because a settlement with a bank was kept secret; in response, they released the agreement.[86]

With this new deferred prosecution tool in hand, corporate prosecutions did not become more frequent, despite a rash of corporate scandals. Even as deferred prosecution and non-prosecution agreements began their rise in 2003, corporate convictions actually began to decline. Convictions of smaller corporations and non-public corporations remained stable, but large and public corporations increasingly received agreements allowing them to avoid a conviction.

What crimes do companies get prosecuted for? Among the deferred prosecution agreements, the biggest category of crime was fraud (36 percent, or 92 of 255 agreements), followed by violations of the Foreign Corrupt Practices Act (25 percent, or 63 of 255 agreements). Other cases involve kickbacks, usually in medical and pharmaceutical sales (16 agreements), bank secrecy act provisions designed to prevent money laundering (13), immigration violations (10), violations of the International Emergency Economic Powers Act (9), antitrust violations (7), and a range of other crimes. Each federal crime has detailed provisions and is enforced differently. Though it is impossible to do full justice to the vast array of federal crimes, in the rest of the book I will discuss some of the major crimes in detail, using important cases as examples.

KPMG was prosecuted for fraud, the most common type of crime among companies entering deferred prosecution agreements, as well as tax crimes. Prosecutors described KPMG's crime as helping to prepare tax returns and other documents that were false and fraudulent in order to hide the true nature of the tax shelters in question. The federal crime of fraud is typically defined in flexible terms, involving a willfully conducted "scheme to defraud," a "material" misrepresentation with intent to deprive another person of property or "honest services," and the use of the mails or wires as part of the scheme.[87] The mail fraud statute was enacted in the late nineteenth century "to prevent the frauds which are mostly gotten up in the large cities ... by thieves, forgers, and rapscallions generally, for the purpose of deceiving and fleecing the innocent people in the country."[88] In 1952, Congress enacted a wire fraud statute for transactions that pass through wires (this now covers the Internet), and there are laws prohibiting health care fraud, banking fraud, securities and commodities fraud, fraud in foreign labor contracting, and fraud involving "the right to honest services," which includes public corruption, a complicated subject of its own.[89] There are separate crimes for conspiracy to defraud the U.S. government (which KPMG was charged with).[90] Securities fraud cases (23 of the 255 agreements) can involve massive fines. Fraud is also a common charge against individual people, with over 8,000 cases brought each year, or about 10 percent of the federal criminal docket.

KPMG benefited from a deferred prosecution agreement, but most companies do not. Only 255 received deferred prosecution or non-prosecution agreements from 2001 through 2012, while more than 2,000 others were convicted. Was there something irredeemable about their corporate cultures? I have collected detailed data on more than 2,000 corporations convicted of federal crimes since 2001. Corporations that are convicted—almost all of which plead guilty—are often prosecuted for environmental violations (501) or one of the various types of fraud (403), along with antitrust violations (167) and more general crimes including false statements (107), violations of the Foreign Corrupt Practices Act (34), food and drug violations (68), import and export violations (112), and others. These data reflect the most specific "lead" charges against the companies; often, for example, environmental or FCPA charges are accompanied by more general fraud or false statements charges. A mere three companies were convicted of securities fraud; these cases were instead almost entirely brought as deferred prosecution or non-prosecution agreements. And generally, banks and other financial institutions received deferred prosecution or non-prosecution agreements, not convictions.

Although the prosecutors who pursue financial malfeasance have adopted a lenient approach, other prosecutors do not follow it. Few companies prosecuted for environmental crimes get deferred prosecution agreements, for example. Why? The DOJ's Environmental and Natural Resources Division

(ENRD) believes that if a firm does not deserve criminal punishment, it should get a civil fine. The Antitrust Division has its own distinct approach to prosecuting companies, giving amnesty to the first company to report antitrust violations, such as price fixing, bid rigging, or other illegal dividing of markets.

There was a rare window into this process in 2010, when prosecutors announced that Bank of America would pay $137.3 million in restitution, but no fine. It was the first and only conspirator to come forward and admit to rigging bids in the municipal bonds derivatives market.[91] Such cartels can involve hidden agreements to raise prices and are viewed as extremely serious conspiracies. Prosecutors almost always keep such agreements secret, and as a result, antitrust amnesty deals are not included in my data. The first company to cooperate may still pay a large fine as part of its amnesty agreement, but prosecutors disguise its role to better use its information against other cartel members, though the identity of the amnesty-receiving cooperator may become obvious later once the other companies in the cartel are convicted. As a result of this amnesty approach, there are few deferred prosecution agreements (seven) for antitrust violations and the focus is not on culture or compliance but rather on punishing price fixing. The corporations that do not turn themselves in typically receive convictions.

Some of those convicted are public corporations or their subsidiaries, and some are large private companies. However, most convicted companies are small and do not have much of a culture that can be rehabilitated, so maybe it makes sense to convict them. Some are closely held, with just a few owners, or they are small partnerships. These tiny mom-and-pop organizations are very different from the likes of KPMG and often cannot pay much of a fine. Nor do they have a complicated structure or culture. Convicting the owner or partners may be the most practical way to punish them.

The deferred prosecution approach has attracted a wave of scrutiny from both the right and the left. Members of Congress in both houses questioned the tactics used by the DOJ, as did the American Bar Association and business groups. Federal legislation was introduced, the General Accountability Office investigated features of corporate prosecutions, and the DOJ sought to mollify such critics. White-collar defense practitioners complained that federal prosecutors "exploit[] their virtually unchecked power to extract and coerce ever greater concessions."[92] Law professor Richard Epstein commented that deferred prosecution agreements "often read like the confessions of a Stalinist purge trial."[93] Other critics of the DOJ strategy offered the opposite perspective: Ralph Nader called failures to convict organizations a "shocking" and "systematic derogation" of the DOJ's duty to seek justice.[94] The Government Accountability Office offered criticism of the way prosecutors decided whether an agreement would involve deferred prosecution or non-prosecution.[95]

Following the Money

In 2011, only thirty-six companies were convicted of fraud, and they were ordered to pay over $100 million.[96] The KPMG agreement alone included a much larger payment, $456 million, than all of the other fraud fines paid that year. However, most of that payment was not a fine but a disgorgement of fees ($128 million) and restitution of money to the U.S. Treasury for what the IRS lost in taxes ($228 million). The IRS had already recovered large sums from taxpayers, but it might not be able to get all of the lost taxes back, notably because of a three-year time limit for the IRS to collect back taxes. KPMG agreed not to deduct the fine from its own federal taxes; if it used insurance to recover any of that money, half of the proceeds would be provided to the United States.

The punishment, perhaps, was slight, something KPMG had counted on when deciding whether to sell the shelters. How about rehabilitation—would the prosecutors really change the culture at KPMG? The company agreed to completely and permanently shut down its entire private tax practice by February 26, 2006. It would no longer market any of the tax shelters or anything at all to wealthy individual clients, nor would it take on any new clients. KPMG was out of the private tax business, but it had avoided another kind of shutdown.

Recall how Arthur Andersen most feared debarment from the SEC, and after it was convicted at trial, it was barred from doing auditing for public companies. KPMG did auditing work for the federal government—in fact, KPMG was hired to audit the books of none other than the Department of Justice! According to the agreement, the debarring official at DOJ decided that suspension or debarment of KPMG was not warranted because KPMG was still a "responsible contractor" for having cooperated and signed the agreement.[97] The next year, in March 2006, KPMG would review accounting at the DOJ and find "four reportable conditions" repeated from the prior year, relating to monitoring grants by the Office of Justice Programs.[98] It is more than just a little ironic that at the same time KPMG was implementing its required new compliance program, KPMG was reporting on inadequate internal controls at DOJ itself.

Was the fine in the KPMG case representative? Fines are not intended to directly fix corporate culture, as the message they send to a firm and to others in industry is secondary to their role as punishment. "While organizations cannot be imprisoned, they can be fined," as the U.S. Sentencing Commission puts it. There are many ways that a company can pay, from the criminal fine itself, designed to punish the firm, to restitution paid to compensate victims. There may be civil suits brought by prosecutors or regulators, and there may also be civil suits from victims themselves.

The trend in corporate prosecutions has generally been toward larger cases and higher average fines, particularly in big cases such as that against KPMG.[99] Antitrust cases, pharmaceutical cases, FCPA cases, and those involving international conduct and foreign firms have driven the increase in fines—more cases are not being brought, but there are more blockbusters. For deferred prosecution agreements, 2010 was a record year, with a total of almost $1.3 billion in fines. The following year saw the imposition of almost $500 million in fines. The deferred prosecution and non-prosecution agreements since 2001 had a total of $4 billion in criminal fines. Adding restitution paid to victims, disgorgement of profits, and forfeiture payments to the mix, the total dollar amounts paid grow by over $7.5 billion.[100]

Firms also paid civil penalties to regulators. In 91 percent of deferred prosecution or non-prosecution agreements (233 of 255), a regulatory agency was involved, most commonly the SEC (69 cases), the Office of Inspector General at the Department of Health and Human Services (25 cases), the U.S. Postal Inspection Service (27 cases), and the IRS (24 cases). In almost two-thirds of the cases, companies faced civil enforcement actions filed by regulators (65 percent, or 165 of 255 cases), particularly the SEC (88 cases). Fines by regulators sometimes dwarfed criminal fines. For deferred prosecution and non-prosecution agreements since 2001, about $12 billion was paid to regulators on top of the about $11.5 billion in fines and restitution separately secured by prosecutors, for a total of over $23 billion. Prosecuted companies also faced private lawsuits and paid at least another $6 billion in civil judgments. Then one can add costs of complying with reforms required by the agreements.

Given these numbers, you would expect large public firms that commit bigger crimes to receive the harshest punishments. Yet punitive fines are often dwarfed by the payments to victims or regulators. Figure 3.1 puts in perspective the different payments by companies entering deferred prosecution and non-prosecution agreements.

The corporate prosecution agreements are even more lenient than the totals suggest. The fines imposed on companies vary wildly, and in almost half of the agreements there was no criminal fine at all (47 percent, or 119 of 255 agreements). Only a few companies were defunct or could not pay, and for the others, prosecutors offered no explanation for not imposing a criminal fine.

The KPMG case and its millions in fines is an outlier; it was the tenth-largest fine among all deferred prosecution agreements, and the top ten fines in the deferred prosecution and non-prosecution agreements add up to $1.7 billion—almost half of the total for *all* such agreements.[101] The biggest fines in deferred prosecution and non-prosecution agreements do not compare to those in blockbuster cases in which a corporation is convicted. The biggest deferred prosecution or non-prosecution agreement fine, of $400 million, in the UBS case, would be outside the top ten fines for convicted firms, a list led by the record $1.3 billion fine paid by British Petroleum for its role in the

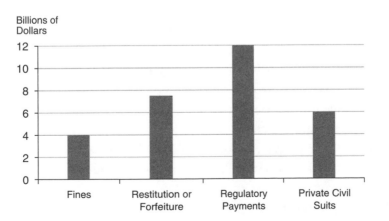

Figure 3.1 Total Payments by Firms Entering Deferred Prosecution and Non-Prosecution Agreements, 2001–2012

Deepwater Horizon spill and the nearly $1.2 billion paid by a Pfizer subsidiary. As shown in the Appendix, the twenty largest corporate criminal fines range from $250 million to $1.2 billion and include eight pharmaceutical cases, seven antitrust cases, three FCPA cases, and one securities fraud case. These blockbuster cases have been growing in recent years: six of those top twenty corporate fines were in 2012, and all but two of the rest were after 2006.

These fines sound significant, but how damaging are they for companies of this size? Take the Pfizer case. The $1.2 billion paid was just 0.6 percent of its market capitalization at the time, or the total value of the outstanding shares of the company. In general, the fines averaged only 0.04 percent of market capitalization—and public companies had the comparatively larger fines—while the total payments made averaged just 0.09 percent of market capitalization.

Rehabilitating KPMG

Prosecutors also try to rehabilitate corporations using structural reforms. Indeed, if the goal of prosecuting a company is to single out significant and systematic violations, one would expect prosecutors to focus on reforming compliance. However, prosecutors use very different tools than a corporate manager would when trying to change a company. Moreover, their guidelines say nothing about what should happen to a company that enters a deferred prosecution or non-prosecution agreement. The nine factors provide guidance on when to prosecute, but not on how to reform. As a result, prosecutors have significant discretion.

There was much more to the KPMG agreement than a confession and a fine. KPMG had to bring in an outsider, an independent monitor, for three years, to implement an elaborate compliance program. The monitor, a former SEC chairman, was picked in consultation with KPMG and had sweeping power to hire lawyers, consultants, investigators, and experts to gather information, make recommendations, and supervise the new compliance program.[102]

Every corporation has some kind of a code of ethics and provides training for employees on the laws and regulations they must follow. But do employees really carefully read the language in their corporate ethics handbook or tune in during trainings? Increasingly, corporations realize that making sure employees follow the law is just as important as making sure they are doing their jobs well. There are many sorts of tools available, including testing employees to see if they understand the rules, creating anonymous hotlines, and performing random audits—like with professional athletes, though not necessarily drug testing. Employers can record calls and randomly check them ("This call may be recorded for quality assurance"). They can put automated systems in place to make sure employees do not bill improperly or fail to report their work on time. They can create new documentation requirements so that there is a clearer paper trail to monitor employees.

Why was a compliance program necessary at KPMG if the firm closed its entire private tax practice? The new compliance program would be company-wide and would create a new whistle-blower hotline to allow anonymous complaints. The program would pay "particular attention to practice areas that pose high risks." There would be a new permanent compliance office that would conduct ethics trainings. There was a meta-dimension to all of this: the compliance effort would itself be audited to measure its effectiveness. The attorney general called this the "most important" part of such an agreement, vital to "help prevent such wrongdoing in the future."[103]

No prosecutor has the resources to oversee reform of an entire company. Instead, prosecutors create incentives for the company to do that itself. For that reason, prosecutors and regulators ranging from the SEC and the EPA to the Department of Health and Human Services all focus on creating incentives for self-policing, giving credit for good compliance, and requiring better compliance when companies lack appropriate mechanisms.[104] The 2010 Patient Protection and Affordable Care Act (colloquially called Obamacare) requires health care providers and doctors to maintain effective compliance and ethics programs.[105] The compliance approach has even gone international—the Organization for Economic Cooperation and Development (OECD) has recommendations for combating bribery of foreign officials with detailed guidance on how to implement a sound compliance program.[106]

Federal prosecutors believe that one key to changing a corporation's culture is an effective compliance program. After all, perhaps the central reason for prosecuting the company in the first place was a breakdown in compliance. The KPMG agreement was typical, as the vast majority of the agreements require that the company create or improve a program to detect and prevent criminal violations. Most agreements required compliance reforms (63 percent, or 160 of 255 agreements) or steps already in place to improve compliance (64 percent, or 162 of 255 agreements), while others cited compliance reforms that regulators required (28 percent, or 71 of 255 agreements). The agreements ask that higher-ups endorse new policies, new trainings of employees, and new forms of supervision of employees, and that they provide periodic reports summarizing their progress. The agreements also note the firing or disciplining of employees involved in the crime.

However, compliance programs are often described in fairly general terms. They refer to "appropriate due diligence" and "effective compliance" without defining it. Some require that the compliance program be updated over time—certain agreements, for example, require an annual review in light of "evolving international and industry standards" in the FCPA area.[107] The agreement says the company must do periodic review and testing of the compliance program.

A smaller number of agreements (9 percent, or 23 of 255 agreements) were designed to change the governance of the business by methods beyond improving compliance. The KPMG agreement closed down the firm's entire private tax practice. Beazer Homes had already shut down the entire offending subsidiary that engaged in fraudulent mortgage practices. Other changes include altering employee compensation; two banking cases changed how senior executives were paid, by allowing banks to claw back prior bonuses to executives "determined to have contributed to compliance failures."[108] Several pharmaceutical cases resulted in plea agreements that changed how sales representatives were paid. For example, the GlaxoSmithKline plea agreement provided that sales staff or managers would no longer be paid based on "volume of sales."[109] The Abt Associates agreement provided that any employee who uncovers and reports a "significant" billing error to the government should be given an on-the-spot award of $100.[110]

More than one-third of the agreements required hiring new employees (35 percent, or 88 of 255 agreements). Perhaps most intrusive, the Bristol-Myers Squibb agreement detailed how the company must separate the positions of CEO and chairman of the board, appoint a new outside director, and report more information to the SEC than required. Most are not so detailed, though some require adding a new chief compliance officer or a compliance committee to the board.[111] Some require prosecutors to approve the people hired. Aibel Group had to secure "prior approval" before selecting a new executive chairperson of its board of directors, a majority of the members of its compliance committee, and the compliance counsel. If prosecutors and the corporation could not agree on names within seven days, prosecutors would have the right to select them.[112] Aurora Foods had to consult with prosecutors on all personnel decisions related to its compliance program.[113] Most idiosyncratically, a company charged with traditional mail fraud, for sending "solicitations that purport on their face to be written by astrologers," was required to have employees make sure the mailings were "reviewed and approved in writing."[114]

Some firms clean house on their own. Prosecutors noted how Academi LLC "replaced all of its executive leadership," including its CEO and general counsel as well as several vice presidents; it also hired a new chief of compliance and added independent members to its board.[115] Prosecutors often named "remedial measures" as a reason for allowing the company to avoid a conviction, and noted prior compliance reforms in a majority of the agreements (162 of the agreements).

While it is easy to add language to an agreement stating that the company must adopt a better compliance program, actually reforming a corporation may be more difficult. Companies often cite progress in repairing their corporate culture. Yet prosecutors may come into the picture only when there is a complete breakdown. For example, after the explosion at the Upper Big Branch mine owned by Massey Energy killed twenty-nine miners and prompted a federal inquiry, the report found violations of safety standards so rampant that they could "only be explained in the context of a culture in which wrongdoing became acceptable, where deviation became the norm."[116] Yet despite a terrible track record of several serious prior violations and the egregious safety breaches that led to these deaths, the new owners of the company received a non-prosecution agreement. Former chief of the DOJ environmental crimes section David Uhlmann called this result timid and an erosion of the rule of law, and he concluded that the "Justice Department did not live up to its name in agreeing not to prosecute Massey for its crimes."[117]

A lingering question is when and whether compliance programs are effective. This question goes to the core of the rationale for prosecuting companies. The pejorative name for compliance programs that are just window dressing is "cosmetic compliance," referring to policies expressing lofty ethical values that are ignored by employees.[118] Whether compliance programs work or not, they are a boon for lawyers and other consultants hired to improve compliance programs. Focusing on compliance may also distract from the role that management might have played.[119] One wonders whether companies can have it both ways: good compliance programs convince prosecutors that no prosecution is necessary, while bad compliance programs earn the company a lenient agreement aimed at fixing them. If true, there would be nothing distinctively serious about the violations by companies singled out for prosecution, or about the consequences of that prosecution. Figure 3.2 depicts the various terms of the 255 deferred prosecution and non-prosecution agreements.

A substantial number of the agreements, nearly one-third, did not even require the company to implement a compliance program (31 percent, or 78 of 255 agreements). If the central purpose of a deferred prosecution agreement is to ensure that the corporation reforms itself, how can an agreement require no compliance at all? Some firms adopted compliance reforms under a separate agreement with regulators (71 of 255 agreements), and almost

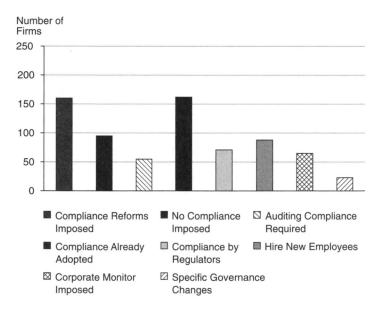

Figure 3.2 Terms of Deferred Prosecution and Non-Prosecution Agreements

two-thirds (162 of 255 agreements) were said to have already adopted compliance reforms on their own—but why not require companies to implement those reforms and assess them before giving a free pass?

As Figure 3.2 depicts, few agreements required a company to evaluate the effectiveness of its compliance program to find out if it was really working or not (22 percent, or 55 of 255 agreements). The agreements typically say that the compliance program must be "clearly articulated," "rigorous," and "effective," but those terms are not defined. The sentencing guidelines say that no compliance program is "effective" if the company does not "evaluate periodically."[120] Yet prosecutors generally do not insist that a company do that—typically only the FCPA agreements have brief language that there must be some kind of periodic testing and review of compliance.

There has been much controversy surrounding corporate prosecutions, but no company has complained that compliance terms are too lenient. The agreements are also fairly short-lived, with an average length of two years and three months. Just two agreements lasted for more than three years. Very few have ever been extended, though in rare cases prosecutors have said more time was needed.[121] Can prosecutors effectively supervise the reform of a major corporation in just over two years, particularly if not required to audit the effectiveness of its reforms? These data suggest that prosecutors are not taking structural reform seriously.

Judges have a role to play in deferred prosecutions, though it is very limited. Federal law provides that a court may approve deferral of prosecution if there is a written agreement allowing the defendant "to demonstrate his good conduct."[122] However, no judge has ever rejected a corporate deferred prosecution agreement. The Government Accountability Office spoke to twelve judges who approved such agreements and found that nine of twelve did not even hold a hearing to review the agreement and its terms.[123] In the KPMG case, the judge did hold a hearing, but the agreement was accepted without changes. As I will discuss in Chapter 10, only a handful of judges have insisted on ongoing supervision over deferred prosecution agreements.

What would happen if KPMG did not comply? Prosecutors would retain sole discretion to decide what to do. They could extend the term of the agreement or ask the monitor to serve for a longer time. Most threatening of all, if prosecutors decided KPMG breached the agreement, they could scrap the deal and prosecute KPMG for federal criminal violations. The agreement

provided that all of KPMG's statements to prosecutors and the IRS—
including its detailed admissions of its guilt—would be admissible against
them.

Despite those stringent terms, judges have said due process prevents the
government from "unilaterally determining" that a defendant breached an
agreement not to prosecute and prosecutors "must obtain a judicial determi-
nation of the defendant's breach."[124] In a closely watched case, the Stolt-
Nielsen company asked a judge to bar an indictment after the DOJ decided
the company had breached its agreement to cooperate under the Antitrust
Division's Corporate Leniency Program. The federal judge found that prosecutors acted arbitrarily, but the appeals court reversed, ruling the judge had
no power to halt a prosecution before an indictment.[125] Only after the company was indicted could the judge dismiss the charges.[126]

Prosecutors can avoid even the limited role a judge plays in approving a
deferred prosecution by entering non-prosecution agreements where nothing at all is filed with a court so long as the firm complies with the terms. Of
the agreements made since 2001, about half (48 percent, or 122 of 255) were
non-prosecution agreements, while 131 were deferred prosecution agreements
(for two, prosecutors have not released the agreements and it is unclear).

Some terms in agreements have nothing to do with improving corporate
culture. Prosecutors required the New York Racing Association (NYRA), as
part of an agreement, to install video lottery terminals at Aqueduct
Racetrack—slot machines, basically.[127] Was NYRA somehow criminally depriving the public of slot machines? The machines had nothing to do with the
case, which was about tax fraud and conspiracy to defraud the U.S. government. The installation of the slot machines, which had already been subject to
a decade-long delay for other reasons, entered the negotiations because state
officials feared that the prosecution might further postpone their installation
at the racetracks, and without that revenue New York State would be unable
to comply with a separate court ruling requiring additional school financing.
The machines could generate an estimated $500 million, and officials were
"counting on the gambling hall to help balance the state budget."[128]

In the Roger Williams Medical Center agreement, the government feared
that indicting a nonprofit hospital for public corruption would jeopardize
health care for poor residents of Providence, Rhode Island. The deferred
prosecution agreement required that the hospital provide $4 million in ad-

ditional free health care to uninsured low-income residents—a form of community service.[129]

The deferred prosecution agreement with Bristol-Myers Squibb stated that the company would fund a new chair in ethics at Seton Hall Law School; the new professor would teach an annual ethics class that the company's employees could attend.[130] The U.S. attorney said the Seton Hall ethics chair was added to the agreement at the request of Bristol-Myers Squibb.[131] However, Seton Hall was the law school the U.S. attorney had attended, causing some to criticize the creation of the ethics chair as not particularly ethical.[132] In response, the DOJ adopted a rule that such agreements should not include terms requiring payments to a person or organization "that is not a victim of the criminal activity or is not providing services to redress the harm caused by the defendant's criminal conduct."[133]

There is also the lingering question of whether additional side deals remain hidden. In 2010, a former employee of American Express Bank International sued after learning of an undisclosed "side letter" to a deferred prosecution agreement with the bank providing that the employee no longer be employed. The employee sued and settled with the Department of Justice; it came out that DOJ supervisors were unaware of this side letter.[134] Perhaps other such side letter agreements exist. In cases where prosecutors found no wrongdoing by particular individuals and do not want to harm those individuals' reputations, then they might be entered for good reason. Without knowing more about the existence or nature of any such side agreements, it is impossible to evaluate them.

Some agreements required the use of corporate monitors to implement changes in corporate culture and ensure compliance reforms (25 percent, or 65 of 255 agreements). KPMG had to permit the DOJ to appoint an "independent monitor" to serve for three years; once his term expired, the IRS would monitor KPMG for two more years. Furthermore, KPMG would pay the salaries and other expenses of the monitor and anyone he or she hired.

The monitor had authority to "take any other actions that are necessary to effectuate his or her oversight and monitoring responsibilities." What if the monitor made unreasonable demands or simply charged excessive fees—or, for that matter, what if the monitor did next to nothing? With such a prominent individual on board, maybe that was not a risk. Regardless, we do not know. As in the other deferred prosecution agreements, neither the KPMG monitor's reports nor any of the monitor's actions have been made public. In Chapter 7, I try to shed more light on how these monitors do their work.

The KPMG agreement quietly ended on December 31, 2006. The DOJ consented to dismiss the case, stating only that "monitorship . . . has been comprehensive and effective."[135] No other information was provided about what had been done. Did KPMG have a new and ethical corporate culture? Were the compliance reforms effective?

Those were not the concerns raised by a number of former KPMG employees who were still being prosecuted; they believed that the judge should scrap the entire agreement. One former employee argued that the deal was too lenient and that it was against public policy to end the prosecution given KPMG's actions. Another group of former employees argued the reverse: that the agreement should be rescinded and fines returned because it provided prosecutors with unconstitutionally broad power over KPMG.[136]

Up until the day the agreement ended, in theory KPMG was under the gun. The DOJ, at its sole discretion, could have found that KPMG breached the agreement, and it could have made full use of all statements and admissions to convict KPMG. But with the charges dismissed, the monitoring continued for two more years, supervised by the IRS, and then that ended as well. With very few exceptions, the other corporate deferred prosecution and non-prosecution agreements also ended quietly and without dispute. Indeed, even companies that appear to have engaged in additional crimes have avoided the consequences of a breach of an agreement. After Bristol-Myers Squibb entered a deferred prosecution agreement, new crimes were uncovered, but the company was not found in breach, as I will describe in Chapter 7. Another company, Wright Medical Technology, had the term of its deferred prosecution agreement extended for a year rather than a finding of a breach. Only once have prosecutors declared a company in breach of a deferred prosecution agreement, resulting in a guilty plea.[137]

Snakes and Wolf Packs

Prosecuting KPMG was not enough to change the culture in the industry. Other companies were prosecuted, and how they were treated very much depended on how prosecutors viewed their corporate culture. The aftermath gives a vivid picture of how prosecutorial discretion can work under the new deferred prosecution regime.

A firm that marketed tax shelters known as "snakes" received far more lenient treatment than KPMG. Ernst & Young, another Big Four accounting firm, was fined $15 million by the IRS. Four Ernst & Young partners, part of a group that called itself VIPER (for "Value Ideas Produce Extraordinary Results"), were prosecuted for their role in marketing a shelter called CO-BRA.[138] Prosecutors apparently concluded that pursuing those partners was enough and that it would not serve a useful purpose to prosecute the firm.

Jenkins & Gilchrist, then one of the largest law firms in the country, faced far more severe consequences. This firm wrote legal opinions approving of the tax shelters. The IRS sought and received the names of more than a thousand of its tax clients. Jenkins & Gilchrist eventually paid $81 million to some of its former clients and $76 million to the IRS. It signed a non-prosecution agreement in 2007, having become practically defunct, suffering great losses and a mass exodus of attorneys.[139] Contrast the law firm of Sidley Austin, which paid $39.4 million to the IRS but was not prosecuted, in part because prosecutors concluded that primarily just one partner had been involved.[140]

At another firm, BDO Seidman, the partners marketing tax shelters called themselves the "Wolf Pack."[141] Years later, in June 2012, its parent company, BDO USA, signed a deferred prosecution agreement. It had to hire a corporate monitor and agree to never again market a tax shelter "listed" by the IRS.[142] It paid a $34 million fine and about $16 million more to the IRS. (Perhaps it is telling that prosecutors saw fit to remind the tax professionals at BDO that no part of its criminal penalties could be declared as tax deductible).[143] A former chief executive at BDO Seidman and six others were convicted. Some pleaded guilty and cooperated, while others took their case to trial along with two former partners at Jenkins & Gilchrist and two former employees at Deutsche Bank.[144] Three trial verdicts would later be thrown out due to juror misconduct, and at a retrial one defendant was convicted and one acquitted.[145]

Deutsche Bank also settled with prosecutors and the IRS in 2010, paying no fine but $553 million in forfeiture. Others fared similarly. HVB Bank, Germany's second-largest, settled a prosecution over its role in marketing the tax shelters in 2006, paying almost $30 million in fines and restitution. One of its former accountants pleaded guilty to tax fraud.[146]

All of these prosecutions had a remarkable impact on the business of marketing tax shelters and advising wealthy clients on tax matters. What changed at KPMG specifically? There have been no more investigations or prosecutions of KPMG, and it closed the entire unit marketing the tax shelters. But it must be emphasized that this agreement, with its detailed structural reforms, looks very different from the majority of agreements I described in this chapter. KPMG is the exception, not the rule, and it should disturb us a great deal if prosecutors are not taking structural reform seriously, since this is a core rationale for prosecuting corporations in the first place. Only the serious corporate violators are supposedly targeted—those who lacked effective compliance, whose misconduct was tolerated by management, or who are recidivists and fail to report their crimes. Such cases demand serious criminal punishments, not just the appearance of compliance.

Even if prosecutors allow corporations to avoid convictions in exchange for reduced fines and too little compliance, some might view that as a good bargain if the company helps successfully prosecute the individual wrongdoers. Unfortunately, even with the company's cooperation, it is not easy to prosecute white-collar criminals. In the next chapter, I describe what happened when prosecutors turned to KPMG employees, and why companies receiving deferred prosecution and non-prosecution agreements typically do not have employees prosecuted. The prosecutions of former KPMG employees did not end neatly, and those cases would change how corporate prosecutions are brought.

≈ 4 ≈

The Ostriches

Roman author and naturalist Pliny the Elder described the ostrich as the greatest of the birds, with incredible speed, height, and strength. Yet Pliny also accused ostriches of having a stupidity "no less remarkable," famously explaining that "high as the rest of their Body is, if they hide their Head and Neck . . . they think themselves altogether concealed."[1] But ostriches do not really hide their heads in the sand. They defend themselves with their powerful beak and legs, and when confronted by their largest predators, they can run away at speeds over forty miles per hour.[2] The evocative image of an ungainly ostrich with its head in the sand is, as Judge Richard Posner puts it, "pure legend and a canard on a very distinguished bird."[3]

Unlike real ostriches, some criminals do put their heads in the sand to escape the largest predators in the legal kingdom: the prosecutor. Corporations may argue that managers did not know about the conduct of "rogue employees" or "bad apples." Formally, an ostrich defense does not work. The corporation does not have to possess any knowledge of wrongdoing under the strict *respondeat superior* rule. Informally, however, corporations can earn leniency or escape prosecution altogether by convincing prosecutors that they should not be punished for conduct that did not reach the higher levels of management. In that way, denying awareness of wrongdoing can be very important for a company. Further, to demonstrate that the higher-ups do not tolerate wrongdoing, a company can threaten to fire employees who do not cooperate, and it can provide prosecutors with the documents, emails, and interview statements to make a criminal case against them. From the moment a criminal investigation begins, individuals are caught in a bind between their employer and prosecutors.

While corporate executives may try to put their heads in the sand, the judge in a federal criminal case may provide the jury with what is nicknamed the "ostrich instruction," explaining that a defendant who was not completely aware of the crime may still be convicted if she deliberately sought to avoid the truth. As one appellate court put it, "An ostrich instruction informs the jury that actual knowledge and deliberate avoidance of knowledge are the same thing."[4] And while it is intended to punish those who engage in this deliberate avoidance, which is sometimes called *deliberate ignorance, conscious avoidance,* or *willful blindness,* the ostrich instruction also raises the risk that a jury might convict a person who had vague suspicions but did not know enough about the crime to deserve punishment.[5]

An ostrich defense can be especially important in white-collar criminal cases, where the ostriches are higher-ups who argue they did not know what was happening among subordinates. As one corporate lawyer said, "A fundamental law of organizational physics is that bad news does not flow upstream."[6] Some corporate crimes, such as what criminologist William K. Black terms "control fraud," are crimes by higher-ups bent on self-dealing.[7] Other corporate crimes may have benefited the company but were the product of corporate policies and culture, and may be difficult to pin on any one person. Reflecting the ostrich problem, higher-ups may have an easier time claiming lack of knowledge and

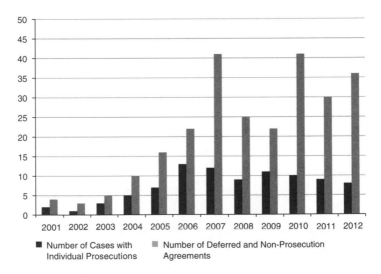

Figure 4.1 Prosecutions of Individual Officers and Employees of Firms Receiving Deferred Prosecution or Non-Prosecution Agreements, 2001–2012

have far more resources to mount a vigorous defense. Yet they may be the most important targets. Low-level employees may have far less to gain by violating the law, and prosecuting them may do little to deter white-collar crime.

The thousands of individuals prosecuted each year for white-collar-related crimes dwarf the 200 or so prosecutions of organizations each year. For example, in fiscal 2012 more than 8,500 people were convicted of fraud in federal courts.[8] Deferred prosecution agreements almost always require the company to help prosecutors investigate any individuals involved. Prosecutors say they are intent on putting people in jail. As a Department of Justice official commented, "It is our view that to have a credible deterrent effect, people have to go to jail."[9]

Given such statements, I was surprised to find that individual officers and employees were often not prosecuted when the corporation was. This was particularly true in the more significant cases involving deferred prosecution agreements and public companies. In about two-thirds of the cases no individual officers or employees were prosecuted for related crimes, while in about one-third of deferred prosecution or non-prosecution agreements (35 percent, or 89 of 255) there were prosecutions of such individuals. This trend has not changed over time; as deferred prosecution and non-prosecution agreements gained popularity, the proportion of cases with individuals prosecuted has remained fairly stable, as seen in Figure 4.1.

The lion's share of the individual prosecutions involved fraud, either securities fraud (16 cases) or some other type (38 cases), as seen in Figure 4.2. While

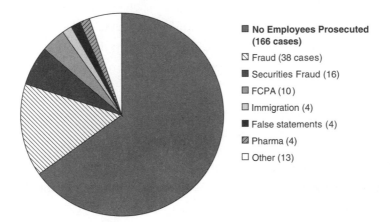

- ■ No Employees Prosecuted (166 cases)
- ◩ Fraud (38 cases)
- ■ Securities Fraud (16)
- ▦ FCPA (10)
- ▢ Immigration (4)
- ■ False statements (4)
- ▨ Pharma (4)
- ▢ Other (13)

Figure 4.2 Type of Crime and Prosecutions of Individual Officers and Employees of Firms Receiving Deferred Prosecution or Non-Prosecution Agreements, 2001–2012

there were few deferred prosecutions of companies in antitrust cases, individuals were prosecuted in three of four antitrust cases. In contrast, no individual officers or employees were prosecuted in cases involving banks violating laws related to money laundering. A similar pattern held true for public companies that were convicted. Slightly fewer (25 percent, or 31 of 125) convicted public companies or their subsidiaries had officers or employees prosecuted.

The mustache-twirling villain is rarely to be found. Prosecutors may eagerly try to convict a big fish, a higher-up who can be blamed and who does not raise a credible ostrich defense, but such cases are few and far between. While the DOJ's Antitrust Division does give outright leniency deals to employees as part of corporate prosecution agreements, most of the time individuals are simply not prosecuted at all. This may be because of a "Where's Waldo" problem, as in the Andersen case, where it is hard to sort out which officers and employees knew what. Or there may be so many low-level employees implicated that prosecuting them all would be pointless or even impossible; prosecutors conserve resources by focusing on the company.

One goal of this approach is to use the corporation as an informant, to help build a case against individuals—but agreements with corporations have not been effective in doing so. Prosecuting interchangeable middle managers may not change anything where corporate culture is to blame, and while prosecuting higher officers may change the culture and affect industry practices, doing so is difficult and can take years. While it may be upsetting to see how rarely higher-ups are prosecuted, prosecutors have limited resources to pursue white-collar cases, and unless that changes, prosecuting the company alone may be appropriate—but only if that actually secures meaningful reforms at the corporate level. Unfortunately, we have good reasons to doubt that it does.

Andersen, Again

In the 1980s, Rudolph Giuliani, then U.S. attorney for the Southern District of New York, famously walked Wall Street bankers in front of the cameras after their arrest to create a media spectacle. In 2002, following post-Enron scandals, "perp walks" around the country included Andrew Fastow of Enron, L. Dennis Kozlowski, the former CEO of Tyco International, John

Rigas, the former CEO of Adelphia Communications, and Samuel Waksal, the former CEO of ImClone.[10] Some, such as Rigas, offered to surrender voluntarily, but prosecutors insisted on a perp walk in handcuffs.[11] As the federal appeals court in New York put it, "a suspect in handcuffs being led into a station house is a powerful image of guilt."[12] The perp walk sends a message that white-collar criminals will be treated just as harshly as gangsters or street criminals.

David Duncan, who pleaded guilty in 2002, was not made to undergo a perp walk. Instead, he cooperated, and at the Arthur Andersen trial, prosecutors pointed out that whatever happened to Andersen, "Mr. Duncan stood up in court and his guilty plea will stand no matter what. It will stand and subject him to a host of problems; criminal problems, civil problems; he faces up to 10 years in jail."[13] Prosecutors charged Duncan with a single count of obstruction of justice, the same crime the company was convicted of. When he pleaded guilty, the judge swore him in. Duncan told the judge that he was satisfied with the advice his lawyer had given him. He had read the written plea agreement, spoken to his attorney, and understood it. The details in his plea suggested he was an ostrich—he had known a crime was occurring. When the judge asked him to "tell me in your own words what it is you did to commit the crime," he said:

> I instructed a number of members of the Engagement team to comply with the Andersen document policy. I did so with the knowledge and intent that those people would destroy documents . . . so that they would be unavailable to the SEC and other third parties.

He added, "I also personally destroyed such documents for such purpose." Finally, he concluded, "I accept that my conduct violated federal criminal law, and I fully accept responsibility for my action."[14]

Having pleaded guilty, Duncan could be sentenced to a maximum of ten years in prison and a fine of $250,000. He could, however, get a downward adjustment on the recommendation of prosecutors, possibly avoiding jail time completely, for his acceptance of responsibility and also for his cooperation. Later, a probation officer would do an investigation of the case and write a report, and the judge would decide how to sentence him.

Duncan was released on a $1,000 bond when he pleaded guilty. As the years went by, his sentencing was put off again and again as the company pursued appeals, through the end of 2005. After the Supreme Court threw out Arthur Andersen's conviction and prosecutors decided not to retry the case, Duncan moved to withdraw his guilty plea. It is not easy to withdraw such a plea, though a judge can approve the motion if the defendant can "show a fair and just reason" for it.[15] Duncan's lawyers argued he had never pleaded to knowing that what he did was illegal and that the Court's decision held that a person can only be guilty of obstruction of justice if there is "consciousness of wrongdoing."[16] Duncan had said when he pleaded guilty that he had "knowledge and intent" that documents would be destroyed. But he had never said he meant to do something illegal. This question of knowledge of an action's illegality is different from the ostrich problem of willful blindness to the action having taken place at all, but both relate to the larger problem of proving what the higher-ups knew in a complex organization.

The judge approved the motion, which the prosecutors did not oppose. Duncan was free of his conviction and never spent time in prison.[17] The SEC had filed charges against him too, but a federal judge dismissed those charges in early 2008.[18] No other former Andersen employees were ever charged.

Was Arthur Andersen the right target, or should it have been employees like Duncan all along? Were Andersen's employees well-meaning people or criminals who ruined the integrity of a great company? The incentives and mind-set of white-collar criminals are obviously very different from those of violent criminals. Businesspeople work for legitimate institutions and may think that what they are doing is not just legal but a valuable contribution to a business or even society. That may drive them to bend or break rules with economic consequences far greater than those of many street crimes.

Most of the employees at Arthur Andersen voted with their feet as the criminal case progressed. In 2001, Andersen had more than 85,000 employees, but by the end of 2002, only 3,000 remained.[19] Many former partners and higher-level employees went on to successful careers at other major accounting firms, but the lower-level employees, perhaps least to blame for what happened, were most likely to be out of a job. Some later complained that while managers were telling them, "We want you to stay. You'll be taken care of," by the time the criminal case ended and everyone knew "the ship was going down," the partners had moved to other firms.[20]

White-Collar Crime

Cases such as Andersen's illustrate just how different white-collar crime is from other types. Sociology professor Edwin Sutherland coined the term *white-collar crime* in the 1940s in his landmark work exploring the causes and nature of business crime.[21] The phrase potentially covers far more than stealing and more subtle forms of fraud, since corporate employees can commit nonfinancial crimes geared toward improving the company's bottom line, such as violating environmental standards. There is a sense that white-collar crimes are not the same as street or violent crimes, though they may also result in deaths, as can happen with workplace safety violations or defective products.[22] On one hand, lines separating appropriate business practices from regulatory violations may be quite blurry. But critics emphasize that the very legitimacy of the business setting makes white-collar crime troubling. Writer and philosopher C. S. Lewis decried crimes conceived "in clean, carpeted, warmed and well-lighted offices, by quiet men with white collars and cut fingernails and smooth-shaven cheeks who do not need to raise their voices."[23]

In 1939, Sutherland complained of the lack of data collected on business crimes, and although the government has not collected much better data since, scholars have conducted case studies, interview research, and experimental work studying the causes and types of white-collar crime. Interview research has suggested that while messages from top management may set the tone, it is the middle managers or lower-level employees who feel pressure to commit crimes.[24] Studies have not found a close connection between the size of a company and likelihood of violating the law.[25]

The causes of white-collar crime may seem distant by the time any criminal case is resolved. Prosecutions of former Enron employees would take far longer than that of Andersen, with former Enron CEO Jeffrey Skilling not sentenced until 2006. Skilling said at his sentencing hearing, "I am innocent of every one of these charges."[26] His appeals continued for years, ultimately resulting in a reduced sentence in 2013.[27] In white-collar cases, there may not be much question whether someone did what he or she was accused of. The question may be, as in Skilling's case or the Andersen case, whether what that person did was a crime.

In a large corporation, there is a lot of sand for ostriches to bury their heads in. The lack of any single villain may enable the largest and most complex organizations to commit the most substantial and damaging crimes.[28] One purpose of an organization, particularly a large one, is to allow work to be specialized and divided among employees. That may make the work more efficient, but it may also make it harder to blame individuals if something goes wrong. Criminologists who study corporate fraud suggest it is usually a "team sport" and the product of "group-think" or collusion among groups of employees.[29] Scholars suggest that managers can be socialized together, with "numbing effects" on their ability to break ranks and question orders.[30] Such crime may not often be detected, so the risks may be perceived as low. Everyone else may be doing it and covering for each other. There may be high pressure to conform, make the numbers, hide embarrassing failures, or conceal violations.

The broader business environment may also play a role. Companies facing tough economic times may have greater incentive to bend the rules. Corporations may not take laws and regulations seriously if they are unclear, weak, or enforced ineffectually. Some who engage in corporate crime may do so for reasons that seem good at the time—to help the company—and not because they are "scheming" or "self-centered" types bent only on their own reward.[31] Employees such as David Duncan are unlikely to see their company as corrupt and incompetent; Duncan's claimed uncertainty about whether he had committed a crime fits the white-collar mold well.

Individuals at KPMG

One corporate scandal can bleed into another, and even as prosecutors learn lessons from one set of cases, the next set raises new challenges. After Andersen, prosecutors targeted KPMG and individuals involved in marketing tax shelters. Nineteen people were ultimately charged—far more than in the typical corporate case. Prosecutions often depend on cooperating witnesses, often "little fish" who are minor players willing to "flip" against "big fish."[32] Here prosecutors had the help of a powerful cooperator—the corporation, KPMG. Did prosecutors use the big fish to prosecute the little fish? And did prosecutors set the "enormous economic power" of the firm, which "faced ruin by indictment," against its own employees? KPMG wanted to avoid being the next Andersen, and it realized that the best defense was to help prosecutors go on the offense.

Informants can be good, bad, or ugly. Jailhouse informants notoriously seek a better deal for themselves by telling prosecutors that they overheard cellmates confess to crimes. The informants may be liars, but sometimes jurors believe them, and DNA and other evidence has proven how lying informants have sometimes helped put innocent people behind bars.[33] More powerful informants are insiders who were a trusted part of a criminal organization—the Mafia turncoat, the co-conspirator who cooperates, or the corporate officer willing to wear a wire and record conversations. In a white-collar case, a whistle-blower may produce information that prosecutors could never obtain otherwise.

A corporation can be the ultimate informant, and it doesn't need to wear a wire. It can turn over all of its employees' emails and documents. It can send lawyers to interview employees to investigate what happened, and employees cannot easily refuse to talk to corporate attorneys if they want to keep their jobs. The power of the corporation over its employees came to a head in the wake of the KPMG deferred prosecution agreement. A judge combed through negotiations between KPMG and prosecutors, and as a result, we know far more about how KPMG negotiated its agreement than in any case before or since. Prosecutors turned over 22 million pages of documents and anticipated a complex trial, with nearly 70 witnesses and 2,000 exhibits totaling more than 150,000 pages. Prosecutors were preparing for a trial against nineteen defendants that might take six to eight months.[34] Yet when the trial finally began, only four individuals faced charges. What happened?

Prosecutors had always been interested in individuals along with KPMG as a whole, and they met with IRS investigators and a confidential informant who used to work for KPMG as they built their cases. Prosecutors charged nineteen people for involvement in the byzantine tax shelters, including seventeen current or former KPMG employees. Only two ever pleaded guilty.

Like many employers, KPMG had a long-standing policy of advancing and paying legal fees if employees were investigated or prosecuted. One of the seventeen who had worked for KPMG had just signed a contract including payment for "all legal proceedings or actions . . . arising from and within the scope of his duties and responsibilities." However, prosecutors "placed the issue of payment of legal fees high on its agenda for its first meeting with KPMG counsel." KPMG argued that not paying employees' legal fees would be a "big problem,"[35] and initially announced that "'any present or former members of the firm asked to appear will be represented by competent coun[sel] at the firm's expense.'"[36] At a meeting on February 25, 2004, prosecutors emphasized that "'misconduct' should not or cannot 'be rewarded,'" and any payment of legal fees would be "look[ed] at . . . under a microscope." Prosecutors seemed "angry" and indicated that avoiding prosecution would be an "uphill battle" for KPMG. Prosecutors delivered the sober warning that "no one has a get out of jail free card."[37]

By the next meeting, on March 2, KPMG had gotten the message. KPMG's lawyer suggested the company might put a "cap" on legal fees, or only provide them to employees who cooperated. On March 11, KPMG proposed sending employees a letter stating that KPMG would pay legal fees and expenses up to $400,000 if the employees would "cooperate with the government and . . . be prompt, complete, and truthful." The payment would "cease immediately if . . . [the employee] is charged by the government with criminal wrongdoing."

Why did KPMG decide to cut off legal fees to employees? It was not because of the cost, although the defense would be expensive. In related civil lawsuits, KPMG paid more than $3 million for most of the same employees' lawyers. Prosecutors later conceded that before 2004, "it had been the long-standing voluntary practice of KPMG to advance and pay legal fees, without a preset cap or condition of cooperation with the government," for its employees in civil and criminal cases. KPMG's new chief legal officer, a former federal judge, testified that he wanted "to be able to say, at the right time with the right audience, we're in full compliance" with the Justice Department's guidelines. One of the prosecutors later commented, "The company was doing anything it could to cooperate."[38] The KPMG lawyers thought it would be a "big problem" to face prosecution. After all, KPMG was acutely aware of the fate of Arthur Andersen.

In addition to telling KPMG that any payment of fees would be looked at "under a microscope," prosecutors apparently "referred specifically to the Thompson Memorandum as a point that had to be considered."[39] Recall how the DOJ, after prosecuting Arthur Andersen, revised its guidelines to encourage the use of deferred prosecution and non-prosecution agreements;

that 2003 revision was popularly called the "Thompson Memo" after the deputy attorney general who issued it.[40] The memo noted that cooperation would be an important factor in deciding whether a company receives leniency, a policy designed to discourage a corporation from circling the wagons. Cooperation requires a "willingness to identify the culprits within the corporation, including senior executives," and the memo noted that supporting "culpable employees" by the "advancing of attorney's fees" or by retaining them "without sanction" might lead prosecutors to think the corporation is being obstructionist. The company should "make witnesses available," "disclose the complete results of its internal investigation," and "waive attorney-client and work product protection."[41] The last phrase was the most controversial, since giving information to prosecutors about who is responsible is standard cooperation, but giving up privileged or protected documents sounds like asking a company to waive its rights.

Corporations have important rights in criminal investigations that give them great power over employees. When lawyers talk about privilege, they typically are referring to an individual right to protect a conversation between an attorney and a client—the attorney-client privilege. There is another type of privilege, work product privilege, that covers the lawyer's notes and memos. If the other side could see a lawyer's thought process, it would be impossible to keep one's strategy private. Corporations "own" privilege in a way that powerfully affects how criminal cases are investigated and litigated. Under the Supreme Court's 1981 decision in *Upjohn v. United States*, the corporation decides whether to assert privilege and protect a lawyer's work product and privileged conversations.[42] This places employees in a bind. If they refuse to speak to company lawyers investigating possible wrongdoing, the company can fire them, as many companies have "talk or walk" policies.[43] If the employees do talk to the company's lawyers, an admission of wrongdoing may be used against them.

They may not understand that the corporation's lawyer is not really *their* lawyer. Lawyers for the corporation typically inform employees that they represent the interests of the corporation and that employees may wish to consult their own separate lawyer.[44] But however well informed the employees are, for them the stakes remain the same. If the company decides to waive privilege, records of those interviews can be turned over to regulators and prosecutors. While difficult for employees, this rule gives corporations great power and control.[45] Corporations have something to offer prosecutors in exchange for leniency: waiver of privilege, granting prosecutors access to materials useful for charging employees.[46] If employees try to play ostrich, prosecutors can turn to the corporation to get information.

KPMG was already in hot water over this issue; a judge had found that in response to a 2002 request by the IRS for documents concerning the tax shelters, the company "misrepresent[ed]" documents as privileged when they were clearly not.[47] That obstructionism helped convince prosecutors to take an aggressive posture, and in response, KPMG abandoned its claims. The deferred prosecution agreement highlighted how KPMG's eventual cooperation was an "important factor" in the decision not to prosecute. KPMG agreed to provide prosecutors with all relevant documents and not to assert any claim of privilege.[48]

There had been howls of protest from the defense and corporate communities in response to the parts of the Thompson Memo discussing waivers of privilege.[49] In fact, most companies did not waive it.[50] Yet many registered fierce objections; the Chamber of Commerce complained that "this policy deals a serious blow to the ability of employees to vindicate their legal rights without suffering financial ruin."[51] In 2005, the DOJ made a small change to the policy, asking each office to review waiver requests to see if they were necessary.[52] Complaints continued that DOJ policy had created a "culture of waiver,"[53] even as most agreements did not include a privilege waiver. From 2001 to 2012, 19 percent of deferred prosecution and non-prosecution agreements (49 of 255) required a waiver, and in eighteen of these forty-nine cases, employees were prosecuted.[54] However, companies can turn over information without agreeing to a formal waiver of privilege.

What if employees do not want to talk to investigators or to federal prosecutors? The Fifth Amendment provides the right not to incriminate oneself. While employees have the right against self-incrimination, the U.S. Supreme Court has held that an organization such as a corporation has no such right to remain silent. A company has a lot of information to offer prosecutors, and the Supreme Court has recognized that "the greater portion of evidence of wrongdoing by an organization or its representatives is usually found in the official records and documents of that organization."[55] Those records will include the fruits of internal investigations. A company can also threaten to fire employees for not cooperating, or for just about any nondiscriminatory reason—and firing employees for suspected wrongdoing can be a good thing.

What if the government tells the company to fire any employees who will not talk?[56] Does that resemble the situation where a detective threatens a suspect in an interrogation room? The Supreme Court in *Garrity v. New Jersey* and subsequent cases held that threatening government employees (not private ones) with career-ending consequences for failing to waive privilege violated the Fifth Amendment. In *Garrity*, a New Jersey law required that police officers agree to be interviewed about misconduct or risk losing their jobs—the choice "was either to forfeit their jobs or to incriminate themselves." Such employee statements obtained in violation of the Fifth Amendment cannot be used at a criminal trial.[57] But in the KPMG case, the individuals involved were not government employees.

As noted, each of the employees under investigation received a letter saying that KPMG would advance up to $400,000 in legal fees, but only if employees would "cooperate with the government and . . . be prompt, complete, and truthful." Almost all of the employees spoke to prosecutors, signing a standard proffer agreement to be interviewed. Two employees chose not to sign and did not talk; one refused to speak with prosecutors, and the other spoke to prosecutors once but refused to speak again except on certain conditions. Attorneys for those two holdout employees received a letter on May 28, 2004, that said:

> Absent an indication within the next ten business days from the government that your client no longer refuses to meet with the government pursuant to its standard proffer agreement, KPMG will cease payment of [the client's legal] fees.
>
> Finally, please note that KPMG will view continued non-cooperation as a basis for disciplinary action, including expulsion from the Firm.[58]

Both of the employees changed course. One agreed to talk, "acting against the advice of his attorney and in order to keep his job," after the prosecutors reported his noncooperation to KPMG, which had "implicitly but unmistakably threatened to fire him if he did not fall into line."[59] The other also agreed to talk, but KPMG ultimately cut off payment of legal fees and fired the employee for being uncooperative.

In July 2006, federal Judge Lewis Kaplan ruled that prosecutors had in effect forced KPMG to force the employees to talk, violating their Fifth Amendment rights.[60] The judge's ruling was unusual. I have studied dozens of disturbing false confessions by innocent people later freed by DNA testing and have found that often judges did not sufficiently consider the coercive impact of lengthy, high-pressure interrogations.[61] In the KPMG case, these were not police interrogations. The company was not acting as an arm of the state. The prosecutors were adversaries of KPMG. Judge Kaplan, though, concluded that prosecutors "quite deliberately coerced, and in any case significantly encouraged, KPMG to pressure its employees to surrender their Fifth Amendment rights." As a result, prosecutors would not be able to use the statements from the two employees or any other "fruits" of the statements. This was undoubtedly a blow to their case, but prosecutors were still moving forward with plans for a major trial.

The judge was clearly troubled by everything that had happened in the KPMG case. He next turned to KPMG's decision to stop paying employees' legal fees, ruling in a lengthy July 2006 decision that prosecutors had in effect forced KPMG to cut off employee legal fees in violation of the employees' Sixth Amendment right to counsel.[62] Of course, most criminal defendants cannot afford lawyers, much less very good ones. The prosecutors made just that point: if these defendants were financially eligible, the federal court could appoint lawyers for them. There is no constitutional right to the very best lawyers. Judges often reject claims by convicts that they were unfairly tried because their court-appointed lawyers were underfunded and inadequate, even in cases where the lawyers were openly sleeping in court or otherwise incompetent.

Judge Kaplan noted that the maximum pay court-appointed lawyers can get is $7,000, and they are paid $94 an hour. That entire federal courthouse had paid less than $20 million a year to court-appointed lawyers. In the KPMG case, defendants had already incurred fees ranging from $500,000 to a high of $3.6 million, and there was a long trial to come. The government agreed that a single defense might cost $3.3 million, and defense lawyers estimated total costs higher than $10 million. For this complex tax fraud trial, the group of lawyers could be paid $50 million or more. That is hardly unique in the world of white-collar defense; in the Enron prosecutions, Kenneth Lay's defense cost $25 million and Jeffrey Skilling's cost $70 million. And the defendants, some wealthier than others, would all have to be "wiped out financially" before they would be eligible for court-appointed lawyers.[63] The judge was concerned that the government had interfered directly with the legal representation KPMG had given the defendants by encouraging KPMG to, in effect, fire their lawyers. KPMG normally paid for lawyers for its employees, changing its policy only when prosecutors pressured them to do so. Despite another setback for prosecutors, the judge had not yet decided whether to dismiss the case.

Larger Ripples: Who Is Going to Jail?

The KPMG case became the focal point for concerns about the role of lawyers and employees in corporate prosecutions. Senator Arlen Specter introduced legislation to bar federal officials from considering a firm's waiver of privilege, payment of employee attorney fees, or employee cooperation with an investigation.[64] The legislation went nowhere, but the bar and business groups carried the cause forward. As noted, most companies receiving leniency do not waive privilege, and no one was suggesting that something should be done to give employees more rights against at-will firing. Nevertheless, the KPMG case eventually would help smooth out matters a little.

In the halls of Congress, prosecutors are apparently damned if they do and damned if they don't. When prosecutors took a more aggressive tack against corporate employees, they faced outrage from the bar, corporate interests, and judges. Now prosecutors face the reverse—outrage that corporations are getting leniency but no employees are being held accountable. In Senate hearings on the Foreign Corrupt Practices Act in 2010, Senator Specter demanded to know why so few individual employees had been prosecuted. He pointed to high-profile cases, such as the Panalpina World Transport case, with $236 million in fines but no individual prosecutions, and the record $1.6 billion in fines in the Siemens case, which at that point involved no individuals. The DOJ said cases were "ongoing," and it had imposed more than $1 billion in penalties in FCPA cases.

Senator Specter pointed out that "fines come out of the corporation . . . but that doesn't deal with the individual conduct violating the law." He put it bluntly: "My question is, who's going to jail?"[65] Perhaps responding to the concern, in 2011 the DOJ announced charges against a group of eight former Siemens executives. The officers were all allegedly involved in paying $100 million in bribes to secure a $1 billion contract to make national identity cards in Argentina.[66] As the DOJ announced, "This is the first time we've charged a board member of a Fortune Global 50 company with FCPA violations." But none of these executives resided in the United States, and arresting and extraditing them to face charges in this country may be impossible. Still, the move pleased Senator Specter, who noted that "just the filing of a criminal prosecution is a salutatory action."[67] Since then, some of the former Siemens executives have settled civil charges with the SEC, but none has been convicted of crimes.[68]

How often are employees targeted? The KPMG case stands out for having so many employees charged. Looking across all of the deferred prosecution and non-prosecution agreements with corporations, most do not involve employee prosecutions. In response to Specter's questions, the DOJ said it had charged fifty people in FCPA cases—far fewer than the number of corporations targeted (more than ninety). The DOJ could point to only a few resulting in jail sentences, the longest of which was eighty-seven months. Of the nearly 100 FCPA prosecutions over the past decade, fewer than thirty involved employee prosecutions. Only ten companies that entered deferred prosecution or non-prosecution agreements for FCPA violations had their officers or employees prosecuted as well. The FCPA does pose special challenges, since it may be hard to arrest foreign employees who were involved. It may require extradition, requiring the cooperation of another government, and some countries do not extradite to the United States, effectively leaving people outside the reach of U.S. authorities unless they travel to the United States or a country that will extradite.

The largest and most serious corporate prosecutions did not result in individual prosecutions. As noted, individual employees or officers of companies were prosecuted in only about one-third of cases involving deferred prosecution or non-prosecution agreements. In addition, slightly fewer (25 percent, or 31 of 125) of the public companies and their subsidiaries that were convicted between 2001 and 2012 had individual officers or employees prosecuted. There is usually not a formal deal to let employees off the hook, or at least not one that is made public. The exception is in antitrust immunity deals, which reward the first company to come forward with immunity for the company, its officers, and its employees. The policy is designed to provide a powerful weapon to prosecute the other companies and employees colluding in a price-fixing cartel. Antitrust agreements often include a promise not to prosecute cooperating employees, but prosecutors also "carve out" and prosecute those employees who do not cooperate, particularly high-level ones.[69] Outside the antitrust setting, I found few deferred prosecution or non-prosecution agreements discussing employees: the exception was an agreement in the AmSouth Bancorp case, which said that if the firm complied, then "the United States will not prosecute any current or former AmSouth employee based upon any of the conduct described."[70] The case was about failure to file "suspicious activity reports" concerning unusual bank transactions, reports designed to detect money laundering.[71] It may have been that no particular employee was at fault, but rather that automated systems were not designed correctly. We do not know. The document describing what prosecutors uncovered in the case is under court seal and cannot be accessed.

Cases in which both the company and employees were prosecuted involved almost exclusively domestic firms: of the eighty-nine companies entering deferred prosecution or non-prosecution agreements, eighty were domestic corporations. This may speak to the difficulty of prosecuting foreign employees of foreign corporations. The cases in which employees were prosecuted had the same average fines. Well over half of the cases, fifty-four of them, involved fraud; only ten involved FCPA violations. None of the banking or currency-reporting violations resulted in individual prosecutions, nor did export violations. Some officers and employees have been held civilly accountable by agencies such as the SEC; they may be debarred from doing work for public companies or pay substantial fines. In such cases, prosecutors may conclude that civil consequences for individuals were enough.

There were a total of 385 individual officers and employees prosecuted in cases related to the eighty-nine deferred prosecution and non-prosecution agreements. Several companies with large numbers of prosecuted employees had violated immigration rules, and low-level employees were convicted for using fraudulent visas. But in some cases, upper- and lower-level employees were prosecuted in large numbers; the twenty-three employees of the New York Racing Association convicted include its director and a vice president. There were the seventeen KPMG employees prosecuted (and two nonemployees). HealthSouth had eighteen officers and employees prosecuted, from the CEO and CFO to the treasurer and a series of vice presidents. What happened to the prosecuted individuals? Most pleaded guilty, like the vast majority of criminal defendants, but some took their cases to trial, and in some high-profile cases, such as that of HealthSouth's CEO, the defendants were acquitted.

There is little data on how many corporate employees have been prosecuted in the past. A study in the mid-1970s by Marshall Clinard and Peter Yeager found that only 1.5 percent of federal enforcement efforts resulted in the conviction of a corporate officer.[72] There may be far more prosecutions of employees of smaller companies, where owners or higher-ups may be closely involved. A study by Mark Cohen in the late 1980s found that in 65 percent of non-antitrust-related federal corporate prosecutions, employees were prosecuted.[73] Such data raise the concern whether elites, such as executives at major corporations, can resist prosecution by hiring high-paid lawyers and arguing a lack of knowledge of crimes by their subordinates.

Sometimes prosecution of employees is considered sufficient. The environmental nonprofit Greenpeace was prosecuted when eleven members trespassed and hiked to the top of Mount Rushmore. On the courthouse steps, one of the hikers explained, "We climbed Mount Rushmore because we wanted to send a message to President Obama that this is an issue that is important to us, and to the future generations who will face the increasing impacts of global warming."[74] When the hikers pleaded guilty and were sentenced to fines and 50 to 100 hours of community service (including work in the park at Mount Rushmore), prosecutors thought that was enough. They dropped the charges against Greenpeace, although it did pay a $30,000 civil fine.

When Morgan Stanley disclosed FCPA violations in its Chinese real-estate business, the DOJ and SEC charged the Morgan Stanley manager in China with violations but announced that they would not prosecute Morgan Stanley itself:

> After considering all the available facts and circumstances, including that Morgan Stanley constructed and maintained a system of internal controls, which provided reasonable assurances that its employees were not bribing government officials, the Department of Justice declined to bring any enforcement action against Morgan Stanley related to Peterson's conduct. The company voluntarily disclosed this matter and has cooperated throughout the department's investigation.[75]

The DOJ and SEC explained that a rogue employee used a "web of deceit" and "actively evaded" the controls that the company had in place in order to get control of a multimillion-dollar building in Shanghai along with his friends and conspirators.[76]

One of the largest immigration raids in history swept a kosher meatpacking plant in Postville, Iowa, in May 2008. More than 300 employees were arrested, all immigrants, and within days more than 250 had been prosecuted and had pleaded guilty to immigration crimes. Prosecutors gave them "exploding" offers of leniency—that is, offers that have an expiration date—for pleading guilty to felonies right away, and they were interrogated without access to immigration lawyers.[77] Prosecutors threatened severe aggravated identify theft charges and denied bail; defendants might have served six to eight months in pretrial detention if they did not accept their exploding offers, which were mostly for only five months of jail time. Congress later held hearings examining what had transpired.[78]

A local Postville official complained, "They don't go after employers. They don't put CEOs in jail."[79] But the government did bring charges against higher-level employees, including the CEO, and the corporation itself, Agriprocessors, Inc. Unlike the cases against immigrant workers, which were fast-tracked and resolved within days, this case plodded along slowly and was intensively litigated. The CEO went on trial in late 2009 and was convicted. The government dismissed all of the charges against Agriprocessors, Inc., but for a good reason—the company was bankrupt, had "ceased doing any business," and had been "effectively divested of all property."[80] The company could not pay a fine because it was "an empty shell." Other corporations dissolve as a consequence of prosecutions, or because an underlying fraud ruins the company, leaving the employees as the only target. This often happens in prosecutions of fairly small companies. For example, a contractor was fined $4,400 for Clean Air Act violations, since the company was basically defunct, but the owner had to pay $303,000 in restitution and was sentenced to six years in prison.[81]

Should more employees be prosecuted? Prosecutors are supposed to prioritize holding real people accountable, not corporate persons. In 2008, the deputy chief of the Justice Department's Fraud Section said that individual prosecutions have gone up "and that's not an accident . . . to have a credible deterrent effect, people have to go to jail."[82] But in most corporate deferred prosecution agreements, no employees are prosecuted, so the credible deterrent must be prosecution of companies.

Systems Failures

In some types of cases, prosecutors do not focus on identifying who knew what in a company. Instead, they focus on structural reforms to prevent future crimes. This is particularly true in prosecutions under the Bank Secrecy Act, a 1970s law that deals with the bank secrecy laws of other countries and includes rules designed to protect against money laundering by requiring banks to track large deposits of cash.[83] Banks must file reports for transactions that involve more than $10,000 in cash, and in particular transport of such sums into or out of the country. Banks file massive numbers of those reports, more than 15 million a year.

There are also tough laws against money laundering—it is illegal to enter financial transactions or transmit funds to and from the United States if one has knowledge that those transactions involve specified crimes, such as fraud, and to conceal or disguise where the proceeds of those crimes came from.[84] Federal law bars structuring transactions to avoid reporting requirements[85] or engaging in money transactions in "criminally derived property" worth more than $10,000.[86] In addition, federal laws, such as the USA PATRIOT Act of 2001, require banks to adopt procedures to identify transactions by suspected terrorists or terrorist organizations.[87]

Violations of laws such as the Bank Secrecy Act absolutely involve compliance failures, since banks are required to have systems in place to flag and report troubling transactions.[88] Yet no U.S. bank has ever been convicted of money laundering.[89] If a bank is convicted of money laundering, federal law requires the comptroller of the currency to terminate the bank's license.[90] This turns a money laundering conviction into a corporate death sentence. Instead, banks typically are charged with Bank Secrecy Act violations, giving the comptroller discretion as to the bank's license, including considering whether the bank cooperated with the authorities and adopted improved "internal controls."[91] Almost all banks receive deferred prosecution or non-prosecution agreements for Bank Secrecy Act violations; only a handful have been convicted. Banks are usually charged with a failure to maintain an effective anti-money-laundering program—a crime of inadequate compliance.[92]

The best-known example is the prosecution of HSBC in the largest money laundering case in U.S. history. Once called Hong Kong Shanghai Banking Corporation, HSBC is now headquartered in London, operates in more than eighty countries, and has $2.5 trillion in assets and almost 90 million customers. The U.S. branch of HSBC became the subject of an inquiry by a U.S. Senate committee concerned about its weak anti-money-laundering program.[93] The committee found that billions of dollars had been diverted to Mexican drug cartels, groups in Iran and Syria, and groups linked to terrorism. HSBC apparently had systems designed to flag suspicious transactions, but employees were told to disregard red flags. The bank also "failed to conduct due diligence" on its foreign affiliate branches opening accounts in the United States despite a law requiring that it do so.[94]

Among the beneficiaries of these lax controls were Mexican drug cartels, who need to get hard U.S. dollars back to Mexico after smuggling drugs in the other direction.[95] It is much easier to wire-transfer the money, but with U.S. banks adopting strict anti-money-laundering controls, cartels took cash across the border and deposited the money in lightly regulated Mexican banks—including HSBC's Mexican subsidiary. The subsidiary was moving billions a year into its U.S. operations. Authorities in Mexico and the United States warned HSBC that the volume of dollars could only be due to illegal narcotics trade. HSBC should have known this would be a problem; when it bought the Mexican bank in 2002, it learned that the other bank did not "in reality, have a Compliance Department." In the late 1990s, this same Mexican bank had been implicated in Operation Casa Blanca, a U.S. undercover money laundering sting.[96]

Prosecutions of other banks should have also been a warning. For example, Sigue, a company that provided electronic transfers of money to Central and South America, faced prosecution for not having adequate controls to prevent money laundering. Sigue was given a deferred prosecution agreement, in part because it was already spending tens of millions to enhance its internal controls. When the agreement was reached, Sigue's lawyer said, "It is important to note, the issues identified did not involve Sigue's officers or employees" but instead involved "a relatively small group of independent agents providing Sigue's services during the period of November 2003 through March 2005."[97]

Banks are also supposed to monitor transactions to the most dangerous persons and countries, places such as Burma, North Korea, and Sudan.

Multiple federal laws make it a crime to violate economic sanctions imposed on such regimes, yet HSBC apparently altered transaction information to disguise links to Iran (to avoid the careful review that regulations require for such transactions). HSBC was active in Asia, Africa, and the Middle East, particularly in Saudi Arabia. Despite "terrorist financing concerns," HSBC reopened business with a Saudi bank and others with possible links to terrorism.[98] One employee pointed out in an email that "over the last couple of months investigators have approached me about cases in the Middle East, especially in Palestine. . . . It appears that most investigators do not understand that the government of Palestine is the terrorist organization Hamas." (Hamas has been designated as a terrorist organization since 1995.) Yet his supervisor angrily responded, "Are you out of your f—— mind?" and "I should fire you right now."[99]

After these transactions came to light, the Senate issued a report calling the culture at HSBC "pervasively polluted." "In an age of international terrorism, drug violence in our streets and on our borders, and organized crime, stopping illicit money flows that support those atrocities is a national security imperative," said Sen. Carl Levin. The head of compliance at HSBC announced his resignation at U.S. Senate hearings in July 2012. He added, "I am happy, however, to be able to say that the bank has learned from its past and is already on a path to becoming a better, stronger banking institution."[100]

One problem was a simple lack of staffing. Despite being one of the largest banks in the world, HSBC had only 200 employees working full-time on compliance, and even fewer on anti-money-laundering compliance. These employees claimed to be "overwhelmed" by the vast number of transactions with anti-money-laundering alerts and complained that they were in "dire straights [sic] . . . over backlogs." The bank kept staffing low to keep costs low; when the head of compliance raised the issue of insufficient staff and resources at a board meeting, she was fired, and her comments were called "inappropriate."[101]

Will HSBC finally shape up its compliance programs now that it has been prosecuted? While money laundering charges were not brought—as we have seen, a conviction on those charges would have led to the bank losing its charter—HSBC paid $1.92 billion in forfeiture and fines.[102] The bank also entered a deferred prosecution agreement that cited its failure to adopt due diligence and have an effective anti-money-laundering compliance program.[103] No employees at HSBC have been prosecuted, although HSBC agreed to cooperate in ongoing investigations. What changed? HSBC replaced all of its top leadership, from the CEO down to the chief compliance officer and anti-money-laundering director. The bank clawed back bonuses for senior officers. It spent $244 million on anti-money-laundering efforts in 2011, nine times what it spent in 2009, and ramped up the number of full-time employees working on those efforts from 92 to 880. It embarked on a $700 million review of all of its clients. It adopted new automated systems to monitor wire transfers and transactions. And the bonuses of senior executives will now be based on "the extent to which the senior executive meets compliance standards and values."[104] Similarly, MoneyGram International Inc. signed a deferred prosecution agreement in 2012 agreeing to evaluate all executives based on adherence to compliance policies.[105] These are remarkable changes to the terms of employment at major banks.

In another banking case, this one involving Barclays, the judge who held hearings before approving a deferred prosecution agreement expressed outrage: "No one goes to jail, no one is indicted, no individuals are mentioned as far as I can determine . . . there's no personal responsibility."[106]

The prosecutor explained, "In every case . . . we look . . . to see is there someone or an entity that has committed a crime. But in this case, there . . . was not someone who we could prove to a court beyond a reasonable doubt . . . had committed an offense."

The judge was incredulous: "There's no paper trail of $500 million being funneled illegally to other countries? I mean, senior management . . . has to know who's responsible for it. I mean, these weren't just computer transfers. Someone had to mastermind this."

The prosecutor responded, "We certainly looked . . . and to date . . . there's no one that we have any charges pending against."

The judge would not let this go: "There's no basis to hold senior management criminally responsible?"

The prosecutor responded that Barclays spent $250 million in internal investigations, but the judge was not impressed. "They spend $250 million and couldn't find anyone responsible. That's just shocking, you know. It is shocking, isn't it?"[107]

No employees were prosecuted, and nor have any HSBC employees been prosecuted. We know from the statement of facts in the deferred prosecution agreement that some of the beleaguered compliance officials at HSBC knew there was a problem and complained, asking for more resources. Perhaps prosecutors could have shown, using an ostrich instruction, that the higher-ups were at least willful blind. Instead, as is typical in Bank Secrecy Act cases, the bank settled its case, and no employees or officers were held individually accountable.

Big Pharma and Corporate Culture

Prosecutions of major pharmaceutical corporations (often known as "Big Pharma"), including several of the largest corporate prosecutions of all time, also involve massive compliance failures but rarely any prosecutions of individuals. These Big Pharma companies can have many thousands of sales professionals, either on staff or as consultants who market drugs to doctors. The Food, Drug, and Cosmetics Act (FDCA) makes it a misdemeanor to cause adulteration or "misbranding" of any food, drug, cosmetic, or device in interstate commerce.[108] Doctors have freedom to prescribe drugs based on their medical judgment, but a drug company must not market drugs to doctors for unapproved or "off-label" uses that have not been tested and approved by the Food and Drug Administration (FDA.)[109] It is also unlawful for drug sales representatives to offer kickbacks to doctors if they prescribe a drug.[110] Other laws make it a crime to falsely report prices of drugs or medical devices. It is estimated that health care fraud in general costs the government tens of billions of dollars a year.[111]

The biggest of the Big Pharma corporations is Pfizer. In 2009 Pfizer and a subsidiary paid $2.3 billion for off-label marketing of a painkiller and an antipsychotic drug. This sum included a criminal fine of almost $1.2 billion, a record at the time. The case began, like most of these cases do, with the accusations of a whistle-blower. One of Pfizer's most widely prescribed drugs was Bextra, a painkiller. (In 2005, Pfizer would remove Bextra from the market after studies showed it created a risk of heart attack.) Sales representatives were paid a $50 reward when they convinced doctors to add Bextra to the standard protocol after an operation.[112] A Pfizer sales representative, whose team of sales reps was nicknamed "the Sharks," recalled, "If you don't aggressively sell your products . . . you're labeled a non-team player." This representative was fired from Pfizer after he complained to supervisors in

2003 about sales of Bextra for unapproved uses. The rep, a Gulf War veteran, lost his $125,000-a-year position and had to take a much lower-paying job, later commenting, "It was a lot of stress on the family. I pretty much depleted my entire 401(k)."[113] He added, "In the Army I was expected to protect people at all costs . . . At Pfizer I was expected to increase profits at all costs, even when sales meant endangering lives."[114]

He turned whistle-blower and filed a *qui tam* suit, which is a lawsuit brought by an individual to report actions that defraud the federal government. Those who file a *qui tam* suit may be motivated by money, since they can take a share of the funds recovered for the government. Such a bounty can be millions of dollars. Federal regulators at the Department of Health and Human Services Office of Inspector General (HHS-OIG), working with DOJ lawyers, may take on the litigation themselves, and criminal prosecutions may follow. The DOJ has created a joint task force to pursue health care fraud cases and has obtained billions in fines.[115]

When the Pfizer case was settled in 2009, the former sales representative received a $51.5 million reward, along with a share of the money recovered by the states. Three other whistle-blowers recovered tens of millions more. Yet it was a Pfizer subsidiary that was convicted, not the parent company. This is because HHS-OIG wields another powerful weapon—debarment from Medicaid or Medicare, which could be the death knell of a major pharmaceutical company. For some crimes a felony conviction requires mandatory exclusion or debarment from participating in all federal health care programs.[116] HHS can offer waivers to avoid that serious sanction,[117] as major companies may be considered "too big to debar" if they sell critical drugs that doctors and patients rely on.[118] Big Pharma companies may pay some of the largest fines in all of federal criminal law, but often a subsidiary pleads guilty to the crime, or the company is convicted of a misdemeanor rather than a serious felony.

The fines may not seem so large after all, given the sums of money involved in health care spending. Consider the case of antipsychotic drugs, on which Americans spend $15 billion a year. In 2012, Abbott Labs paid $1.5 billion, about half of which was in criminal fines, to settle claims about off-label marketing of antipsychotics.[119] In 2010, AstraZeneca settled new charges with the federal government over off-label marketing of antipsychotic drugs (it had previously paid $355 million in 2003). This time it paid a massive $520 million civil fine with no prosecution. Eli Lilly paid $1.4 billion, over one-third of which was a criminal fine regarding off-label marketing of an antipsychotic. In 2007, Bristol-Myers Squibb and a subsidiary paid $515 million regarding marketing of yet another antipsychotic drug.[120]

Perhaps industry practices will eventually change. Take the case of Glaxo-SmithKline, which in 2012 paid almost $3 billion, including nearly $1 billion in criminal fines, as part of a "global" settlement of multiple whistle-blower actions.[121] One of the allegations involved a drug called Wellbutrin SR, an antidepressant. "Operation Hustle" was GSK's nickname for its program to gain a greater market share for this product. Sales representatives were told it was useful for combating a wide range of mood disorders, not just depression. They promoted Wellbutrin as an "add-on" to help prevent weight gain and improve patients' sex lives while on antidepressants. Sales shot up, and Wellbutrin SR became "the product of choice for adding . . . patients who experience sexual dysfunction or efficacy poop-out."[122] Salespeople called Wellbutrin the "happy, horny, skinny pill," according to prosecutors, to remind doctors of unapproved uses.[123] GSK paid its sales representatives by the volume of sales, with special bonuses, such as vacations to Hawaii, for top sellers.

After these violations were revealed, a GlaxoSmithKline spokesperson said the company had "taken action at all levels in the company to ingrain a culture that aligns with our values and puts patients first."[124] A plea agreement, together with a detailed corporate integrity agreement with HHS-OIG, changed how sales representatives were paid, based not on "the volume of sales" but "on business acumen, customer engagement, and scientific knowledge about GSK's products." The plea agreement added a $20,000-a-day penalty for any breach.[125] Other recent agreements have similar language—the Abbott Labs agreement has penalties ranging from $1,000 to $5,000 a day.[126] A detailed agreement entered in 2013 with a Johnson & Johnson subsidiary also included similar language regarding penalties and altering the compensation of employees. In late 2013, GlaxoSmithKline announced that the changes adopted under the plea agreement would be extended to its entire global business: it will no longer pay sales staff based on numbers of prescriptions written by doctors, nor will it pay doctors to promote its products.[127] Whether that is a harbinger of a real shift in industry practice remains to be seen.

Why not prosecute the employees? Pharmaceutical sales employees have not typically been targets, but some doctors have.[128] To prosecute hundreds or thousands of sales employees would be an enormous task, and singling out one or two might seem unfair. Perhaps prosecutors decided only the company can pay fines and prevent improper drug sales and marketing.

The Higher-Ups

Sometimes prosecutors do take on the ostriches and overcome the challenges to holding higher-ups accountable. In the eighty-nine deferred prosecution and non-prosecution agreements in which individuals were prosecuted, 385 people were prosecuted, including ten presidents, twenty CEOs, and twenty-seven CFOs. Among the thirty-one publicly listed firms convicted between 2001 and 2012 that had individuals prosecuted, one chairman, one president, four CEOs, and one CFO were prosecuted. Far more individuals are prosecuted for white-collar offenses each year in cases in which no company is prosecuted, but no good data are kept on how many of those are higher-ups versus lower-level actors. The Department of Justice has occasionally reported on successes in holding higher-ups accountable, although without clearly explaining where its figures come from; one such DOJ report stated that between 2002 and 2008, the members of its Corporate Fraud Task Force prosecuted 200 CEOs, more than 120 vice presidents, and 50 CFOs.[129]

Perhaps the highest-profile individual prosecution related to a deferred prosecution or non-prosecution agreement was that of the former CEO of Kellogg, Brown and Root (KBR), now a subsidiary of Halliburton. He pleaded guilty in September 2008 to conspiring to violate the FCPA, among other federal crimes, as part of a "decade-long scheme to obtain $6 billion dollars' worth of engineering, procurement, and construction contracts" by paying millions of dollars in bribes to Nigerian officials.[130] In his plea agreement, the former KBR CEO admitted to hiring consultants with the expectation they would pay bribes.[131] In addition, he admitted to repeatedly meeting with high-level Nigerian government officials to discuss whom bribes should be paid to, and meeting with Nigerian officials in a London hotel to negotiate the amount of bribe money to be paid. The total paid by KBR to Nigerian officials was reportedly around $180 million.[132]

All of this made it an easy case—he admitted to being personally involved in the bribery scheme. He even admitted an illicit motive, personally obtaining more than $5 million through an illegal kickback scheme. He hired a former employee as a consultant, received portions of the consultant's bonuses from KBR, and sent the money to his secret Swiss bank account.[133] Contrast the guilty plea in this case with the Tyson Foods deferred prosecution agreement, in which the company paid about $5 million in fines and no action taken was against executives, the highest-ranking of which retired, taking a compensation package that included a $1 million payment, a consulting contract for $3.6 million, and other perks.[134]

Perhaps the best-known example of the ostrich instruction in action is the trial of WorldCom CEO Bernard Ebbers. During his early days working as a basketball coach, a warehouse manager, and a motel operator, Ebbers invested in a small long-distance company in Mississippi. Through a series of remarkable mergers beginning in the late 1980s and continuing through the 1990s, he turned the company into WorldCom, a global telecommunications behemoth with 90,000 employees and billions in annual revenue. Yet in 2000, WorldCom's financial situation began to crumble. In the last quarter of 2000, when $800 million in costs surfaced, accounting gimmicks were used to hide them. As actual earnings continued to disappoint and costs rose, a "Close the Gap" program was created to continue concealing the true scope of the problem from investors and regulators. The CFO called these techniques "accounting fluff," "one-time stuff," and "junk."[135]

After WorldCom's true financial situation came to light, the company collapsed in bankruptcy. In 2002, federal prosecutors charged the CFO with securities fraud, and he pleaded guilty. They also charged Ebbers, alleging he routinely reviewed WorldCom's financial situation and ordered his CFO to fraudulently report high profitability. They said Ebbers had a selfish motive—he owned large quantities of WorldCom stock and had large debts. Ebbers's lawyers argued he was unaware of what the CFO and others were doing.

At trial, the CFO testified that Ebbers intimidated him into committing the fraud by ordering that WorldCom must meet Wall Street expectations. Ebbers also took the stand. He testified that he made deals but left the details of running the company to the CFO. He threw out budget reports without reading them and signed documents without reading them—was that willful blindness? On the stand, he politely denied knowing anything:

> Q: Did you ever believe that any of the statements contained in those public filings were not true?
>
> A: No, sir.
>
> Q: Did you ever believe that WorldCom had reported revenue that it was not entitled to report?
>
> A: No, sir.
>
> Q: Did you ever believe that WorldCom had an obligation to announce changes in accounting practices that it had failed to announce?
>
> A: No, sir.
>
> Q: Did you ever believe that WorldCom was putting out bad numbers in its financial statements in any way at all?
>
> A: No.[136]

The judge instructed the jury that conscious avoidance or willful blindness could be a reason to convict: "You may consider whether the defendant deliberately closed his eyes to what otherwise would have been obvious."[137] The jury could treat "deliberate avoidance of positive knowledge as the equivalent of knowledge."[138] In March 2005, after eight days of deliberating, the jury found Ebbers guilty of all nine counts. He was sentenced to twenty-five years.[139] The jurors apparently concluded that Ebbers's claims of ignorance were simply not true.[140] On appeal, the judges agreed the ostrich instruction was proper, saying that based on all of the evidence, "a rational juror could find [that Ebbers] was consciously trying to avoid knowledge that the financial reports were inaccurate."[141] If higher-ups keep themselves in the dark, they can be convicted.

There is another way to hold higher-ups accountable besides the ostrich instruction—the "responsible corporate officer doctrine." Some statutes allow an executive to be convicted of a crime without knowing anything about it, so long as the executive was responsible for that area of the company's operations and it was a "strict liability" type of misdemeanor offense that did not require knowledge of the wrongdoing. This weapon has rarely been used, coming up mainly in violations of pharmaceutical regulations. Misbranding under the FDCA is a strict liability offense and executives can be held responsible even if it cannot be proved they knew what was happening. However, the FDA tends to recommend prosecutions only if executives were aware of what was going on, or if they were reckless.[142] For example, three executives of the Purdue Frederick Corporation, which itself pleaded guilty to misbranding OxyContin by promoting it as less addictive than it was, pleaded guilty as responsible corporate officers. The three were sentenced to 400 hours of community service, a $5,000 fine, and five years of probation each—the crime was a misdemeanor. They also had to disgorge compensation totaling approximately $34.5 million. This was no trivial punishment for a crime where prosecutors did not have to prove executives had any knowledge or consciously avoided having it.[143]

Regulators can also hold individuals accountable. Some employees have faced civil actions by regulators, while some executives have been barred from work in an industry. When the CEO and president of Forest Labs, a pharmaceutical company, was told HHS-OIG was considering barring him from federal health care program work, the firm's general counsel called this "unjustified," adding that doing so would "create uncertainty throughout the industry and discourage regulatory settlements." Exclusion is meant to "alter the cost-benefit calculus of the corporate executives," said the chief counsel for HHS-OIG, though ultimately HHS decided not to pursue this case.[144] Civil sanctions have been challenged—including by the Purdue Frederick executives, who argued HHS overreached by excluding them for twenty years, with "career ending" consequences. On appeal to higher-level HHS administrators, this was reduced to twelve years, but the executives sued to regain their employment. A three-judge panel then reversed the bar completely, suggesting that misdemeanors that did not require intent to do wrong were insufficient to justify a lengthy exclusion.[145]

Few results look worse than the prosecution of a few underlings while higher-ups are let off the hook completely. Massey Coal was prosecuted following a massive explosion at its Upper Big Branch Mine in West Virginia that killed twenty-nine workers. After the company was bought out, it received a deferred prosecution rather than a conviction. Families of victims expressed concern that no higher-ups were targeted, including the

CEO, who left with a multimillion-dollar package before Massey was sold. Building a case that can overcome an ostrich defense can take time and resources. A superintendent and a president of a subsidiary have pleaded guilty and are cooperating, but so far the former CEO has not been prosecuted.[146]

Other Strategies: Corporate Conspiracy Theory and Victims of the Corporation

A company may be charged with conspiring with its employees—an odd concept, since the company cannot act except through employees. Judges have ruled this is impossible for a sole owner and operator of a company, but many companies are convicted of conspiring.[147] One of the most common charges is conspiracy to defraud the United States.[148] Even if the employee is acquitted, the company can still be convicted; judges have said, following the usual rule in the law of conspiracy, that you can convict one co-conspirator even if the others are found not guilty.[149] Companies can also conspire together, for example in cartels to fix prices, but a company can leave a conspiracy only by renouncing the conduct and cooperating with prosecutors.[150]

Some corporate cases involve a united front, where the corporation stands by its employees and they all act as one giant ostrich denying wrongdoing together. This may happen more often when top executives are allegedly involved in the crime, or in antitrust cases where the company could face massive civil suits for price fixing. If the united front breaks down, fingers can be pointed in both directions—the company blames rogue employees, while employees say they were following orders. If the company is on trial along with employees, a unified defense may hurt the firm. After all, the company may argue that an employee was a rogue and that the company should not be blamed just because one person broke the law. Perhaps it could not be expected to hire a "cop looking over everyone's shoulder."[151]

In one jury study, a set of mock jurors was presented with a case where both an employee and the corporation were tried for a crime. All of the jurors heard the same facts, but in one version, the lawyers for the employee argued that he was a "victim of the corporation's attempt to avoid responsibility." The results were dramatic: the rate of acquittal doubled when the defendant made this "victim of the corporation" argument.[152] This suggests that the role of the corporation will be crucial in a white-collar trial.

KPMG: The Outcomes

In July 2007 Judge Kaplan finally dismissed the cases against most of the KPMG defendants. Sixteen defendants had complained that KPMG had refused to pay their legal fees, and the judge found that prosecutors had violated the constitutional rights of most of them. Mincing no words, the judge said: "Justice is not done when the government uses the threat of indictment—a matter of life and death to many companies . . . to coerce companies into depriving their present and even former employees of the means of defending themselves against criminal charges in a court of law."[153] The judge said prosecutors had been "economic with the truth." He added: "Prosecutors used KPMG to coerce interviews with KPMG personnel that the government could not coerce directly," "used its leverage over KPMG to induce KPMG to coerce proffers by certain defendants," and denied the indicted defendants the "means of defending themselves."[154]

The judge also suggested the Thompson Memo might violate the Constitution's due process clause, adding that the government's "outrageous misconduct" in the case "shocks the conscience." This "shocks the conscience" phrase is very rarely invoked, and only in cases of highly intentional and abusive conduct. The judge argued prosecutors "used KPMG to strip any of its employees who were indicted of means of defending themselves that KPMG otherwise would have provided to them." Very few criminal defendants can afford a lawyer, and the judge admitted this—but held that the government had interfered with lawyers the company already provided. The judge dismissed charges against thirteen defendants, and the appeals court approved, deferring to the judge's findings.[155] Two more KPMG employees pleaded guilty, and four went to trial.

Even for those who went to trial, the "largest criminal tax case in American history" ended with more of a whimper than a bang.[156] The four remaining defendants showed how complicated it can be to hold individuals accountable in corporate cases. Of the four, two had left KPMG before the prosecutions and formed their own company. A third left under "strained circumstances," and the judge concluded KPMG would not have paid that person's fees regardless. A fourth had worked for a law firm that provided opinion letters for the tax shelters.

The jury had to decide if there was a reasonable possibility tax shelters had economic substance or whether there was "no reasonable possibility that the transaction would result in a profit."[157] The question was whether these people willfully evaded federal taxes, or conspired to willfully file false tax returns.[158] The judge did interpret the tax evasion statute as broadly applying to "any person" attempting to "evade or defeat" federal taxes. There was not much law on what makes a transaction a sham versus one with economic substance that might turn a profit, but at trial there was testimony from several of the people involved in the scheme that the chances of profiting from the investments was remote or "basically zero."[159] A star witness for the prosecution was one of the promoters of a shelter who pleaded guilty and cooperated (he faced 195 years in prison and instead received five years).[160] This witness testified that the chance these schemes could lead to a profit was "by far less than 1 percent," and a "pie in the sky or zero" possibility that would take an "unbelievable miracle."[161]

Ultimately, one defendant was acquitted—a former tax partner at KPMG— and the other three were convicted of tax evasion, receiving about ten years each. The judge commented: "There does come a time when a scheme is so raw, so brazen, and so outrageous that it crosses the line that separates bad or incompetent or unsuccessful tax planning from crime." More colloquially, the judge said, "Anybody who thought this was on the whole . . . really an investment transaction was smoking weed." Speaking of the trial's outcome, the judge added, "I personally considered it an intelligent, a thoughtful, and careful verdict."[162] The convictions were upheld on appeal.[163] No KPMG employees were convicted, but two former employees who worked at the separate "promoter" firm were. Other cases against those involved in the shelters fared similarly, with companies ranging from law firms to accounting firms and major banks prosecuted and settling with the government. Additional employees were prosecuted and convicted; however, the appeals court reversed convictions of two of three Ernst & Young partners, finding insufficient evidence against them.[164] All of this highlights how hard it can be to hold employees responsible.

How important were the key phrases in the DOJ memo that the judge fixed on when deciding to throw out most of the KPMG prosecutions?

Another court called the DOJ policy "unquestionably obnoxious."[165] The Department of Justice made a series of revisions to the policies on the eve of congressional hearings in 2006 and again in 2008, taking seriously several "important policy considerations" raised by critics. It restricted pursuit of privilege waivers to cases raising a "legitimate" need, with procedures to limit the scope of such requests, and required written approval from the main DOJ office.[166] The DOJ also emphasized that a company following policies on paying legal fees "cannot be considered a failure to cooperate," and prosecutors "generally should not take into account" such payment of legal fees.[167]

After criticism from a "broad array of voices," in 2008 the Department of Justice made the rule on privilege waivers simple and direct: "Prosecutors should not take into account whether a corporation is advancing or reimbursing attorneys' fees or providing counsel to employees, officers or directors under investigation or indictment." The policy allows a company to waive privilege or work product, but only if the corporation "voluntarily chooses to do so," and prosecutors "are directed" not to ask a company to do so.[168]

In the years after the changes, fewer companies signing deferred prosecution or non-prosecution agreements waived privilege. The practice was never a dominant one, although it has not disappeared, either—nineteen of the forty-nine deferred prosecution and non-prosecution agreements requiring a privilege waiver were entered since December 2006, when the DOJ first changed its policies. Eight more cases since then noted that withholding documents based on privilege may be considered as a factor in deciding whether the company fully cooperated. In no other area do federal prosecutors provide such detailed guidelines for how they exercise their discretion, particularly in ways that can significantly limit it.

It is common to hear complaints, including from prominent politicians, judges, and commentators, that the government "has prosecuted only a handful of individuals in the Wall Street meltdown of 2008."[169] I have described the difficulties in doing so, and the result: deferred prosecution and non-prosecution agreements are typically not accompanied by individual prosecutions. In certain areas in particular, including in cases of bank violations, individual prosecutions are especially rare. Although an important justification for corporate criminal liability is the firm's ability to locate the wrongdoers and turn them in, the full cooperation of the company is not enough, as the KPMG case illustrates.

The lack of individual prosecutions is also understandable given the ostrich problem and other challenges that make white-collar cases so difficult to bring against corporate officers and employees. These cases require massive resources and can be hard fought. In the wake of the dot-com bust and corporate scandals such as Enron, high-profile CEOs were prosecuted and convicted, including Bernard Ebbers of WorldCom, Ken Lay and Jeffrey Skilling of Enron, and L. Dennis Kozlowski of Tyco. However, some of the highest-profile white-collar prosecutions ended in acquittals, such as the 2009 prosecutions of two Bear Stearns hedge fund managers.[170]

White-collar prosecutions of individuals have not declined, though that may not reassure those critical of how rarely such prosecutions occur. No statistics are kept on white-collar crime as a category, and there are important debates about how to define it. There are statistics kept on fraud prosecutions, however, and although fraud includes everything from minor offenses to massive financial schemes, these data on fraud prosecutions provide at least a rough sense of how white-collar prosecutions are handled. The number of federal fraud convictions rose between 1996 and 2012 from about 6,000 cases per year to more than 8,000 cases per year, though they fell as a percentage of the federal docket. Average fraud sentences nearly doubled during that time, yet judges often grant more lenient fraud sentences than the sentencing guidelines call for.[171] Some judges may be sympathetic to nonviolent white-collar offenders; a twenty-year sentence might be in effect a life sentence for older offenders, and even a short sentence may be enough to end a person's career and prevent him or her from committing corporate fraud again.

People should be concerned when a company admits to its wrongdoing in detail and yet no individuals are held criminally accountable. When corporate culture is to blame, just prosecuting the company is certainly better than not prosecuting at all, but such a corporation-focused prosecution strategy works only if prosecutors vigilantly pursue criminal punishment and reform of the company. The lack of employee prosecutions makes it all the more troubling that prosecutors are likely to offer corporations alternatives to a conviction without insisting on strict compliance. The ostrich problem, together with all of the other practical and legal difficulties in prosecuting officers and executives, makes it all the more crucial that we effectively prosecute the corporation as a whole. Prosecutions should hold individuals and corporations accountable for serious crimes. Far too often, both are let off the hook.

⟫ 5 ⟫

The Victims

The Foreman was driving a forklift early in the morning on March 23, 2005, at a refinery complex in Texas City, Texas. The facility was owned by BP, the British multinational oil and gas company. A hundred yards away was a double-wide office trailer where his wife and father-in-law, who both also worked at the refinery, were in a meeting. Suddenly he heard an explosion behind him, in the direction of the trailer. He recalled:

> I turned and looked around in time to see, hear and feel two more explosions, much larger than the first. There was a giant fireball shooting into the sky taking flaming debris up with it into the air.[1]

The Foreman saw the trailer, with his wife, father-in-law, friends, and colleagues inside, "fall to one side, then disappear, flattened by the force of the explosions." He ran toward it.

> The world had turned into smoke and flames; there was burning debris falling from the sky and black, thick, acrid smelling oil smoke everywhere. All I could see of the trailer was a flattened mass of burning wreckage. I jumped on the trailer and starting digging.

Another explosion blew him over. He got up and found a forklift, which he used to move a burning truck from the wreckage covering the trailer. Meanwhile, "it was amazing how long burning stuff kept falling from the sky." He moved "about six cars" from the top of the trailer, and "most of them exploded while being moved." He then "jumped on the trailer and through the debris." He was not leaving without finding his wife.[2]

High Octane

The Texas City Refinery is the third-largest in the United States. It refines 475,000 barrels of crude per day and occupies a massive 1,200-acre site. This makes it one of the most important energy facilities in the country, refining almost 3 percent of the gasoline used in the United States in 2005.[3] March 23, 2005, would be the worst day in its history.

Anyone who has driven by a refinery has likely seen a bewildering complex of smokestacks, storage tanks, flares, and other intricate industrial structures. Every refinery is different, but in general, that equipment is used to turn crude petroleum into useful products, including gasoline, jet fuel, and diesel fuel. A single refinery complex is made up of many smaller refineries that make those products. The Texas City Refinery had more than thirty separate units at a sprawling site and more than 2,000 workers. One such unit produced high-octane gasoline.[4]

High-octane gasoline detonates relatively slowly, resisting what carmakers call premature ignition, or engine knock. This makes it valuable for high-performance engines, where precise timing of pistons in the engine is important. High-octane gasoline is made by distilling a higher-octane liquid and blending it into normal gasoline. The factory complex used to make the higher-octane liquids is called the isom unit, short for isomerization unit, and it used a raffinate metal tower, 12.5 feet wide and 170 feet tall. The bottom of the tower had a large furnace that boiled low-grade hydrocarbons, causing high-octane liquids to rise in vapors to the top of the tower, where they were collected.

That morning, the tower was being restarted after having been shut down for several weeks. The start-up of a massive industrial distillery is a significant operation, but the topic was not discussed at the morning's safety meeting.[5] Why? The tower was not supposed to be restarted that day, but somehow supervisors never told the workers to leave the tower idle, and many others on-site had no idea it was being restarted. The workers at the isom unit were also exhausted from working twelve-hour shifts for almost a month straight.[6]

BP had not kept the tower's safety measures in shape. If there was too much pressure, the overflow was shunted through pipes to a container off in the corner, called a blowdown drum. This particular blowdown drum, though, had been built in the 1950s and had a history of catching fire, releasing flammable vapors, and corrosion problems—yet BP had never repaired it.[7] BP should have installed a flare at the top of the drum's smokestack; the flames from such flares may look ominous, but they can safely burn off excess liquids in a controlled burst. Engineers and regulators had been saying for years that BP should install a flare, but their requests, along with many others, had been ignored for cost reasons. The blowdown drum was also too small, and with the hot high-pressure fuel needing to go somewhere, it began to erupt from a 113-foot-tall smokestack connected to the drum.

The Foreman recalled that he and others working at the office trailers close to the blowdown drum—only 121 feet away—did not initially notice anything happening. After all, they "were not working on the isom unit and had nothing to do with it." The drum was supposed to be put in an out-of-the-way place, and it was unsafe for workers to be near it. He recalled that "it was not common for our trailers to be located so close to an operating unit" and that his father-in-law "was not happy with the location, but we had to follow BP's directions." The workers in the trailers had no way of knowing that the unit was being restarted that morning or that there was a problem with it.

Highly explosive fuel began shooting out of the blowdown drum smokestack into the air like a geyser. Raining back to the ground and evaporating, the hot fuel formed a growing vapor cloud that could explode at any time. A cloud of toxic fumes spread from the site, but workers in office trailers nearby had no idea of the danger. No alarms or sirens went off; they were broken.

Some refinery employees eventually noticed what was happening and started to run away—but not fast enough. A diesel truck was out of place, parked and idling about twenty-five feet from the blowdown drum. It backfired, and sparks from the truck landed in the growing pool of hot liquid fuel, igniting a massive blast.[8]

The Foreman, having survived the explosion and cleared the exploding vehicles from on top of the flattened trailer, combed through the debris and

found his father-in-law. He was dead. "At some time I stopped long enough
to say a prayer over his body." Finally, he found his wife's office:

> A bookcase had fallen over on her while she was at her desk and,
> I guess, it partially shielded her. She was in an area where there
> was fire and smoke and was burned and unconscious. I was ter-
> rified that she would die. . . . I lifted the bookcase with my
> shoulder and picked her up. . . . she was carried to a lifeflight he-
> licopter and I saw it fly away.

Fifteen people died, all employees in or near those office trailers, and more
than 170 were injured. Debris rained on nearby Texas City, and people working downtown felt the ground shake, as if there had been an earthquake.
Houses were damaged "as far away as three-quarters of a mile" from the explosion.[9] There were billions of dollars in damage.

The Foreman's wife survived. She was "unconscious for about 90 days,
and was in the burn unit ICU after that." Injuries to her lungs from the toxic
vapors are permanent. She "is frequently short of breath; her lungs create
fluids all of the time, and she coughs constantly."[10]

A Systems Failure

For years, employees asked that added safety precautions be installed at the
refinery, including fixing smokestacks and adding flares. BP bought the plant
in 1999, and to be sure, it was an old plant with long-standing problems. The
local BP manager asked for a report on the refinery in 2002, which found
serious problems, concluded the facility was "in complete decline," and expressed "serious concerns about the potential for a major site incident." Far
more spending was needed to fix up the refinery, but BP was not willing to
pay those costs.[11]

The corporate culture may have had something to do with this. BP had a
"Getting Health, Safety, and the Environment Right" program, which
sounded very conscientious. However, an audit in 2003 found that there was
a "checkbook mentality" in which budgets were not sufficient to "achieve all
commitments and goals."[12] The Occupational Safety and Health Administration (OSHA), the federal agency responsible for worker safety, had cited

the plant for the unsafe condition of a similar type of smokestack, but repairs were not made. The U.S. Chemical Safety Board did a review after the explosion and found "extensive evidence showing a catastrophe waiting to happen."

Meanwhile, BP had been rebranding itself as the environmentally friendly oil company, changing its logo to a green and yellow flower or sunburst and introducing the slogan "Beyond Petroleum." CEO John Browne made a statement the day after the explosion at city hall in Texas City, telling reporters this was a "dark day in BP's history." He had been at BP for thirty-eight years, he said, and "it is the worst tragedy that I've known." He assured families of the victims that BP would "help in whatever way we can do it to make the future feel a bit better. To make tomorrow better than yesterday."[13]

Enter the Lawyers

Lawsuits over the refinery explosion quickly multiplied. To respond to this tragic accident, BP immediately fired six operators and employees at the refinery. A BP internal investigation report blamed those employees for misusing equipment and failing to take emergency action. Those six employees sued and they eventually settled their cases.[14] Meanwhile, victims of the explosion, like The Foreman, filed thousands of lawsuits blaming the company. BP began to quietly settle those cases as well. Such settlements of civil lawsuits are typically confidential; a company like BP may prefer to avoid the publicity.

The Foreman described how he and his wife had "settled our case against BP very early; we did not want to go to court; we wanted to get it over with and try to rebuild our lives." While BP agreed to pay his wife's medical bills, "after the settlement, they didn't do it." After "many letters and phone calls" and finally filing another lawsuit, it "took over a year to get BP to move," and then they demanded a discount from the hospital and "only paid about half of what was owed on the bills."[15]

Unlike private civil settlements, criminal cases are typically public. The goal is to punish criminals so they suffer the stigma of society's most serious sanctions. Federal prosecutors decided to prosecute BP under the Section 112(r) of the Clean Air Act, nicknamed the "Bhopal Provisions," after a catastrophic 1983 release of tons of poisonous gases at the Union Carbide pesticide plant in Bhopal, India killed tens of thousands of people. The law was designed to ensure that nothing similar ever happened in the United States. It criminalized "knowing" failure to comply with detailed measures to detect and prevent releases of hazardous substances into the air.[16] BP was the first company prosecuted under the Bhopal Provisions. An official with the Environmental Protection Agency (EPA), which enforces federal environmental laws, commented that the case would send "a message that these types of crimes will be prosecuted."[17] What part would the victims of the blast have, if any, in this major criminal prosecution?

The Victims of Corporate Crime

Victims play an important role in our criminal justice system. They are no longer expected to "behave like good Victorian children—seen but not heard."[18] In the English common law system that formed the basis for our own, there were no prosecutors. Victims typically had to ask judges to arrest wrongdoers, and they had to bring cases themselves in order to punish criminals and be compensated for their injuries. Beginning in colonial times, professional police departments and prosecutors began to represent victims, rather than letting them bring cases, and prosecutors focused more on incarcerating convicts than on compensating victims.[19]

Lawmakers have increasingly created space for victims to be heard in criminal cases. Many states enacted victims' rights laws over the past few decades, giving victims or their family members the right, for example, to make a statement at sentencing, explaining how the crime affected them. Laws also aim to protect the privacy of victims, shield them from intimidation, require greater sensitivity to their concerns, and allow participation in criminal cases. Restitution has long been awarded to victims in criminal cases to compensate for their injuries, and in the past few decades, lawmakers have expanded restitution by making payments mandatory for more crimes and making it easier for victims to collect compensation.

There are debates about whether this kind of victim role is appropriate, but none of these have considered the role victims of corporate crimes should play, especially in light of the increasing use of agreements that permit a corporation to avoid standing trial. Victims' rights can mean something very different in corporate prosecutions, and it is not clear that lawmakers thought through what would happen if victims became an important part of the process in these large-scale cases. A corporate crime may be nothing like a street crime in which one person injures another. The corporation is being prosecuted for acts of its employees; it is an artificial or legal entity. Can a victim achieve closure by speaking at the sentencing of a corporation? In a corporate prosecution, there may be thousands or hundreds of thousands of victims, and identifying and contacting all of those affected by the crime may be difficult.

The prior chapters have described how prosecutors increasingly allow corporations to avoid a conviction and reduce fines in exchange for adopting structural reforms, but it is often doubtful whether meaningful changes are required. The victims could theoretically play an important role in insisting on stronger accountability, and if prosecutors accept insufficient fines, victims could insist on compensation for their injuries. I wondered how victims' rights would work in complex financial crimes, or whether large numbers of victims could provide meaningful input. As I will describe, victims are indeed an increasingly important part of corporate prosecutions, and payments to such victims are in the hundreds of millions of dollars each year. Victims can speak to the public interest in holding a company accountable, but they are not always heard.

Along with the right to participate, federal laws provide for victim compensation, which is known as restitution. Victims can receive monetary awards separate from any criminal fine in order to try to make them whole for their injuries. Restitution is now mandatory in many federal prosecutions, mostly due to two laws: the Victim and Witness Protection Act of 1982, which states that a judge "may order" restitution to victims when sentencing a defendant for certain federal crimes, and the Mandatory Victims Restitution Act of 1996, which states that the judge "shall order" restitution to victims of certain federal crimes, including crimes of violence, fraud, and property crimes.[20] Under the sentencing guidelines, restitution is always an option for organizations so long as there is an "identifiable victim."[21] The victims do not have to request restitution—prosecutors will work to identify the victims and the judge will ensure they are paid—and it is ordered regardless of the defendant's ability to pay at the time of sentencing.

A restitution payment is considered part of the criminal punishment, and it can be made a condition of probation. The judge may set a schedule for payments—an installment plan—if the defendant cannot afford to pay it all at once.[22] There is also a process for distributing restitution, with private victims paid first, before the government, and direct victims getting priority over insurance companies and other third parties.[23] Victims cannot recover twice: any money received from civil lawsuits or insurance is deducted from restitution.[24]

Forfeiture provides a second way to compensate victims in federal criminal cases. Criminals' cars, artwork, jewelry, and other assets can be forfeited and auctioned off. This can occur in a criminal case or in a separate civil or administrative proceeding against the property itself. Giving forfeited assets and money to victims is called remission. Unlike restitution, this does not cover lost income, lost profits, or bodily injury, and victims just receive the fair market value of property lost after filing a petition requesting compensation.[25] The Asset Forfeiture and Money Laundering Section at the Department of Justice handles complex forfeitures, and it returned more than $400 million to victims in 2008 alone.[26] In addition, forfeited money can be added to a restitution fund, a process called restoration. Forfeited assets can also be given to law enforcement (the vast bulk go to state and local law enforcement).[27]

JPMorgan paid the largest forfeiture in any corporate prosecution agreement—the sum of $1.7 billion—in early 2014 for the failure to report "suspicious activity" concerning Bernard Madoff's use of accounts at the bank as part of his Ponzi scheme. Had JPMorgan paid a criminal fine, the money would have gone to the U.S. Treasury. Instead, prosecutors pursued the $1.7 billion forfeiture for property "traceable to the Ponzi scheme" so that the money would go to a fund set up to compensate the victims of the scheme.[28]

Corporate crime can turn victim participation and restitution into complex litigation all its own. Restitution does not have to be awarded if the "number of identifiable victims is so large as to make restitution impracticable," or if calculating restitution involves resolving "complex issues of fact" and would unduly delay sentencing.[29] However, there are ways for a judge to handle cases with large numbers of victims and complex facts, including by appointing a trustee to help administer the compensation process.[30]

We normally think of criminal fines as a form of punishment and not as a way to compensate victims, as they can file civil suits to claim damages for their injuries. As I collected data on corporate prosecutions, I did not expect to see compensation for victims to be such a prominent part of the cases. Yet in some of the largest corporate prosecutions, prosecutors create enormous funds to compensate victims, sometimes in cooperation with civil lawyers and regulators. The restitution amounts can dwarf the fines paid.

Figures 5.1 and 5.2 include total fines, restitution, and forfeiture from 1994 until 2012. The U.S. Sentencing Commission's data are depicted in black, and the data I collected manually from federal docket sheets are in lighter gray. Corporate fines are in the hundreds of millions (if not billions) of dollars each year and increasing. Restitution and forfeiture awards are more modest but can also be large, often totaling in the low hundreds of millions each year, and there have been several blockbuster awards.

There are striking differences between data collected from court dockets and the Sentencing Commission's data. The commission is missing what I believe to be the largest restitution award to date in a criminal case, $606

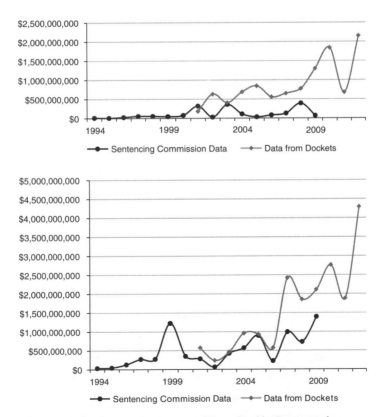

Figures 5.1–5.2 Total Restitution and Fines Paid by Prosecuted Corporations, 1994–2012

million paid by Republic Securities, a subsidiary of the multinational bank HSBC, in 2002.[31] The commission does not collect data about deferred prosecution agreements, which add still more massive fines, restitution payments, and forfeitures, the last of which may occur in separate civil proceedings that would not be reported to the commission or necessarily reflected on criminal dockets. The average restitution paid by convicted companies was just under $3 million, while the average restitution and forfeiture in deferred prosecution agreements was $94 million.[32] For deferred prosecution and non-prosecution agreements from 2001 to 2012, there was over $7.5 billion in restitution, disgorgement, and forfeiture.

Just as the lion's share of fines comes from a small number of corporate prosecutions, the vast majority of restitution money comes from a few blockbuster cases. A minority of the deferred prosecution agreements involved awards to victims (31 percent, or 80 of 255, paid restitution or forfeiture), but some involved enormous awards, such as the $1.7 billion forfeiture by JPMorgan, $1.256 billion in forfeiture by HSBC, $310 million in restitution paid by ING Bank, N.V., and $370 million in restitution paid by Science Applications International Corp. A similar number of convicted corporations pay restitution, but most pay none at all. For example, in 2008, when the Sentencing Commission reported that companies paid $390 million in restitution, that amount came from fewer than one-third of the corporations involved. The rest paid none. The big numbers for 2008 came from just a handful of cases—a mail fraud case against Health Visions Corp. with an almost $100 million restitution award, and three others with awards of $78.4 million each.

Even large restitution awards may disguise how hard it is to recover money for victims. The Sentencing Commission reported the three companies above as being sentenced to $78.4 million in restitution in 2008. In that case, three people jointly controlled a fake hedge fund that defrauded investors of almost $200 million.[33] Nothing close to that amount was ever recovered. Under the statute, mandatory restitution must be ordered regardless of the defendants' ability to actually pay, so huge restitution awards imposed by the judge may not reflect what the victims actually recover. The victims claimed over $130 million in losses. The receiver sold off mansions, country club memberships, jewelry, and cars but recovered only about $6.6 million in assets and distributed $2.8 million to victims, all while spending over $3 million in legal and administrative costs, even more than the typical 30 percent consumed by costs in such cases.[34] Obviously, perpetrators may spend the money before being caught, leaving little for victims to recover.

In the case of Bear Stearns, the bank whose collapse helped trigger the global economic crisis in 2007, the Securities and Exchange Commission entered a settlement with managers of two hedge funds responsible for $1.6 billion in losses. JPMorgan bought out Bear Stearns, and while the managers were acquitted at their criminal trial, the SEC's civil suit went forward. The settlement involved just over $1 million, an amount the judge called "chump change" in comparison to $1.6 billion in losses to investors. He asked the parties to reconsider, but eventually concluded he had to approve the settlement, saying it was "little wonder that many believe that the SEC is simply not up to the task of enforcing the securities laws."[35] While the defendants lacked assets to cover much of the losses, perhaps the judge should be applauded for asking whether a settlement was fair and in the public interest.

Under Seal

In the BP case, the judge did not initially tell victims that plea negotiations were under way. Most had already settled cases with BP and received compensation, but they wanted to participate in the criminal case to ensure that BP was held accountable. Under the 2004 Crime Victims' Rights Act, victims of crimes have a right to be given notice and to participate in criminal cases even if not entitled to restitution.[36] Giving notice to a large group of victims may be complicated and expensive, and judges can decide what is reasonable and order defendants to defray the cost of notifying victims.[37] The Crime Victims' Rights Act defines a "crime victim" as a person "directly and proximately harmed as a result of the commission of a Federal offense."[38] Sometimes no victims can be readily identified, and judges also look at what the crime is and ask whether the alleged victims were really harmed by the crime or not.[39]

Very few corporate criminals are required to give notice to victims in federal courts.[40] In the Texas City refinery case, the criminal case was filed under seal so that it would not be public. Two days later, the plea agreement was signed, and prosecutors soon publicly announced it as a done deal—without any involvement by the victims.

The victims were not hard to find. They and their families had filed more than 4,000 civil suits against BP. To be sure, some who filed lawsuits were not injured in the blast or were not family members of those killed, but instead had suffered less direct property damage.[41] Still, the most directly injured victims could easily be reached. Prosecutors asked for the proceedings to be filed under seal, yet the statute gave the victims a right to be involved and informed, and the Department of Justice's own guidelines said that federal prosecutors "should be available to consult with victims about major case decisions" such as plea negotiations.[42] Still, these prosecutors apparently did not keep the victims informed of what was happening.[43]

Only after the plea was publicly announced did prosecutors finally send out notices telling victims they could participate. The victims were not happy to have been told about an already done deal. Still, the judge sided with the prosecutors, citing the large number of victims and the "extensive media coverage" that might result from victim participation and "prejudice" BP by hurting its reputation.[44] The judge concluded that victims could submit letters and participate in a sentencing hearing to lodge their objections, after the fact, to the plea agreement. The court added that victims could have reached out to prosecutors during the investigation.

At this hearing, victims' lawyers presented their objections to the plea agreement and asked why they had been left out of the process. Later, 134 victims provided victim impact statements to the judge, describing how they had been injured by the Texas City Refinery blast. The Foreman's statement was one of those. In addition to describing his family's ordeal and losses, he noted he was "unspeakably angry" that "the doctors, and hospitals and nurses who slaved to save lives should get stiffed on their bills by BP. And it tells us that BP cannot be trusted to keep their word about what they will do." He added that if BP was emphasizing to the judge "all they have done to pay the damages," the judge should be concerned that BP was not really assuming responsibility for what happened.[45]

Environmental Prosecutions

Environmental prosecutions of corporations stand out for their numbers. A quarter of the corporate convictions from 2001 to 2012 that I studied were environmental prosecutions (25 percent, or 502 of 2,016). Environmental violations can involve air or water pollution, rules for handling hazardous wastes, and protections for fish and wildlife. Each area has detailed regulations, and those rules can be accompanied by criminal penalties. For example, it is a crime to negligently discharge pollutants by failing to exercise ordinary reasonable care to prevent the pollution, and there are more serious penalties for "knowing" violations made with some awareness.[46]

Environmental laws are highly technical, and the Department of Justice has a specialized Environment and Natural Resources Division that handles such cases in cooperation with the EPA.[47] Very few deferred prosecution agreements are environmental cases (only 6 of 255 agreements), because this division's prosecutors have long believed that an environmental case should either be handled as a civil matter by the EPA or result in a criminal conviction.[48] That said, a criminal case will usually be settled in a plea bargain, and how serious a punishment that criminal conviction imposes will depend on the deal the company reaches.

What were the terms of BP's plea agreement, and was it in fact a done deal? The agreement required BP to admit guilt, pay a $50 million fine, and serve three years of probation. As I discuss in the next chapter, corporate probation means that a company may have to submit reports to the probation office, and any new criminal offense may violate probation. The victims felt that this was a sweetheart deal, and they argued that they should have been allowed to provide input and that the agreement should be changed. However, a federal judge, despite considerable power, has little leeway to change a plea bargain the sides reach in a criminal case. A judge may not rewrite a plea agreement, though in unusual cases a judge may reject one outright.[49] Judges have rejected agreements that offer a defendant "undue leniency" or that go against the public interest.[50] The victims may offer input on that question; this is one reason they have a right to participate.

On October 25, 2007, BP formally pleaded guilty in court. At the hearing, victims and their lawyers were finally permitted to speak, and they asked the judge to reject the plea agreement. The victims were not looking for money; they did not need restitution, as most had settled civil cases. Instead, they wanted BP to be effectively deterred from endangering more lives. They pointed out that this agreement did not impose a corporate monitor to supervise a compliance program to make sure that more workers were not harmed in the future. In addition, they argued the fine was far too low, and called the entire agreement "shockingly lenient."[51] Later that month, the judge rejected the victims' objections and approved the plea agreement without any written explanation. The victims filed an emergency appeal.

The Pinto Again?

BP pleaded guilty to violating detailed environmental statutes, but could the company have been prosecuted for something more serious, such as homicide? According to one of the victim's lawyers, "The fact is, they are a serial killer."[52]

Federal courts stated in the early twentieth century that a "corporation can be guilty of causing death by its wrongful act."[53] Yet rulings by judges since then have been mixed. In the 1970s, several state laws allowed corporate criminal liability for homicide, and there were a series of noteworthy criminal trials.[54] But most states had laws like New York's, which defined manslaughter as "the killing of one human being by . . . another."[55]

The best-known corporate homicide trial is that involving the Ford Pinto. In 1977, media reports described how the Ford Pinto might be prone to fires even in fairly mild rear-end collisions because of the placement of its gas tank.[56] Documents suggested that Ford executives, desperate to sell a small, fuel-efficient car during the oil crisis, knew of the danger but decided that changes would not be cost effective. A federal investigation by the National Highway Traffic Safety Administration ensued, as did civil suits by crash victims, with some resulting in millions of dollars in damages.[57] Ford eventually ordered a recall telling owners that the government had found an "unreasonable risk of substantial fuel leakage" in a collision, and it asked dealers to add a new shield to the gas tank. But in 1978, before the recall letters were sent out, three teenage women died in Indiana when their Pinto exploded after a rear collision.[58]

The local prosecutor decided to prosecute Ford—the first attempt to hold a company criminally accountable for an unsafe product. State courts allowed the case to go forward, finding that Ford had had "sufficient notice" that it could be prosecuted for "reckless homicide."[59] The trial lasted about a month, with detailed exhibits showing how the Pinto had been designed and dozens of witnesses.

After almost becoming deadlocked, the jury ultimately acquitted Ford. Perhaps the jurors decided the particular car was driving so fast that even a safer car might have had a gas tank leak in a crash.[60] The judge commented, "I won't quarrel with the verdict. It was the right one."[61] Back at Ford's headquarters, the board of directors was assembled for Henry Ford II's retirement, and they erupted into applause when they heard that the company had been found not guilty.[62]

Today, judges are reluctant to hold corporations liable for manslaughter or reckless homicide.[63] Prosecutors may have been right to charge BP under environmental laws and with homicide—but that does not mean that they reached the right plea deal with the company.[64]

Victim Statements

One of the main rights of a victim under the federal law is simply to be heard. Those affected by explosions or environmental disasters may suffer physical harm, but what about financial crimes? Recall the WorldCom case, in which former CEO Bernard Ebbers was convicted of fraud. One victim who made a statement at sentencing was a former shareholder and employee of World-Com. He described how he represented "the working professional," one who suffered "indescribable trauma" as a result of the crimes. He had to deal with "abuse and skepticism" from clients who no longer trusted him after hearing about misconduct at the top of WorldCom. Laid off as WorldCom collapsed, he lost his savings, medical benefits, and retirement benefits, and wanted to have the record reflect the experiences of people like him, who were "trying to piece back the broken pieces of our lives in the wake of this disaster."[65] Such written statements are sent to the probation office and may contribute to the pre-sentence report prepared for the judge.

Victims can also speak in person at the sentencing hearing, though it may be difficult to know whether this has any influence on the resulting sentence. The victim statements in the WorldCom case may have helped to counter efforts by Ebbers's lawyers to seek leniency, including more than 150 letters from friends and family mentioning his charitable giving, age, and declining health. The judge said it was not possible to "overstate the seriousness of the fraud," and sentenced him to fifteen years in prison.[66]

Who would be heard in the BP case? In the emergency appeal by the victims to the Fifth Circuit Court of Appeals, the appellate judges quickly ruled that keeping the plea deal secret violated the Crime Victims' Rights Act, as there were fewer than 200 victims and they could be easily reached. However, the appellate judges said they were sure that, going forward, the "conscientious" district judge would now take the time to "fully consider the victims' objections and concerns."[67]

The judge did allow the victims to speak at a hearing in October 2008—this time *before* the plea agreement was finalized.[68] At the hearing, prosecutors walked a fine line between expressing sympathy for the victims and defending their work. While "nothing can bring back the 15 dead," they said, the plea agreement was effective. Prosecutors admitted that in 2007 they had told BP there was a "significant problem," as they were not satisfied that the company was complying with OSHA's requests, but that the disagreement eventually had been resolved. Prosecutors emphasized how two agencies—OSHA and Texas environmental regulators—would make sure the refinery was fixed. And probation could be extended if BP failed to comply.[69] Prosecutors did not try to defend the size of the fine, but called it "adequate."[70]

The victims said regulators were not doing enough to restore safety at BP. They implied that OSHA was giving BP a "sweetheart deal, and they suggested OSHA lacked adequate resources to monitor BP."[71] Major problems had still not been fixed. Equipment had still not been tested for mechanical integrity. OSHA did not ensure that workers had basic safety information for devices throughout the refinery, and it had postponed documenting certain improvements until 2012. OSHA had inspected the refinery in the years before the explosion in response to prior worker deaths but had not noticed the "likelihood for a catastrophic incident."[72] Meanwhile, more than three years had already passed since the explosion, and BP was saying improvements would take years more.

While victims called for an independent monitor to oversee compliance, BP's lawyer countered by saying "good progress" had been made in upgrading equipment.[73] The judge found the reasoning of BP and the prosecutors persuasive. OSHA regulators were using this as a "poster child" case to improve their methods.[74] The judge did not have the power to "rewrite the plea," and could only "find it so deficient as to reject it."[75] The victims suggested the judge could accept the plea but impose special conditions of probation, such as a monitor or a special master to help ensure compliance. The judge declined to do so.

The judge once again approved the same plea agreement, with its $50 million fine and three years of probation. There would be no special conditions of probation or oversight, as the victims had requested. To be sure, BP would have to comply with its settlement with OSHA to remedy conditions at the refinery and with an agreement with the Texas Commission on Environmental Quality.[76] By late 2007, BP had paid $1.6 billion in compensation to victims and $21.4 million to OSHA.[77] It had also spent $1 billion in making safety improvements to the refinery and would spend billions more.[78]

The $50 million fine could have been much larger. The criminal law that BP was convicted under had a maximum fine of just $500,000, but as the next chapter discusses, under a federal law called the Alternative Fines Act, a company can be ordered to pay up to twice the "gross gain or loss" from the offense.[79] How is that calculated? Perhaps it was based on the profits at the refinery in the months or years prior to the explosion—or the loss caused to lives and property. BP could certainly afford to pay a lot more. At the time, it was ranked second on the Global Fortune 500, with a market capitalization of $225 billion and annual profits over $20 billion.[80]

The victims pointed out that BP had obtained a local property tax reduction of $12 million per year, "based on the deteriorated (and unsafe) condition of the plant," and that "the proposed fine is less than the plant property taxes for two years."[81] This was not the largest fine in an environmental disaster; Exxon had paid far more in criminal fines, $125 million, after the massive Valdez oil spill in Alaska, and in that incident no people had been killed. Interestingly, in the Valdez case the judge had rejected an initial plea agreement with a fine of $100 million, explaining that the spill was "off the chart" in its seriousness, and saying, "I'm afraid these fines send the wrong message and suggest that spills are a cost of business that can be absorbed."[82] The judge in the Texas City Refinery case did no such thing.[83]

A Recidivist

A month before the final hearing about the BP plea agreement, another worker was killed at the Texas City Refinery. BP had argued it had a history of two prior violations; the victims noted "at least" thirty. They pointed out that the same key employees were still in their jobs, or had since been promoted or retired with generous benefits.[84] In his victim impact statement, The Foreman argued that "this criminal agreement would let them off with paying just a few pennies on the dollar of the billions of dollars they made, and let them keep breaking promises. This isn't justice, and it isn't punishment, and it isn't fair."[85]

The victims also pointed out that "prior history" is supposed to enhance the punishment of a corporation, but that as a recidivist, BP provided "spills, fines, probation and the promise to do better."[86] After a March 2006 oil spill from the Trans-Alaska Pipeline caused a shutdown of the largest oil field in the United States,[87] BP pleaded guilty to Clean Water Act violations, paid a $12 million fine plus $8 million in community service to fund environmental research, and was placed on three years of probation. The guilty plea in this case was announced in October 2007, around the same time that BP pleaded guilty in the Texas Refinery prosecution.[88] There was a third October 2007 case: BP North America entered into a deferred prosecution agreement for commodities and wire fraud regarding the market for Texas propane, resulting in $100 million in criminal fines and $200 million in civil fines and restitution.[89]

The victims argued "BP is back to its old ways."[90] Even after the explosion, "nothing meaningful is being done to actually bring the plant into full compliance with Federal law." They concluded that "meaningful change will occur only if forced by strict oversight through the court system." Consumer rights advocates also expressed outrage about the settlement: "These accommodating prosecutors march into court and announce that all this human wreckage is not worth even a single day of BP's precious profits." The head of Public Citizen said, "A democracy cannot tolerate two standards of justice—one for street criminals and another for corporate criminals."[91]

After the victims' protests were waved away and the plea agreement was approved, BP did not properly fix the refinery. OSHA would later conclude that after the explosion, BP "allowed hundreds of potential hazards to continue unabated."[92] It was exactly what the victims had said would happen. In 2009, OSHA issued hundreds of notifications of failure to abate and hundreds more notices of "willful violations" for failures to follow industry safety controls, with penalties totaling over $87 million.[93] Employees continued to die at the refinery. On July 22, 2006, a contractor was crushed between a "scissor lift and a pipe rack." On June 5, 2007, a contractor was electrocuted "on a light circuit." On January 14, 2008, an employee was killed when the top of a pressure vessel blew off. On October 9, 2008, a contractor was hit by a front-end loader and died from his injuries.

In December 2010, the EPA entered into a civil consent decree with BP, which included a $15 million penalty and a requirement of regular reports for three years regarding leaks and fires at the refinery, two of which took place just months after the explosion.[94] While one might think a serious criminal matter would require more oversight from a judge than a civil case, the judge often plays a greater role in a civil case. The judge can decide whether or not to approve a civil consent decree based on whether it is "fair, reasonable, and consistent" with the purposes of the laws or regulations.[95] A judge will still defer to the agency's decision that a settlement is appropriate, but the judge can examine its terms, hold hearings, and consider input from the public. Once the consent decree is finalized, the judge's role does not end, as the judge supervises compliance with the decree and resolves any disputes that arise. I believe that this broader judicial role is justified in criminal corporate settlements as well.

When settling the case, the EPA cited BP's ongoing program of corrective actions at the refinery, "currently estimated to cost almost $2 billion."[96] The agency noted $500 million in changes made in 2010 as a result of violations of the 2005 agreement with OSHA.[97] And it claimed that a "penalty of this magnitude provides a strong deterrent to BP Products and the regulated community against future non-compliance."[98] No mention was made that the $15 million fine was less than the $50 million paid after the refinery explosion, and the earlier settlement had apparently not been a "strong deterrent."

Once again, there was no new prosecution. The victims returned again, claiming to have been right all along and that BP should be prosecuted in earnest now that it had violated the terms of its probation. Yet there was no effort to resurrect the criminal charges or find BP in violation of its probation. In fact, the Department of Justice considered taking stronger action, telling BP in early 2010 that "if it failed to resolve the allegations of non-compliance to OSHA's satisfaction, the government might seek revocation and/or extension of probation." Yet the DOJ ultimately decided not to do more, stating it "is not seeking a revocation or extension of probation at this time." Instead it gave BP even more time to try to fix the refinery.[99] A former EPA investigator later complained to the press that the EPA and the DOJ simply gave in to pressure from BP. He recalled: "I was smelling blood in the water and they wanted to drain the pool."[100] Victims may now have a stronger right to be heard in federal court, but their stories may not change the minds of the prosecutors who decide how to handle a criminal case.

Who Is a Victim?

Victims are supposed to have a voice, but defining who is a victim is not always as simple as in the BP case. Recall that the 2004 Crime Victims' Rights Act obliges prosecutors to involve victims in the process, give them notice, and allow their views to be heard in the courtroom. The victims entitled to these rights must be people "directly and proximately" harmed as a result of the crime.[101] Some corporate crimes do not have clearly identifiable individual victims (foreign bribery); others harm the U.S. Treasury (tax fraud) or the environment (pollution), or they assist criminals without harming identifiable victims (money laundering).

Even for crimes with direct victims, there may be hard questions as to whether a particular person was harmed. In another environmental prosecution of a refinery in Texas, CITGO was convicted in 2007 for toxic emissions. At sentencing, prosecutors argued that more than 300 members of the nearby community had been exposed to emissions of benzene, a toxic substance, and should be compensated as victims. CITGO moved to have these people excluded as "purported" victims. Initially the judge ruled that they lacked victim status, finding no proof that refinery emissions had caused their health problems. Many were elderly, smoked cigarettes, or had other medical conditions, so their injuries might have been caused by other factors.[102] A year later, the community members tried to raise new arguments, but the judge said it was too late. The appeals court reversed and directed the judge to look into the matter further, saying that there is no "time limit" under the Crime Victims' Rights Act.[103]

The judge, moved by the testimony of community members who said "they suffered symptoms such as burning eyes, bad taste in the mouth, nose burning, sore throat, skin rashes, shortness of breath, vomiting, dizziness, nausea, fatigue, and headaches," concluded they should be allowed to give victim impact statements at sentencing and seek restitution, including medical monitoring of their health.[104] Although CITGO was convicted in 2007, almost seven years later, the judge finally finished reviewing over 800 victim impact statements. The government had asked for $25 million in restitution, but the judge ruled that calculating restitution would be too complex, and no restitution at all would be provided to the victims.[105] The victims are appealing.

Civil Suits

Paying restitution to victims is particularly important where they are unable to hire lawyers and be compensated in civil suits. In many corporate crime cases, though, victims do file separate civil suits, and the company knows that settling with prosecutors can mean admitting wrongdoing and giving ammunition to the victims.[106] Lawyers call facing multiple types of lawsuits "parallel litigation," and it can include criminal prosecutions, civil suits, and regulatory suits by both state and federal officials. It is a new thing for prosecutors to compensate large groups of victims, and it is also fairly new for regulators to act like a massive collection agency.[107] The Sarbanes-Oxley Act, passed in response to the Enron-era scandals, gave the Securities and Exchange Commission the power to collect money for victims of securities fraud, and the SEC now supervises multimillion-dollar funds to compensate shareholders.[108]

There is no official information about how many companies face parallel civil litigation while being prosecuted. I collected data on the 255 companies that received deferred prosecution or non-prosecution agreements from 2001 to 2012 and whether they faced civil suits, finding such suits against 36 percent, or 93 of the 255 companies. While not all civil settlements may be public, I identified $6.1 billion in civil settlements in those cases, far more than the $4 billion in criminal fines imposed by federal prosecutors. Although regulatory enforcement and civil suits may provide more compensation for victims than restitution efforts by prosecutors, the latter can fill an important gap when civil or regulatory remedies are inadequate.

Some of the biggest civil suits filed against companies facing prosecution were class action suits. At least 35 of the 255 deferred prosecution and non-prosecution agreements studied had parallel class actions. A single person can file a case representing the entire class of injured people, a group that can number in the thousands or even in the millions. One main goal of class action lawsuits is efficiency; if a group was injured in the same way, there is no sense in forcing each to hire lawyers and bring separate cases. If 1 million stockholders each lost $15 because of securities fraud, none would bother to pursue a case individually. But if they can sue collectively in one class action, the company may have to pay for the entire $15 million in injuries—and a $15 million case is one that lawyers will clamor to bring.

There are detailed rules for how the judge decides whether to approve a class action. For example, the lawyers and injured parties leading the case must be fair representatives for the class and must share common interests and claims. In the Computer Associates case, victims brought a securities fraud class action alongside the criminal prosecution. The prosecution resulted in a $225 million restitution fund for anyone who purchased Computer Associates stock (or stock options) from early 1998 through early 2002. The prosecutors asked that a professional administrator develop a road map for how the funds would be distributed, and the choice could not have been more famous: Kenneth Feinberg, known for his work administering complex class action funds and government compensation funds, including the September 11, 2001, victims' fund.[109] The prosecutor asked for input from shareholders on distributing the funds. None responded.[110] Feinberg then came up with a plan to distribute the funds, which the judge approved.[111] An expert was consulted to calculate how much Computer Associates' stock had been inflated due to the securities fraud. Victims had to file a proof of claim, showing they really did purchase stock during the right time period, and almost 100,000 victims responded. Another firm was hired to distribute the money, and accountants were brought in when human error resulted in some victims getting incorrect payments.[112] Outside of this process, other victims filed class actions, which settled for millions of dollars. Victims could not get double payments, of course, so they had to choose compensation from class actions or from prosecutors.[113]

If the company is itself a victim of bad management, companies can be sued by shareholders in a manner designed to compensate the company itself, rather than the victims. At least twenty of the companies that received deferred prosecution agreements faced derivative lawsuits. These are called derivative suits because shareholders are suing in the name of the company to force the management personnel who harmed the company to compensate it. For example, Bristol-Myers Squibb entered into a deferred prosecution agreement and a consent decree with the SEC, paying a $100 million civil penalty and $50 million to compensate shareholders. Shareholders also filed eight derivative actions, all consolidated in the Southern District of New York, and ultimately settled. Plaintiffs brought another set of derivative lawsuits against PriceWaterhouseCoopers, the firm that had audited BMS's books.[114] Some of those lawsuits settled, while others were dismissed.[115] The money recovered in such a derivative lawsuit may benefit the company, or the shareholders indirectly, and the plaintiff's attorneys may recover fees.

There are not clear rules on how prosecutors or judges should handle parallel and competing lawsuits. One way to handle logistical problems is to consolidate the lawsuits before the same judge. For example, when Eli Lilly was prosecuted regarding the drug Zyprexa, victims had already reached a $1 billion settlement.[116] Prosecutors then sought an additional $1 billion in restitution.[117] A judge in the Eastern District of New York was asked to coordinate all of the cases against Eli Lilly, to ensure that all victims were compensated but that none were paid twice. Other courts have decided it was too difficult to compensate victims in a particular case. Newspaper publishers Newsday and Hoy agreed to pay $15 million in forfeiture to the United States, but the judge rejected a recommendation that they should also provide $5,966,000 in restitution to 30,724 of their commercial advertisers in the amount of about $25 each.[118] The judge concluded that such restitution, even if normally mandatory, would prolong and burden the sentencing process.[119] The victims had been given a chance to claim forfeited funds, and a year later, not one had done so. The $15 million in forfeited money would go directly to law enforcement.[120] (In contrast to forfeiture, unclaimed restitution goes not to law enforcement but to the U.S. Treasury.)[121] When people lose large amounts of money in a Ponzi scheme, they may quickly file lawsuits. But when a card arrives in the mail saying that filling out a form will mean a $25 refund from a lawsuit, most people do not bother.

In civil class actions, lawyers represent the victims, and the lawyers are required under federal rules to send out notices to them. A judge must supervise the process, and must approve any settlement after a second round of notice to victims. Those protections do not exist in criminal cases. Yet corporate prosecutions can involve vast restitution funds that dwarf the fines.

The judge may appoint a special master to help, or she can "fashion a reasonable procedure" if there are multiple victims who might be hard to locate or reach, but there are no clear rules for how to do so.[122] The system should ensure adequate notice to victims, adequate representation of victim interests, and coordination with parallel civil cases. Law professors David Jaros and Adam Zimmerman argue that criminal restitution funds are like a "criminal class action" and deserve some of the same protections.[123] There should be clear procedures for "complex restitution" just as there are for class actions in civil cases.

Victims and Deferred Prosecutions

A judge must approve a plea agreement, and federal law requires that victims play some role—but can that role include intervening to object to deferred prosecution agreements? This agreement is filed in court, but a judge has limited supervision. A non-prosecution agreement is never filed in court at all, so there is no opportunity for victims to be involved. Victims have not objected that such agreements harm their rights, but perhaps they should.

In a creative move, the state-owned electric utility company in Costa Rica, the Instituto Costarricense de Electricidad (ICE), objected to a deferred prosecution agreement, claiming it was the victim of bribery by Alcatel-Lucent. Alcatel-Lucent had entered a deferred prosecution agreement, and three of its subsidiaries pleaded guilty to Foreign Corrupt Practices Act violations in Costa Rica. Prosecutors alleged that officers and directors of ICE accepted bribes in exchange for telecommunications contracts with Alcatel-Lucent, but ICE asked to be recognized as a victim and sought restitution. The prosecutors kept ICE informed of developments in the case.

At hearings in 2011, ICE argued that "this case involves worldwide corruption," but the Department of Justice refused to return the money to Costa Rica.[124] They said only a handful of employees at ICE were involved in bribery, and that they were "brought to justice."[125] Major phone line purchases were never delivered due to the bribery scandal, but there was already a settlement with the government of Costa Rica for $10 million.[126] The prosecutors emphasized: "We're talking about a $147 million resolution. It is one of the largest resolutions in the history of the Foreign Corrupt Practices Act."[127]

The judge asked who the victim was in the case.[128] Was it the electric utility or the people of Costa Rica? The judge said evidence indicated that even higher-ups at ICE were involved in the bribery—"basically it was 'Bribery Is Us.'"[129] The judge concluded there was no need to figure out who was harmed by the bribery. On appeal, the Eleventh Circuit agreed and ruled that participants in a crime cannot usually be entitled to restitution or status as victims.[130]

In other cases, foreign victims have been compensated. A prosecutor agreed not to prosecute Chevron for violations related to the U.N. Oil for Food program, which operated while Saddam Hussein controlled Iraq, but the company agreed to pay $20 million to "the Development Fund of Iraq as restitution for the people of Iraq."[131]

Corporate Community Service

A few corporations perform community service, but rather than sending employees to clean up graffiti or pick up litter, they send money. Corporations donate to environmental cleanup or awareness groups; payments to the National Fish and Wildlife Fund are common in environmental cases. The average community service payment was $160,500, but I found that only 12 percent of prosecuted companies paid community service (262 of 2,262 companies). The largest community service awards were paid by BP (a record $2.75 billion payment, described below), Alpha Natural Resources ($48 million), AIG ($25 million), BP again ($25 million), Blue Cross Blue Shield of Rhode Island ($20 million), and General Reinsurance Corp. ($19.5 million). More creatively, when the U.S. Attorney's Office of the Western District of Virginia prosecuted the ITT Corporation for exporting unlicensed and secret night vision technology, causing harm to the military's technological edge, the agreement allowed some of the fine to be spent on research for improving U.S. night vision technology.

Sometimes the community gets an apology. Style Craft Furniture, pleading guilty to importation of baby cribs with an endangered type of Indonesian wood protected by international treaty, agreed to run advertisements in Mandarin in China and in English in the United States describing "a commitment to ensure that our entire wood supply chain is legal" and urging "other manufacturers to do likewise, both for their own business interests, and for the protection of the forest resources for our children."[132]

Corporations can also perform community service the traditional way. In another export-violation case, Metric Equipment Sales, Inc. was ordered to do 250 hours of community service through its employees. The Roger Williams Medical Center in Rhode Island was asked to contribute to health care for the poor.[133] Sometimes prosecutors may not be the best judges of what types of service are useful to the community, and the DOJ responded to criticism with a new policy stating there would be no more "extraordinary restitution" in corporate prosecution agreements.[134] That did not mean community service could not still be required as part of a sentence, but it has to be closely related to remedying the harm experienced by victims.

The Public Interest

Whether a settlement serves the public interest can decide whether it is approved. Merck, a major Big Pharma company, faced a mass of litigation surrounding its marketing of the painkiller Vioxx, which was linked to heart attacks and withdrawn from the market in 2004. The judge delayed the settlement to examine objections by victims, though Merck had already created a $4.85 billion settlement fund to compensate victims and spent $1.9 billion in legal costs.[135] Finally, in April 2012, the judge approved the settlement, stating, "I'm certainly going to accept this agreement because I think it's in the public interest."[136]

In contrast, another judge expressed concerns about a plea agreement in a case about defrauding Medicare, one where Orthofix International N.V. entered a deferred prosecution agreement and a subsidiary pleaded guilty. This judge commented: "It seems in this case the court's hands ought not be tied. . . . I have extreme unease of treating corporate criminal conduct like a civil case."[137] Six months later, the judge rejected a proposed guilty plea, which carried a fine of almost $8 million and five years of probation, saying the agreement did not "ensure the public interest."[138]

We should rethink the way that victims are involved in corporate prosecutions, as they may speak for the public interest and sometimes have an impact even if a judge does not have to formally consider their views. There is little need for restitution when victims can get compensated through private suits, but there is no current substitute for their role in influencing the terms of the plea bargain. Law professors Richard A. Bierschbach and Stephanos Bibas have argued that public participation could also play a far greater role in improving the sentencing process.[139] This may be particularly true in corporate prosecutions. As noted, in a civil decree, a judge must consider the public interest, public input, and the fairness of the settlement. Once the agreement is reached, a judge supervises its implementation. Judges should exercise similar oversight over deferred prosecution agreements by carefully considering the public interest. In Chapter 10, I discuss possibilities for greater judicial oversight of plea agreements and deferred prosecution agreements. Formal rules for ensuring participation of the victims should be put into place to ensure that corporate settlements are fair. And the public or public interest groups should be given a chance to contribute their views as well.

Macondo

Macondo is the name of the fictional town in Colombia where Gabriel García Márquez set his classic book *One Hundred Years of Solitude*. The town begins as a spot on a riverbank, but when a banana plantation brings great wealth, a larger city springs to life. After seven generations—apologies for spoiling this part of the ending—a massive hurricane destroys the town, returning it to dust.

Those charged with naming a new oil well, one located 5,000 feet under the sea off the coast of Louisiana in the Gulf of Mexico, were probably not thinking of the disastrous fate this fictional town suffered when they named the well the Macondo Prospect. Apparently a group of BP employees won a United Way contest when they picked Macondo.[140] Maybe the employees and the judges of the contest had not read to the disturbing end of Márquez's beautiful book when they named the well. Or maybe they had a very dark sense of humor.

While the name may have been accidentally prophetic, the victims of the Texas City refinery explosion were quite specific with their repeated predictions that the corporate culture at BP would result in new fatal disasters unless change was mandated. Just a few years after that explosion, on the evening of April 20, 2010, a massive flow of water, oil, and gas blew out of the drilling pipe on the *Deepwater Horizon*, a giant mobile offshore rig that was drilling at the Macondo site.

There were several explosions, and after burning for a day and a half, the *Deepwater Horizon* sank into the Gulf of Mexico. Eleven workers were killed. Others evacuated in lifeboats or jumped into the water, and many were rescued by the heroic efforts of those in nearby boats. A fireball could be seen for miles, and the oil from the well continued to gush for months, until it was finally capped and sealed.[141] The problems—failures to detect high pressure and malfunctioning of defenses and emergency alarms—were much like the systemic problems that had led to the refinery explosion at Texas City.

Afterward, a presidential commission found that "underlying failures of management and communication" contributed to the disaster. These "systemic failures" were so serious that they "place in doubt the safety culture of the entire industry."[142] The presidential commission highlighted "the importance of organizational culture" and noted that BP's inadequate "safety culture" had played a role in the Texas City Refinery explosion as well.[143] Another report stated that the "corporate culture" at BP had been "embedded in risk-taking and cost-cutting," and "when given the opportunity to save time and money—and make money—tradeoffs were made for the certain thing"— oil production and money.[144] This was not just an unpredictable accident but a systems failure rooted in organizational culture. The victims had been saying all along that unless there was an independent monitor or outsider to ensure change, it would happen again.

The newest victims brought lawsuits, and BP created a multibillion-dollar restitution fund. This time, prosecutors began investigating employees at BP and built their case step by step. In April 2012, a BP engineer was charged with obstruction of justice for deleting hundreds of text messages sent during the early days of the spill discussing how much oil was leaking from the well.[145] The resulting criminal complaint hinted that more might be coming. Some of those text messages were recovered from the engineer's iPhone, and they apparently suggested that BP officials knew more oil was flowing from the leak than the company had publicly acknowledged. Some of the deleted texts indicated that the engineer and others knew that the first effort to stop the leak, a "top kill" tried in May 2010, would not work.[146] Yet at the time, BP was reassuring the public that the top kill had a high probability of success.

Meanwhile, BP remained in trouble over its refineries. The company was prosecuted for emissions violations at a refinery in Whiting, Indiana, paying a penalty of just $8 million despite once again being in violation of a prior consent decree with the EPA.[147] Ordinarily, people face greater and greater punishment each time they are recidivists. Yet these new violations by BP did not lead to criminal charges.

In November 2012, BP settled the *Deepwater Horizon* case with federal prosecutors, pleading guilty and paying the largest criminal fine of all time—$1.256 billion. BP pleaded guilty to several counts, including Clean Water Act violations, obstruction of Congress, and—much like in the Ford Pinto case—negligent manslaughter of sailors on the *Deepwater Horizon*, under a law that makes it a crime for a person on a vessel to cause deaths through negligence or misconduct.[148] BP also agreed to pay the largest community service payment of all time: $2.4 billion to the National Fish and Wildlife Foundation and $350 million to the National Academy of Sciences.

BP also paid about $500 million to the SEC regarding charges that its statements mislead investors.[149] Meanwhile, a class action lawsuit by victims may result in an almost $8 billion settlement. Civil environmental fines paid to regulators may dwarf anything paid in the criminal cases, however, and may top $17 billion. BP is taking that case to a lengthy trial, disputing whether it was "grossly negligent" and must pay enhanced fines. Alongside these other penalties, the criminal fine is a drop in the bucket.

Five years after the Texas City victims stood in front of a judge and demanded more accountability and oversight, prosecutors finally did the same. BP was placed on probation for five years. BP was required to hire two corporate monitors for four-year terms: one to supervise safety procedures and another to focus on ethics and compliance. BP was to revise its oil spill response plan within sixty days, conduct annual oil spill response drills, create a new compliance program, hire outside auditors, and post information online about lessons learned, annual progress reports, and safety incidents. The government also suspended the company for over a year from entering new contracts with the federal government.[150] Whether this changes a corporate culture of risk-taking and cost-cutting remains to be seen.

The BP cases show how victims tend to play only a sideline role in corporate prosecutions. Regulatory enforcement and civil suits provided far more compensation for victims than restitution from criminal cases. Victims can stand in for the public interest, but despite their right to participate, their voices are often not heard. The story of victim litigation in corporate prosecutions suggests that unless fundamental changes are made, victims will not be the ones to ensure that corporations are held fully accountable. The next chapter turns to the judges and asks whether they can use sentencing guidelines to better hold a company accountable. Already, we have seen how judges may ignore problems raised by victims and remain reluctant to review plea deals between prosecutors and corporations. Unfortunately, as the next chapter discusses, one of the reasons for judicial ambivalence is that the sentencing guidelines provide little guidance on how to properly sentence a corporation.

Meanwhile, residents of Texas City are still suing BP. At the same time that the *Deepwater Horizon* spill was occurring in the Gulf of Mexico, the Texas City refinery was emitting 500,000 pounds of toxic chemicals, including carbon monoxide and benzene. More than 50,000 residents have sued in separate lawsuits and in a class action saying these emissions made them sick.[151] BP has now sold the Texas City refinery.[152]

Asked about his reaction to the *Deepwater Horizon* disaster, The Foreman's view was simple: "They're still doing it. . . . If you get hurt, they throw a little money at it and go on."[153]

≈ 6 ≈

The Carrot and the Stick

"We will go to our grave saying we are not guilty."

This statement, according to the lawyer for Arthur Andersen who made it at the company's sentencing hearing, "is not defiant . . . We truly believe our people were not guilty." By this time, in October 2002, Andersen had just about gone to its grave. It was a shell of the Big Five accounting firm it had been a year before, with only 1,000 employees and no remaining auditing work for public companies. The prosecutor argued Andersen should receive the maximum penalty of a $500,000 fine and five years of probation, as "the government did not destroy Arthur Andersen, the management destroyed Arthur Andersen."[1]

What happens when a corporation is convicted of a crime? How is the corporation punished? A federal judge first looks to the U.S. Sentencing Guidelines. The Supreme Court has ruled that a judge has discretion to impose a harsher or more lenient sentence, but judges begin by calculating the range that the guidelines recommend, and they often impose a sentence within that range.[2] The guidelines for individual defendants, which took effect in 1987, include a large grid with six vertical columns based on a person's criminal history, and forty-three horizontal rows based on points calculated using complex provisions that score the seriousness of a crime.[3] Adding just a few points can double a person's possible sentence. Since many of these provisions would not apply to corporations, judges use separate organizational sentencing guidelines, but the concept of points is still relevant.[4] These organizational guidelines also inform the settlements that prosecutors enter with corporations, and their structure helps to explain why corporate prosecution settlement can be so lenient, regardless of whether prosecutors settle with a company or a judge sentences it.

The judge gave Andersen a fine of $500,000, the maximum fine listed in the statute for obstruction of justice.[5] The sentencing guidelines for organizations ask the judge to calculate a fine based chiefly on the seriousness of the crime and the characteristics of the firm. The company might get a small break if it accepted responsibility, self-reported misconduct, or had a good compliance program. Andersen had not accepted responsibility and was still proclaiming its innocence. The judge noted that Andersen was a recidivist, having violated a prior Securities and Exchange Commission consent decree. Along with the fine, the judge ordered Andersen to save all documents, refrain from doing auditing work, and tell others it had a criminal record. What was left of Andersen was now branded a criminal—at least until a 2005 Supreme Court decision reversed the conviction resulting in the $500,000 fine being refunded.[6] That was small consolation, though, because by then the company was defunct.

Carrots and Sticks for Corporations

Do you need both a carrot (a reward) and a stick (a punishment) to discipline a corporation? We mostly punish criminal convicts with sticks—lengthy prison terms. Juveniles or first-time offenders are sometimes treated more leniently to give them an opportunity to learn from their mistakes. Companies are treated a bit like children, as neither can be put in prison. Instead, judges may order them to pay fines and to make reforms. However, companies are also rewarded with carrots in the form of leniency, such as reduced fines, to encourage them to report crime, cooperate, and help to prevent future violations.

When prosecutors offer carrots and sticks together, it is rarely clear how they exercise their discretion. For example, when settling with Johnson & Johnson in 2011, they cited the company's "effective" compliance program—but should that have been relevant, given that the program hadn't been effective enough to prevent the crimes from occurring? Prosecutors then listed eleven factors and five more subfactors as "relevant considerations," ranging from compliance to cooperation to self-disclosure of the conduct—but they did not say what role each played.[7] We have seen how prosecutors offer corporations leniency and forgo prosecution in exchange for ill-defined compliance and rarely useful cooperation in pursuing charges against individual employees. And we have seen how, even when victims intervene, the terms of the prosecution settlements typically do not change.

Perhaps judges could more carefully wield carrots and sticks, focusing on deterrence more single-mindedly than prosecutors, who take so many other factors into account. A judge must at least explain the reasons for the sentence, and this sentence can be appealed. Unfortunately, as I will show, a judge's decision how to punish a company often depends on a similar weighing of multiple factors, beginning with those found in the organizational sentencing guidelines. This chapter explores how sentencing for organizations works and how prosecutors and judges actually punish companies—typically quite leniently—in practice.

These concerns are borne out by data concerning the use of fines as a stick to deter corporate misconduct. When I finished collecting information about 2,262 companies prosecuted federally between 2001 and 2012, I was surprised at how inconsistent and how lenient corporate fines were. After all, federal sentences are known for being severe. In fact, the guidelines were adopted because Congress wanted to get tougher on crime, particularly white-collar crime, and Congress has repeatedly enhanced the sentences for white-collar offenses in recent years.

Large numbers of companies paid no fine at all. Almost half of the deferred prosecution agreements, 47 percent (119 of 255 agreements), included no criminal fine. Of convicted corporations, 23 percent paid no fine (455 of 2,008 companies). Some were defunct or unable to pay a fine, while others were given credit for payments to regulators. In some situations, the owners are the party able to pay, and the brunt of the punishment falls on them. Other companies may forfeit property or pay restitution to victims or community service rather than pay a fine. At the other end of the spectrum is the largest criminal fine ever, the approximately $1.2 billion paid by BP. Yet prosecutors rarely explain how they calculate fines, even in the biggest corporate cases.

In deferred prosecution and non-prosecution cases, a judge is not involved in approving a sentence, so no justification must be given. Prosecutors apparently feel little need to volunteer one—in only a few deferred prosecution and non-prosecution cases did prosecutors provide a calculation of the fine (12 percent, or 30 of 255 agreements). Almost without exception, they explained that the fine was at or below the very bottom of the guidelines range, even for cases involving large public companies. Only three agreements noted fines at the top of the range. But even when a company is convicted and sentenced by a judge, similar patterns are apparent, although far more convicted companies are small and unable to pay any kind of fine.

Which companies are fined the most? I wondered whether larger fines were correlated with certain types of companies or certain types of crimes. The results of regressions conducted to analyze those relationships are presented in the Appendix. I found that public companies received fines four times larger on average than other companies, controlling for the type of crime and certain other characteristics of the cases. This is reasonable, as larger public companies may commit more substantial offenses. Foreign companies were punished more heavily, paying average fines over seven times larger.

Prosecutors secured the lion's share of the blockbuster fines in cases involving antitrust violations, violations of the Foreign Corrupt Practices Act, and pharmaceuticals. I knew there were record-setting fines in each of those areas, but I did not expect the degree to which those cases stood out, even when controlling for characteristics such as whether companies were public. The average fine levied in antitrust cases was a remarkable 102 times larger than the average fine in other comparable corporate prosecutions. FCPA cases received an average fine 76 times larger, and pharmaceutical cases received a fine 53 times larger. In contrast, more run-of-the-mill federal crimes such as fraud or money laundering did not involve much larger fines.

Fines are not the only way to punish a criminal convict. Just as individual convicts can be put on probation and must report to a probation officer, companies can also serve probation. But very few such companies are carefully monitored. I found that the average amount of time a company is put on probation or kept on a deferred prosecution agreement is just over two years. That is minimal. Nor are the collateral consequences of a conviction typically very serious. The true death sentence for Arthur Andersen was not the $500,000 fine but the SEC debarment. However, suspension and debarment are highly uncommon. One might expect prosecutors to treat recidivist companies more harshly, but there is little evidence of that happening.

Siemens Pleads Guilty

The role of a judge in sentencing a corporation can be quite deferential and limited, and observing a typical sentencing hearing gives a sense of why. The sentencing hearing for Siemens, in the biggest foreign bribery case of all time, was a genteel affair, with a touch of the celebratory. Siemens and three subsidiaries all pleaded guilty, and the judge began by complimenting the lawyers for Siemens and the prosecutors: "this is not the typical everyday criminal case we get in this courtroom, and an awful lot of hard work from both sides has been put into coming up with a resolution in the case that is in the interest of the United States and in the interest of the parties."[8]

Who could plead guilty for a major multinational corporation? A lawyer introduced himself by saying, "I'm a member of the managing board of Siemens AG and its general counsel." The judge asked, "You've been authorized duly by the Corporation to represent them in the taking of this plea today?" He answered, "Yes."[9] A second lawyer was authorized to take pleas for Siemens of Argentina, Bangladesh, and Venezuela. Signed corporate authorizations were given to the judge. The judge asked more specifically: "Have the boards of directors of these corporations authorized you to enter pleas of guilty to the charges set out in the information pending against them?" The lawyers answered, "Yes."[10]

Normally the defendant must be present in court for the initial arraignment, trial, and plea or sentencing. Failure to appear will subject the defendant to arrest. However, the Federal Rules of Criminal Procedure say an organization does not have to appear in person when it pleads guilty if its attorney is present.[11] Some judges have nevertheless been upset when a company pleads guilty through a lawyer, rather than sending the CEO to personally acknowledge responsibility. This judge did not mind.

The judge next asked the same questions that are posed to any individual who pleads guilty, though the questions make less sense for a corporation. The judge asked if counsel for either side had any question as to the defendant's competence to enter a plea. Could a corporation be incompetent to understand criminal charges or stand trial—a criminally insane corporation? No such concept exists, and no one had questions about that possibility. The judge then asked if they had "had adequate time and opportunity to discuss this case with your attorneys" and if they were "satisfied with your

attorney's representation." Unsurprisingly, given that the attorneys themselves were sent to enter the plea, they were satisfied. The judge asked if the
companies understood they were waiving the right to a jury trial, to cross-
examine witnesses, to present evidence, to have a day in court, and to appeal.
The judge explained, "If there were a trial, each would be presumed to be innocent," and the government would be required to prove each was "guilty by
competent evidence beyond a reasonable doubt." They understood.[12]

The judge then reached the details of the charges—internal controls and
books and records violations of the FCPA by Siemens and its subsidiaries
(with the Bangladeshi and Venezuelan operations also pleading guilty to
bribery violations). The judge asked if the companies "understand the nature
of the offenses," and the lawyers said they did. The lawyers had not been involved in the crimes themselves; as the prosecutor noted, "Obviously, none of
these gentlemen have personal knowledge of the facts that they have agreed to
here today. Instead, it's based on information and belief." The judge asked the
prosecutor to describe the charged crimes. Since this was perhaps the largest
international bribery case of all time, the judge cautioned, "Hit the highlights." Otherwise the hearing might have taken days. The lawyers for Siemens agreed that the description of the case was "fair and accurate." The judge
emphasized, "So, in the case of each of your companies, they are pleading
guilty because they are in fact guilty; is that right?" They answered, "Yes."[13]

The judge walked the group through the potential fines for Siemens and
the subsidiaries. He asked about the other conditions of the plea agreements:
"In signing those, the company acknowledges that they not only understand
those conditions, but they're agreeing to comply with those conditions?"
Now the prosecutor enumerated the terms of the detailed plea agreement,
describing the $450 million in fines to be paid by Siemens and its subsidiar-
ies, the responsibilities of the corporate monitor, and the continued cooperation with the SEC, IRS, and prosecutors in the United States, and Germany.
"Has anyone threatened your companies in any way to enter into these plea
agreements?" the judge asked. They answered, "No."[14]

The judge noted that the proposed $450 million fine, while large, was well
below the sentencing guidelines range of $1.35 billion to $2.7 billion. And
Siemens pleaded guilty only to violations of FCPA accounting requirements
and not to payment of illegal bribes, which are also prohibited by the FCPA.
There was more leniency. Investigators had uncovered over $1 billion in

worldwide bribes by Siemens, but the fine was based on a calculation that only represented bribery related to the U.N. Oil for Food Program in Iraq.[15] The fine could have been up to twice the pecuniary gain derived from the offense, which was $843,500,000.[16] How about the gains from other Siemens bribery schemes around the world?

The judge did not have to accept the amount that the parties had agreed on, and asked the prosecutor to explain why this reduced fine was "nonetheless . . . fair and appropriate and in the best interest of the United States in this particular case." The prosecutor described "thousands of man hours" spent on the case and noted the crimes were "farther reaching in scope and magnitude than the Department has ever seen in any previous Foreign Corrupt Practices Act case." What justification was there for so deeply discounting the fine in the most serious foreign bribery case of all time? The prosecutor noted "extraordinary efforts with respect to cooperation and remediation," and filed a sealed document with the judge explaining which individuals and corporations Siemens provided important information about. That was why the corporation received a "substantial reduction from the low end of the guidelines range." Siemens had already paid approximately $856 million to Munich prosecutors and $350 million to the SEC in disgorgement of profits, amounting to a total of $1.6 billion. Siemens was cooperating extensively, but at the same time, the company had not self-reported the conduct, keeping it concealed for years.

Obviously, Siemens had no reason to complain about a reduced fine. Even if victims or others had intervened to raise that issue, as discussed in the last chapter, little may have changed. The judge concluded, "Well, it's the finding of the Court that the plea agreement in this case is a reasonable and fair resolution of this matter."[17] The judge did not rely heavily on the guidelines, instead deferring to the judgment of the prosecutors. The judge notified the companies of their right to appeal, asked if they had anything to add, and then called an end to the proceedings. Siemens was a sentenced criminal convict.

Too Lenient

In another case, outsiders did express concern that a corporate plea was too lenient. The Guidant Corporation made medical devices, including defibrillator implants, devices implanted in the chest of people with heart problems in order to detect abnormally fast heart rhythms and use electric shocks to prevent heart attacks. More than 20,000 patients received the devices. According to the plea agreement, Guidant changed how it made those implants in 2002, correcting a flaw that could cause them to short-circuit and shut down. Rather than recalling the devices, Guidant merely stopped shipping them. A patient died in Spain in 2004, after Guidant had already heard of four prior short-circuit incidents. Only in March 2005 did Guidant send a nondescript product update, one that did not mention the short-circuit incidents or the patient's death. When it later pleaded guilty, Guidant admitted that only in June 2005 did it notify the Food and Drug Administration about the problem, even though it was required to tell the FDA within ten days.[18] The plea agreement included a $254 million fine and $42 million in forfeiture of funds to the government.

At the sentencing hearing, the judge noted that a plea agreement presented as "binding" is normally either accepted or rejected as a whole.[19] However, the judge could not decide what to do here, noting the "unique contours" of the case. The parties had agreed on a settlement, but the judge also heard from victims' lawyers who argued that Boston Scientific, which had purchased Guidant after these events, was not itself being punished or put on probation. In response, the prosecutor explained, "As far as the Government knows, [Guidant] is no longer operating," making it "absolutely meaningless" to impose probation on a subsidiary that no longer existed.[20] In addition, doctors who had treated a college student who died when a Guidant device short-circuited wrote a letter asking the judge to reconsider the plea deal: "At issue in this case is the safety of future generations of patients who receive medical devices."[21]

The judge decided that a company should not be allowed to "avoid probation simply by changing" its "corporate form" and doing so "less than two weeks" before the government filed charges. The judge noted that the guidelines might call for a better compliance and ethics program, or community service.[22] Ultimately, given "the public's interest in accountability," the judge decided not to accept the agreement "as currently drafted," saying the parties were free to submit a new agreement with probation and compliance requirements.[23] A year later, the judge accepted a revised plea agreement providing for three years of supervised probation.[24]

The Organizational Sentencing Guidelines

In the past, corporations received minimal fines from federal judges, and it made little sense to bother prosecuting companies if the fine might only be a few thousand dollars.[25] All of that changed with the birth of the sentencing guidelines. These had many goals—to eliminate racial disparities in sentencing, to require judges to follow reliable factors when sentencing, and to raise sentences for white-collar offenses. According to Justice Stephen Breyer, one of the architects of the guidelines, "Too many different judges were imposing too many different sentences upon too many similar offenders who had committed similar crimes in similar ways."[26] Organizational fines were very low, averaging less than $50,000 before 1984, and they varied depending on the judge.[27] Congress increased maximum penalties in the 1980s, but there were no rules for how to sentence corporations.[28]

The newly established U.S. Sentencing Commission studied fines paid by corporations and found they were so low that they paled in comparison to company profits or the losses caused by the crimes.[29] The commission ultimately decided on a separate set of Organizational Sentencing Guidelines, which took effect in 1991, and the result was a rise in fines for corporations.[30] Following the Supreme Court's 2005 ruling in *United States v. Booker*, those guidelines are now "advisory" for judges rather than mandatory, but they form the starting place judges use when sentencing companies. They also inform negotiations between companies and prosecutors.[31]

When the corporate guidelines were being designed, some argued the commission should aim for optimal deterrence—a fine big enough to incentivize the company to stop the behavior.[32] The commission ultimately rejected a pure deterrence approach, deciding that it was too hard in practice for a judge to estimate what fine it would take to prevent a company from doing it again or from hiding misconduct. Even the right fine might not have the right effect, since the company might pass the costs to shareholders or customers. The commission wanted to reward companies that genuinely tried to prevent and detect wrongdoing. After all, without a strong compliance defense, as law professors Jennifer Arlen and Reinier Kraakman have argued, a company will have no incentive to uncover wrongdoing, report crime to the authorities, and prevent crime.[33] There must be a large carrot.

The emphasis on compliance has spread to prosecutors, who now offer deferred prosecution and non-prosecution agreements to corporations that self-report, cooperate, and adopt compliance programs. Others followed suit. In 1996, the Delaware Court of Chancery held that a corporate director may be held liable for a failure to implement adequate compliance systems.[34] The SEC announced it would tend to pursue civil charges when a company lacks adequate compliance. In 2010, the SEC announced a "cooperation initiative" and now enters its own deferred prosecution agreements. Other federal agencies emphasize compliance—for example, the Office of Inspector General at the U.S. Department of Health and Human Services has long secured "corporate integrity agreements" with health care providers.

The Death Penalty

Behind this wave of deterrence, the so-called corporate death penalty lurks in federal courthouses, but very few companies are actually sentenced to "death." A special provision in the guidelines allows a judge to set the fine so high as to fine a company out of existence. The goal is to divest a company that "operated primarily for a criminal purpose or primarily by criminal means" of "all of its net assets."[35] Take Nexus Technologies, a small Philadelphia-based export company. The firm pleaded guilty in 2010 to multiple violations of the FCPA, money laundering, and violations of the federal Travel Act, and it agreed to cease all operations as part of its plea. Apparently Nexus paid almost $700,000 in bribes over nearly a decade to secure contracts to sell equipment to the Vietnamese government, including "underwater mapping equipment, bomb containment equipment, helicopter parts, chemical detectors, satellite communication parts and air tracking systems."[36] The government argued the corporate death penalty was appropriate because "Nexus did not slowly fall into bribery in order to compete—bribery was Nexus' business model" and that "Nexus not only paid bribes on every contract it won, it offered a bribe on every contract on which it even submitted a bid." This hurt the people of Vietnam, who paid for inflated contracts, and Vietnamese officials had been working hard with the United States to clean up corruption problems that had helped put the country in a "severe economic crisis."[37] The amount paid in bribes "represent[s] the yearly income of more than 200 Vietnamese citizens."[38] The judge agreed and ordered that the company "shall cease all operations permanently and turn over all net assets to Clerk of Court as a fine."[39]

This remains rare. According to the Sentencing Commission, no firms at all received the death penalty from 2000 to 2008—although the commission's data are not entirely complete, and I have found a few examples. In 2002, a Texas judge ordered Pillbox Medical Center and S&H Scripts, both convicted of distributing controlled substances, to be dissolved and all of their assets seized. Far more common is the situation in which small mom-and-pop corporations are unable to pay the entire fine. A judge can make a preliminary decision that the firm cannot pay the full amount of restitution to victims or of a fine, and can order the firm to pay what it can.[40] For example, in 2008, 48 of 199 firms convicted were unable to pay the entire fine imposed, and 63 received no fine (some fell into both categories).[41] Sometimes judges even order companies to pay fines on an installment plan because they cannot afford the cost up front.

Fining the Corporation

Fines may or may not affect senior managers or those who actually committed the crime in question. In hearings regarding the Barclays deferred prosecution agreement, entered in 2010 concerning violations of international sanctions, a judge asked of a $298 million fine: "Who pays that? Does that come out of the shareholders?"[42]

"That comes out of company profits which would ultimately be borne by the shareholders, yes, Your Honor," the lawyer for Barclays responded.

The judge responded, "There's no alternative source of income to pay this?"

"No, Your Honor," the lawyer responded.

"The shareholders pay for this. All right. So it's just a risk of investment then?"

"Yes, Your Honor," responded the Barclays lawyer.

The judge wondered, "Why should the shareholders have to pay for the Bank's irresponsibility? I don't understand that."[43]

While the judge cannot decide who pays, the judge can set the amount. The judge's priority is to ensure that victims are compensated, as discussed in the last chapter.[44] A fine is then set under the guidelines, though not all companies are punished under them. Environmental offenses, obstruction of justice, export violations, and other crimes are treated differently under separate statutes, as they involve harms that are hard to translate into a dollar figure.

An organization can also be fined under an alternative fines provision, a federal law that says a corporation may have to pay up to twice the amount of either its gains from the crime or the losses it caused to others.[45] "Loss" and "gain" are notoriously hard to calculate, even just to provide a reasonable estimate. In antitrust price fixing cases, mathematical models are used to assess how much customers paid due to the higher prices. In a securities fraud case, it may be complicated to figure out how much the failure to disclose material information affected stock prices. Judges have scathingly critiqued calculations under a guideline that applies in many financial crimes, calling them "a black stain on common sense," an "utter travesty of justice," and a "fetish with abstract arithmetic."[46] If the scheme was a sting operation by federal agents, it might include a harm that never would have happened in the absence of the sting.[47]

If the alternative loss or gain provision is not used, the guidelines calculate a fine based on the same base offense level used to punish individual people. The fine rises with the number of offense level points the organization gets, from just $5,000 for six points or fewer to over $70 million for thirty-eight or more points. Those complex calculations provide the starting place (the base fine). If that is not enough to take away any gain the corporation got from its offense, the court should add more to the fine (the disgorgement) to keep the company from profiting even after being caught.[48] The factors are numerous, and it is more of an art than a science to calculate a corporate fine.

The Bigger Stick

Under the guidelines, the companies that get a bigger stick are the ones that (1) were involved in or tolerated the criminal activity, (2) had a prior history of violations, (3) violated an order, or (4) obstructed justice.[49] Those four factors increase a "culpability score," which can make the fine many times higher due to a multiplier.[50] The guidelines give more points if high-level personnel participated in, condoned, or were willfully ignorant of the offense. The biggest sticks are reserved for the biggest corporations, with the most points (five) for large companies with 5,000 or more employees and only one point

for those with ten or more employees where someone with substantial authority was involved.[51] The other factors increasing punishment are less
common, such as outright obstruction of justice, which can add three points.
A company that earns five culpability points can have its fines doubled, and
an organization with ten or more points can have them quadrupled.

The Compliance Carrot

Good corporate citizens can have points taken away, cutting fines in half or
more.[52] Two factors can reduce the fine: (1) an effective compliance and ethics program, and (2) self-reporting, cooperation, or acceptance of responsibility. Few companies ever get that first carrot, so it is hard to say what counts
as an effective compliance program. From fiscal 2009 through 2012, the
Sentencing Commission reported no companies as having received that
credit, and only five companies out of over 3,000 sentenced have *ever* received
it.[53] But this is not a sign of strict punishment, as small family businesses and
little companies may not have compliance programs, and big companies often get deferred prosecution or non-prosecution agreements and avoid a sentence from a judge.

The Sentencing Commission cares more about compliance than it used
to; it moved the description of effective compliance from footnoted "commentary" into the guidelines themselves. It also added details about what
should be in place, including training, monitoring, anonymous reporting of
misconduct, and evaluation.[54] In 2010, the commission made clear that if the
company really was committed to compliance, then it could still get a reduced sentence even if a high-level employee committed a crime.[55] It remains
to be seen whether this means that more companies will get their sentences
reduced for having "good" compliance. None have received such a credit yet,
nor have prosecutors cited that reason for reducing a fine when entering deferred prosecution and non-prosecution agreements, although prosecutors
have often more generally recognized that corporations had created good
compliance programs. (Prosecutors also tend not to provide sentencing
guidelines calculations in such agreements.)[56] Slightly more companies get
credit for self-reporting crime before the authorities began their investigation, but not many; for example, only four companies in 2008 received such
credit.[57] The guidelines will not effectively encourage self-reporting of crimes

or compliance if they do not give meaningful credit for good corporate conduct, and even after these changes, law professor Jennifer Arlen has called the guidelines a "failure."[58]

Accepting Responsibility and Cooperating

Companies can also get credit for accepting responsibility for their crimes early on, or promptly reporting the offense and cooperating fully.[59] According to the Sentencing Commission, 29 percent of companies did so in 2012, receiving five points off their culpability score.[60] They get less credit (two points off) if they fully cooperate and accept responsibility later on.[61] Most convicted companies cooperate (51 percent in 2012),[62] but few companies self-report their crimes—only 3 percent received sentencing credit for self-reporting in 2012.[63] A judge can also give credit for providing "substantial assistance" in investigations of others.[64]

Cooperation can be grudging and delayed; the Panalpina corporation, a Swiss logistics and contracting company, did not report bribe payments, and when clients turned Panalpina in and the Department of Justice started to investigate, it still did not cooperate. According to prosecutors, Panalpina also "did not stop the illegal payment of bribes that was occurring on multiple continents."[65] The next year, prosecutors demanded documents, and only then did Panalpina decide to help. At that point, the company "exhibited exemplary cooperation" and hired outside lawyers to do a global investigation, providing "voluminous and helpful" information about others who knew about the bribes and participated in the schemes. The company turned informant, and the revelations sparked an "industry-wide" investigation by the DOJ, with three more companies prosecuted.[66] As a result, prosecutors recommended Panalpina get a $70.56 million fine, which the judge imposed, although it was less than the range of $72 million to $144 million the guidelines suggested.

This approach may give companies an incentive to cooperate once no other options are available, but it certainly does not give much incentive to self-report or cooperate quickly. In deferred prosecution and non-prosecution agreements, prosecutors do not always mention the reasons for offering an alternative to an indictment and conviction, doing so in 191 of 255 agreements. When prosecutors did state their reasons, they mentioned cooperation most of the time (70 percent, or 133 of 191 agreements) but rarely mentioned self-reporting of the offense (17 percent, or 33 of 191 agreements), and often used vague language such as "timely and voluntary disclosure," failing to say whether the company came clean before the government learned of the crimes. Prosecutors should be far clearer in rewarding effective compliance, cooperation, and self-reporting, and also more clearly punish poor compliance, lack of cooperation, and failure to report.

Comparing to Individuals

The guidelines are more bark than bite—not just because judges have discretion to depart from them, but also because of how prosecutors negotiate with companies. Ultimately, in the midst of heated negotiations prosecutors offer far too many carrots to companies that seemingly deserve a stick. Compare this practice to the off-the-charts sentence Bernard Madoff received for masterminding the largest Ponzi scheme of all time. The guidelines impose sentences for fraud based on the size of the monetary loss to the victims.[67] In the Madoff case, victims lost a "conservative estimate" of $13 billion over two decades, but it may have been many times more.[68] Madoff pleaded guilty to eleven counts of fraud, money laundering, perjury, and other crimes, and prior to the sentencing, many victims wrote to the court or testified at the hearing about losing their life savings and how Madoff abused their trust, and they asked that he be given the maximum sentence.[69] One recounted how in Dante's *Divine Comedy*, the perpetrators of fraud were placed in the "lowest depths of hell," beneath violent criminals, and expressed hope that in the afterlife Madoff would suffer a similar fate.[70] Madoff's lawyers admitted that he was "flawed," but added that he "chose not to flee" or "hide money."[71] They pointed out that he was seventy-one and had an estimated life expectancy of thirteen years, and they asked for a twelve-year sentence.

"I cannot offer you an excuse for my behavior," Madoff said on the stand. He said he had not intended to do harm, but had made mistakes as a money manager and concealed them by using assets from new investors. The more he tried, "the deeper I dug myself into a hole." He described living in a "tormented state"—"I will live with this pain, with this torment for the rest of my life." Madoff apologized to victims: "I will turn and face you. I am sorry. I know that doesn't help you."[72] There is usually no such personal admission of guilt and responsibility in the sentencing of a corporation. Still, Madoff was sentenced to 150 years in prison.[73] The judge admitted that a sentence above his life expectancy was "largely, if not entirely, symbolic," but it was "important" to send the message that these crimes constituted "extraordinary evil" and not "bloodless financial crime that takes place just on paper."[74]

Average sentences for fraud have doubled over the past decade, perhaps due to harsher sentencing provisions or because prosecutors have brought more serious cases.[75] That said, one readily finds fraud cases imposing sentences of just a few years when longer or even life sentences were available under the guidelines. One of the highest-profile recent insider trading prosecutions, that of hedge fund manager Raj Rajaratnam, resulted in the longest-ever sentence for insider trading: eleven years. The judge commented that the crimes "reflect a virus in our business culture that needs to be eradicated." Yet eleven years was half of the guideline sentence prosecutors pushed for.[76]

When Corporations Plead Guilty

We generally know little about corporate convictions and guilty pleas. As noted, deferred prosecution and non-prosecution agreements have received scrutiny by Congress, the General Accounting Office, the Department of Justice, judges, the bar, scholars, and corporations. But there are far more corporate convictions, chiefly guilty pleas, than deferred prosecution or non-prosecution agreements, and these plea agreements deserve careful attention. A few firms, such as Arthur Andersen, risk a trial each year. But just as in prosecutions of individual persons, the vast majority of corporations, more than 90 percent, plead guilty. According to the Sentencing Commission, only 8 percent of firms go to trial.[77]

Unlike a deferred prosecution agreement, plea agreements must be approved by a judge. Typically, prosecutors and defendants negotiate a plea agreement, and prosecutors may also recommend a sentence or include a binding sentencing calculation.[78] But even for so-called Type C agreements (named after Federal Rule of Criminal Procedure 11(c)(1)(C)), which are binding, judges have discretion to reject an agreement as unfair, contrary to the interests of justice, or contrary to the purposes of the guidelines. In one case a judge scuttled a plea agreement, reasoning that the firm's employees rather than the firm itself should be held responsible; the employees were then prosecuted individually.[79] A judge can also reject a plea agreement that fails to consider victims' interests. A judge threatened to reject a binding plea agreement with Samsung, complaining, "You are trying to run this through like a railroad train" and that he would not be "stampeded." The judge wanted to know what restitution would be paid to victims, and though the agreement was later approved, the judge held hearings to examine that question.[80]

The DOJ offers only general guidance on how prosecutors should exercise their discretion when entering a plea agreement with a corporation. The *U.S. Attorney's Manual* emphasizes that a guilty plea should be sought in a serious case, one that involves participation of higher-level corporate officials and in which neither civil actions, prosecutions of individuals, nor a deferred prosecution agreement would be sufficient. Corporate pleas should impose "substantial fines, mandatory restitution, and institution of appropriate compliance measures, including, if necessary, continued judicial oversight or the use of special masters or corporate monitors." Not only may the terms be more punitive than in a deferred prosecution, but a criminal conviction may bring reputational and collateral costs. The company must admit guilt, which may provide ammunition to private parties or regulators suing the company.[81]

Corporate Probation and Court-Ordered Compliance

A convicted corporation not only pays a fine but, in a way, can do time. More than two-thirds of convicted corporations are put on probation.[82] Companies may be put on probation if they lack an effective compliance program, and probation can be more active if "special conditions" are imposed to make sure "changes are made within the organization to reduce the likelihood of future criminal conduct."[83] Just like individuals, the company agrees not to violate the law again—any sentence of probation includes "the condition that the organization not commit another federal, state, or local crime during the term of probation."[84] Early on, however, the guidelines suggested that probation would do very little. The Sentencing Commission was concerned that probation had been abused by judges who required firms to do "community service" by donating to charities and the like.[85] Only in extreme cases were monitors appointed.

The Con Ed case started to change that. One summer evening in 1989, a steam pipe exploded in the Gramercy neighborhood in Manhattan.[86] Three people were immediately killed, and a plume of debris settled over the crowded area. Consolidated Edison, the New York utility, known as Con Ed, did not tell residents something important about that debris: it contained asbestos. It was residents who performed their own tests and figured it out themselves. Federal laws require immediate reporting when dangerous substances are released, and federal prosecutors brought a case against Con Ed, which went to trial.[87] Days into the trial, Con Ed capitulated and pleaded guilty. It opposed the appointment of a monitor, but the judge imposed one anyway, explaining:

> One of the things I found disturbing here was the sense that there were people at Con Edison, who testified at the trial, who clearly knew and who should have been jumping up and down saying, there is asbestos here, we know it. It was obvious they didn't say it because they were intimidated from saying it, because they didn't think that was the corporate culture; and that was not the corporate culture that came across to me in this trial.

The judge added, "I want to be sure that, on an ongoing basis, people will know that this is real and that there is an avenue outside the company for them to go to."

The guidelines have been amended to encourage probation to do more. But these new powers are not commonly used. The court, while it may only appoint a special master or trustee in serious cases, may "employ appropriate experts" to review a compliance program.[88] The company may receive unannounced visits by probation officers to examine books or records or by an expert appointed by the judge, including to conduct an "interrogation" of employees.[89] Nevertheless, probation is still typically unsupervised.

What has changed is that judges more frequently order a company to adopt a compliance or ethics program. According to the Sentencing Commission, 36 percent of organizations sentenced had a judge order compliance in fiscal 2012, compared to only 6 percent in 2008.[90] How closely judges can supervise such an order without the help of a special master or supervised probation is unclear.

There is one more penalty, one that any company can afford but which judges impose rarely—the public apology. In a small example, the Midwest Sheets Company was ordered to print an apology in a Tipton, Indiana, newspaper and a trade journal for violating the Clean Water Act. Large companies do not normally have to do that, and judges and prosecutors should require an apology far more routinely.

Recidivist Corporations

There is a surprising amount of recidivism in white-collar offenses. The Sentencing Commission found that recidivism rates for fraud and larceny were low overall, but that over 50 percent of the most serious fraud and larceny culprits were recidivists—about the same as robbery and firearms offenders, and far higher than drug traffickers, who have some of the lowest rates of recidivism.[91] And the rates for white-collar offenders may be conservative, as such offenders are not easy to catch or convict.

Few companies convicted each year are officially recidivists. From zero to just over 1 percent of organizations have a history of similar convictions in the past ten years, but these commission data are missing information on recidivists in the environmental area not sentenced under the guidelines and companies entering deferred prosecution agreements.[92] Several companies have been convicted multiple times, and some violated probation by committing another crime.[93] Others receive multiple deferred prosecution agreements. Still others were under consent decrees with regulators, promising not to violate the law again—but they did.

There is no three-strikes rule for corporations, but recidivists can be sentenced more harshly under the guidelines. The guidelines call for a more severe sentence for a company that committed a crime less than ten years after a crime based on similar misconduct, or civil or administrative cases based on two or more instances of similar misconduct, and still more severe penalties if the prior similar crime was only five years in the past.[94] However, what counts as "similar" may be open to interpretation. Many deferred prosecution agreements also call for consequences if a company engages in additional crimes during the term of the agreement, but often only if it is a similar offense. Some companies have received multiple deferred prosecution and non-prosecution agreements not many years apart, but for different crimes presumably not deemed sufficiently similar. And companies are rarely sentenced using guidelines—they receive deferred prosecution and non-prosecution settlements.

It is not at all clear that prosecutors take corporate recidivism seriously. Some settlements reflect prior crimes, but often they do not appear to do so. Companies with several environmental convictions include BP, ExxonMobil (with four convictions since 2001), McWane Inc., and a series of ocean shipping companies. Outside the environmental area, in Big Pharma cases, take the example of Pfizer. Its subsidiary, Pharmacia & Upjohn, had two convictions and a deferred prosecution agreement, while the parent, Pfizer, received a non-prosecution agreement, and another subsidiary had a deferred prosecution agreement for FCPA violations. ICN Pharmaceuticals had two convictions, and GlaxoSmithKline had a conviction and a non-prosecution agreement. There has been much public discussion of cases involving major financial institutions such as AIG, Barclays, HSBC, JPMorgan, UBS, and Wachovia, which each received multiple deferred and non-prosecution agreements over the past decade. These cases do not show clear signs that prosecutors treat recidivists more harshly. If they truly mean to reward compliance and self-policing by firms, then they must also punish recidivism more severely.

One judge questioned whether a big corporation can be a recidivist if different employees or subsidiaries are involved. In a case dealing with groups of related corporations, in 2004, ABB Vetco Gray and a related U.K. firm pleaded guilty to FCPA violations involving years of bribing officials in Nigeria. They paid over $10 million in fines and disgorgement, and were sentenced to five years of probation.[95] They were both part of the ABB Group, a mass of more than 500 companies all controlled by ABB Ltd., a Swiss holding company, with a major division focusing on oil and gas exploration.[96]

Three years later, in 2007, three subsidiaries in the same group pleaded guilty to FCPA violations involving bribes to Nigerian officials concerning deepwater oil drilling, paying $26 million in fines. One of the subsidiaries, Aibel Group, Ltd., also entered a deferred prosecution agreement.[97] In 2008, Aibel reported that it continued to violate the FCPA, breaching the deferred prosecution agreement. Having breached, the firm negotiated a guilty plea.[98] That, perhaps, was the punishment for recidivism—the firm did not get a deferred prosecution.

There was a fourth time. In 2010, additional FCPA violations were reported by another collection of ABB-related entities. The parent company, ABB Ltd., negotiated a deferred prosecution agreement, as did its Jordanian subsidiary. The U.S. subsidiary, ABB Inc., negotiated a guilty plea.[99] Would some part of the company ever receive a harsher sentence as a recidivist? In September 2010, the judge held a hearing on the guilty plea.[100] As part of the plea, the government was offering ABB Inc. a fine at the bottom of the range.[101]

But the judge changed the topic and asked, "How many employees does ABB have?" Its lawyer answered, "ABB Inc. has approximately 10,000 employees in the United States."

"How many worldwide?" the judge asked.

"More than a hundred thousand," the lawyer answered.

"In how many countries does it operate?"

"Over a hundred countries."

"Isn't calling ABB Inc. itself a recidivist a little harsh given that just—how many people work at the Justice Department?"[102]

The prosecutor guessed about 9,000 (in actuality it is well over 100,000).[103] The judge parried, "Is it the case that occasionally people at the Justice Department violate the law?" The judge added, "Would it not be remarkable [with] 200,000 people, many of whom work in countries that have a level of integrity, especially in the government, that are abysmal, that somebody doesn't weaken in the name of the company . . . ?"[104]

The judge would not let it go: "You would not call ABB Inc. a murderer because one of its employees in Australia murdered somebody, would you?" Actually, as noted, a company may not be prosecuted for murder, but for other crimes, such as FCPA violations, a company really is liable for the acts of its employees in the scope of their duties. The judge was questioning the entire concept of corporate criminal liability as recognized by the Supreme Court.

The judge ignored the plea agreement and concluded the company should not receive an enhanced punishment as a recidivist. The judge wanted a much lower fine that did not include any enhancement based on recidivism and would not sentence ABB Inc. to any probation. The prosecutor said, "I'm sure Your Honor is aware that that is not the agreement of the parties," and pointed out that the sentencing guidelines call a company a recidivist even if it is a different part of the company that committed the new crime.[105] The guidelines refer to an organization "or separately managed line of business."[106] There is a good reason for that—a company could just close down or rename any subsidiary business that pleaded guilty to a crime and wipe its own record clean.

The judge countered that this company was "earnestly trying to avoid this kind of problem." The prosecutor responded that the conduct in Nigeria had occurred from the 1990s through 2004, the very same time period covered by the prior 2004 plea agreement.[107] Still, the judge concluded that the guidelines would not be applied, saying, "Do I look like a rubber stamp?"[108] Instead of a $28.5 million fine, the judge imposed a $17.1 million fine, removing the recidivism enhancement. Under the judge's approach, the larger the company, the more protection it receives from multiple criminal violations. This is a very troubling argument.

For Shame

One view of corporate prosecutions is that they serve to bring shame on the company—to harm its reputation and place it in the equivalent of the stocks for everyone in the community to see. Law professor Samuel Buell has argued that corporate criminal liability has an important "blaming function."[109] One study suggested that shame can "work wonders" to cause a corporation to "shape up after its wrongdoing."[110] But a firm's reputation may not be hurt much at all; it depends on the firm and the crime.[111]

Arthur Andersen took a direct hit to its reputation, and the prosecution led to its being debarred by the SEC. However, customers who buy Siemens kitchen appliances may not have been particularly troubled by reports of payment of bribes in third-world development projects. And companies can manage the news of their prosecution. For example, the same week Deutsche Telecom entered a settlement and had three executives charged by the SEC, the company made two major announcements: that AT&T had ended its bid to buy T-Mobile, a unit of Deutsche Telecom, and that the German firm might bid for the rights to broadcast the country's popular Bundesliga soccer league via satellite. After the Upper Big Branch mine disaster case settled, with civil and criminal penalties, newspapers reported that Massey Coal's stock was down 1.1 percent but that "indicators for the stock are neutral." One commentator suggested it would be a good company to bet on.[112]

Of course, even if the prosecution does not hurt the company's bottom line, executives may feel shame and may be embarrassed (in addition to personally facing prosecution). As law professor Dan Kahan puts it, the average corporate executive "probably cares a lot about what his family, his colleagues, his firm's customers, his neighbors, and even the members of his health club think."[113] There is also a sort of CEO "walk of shame" provision in the guidelines. The judge can require a corporation that has accepted responsibility for its crime to send its CEO to appear in court and receive the sentence, and perhaps personally accept that responsibility and explain why the corporation will not violate the law again.[114] CEOs do not relish a visit to a courtroom, but in a few high-profile cases judges have insisted that the CEO or executives come in person.[115]

Probation can also include an order that the company publicize the offense, including the conviction and the punishment. It is apparently not something courts do often, just as they rarely require apologies.[116] Sometimes prosecutors actually try to protect the reputation of the company. One corporate plea agreement included a stipulation that prosecutors would not ask for a press conference or write a press release about the conviction.[117] Almost two dozen corporate deferred prosecution and non-prosecution agreements are sealed—not by a court order, but because prosecutors agreed not to disclose them.

Corporate Parenting

Companies are slippery creatures. They cannot serve jail time, but they can have immortal life and countless subsidiaries. They can merge with another company, or split themselves into pieces. For small companies, judges may hold owners in contempt for failing to ensure that a company pays its fine. In one example, the owner of a trucking company was sentenced to six months in prison for failing to pay a $25,000 fine and $9,000 to victims.[118] But what if the company is more complicated? Do you punish the subsidiary or the parent company? Perhaps the parent corporation controlled its subsidiaries, set the tone, and for all practical purposes will pay the fine.

The government has spared parent companies from some effects of a criminal conviction. In the Pfizer case, subsidiary Pharmacia & Upjohn Co. Inc., rather than Pfizer, was charged with illegal marketing of generic drugs. Reporters examining the case concluded this subsidiary was "nothing more than a shell company whose only function is to plead guilty."[119] Pfizer owns Pharmacia Corp., "which owns (b) Pharmacia & Upjohn LLC, which owns (c) Pharmacia & Upjohn Co. LLC, which in turn owns (d) Pharmacia & Upjohn

Co. Inc." The company that was convicted was "the great-great-grandson of the parent company." Why pin the blame on a great-great-grandchild? The conduct was so serious that the company could be permanently excluded from Medicare and Medicare; in such circumstances, according to an official, the Department of Health and Human Services must "ask whether by excluding the company, are we harming our patients"? Rather than using a deferred prosecution or non-prosecution agreement, prosecutors can convict the subsidiary but permit the parent to avoid the collateral consequences of a conviction.

Mergers and Acquisitions

Since companies can share in the responsibilities for their subsidiaries, they have to be very cautious about buying a subsidiary or merging with another company, as a company that buys another company may assume its criminal liabilities.[120] The rise in corporate prosecutions has given companies incentives to be far more diligent when investigating whether a company they are purchasing has compliance issues. Indeed, wrongdoing has often come to light when such a company was being considering for purchase, and some planned mergers have been abandoned due to possible criminal violations. For example, Lockheed had planned to buy the Titan Corporation before it found out about possible FCPA problems.[121]

Only in the corporate world can a criminal divide itself into a blameless half and a half to be punished. Abbott Laboratories was prosecuted and faced massive fines for illegal off-label marketing of Depakote for treatment of schizophrenia and other disorders and conditions. It paid about $560 million in fines when it pleaded guilty in May 2012 and another $241 million to state governments. Just weeks before its plea, it announced its plan to separate into two public companies—a "diversified medical products company" that "may retain the Abbott name" and a pharmaceutical company.[122] The pharmaceutical branch had been involved in the illegal marketing, and the agreement released the other branch from prosecution.

Plea and deferred prosecution agreements typically say that despite a sale of all or "substantially" all of a company's assets, the purchaser is still bound by its terms.[123] As the judge that sentenced BP after the Texas Refinery explosion put it:

BP Products may not dissolve, change its name, or change the name under which it does business unless the judgment and the criminal monetary penalties imposed by this Court are either fully satisfied or equally enforceable against BP Products' successors or assignees.[124]

But my research has shown that there is rarely much in the way of consequences to attach to any successors or assignees. Judges approve lenient corporate fines that undermine the legitimacy of corporate criminal liability, and they take a hands-off approach to probation conditions that might reform a company. Meanwhile, prosecutors do not seek to impose maximum fines—or in many cases even minimum fines—as calculated under sentencing guidelines. The guidelines can also be bypassed entirely through the use of deferred prosecution and non-prosecution agreements. It is not clear that companies receive these lenient fines as a real reward for meaningful cooperation, self-reporting, and compliance. If prosecutors offer leniency or drop a criminal case regardless of whether a company actually self-reported and had effective compliance, then companies have truly perverse incentives.

Critics argue that no firm should be treated as "too big to jail" and allowed to avoid conviction with deferred prosecution and non-prosecution agreements. Convictions are usually the appropriate resolution where a crime was committed, but as I have described in this chapter, just convicting a company is not enough if the fine is too lenient, repeat violations are disregarded, and serious violators are not sufficiently incentivized to adopt meaningful structural reforms. In the next chapter, I turn to a tool prosecutors use to try to ensure that a company has the supervision to properly reform itself—the corporate monitor.

7

Enter the Monitors

The mythological Greek hero Theseus sailed from Athens to the island of Crete to slay the fabled Minotaur, who was half bull and half man. As the Greek historian Plutarch told the tale, after Theseus returned from his adventures, Athenians preserved his ship as a monument: "they took away the old planks as they decayed, putting in new and stronger timber in their place." The classic philosophical puzzle about this ship asked: if every plank and piece of it was gradually replaced over time, was it still the Ship of Theseus? This question generated much debate among the thinkers for which Athens was famous. "This ship became a standing example among the philosophers . . . one side holding that the ship remained the same, and the other contending that it was not the same."[1]

Like a ship made out of many planks, a corporation is a collection of people. A company can be as immortal and as mutable as the Ship of Theseus; it can change leadership, employees, headquarters, business models, and product lines. It can be bought out, change its name, acquire new subsidiaries, or go through bankruptcy. Prosecutors do not seek to reform the entire structure, however, and the question they must ask is more practical than philosophical: how much change is enough to make it a company that will not commit more crimes? Prosecutors usually lack expertise in overseeing such structural reforms, but they can bring in a specialist to supervise the process: a corporate monitor.

Siemens's New Leaf

Siemens is a study in corporate metamorphosis on a grand scale. As you may recall from Chapter 1, Siemens is ranked in the Fortune Global 500 and operates in more than 190 countries. It also pleaded guilty in 2008 to paying billions of dollars in bribes to government officials around the world. The plea agreement called for a new compliance program, and at the time, prosecutors lauded Siemens for "uncommonly sweeping remedial action" in which the company committed itself to becoming a "worldwide leader" in "responsible corporate practices."[2] How would Siemens do that?

The company replaced most of its top leadership, including its CEO, chairman of the board, general counsel, and chief compliance officer. The new CEO described how, within two years of his arrival, half of the top 100 managers were replaced.[3] Siemens also hired more than 500 full-time compliance staff around the world and a new chief audit officer with a staff of 450. New policies, handbooks, and training were adopted.[4] Auditors from PricewaterhouseCoopers were hired to create an "anti-corruption tool kit." Siemens stopped entering any new business consulting agreements until reviews were conducted.

The plea agreement required four years of monitoring, and prosecutors asked Siemens to retain not one but two corporate monitors. The lead monitor, Dr. Theo Waigel, could not have been more prominent. Dr. Waigel had been German minister of finance and was the first non-American monitor appointed in a federal prosecution. An independent U.S. counsel was appointed to collaborate with and assist him.[5] Dr. Waigel and Siemens would forge a strong relationship, but as another high-profile case shows, not all prominent people work smoothly with the companies they are selected to monitor.

The Bristol Monitor

Bristol-Myers Squibb, often referred to as BMS, is one of the largest pharmaceutical and health care companies in the world, with billions of dollars in sales each year. In 2005, BMS admitted to "channel stuffing," or encouraging wholesalers to buy extra product to make sales and earnings appear $1.5 billion higher.[6] BMS was prosecuted in New Jersey, where its Medicines Group was based, for conspiracy to commit securities fraud. The company admitted wrongdoing and entered a deferred prosecution agreement.

Two years later, this corporate giant was pronounced cured, with the U.S. attorney for New Jersey announcing, "We promised that federal oversight would help to make Bristol a better company. The objective facts prove that goal has been achieved."[7] The prosecution agreement had come to an end.

What ensured BMS had good compliance by the time the agreement was concluded? Changing corporate culture means more than just checking off the boxes (training, check; code of conduct, check). But prosecutors cannot be on-site for years evaluating a company, and neither can judges. The BMS agreement was instead supervised by a former judge: retired U.S. district judge Frederick B. Lacey. As the monitor, Judge Lacey announced a successful end to the project, as BMS had "undergone a remarkable transformation" and now "is governed by the highest standards of integrity, ethics and accountability."

Yet in the same report, Judge Lacey noted it "cannot be ignored" that BMS had just pleaded guilty to another crime, this time making false statements to the Federal Trade Commission. BMS was forced to pay a $1 million fine over marketing of its drug Plavix. Such was the "transformation." But whether BMS was a recidivist or not, federal oversight of the company would still come to an end.

What Is a Monitor?

I was surprised at how rarely prosecutors required companies to hire monitors to oversee the implementation of prosecution agreements. After all, prosecutors do not typically impose the maximum fines, as discussed in the last chapter, instead focusing on compliance as a goal. If both prosecutors and judges lack the resources to supervise compliance, then insisting that the company retain a monitor would make sense. Yet only 25 percent of the deferred prosecution and non-prosecution agreements entered into between 2001 and 2012 required a monitor (65 of 255 agreements). There is no trend over time toward imposing monitors more often, and if anything, a surge in use of monitors in the period 2004–2007 was followed by a slight decline in recent years, as Figure 7.1 illustrates.

The Department of Justice says that its test for whether to hire a monitor is whether the company lacks "an effective internal compliance program, or where it needs to establish necessary internal controls."[8] Since almost all corporate prosecution agreements require new compliance measures, presumably because previous ones were lacking, one would think a monitor is often appropriate. Instead, compliance is usually unsupervised, and companies simply file reports with prosecutors or a separate regulatory agency.

What is a monitor, exactly? The agreements that do require their use include all sorts of different terms: *independent monitor, independent examiner, independent consultant,* or possibly *corporate compliance monitor, compliance consultant,* or *special compliance officer.* Perhaps it is called an *outside consultant.*[9] What they have in common is they are outsiders, not employees, and they are hired to investigate, make recommendations, and report back to the company and to prosecutors.

The monitor is a third party and an independent actor.[10] Although the monitor may be a lawyer, the corporation is not hiring someone to give it legal advice or representation. Although paid by the company, the monitor does not work for it or for the prosecutors. The monitor's job is to make sure the corporation has a solid compliance program in place and that crimes are no longer committed. In its brief guidelines on using corporate monitors, the Department of Justice says that this person must "assess and monitor a corporation's compliance."[11] A company that already has a very good compliance

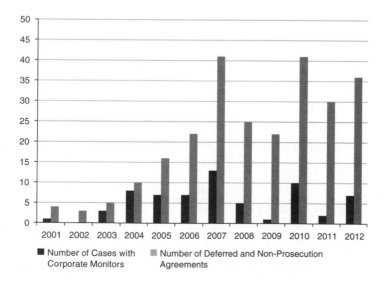

Figure 7.1 Corporate Monitors and Deferred Prosecution or Non-Prosecution Agreements, 2001–2012

program does not need the expertise of a monitor, nor does a company that has closed down its operations. But when prosecutors conclude a company needs to improve its compliance and cannot do it alone, they should demand that the company hire a monitor. As of now, we have very little information about how this important task should be handled, as monitors do not make their work public or report to judges. What is clear is that monitors are highly paid, have ill-defined roles, and are chosen by prosecutors with little oversight.

Structural Reform Litigation

The idea of having an independent monitor is not new. One of the first deferred prosecution agreements, with Prudential Securities in 1994, required a monitor. In other types of cases, prosecutors may ask that the court appoint a special master or trustee to supervise a consent decree. As law professor James Jacobs has described, prosecutors in the 1980s began using the RICO anti-racketeering statute to reform unions infiltrated by organized crime. They settled the cases in consent decrees overseen by judges, who often appointed trustees to temporarily take over entire unions.[12] In the biggest union consent decree of them all, a federal court described how three special masters oversaw reforms at the International Brotherhood of Teamsters over many years, though they faced "incessant attacks" against their authority.[13] Prosecutors and other government agencies may also impose monitors when they bring civil actions to reform government institutions.

Structural reform litigation is the term lawyers use to describe cases, usually civil rights cases, in which the goal is to reform organizations with systemic problems.[14] There is a long history of this type of litigation, including the real need for structural reform in the wake of the Supreme Court's decision in *Brown v. Board of Education* as federal courts struggled to oversee the racial desegregation of schools. Desegregation cases became a "prototype for the judiciary's new supervisory role," and in the 1970s, parties brought litigation to reform hospitals, police departments, prisons, public housing, and special education facilities.

In a famous article, law professor Abram Chayes described the role of the judge as fundamentally different in a structural reform case than in a traditional civil case in which private parties settle disputes. Such a judge supervises litigation in which "masters, experts, and oversight personnel" monitor "a complex, on-going regime of performance."[15] Structural reform litigation can involve lengthy judicial supervision. After all, it can take time to create safe conditions at a prison, desegregate an entire school system, or eradicate the influence of organized crime at a labor union. In the classic model, judges serve the public interest by acting as an impartial power broker in an ongoing bargaining process between citizens and government. Judges appoint experts (typically called *special masters*) to supervise these complicated cases, and they may ask for detailed reports and updates over many years.

Structural reform litigation can be quite controversial. There are major public disputes about the costs and the wisdom of reducing prison overcrowding, using busing to integrate schools, or ordering police to change their practices. The Supreme Court developed a body of law to regulate when judges may change the terms of an agreement as a result of changed conditions or unforeseen difficulties.[16] Some view those decisions as far too restrictive of civil rights, but structural reform litigation is still common.

In a range of areas, best practices have emerged over time that help judges to use a defined set of effective remedies.[17] Yet in corporate prosecutions, prosecutors have ignored these hard lessons. Corporate monitors typically do not report to any judge, only to prosecutors. Their work occurs out of the public eye; few monitor reports have ever been made public.[18] There is no effort to test and evaluate best practices over time. Complicated methods for selecting and overseeing corporate monitors could be made simple—a judge should decide if a monitor is needed, approve the monitor's selection, and supervise with input from all of the parties. Federal prosecutors have been allergic to involving judges in supervising corporate prosecutions, but corporate prosecutions are too important to proceed without their oversight.

When Monitors Are Appointed

As noted, there were monitors in one-quarter of the deferred prosecution and non-prosecution agreements examined, most commonly in cases involving securities fraud or violations of the Foreign Corrupt Practices Act (twenty-three monitors each). FCPA and securities fraud cases were often handled in conjunction with the Securities and Exchange Commission, which itself began to impose monitors in its civil cases. Prosecutors appoint

monitors quite unevenly, with results varying by the type of prosecution and
the prosecutor's office. In some years few monitors are appointed, while in
some years there are double-digit numbers. These erratic numbers may be
due to variations in how many securities fraud and FCPA cases are resolved
in a given year, but this does not explain why agreements in so many other
types of cases lack any kind of monitor.

In contrast, judges in large corporate convictions commonly appoint monitors or special masters, particularly in environmental and foreign bribery
cases.[19] The prosecutors at the Environment and Natural Resources Division have made it a standard requirement. The available plea agreements
and press releases show that of more than 2,000 corporate convictions from
2001 to 2012, at least 110 had a monitor or special master reporting to the
judge, and as I will describe, judicial oversight can strengthen the monitor
system.

Who Picks the Monitor?

Corporate monitors can exercise vast powers, including "extensive supervisory and monitoring responsibilities" over a large company such as Bristol-
Myers Squibb. These are plum positions and can pay very well, making the
selection process important. Unfortunately, there is no standard process.
Most common are joint processes that allow the company, some say, but give
prosecutors final discretion in making the appointment; some version of this
was used in forty cases. In other agreements, practices varied; the company
chose five monitors, prosecutors chose fourteen, regulators chose one, prosecutors and regulators together chose four, and judges chose only one (and
were involved in choosing a total of three.)[20] Regulators were involved in
some manner in eight selections. The DOJ says there is "no one method" to
select monitors, and the data reflect this.

This makes no sense, and as I will describe, prosecutors have faced charges
of nepotism or cronyism regarding their role in picking monitors. The names
of eleven monitors have not even been made public, and some companies
have declined to disclose their identity. With prosecutors picking so many
monitors, perhaps it is no surprise that over half of those we know of were
former prosecutors (at least thirty-eight). Maybe they were the best for the
job, but there is the concern that these lucrative positions are being given to

members of a "club" of former prosecutors.[21] As in traditional structural reform cases, judges should help select and supervise the monitors.

Where Were the Lawyers?

Federal judge Stanley Sporkin famously asked in a savings and loan scandal
case, "Where were these professionals.... Where were the ... attorneys
when these transactions were effectuated?"[22] Perhaps if lawyers had intervened at the time, prosecutors and corporate monitors would not have had to
intervene later. Was Judge Sporkin suggesting that lawyers should have
turned in their clients? Lawyers have long thought of their role as that of
advocates who must vigorously defend their clients to the hilt and keep their
work and discussions privileged and confidential. However, they increasingly
have a new role as "gatekeepers"—raising new questions about what they are
supposed to do when misconduct comes to light.

Companies have increased incentives to hire outside lawyers to conduct
internal investigations, even before there is a prosecution. This involves not
defending the company but rather investigating wrongdoing.[23] The Enron
scandal changed the role of corporate lawyers, as not only did the Enron accountants fail to detect wrongdoing but so did the legal department. As Sen.
Jon Corzine put it at the time, "When executives and accountants have been
engaged in wrongdoing, there have been some other folks at the scene of the
crime—and generally they are lawyers."[24] Of course, one reason corporations and executives may argue they should not be prosecuted is that they
asked lawyers all along whether they were doing anything wrong and were
told their behavior was legal. Advice from lawyers may be used as a defense
in corporate prosecutions. Perhaps the lawyers in these cases were trying to
cultivate and please their clients. Maybe the law was vague. Both may have
been true.

In the wake of the Enron scandal, the American Bar Association convened a task force that recommended changes to the traditional approach
where lawyers must keep a client's information in confidence, namely, by
changing the concept of who the client is. Is senior management the client, or
is there a broader duty to the shareholders to prevent harm to the company?
The association included a new recommendation that lawyers report confi-
dences to prevent corporate fraud from happening, and if it does happen,

requiring lawyers to report misconduct "up the ladder" to senior management.[25] Congress included that change in the Sarbanes-Oxley Act and also asked the SEC to develop new rules requiring lawyers who learn of misconduct to report it to the CEO or chief legal counsel. If neither of these individuals responds appropriately, lawyers must then go to a separate audit committee, some other committee of independent directors, or the board of directors.[26] The audit committee and independent directors themselves take on a new role to respond to misconduct, and the lawyers serve as gatekeepers who have an obligation to protect the company.[27]

As a result, firms commonly conduct internal investigations on their own, even before criminal prosecutions occur. It is simply good management to find out whether there is a problem and solve it before it becomes more serious, although an investigation may be mishandled, as the Andersen engagement team did. In addition, an audit committee may hire outside lawyers to conduct an independent investigation. Often a lawyer leads the investigation, allowing protection of confidentiality via attorney-client privilege and work product rules. Since the firm's legal rights and liabilities may be at issue, a lawyer can provide legal advice. That said, other types of specialists with more expertise and a broader focus can be important to investigations. Outside lawyers may also be brought in, although people inside the firm may not readily trust them.

Meanwhile, the internal investigator has to figure out the goal of the project. The first question to ask is whom one is investigating for. Is it a management team? Is it the board of directors, or the CEO, or the general counsel? Investigators will try to assemble documents and interview employees to get to the bottom of what happened, knowing all the while that the record they create may be eagerly sought after by regulators, prosecutors, and others.[28]

An internal investigation may cost millions, more than entire public defender systems or government enforcement budgets. In 2011, Avon Products spent $93.3 million to investigate potential FCPA violations, which was actually less than the $95 million it spent the year before.[29] Siemens paid $1.6 billion in fines, as described, but also spent over $950 million to conduct its global investigation—an amount that was "almost triple the $324 million annual budget of the SEC's enforcement division when the case was resolved in December 2008."[30] In another FCPA case, Daimler apparently paid at least $500 million for a five-year internal investigation.[31] Some companies retain independent lawyers to oversee compliance efforts and may avoid the imposition of a corporate monitor by doing so.

Lawyers may also be held accountable if they became part of the criminal scheme rather than merely giving advice to the corporation on what the law required. Recall that in the tax shelter prosecutions, lawyers had given opinions that the different tax shelters were legal. The law firm of Jenkins & Gilchrist was prosecuted, signed a non-prosecution agreement, paid a $76 million fine to the IRS, and eventually closed its doors as a result.[32]

After an investigation, a company may improve compliance on its own to make sure problems do not recur. Quite a few deferred prosecution and non-prosecution agreements recognize that the company has already brought in outsiders to conduct audits and supervise improved compliance. Some agreements required the company to retain compliance officers or professionals (27 of 255 agreements) or create new positions internally (88 of 255 agreements), though these lack the independence or oversight of an independent monitor.

Structural Change

Returning to the Bristol-Myers Squibb case, major changes had already been made before prosecutors entered the picture. BMS had replaced both its chief financial officer and the president of its Worldwide Medicines Group, as well as creating a new chief compliance officer and hiring a new lawyer specializing in securities law. The company changed its budget process, created a new management group to focus on risk and disclosure, and adopted new training and internal controls. It created a confidential hotline and email so that BMS employees could tell higher-ups of any concerns about "channel stuffing" or anything having to do with "integrity of the financial disclosures" or books and records.[33]

As monitor at BMS, Judge Lacey would be independent and not the attorney for the corporation, though the corporation would pay him. He would send quarterly reports to prosecutors and keep the SEC informed. The agreement called for BMS to adopt detailed changes to its practices, and the monitor would make sure that each was carefully implemented. The monitor would have the power to require BMS to "take any steps he believes are necessary" to comply with the agreement, though BMS could object to a

recommendation by the monitor, and if prosecutors agreed, the company
need not follow it.[34]

Judge Lacey had quite a task ahead of him. Prosecutors described how
BMS "promoted a corporate culture in which meeting or exceeding company
budget targets and the consensus estimates was considered mandatory." For
example, BMS had announced a "Mega-Double" goal, a plan to double year-
end 2000 sales and earnings by the end of 2005.[35] While the company was
required to file quarterly reports with the SEC containing information about
sales and earnings, when it was asked about these earnings, executives at Bristol said nothing was wrong. At an April 2001 conference call, a market analyst asked about wholesaler inventory levels, which we now know were artificially inflated. An executive responded, "There are no unusual items that we
see." Similarly, in 2000, an executive told an analyst, "I don't think there was
any significant wholesaler inventory activity."[36] Meanwhile, executives were
sending emails saying things like "We need to make our May target!"

In 2001, BMS came clean and restated its earnings. It later agreed to pay
an additional $300 million in restitution to victims of the fraud scheme,
along with a $100 million civil penalty, $50 million for a fund to shareholders, and a $300 million settlement of class actions by shareholders.[37] BMS
was to have a meeting for senior executives where prosecutors would describe
the goals of the agreement. A new director would be appointed—with the
agreement of the U.S. Attorney's Office—whose job it would be to foster "a
culture of openness, accountability and compliance throughout the Company."[38] Most surprising was that BMS agreed to endow a chair at Seton Hall
University Law School for teaching business ethics.

The monitor attended board meetings, wrote quarterly progress reports,
and oversaw implementation of a new compliance program. We do not know
how effective that work was, since, as is typical, none of it was made public. But
we do know that new wrongdoing came to light, this time related to Plavix, a
top-selling medication. In 2006, BMS apparently tried to keep a competing
generic version off the market, and the DOJ opened an antitrust investigation.
This issue had nothing to do with the accounting troubles that had prompted
the deferred prosecution agreement, so was it a violation of that agreement?
Should the monitor have been able to prevent this conduct? The agreement
said BMS was obligated to notify prosecutors of "any credible evidence of
criminal conduct." Furthermore, the agreement said BMS would cooperate

by not "engaging in or attempting to engage in" any such crimes. A breach could result in the company's prosecution.[39]

The monitor apparently told the board to fire the CEO, and it did, along with the general counsel. The press reported that the stock price went up when this was announced.[40] The monitor did not speak publicly about any of this, and while his reports were kept private, the executive summary of his final report was released when the agreement ended in 2007. This summary was short and self-congratulatory, citing improvements in the budget process, an "environment that embraces openness and transparency," and an "outstanding global compliance program" among other things. As for the new crime, the monitor called it "unfortunate" but said that the response to it, including a "prompt" internal investigation and cooperation, show how BMS has changed for the better. In its quarterly report to the SEC, BMS said the monitor did not think anything more needed to be done and that the new problem was "fully remediated."[41]

Perhaps, like the Ship of Theseus, one could argue this was a new company. But we do not know the details of what the monitor did or what changes were actually made. This was not like a structural reform project supervised by a sitting judge, and it was not like the Ship of Theseus, rebuilt in public by the citizenry. Whatever changes were made to this company occurred privately.

Siemens's Monitor

Dr. Theo Waigel, the former German finance minister appointed to monitor Siemens, told me in an interview that his first question when approached about the position was whether the job would require a great deal of time. There had not been monitors appointed in Germany before; corporate criminal liability does not exist in Germany, so this was not a role that anyone in the country was accustomed to. Dr. Waigel had the impression that the position would involve some travel but that he might continue his law practice and other work. He was mistaken.[42]

The Siemens monitor had to supervise compliance efforts on a grander scale than perhaps any of his counterparts before or since. The agreement called for the appointment of a corporate monitor for four years and a separate American lawyer to help monitor FCPA compliance.[43] Dr. Waigel recalled that the work required about two-thirds of his time over those four years. It was not enough to simply review documents, although there were tens of thousands to review. He had to visit twenty countries around the world, some of them multiple times, and travel to nearly every continent. There would be multiple visits each year to the United States to speak with prosecutors, and meetings with more than 1,500 people in total.

Despite the enormous size of the job, Dr. Waigel fondly recalled the work as an "exciting experience" and a "highlight of my life." Upon accepting the position, the first thing that he wanted to make clear was the importance of his independence. He had had no business contact with Siemens before accepting the position, and he told both Siemens and the federal prosecutors that he would be "absolutely independent." If he felt that he could not satisfactorily do the work, then he "would quit at once."

Upon beginning his work, a new team had to be assembled. There was a project team with employees from Siemens, all experienced in its operations; the lawyers at the U.S. firm serving as the independent consultant; and those Dr. Waigel brought from his law firm. The monitor had to spend several weeks familiarizing himself with the scope and structure of Siemens's global operations. It was necessary to have complete access to all of the documents concerning compliance, financial controls, and internal audits to understand how the system worked and how it could be improved. Tellingly, as monitor, Dr. Waigel did not do all of his work off-site. He recalled he had "the best office" at Siemens, one "not in the background" but just past the main entrance to the headquarters. This made it clear at the outset that the monitor literally had "an important place" at the company.

The Work of the Monitor

Dr. Waigel recalled the best single sentence he heard anyone utter in his four years as monitor: the new CEO told employees, "Only clean business is Siemens business." Tone from the top can be very important in changing an organization. However, that tone must also translate to real change further down the chain of command. Far more important than a new code of conduct was making sure rules were effectively implemented across Siemens's sprawling global operations. The company speaks of "continuous improvement" since then and how compliance has been built into all of its operations, reflecting a "zero tolerance" policy toward corruption.[44] Detailed guidelines were adopted for business conduct and the conduct of business partners. Siemens created new due diligence programs for gifts and hospitality and began a new program of risk analysis to detect compliance problems.[45] Systems were put into place to catch corruption, including new requirements that transactions be documented and approved.

Dr. Waigel recalls that his first report as monitor included more than a hundred recommendations and that "Siemens accepted all of them." In the second year, he made a little more than thirty recommendations. In the third year there were just nine or ten. Each time, all of the recommendations were accepted. Dr. Waigel's counterpart in the United States, Joseph Warin, described a "seismic change" at Siemens during those years.[46]

To reach employees around the world, Siemens held trainings and surveyed tens of thousands about their understanding of compliance at the company. Siemens used "risk-based internal audits" to assess possible trouble areas. Roundtable discussions with midlevel managers were held, without supervisors present, to discuss the rules and practices. Help lines to report misconduct were tested by placing mock complaints and assessing the response. And the monitor team would sit in on planning meetings, human resources meetings, and other management meetings to be sure that midlevel managers really understood the rules. In its annual report to investors in 2011, it included a report from the monitor and examined how well the new compliance program might work in the long term. The monitor certified that the compliance program was "reasonably designed" but also suggested improvements.[47]

To test whether compliance is working, especially with the danger of misconduct such as bribery in far-flung global operations, several techniques are used. Warin described those used to audit compliance across Siemens's complex operations. Random sampling involves carefully analyzing ten or twelve transactions from each area of business for any improper payments. If the transaction involved business development expenses, one can go on-site and question the chief salesperson, examine expense reports, and review records line by line. Risk-based analysis can be used to select particular countries or areas to focus the random spot-checking.

More than 600 Siemens employees all over the world currently do compliance work; the number was once fewer than fifty. Particularly important, Dr. Waigel recalled, was that compliance work is not seen as the end of a career but a useful part of it. Indeed, one head of compliance was chosen to run all of Siemens's operations in Indonesia. A new disciplinary committee was created and new employees were added at levels ranging from the managing board to local disciplinary committees. Different offices would also think of their own practices to improve compliance for their employees. For example, employees in Turkey would be given a daily quiz with a compliance-related question before they could log on to their computers.

A particularly important challenge came during the Arab Spring unrest in the Middle East, where Dr. Waigel had an opportunity to see a complicated ethical situation firsthand. Siemens could use only one bank in Egypt at that time, but the firm had to continue its work. He wondered, "How is it possible in such situations to have compliance, to have no secret accounts, to work with cash?" Dr. Waigel recalled how compliance personnel followed the events carefully, made sure the work was "transparent," and ensured careful compliance during a "difficult situation."

Reflecting on this work, Dr. Waigel commented that he was very "proud" of what had been accomplished. The work was not only extensive but "as interesting as being finance minister." Most important, he concluded, "I can give a certification that Siemens is working well, that Siemens has an excellent compliance system" and an "impressive tone from the top." He noted that in such a large company, with 400,000 employees, uncovering occasional new violations would be inevitable, but what was impressive was that "Siemens reacted at once" to any problems and did so effectively. Dr. Waigel added, "I can say at the end of my work, there is no systemic risk." Similarly, the CEO similarly commented in a speech, "Last year, incidents in Brazil and in Kuwait required rigorous enforcement. And we acted accordingly."[48]

Corporate Czars?

With few monitors publicly describing their work, critics have had to speculate about whether corporate monitors have too much power or use it unwisely. Some have called monitors "corporate czars," while others describe an independent outsider as essential if a corporation is to build a culture of ethics.[49] Others question whether monitors serve long enough to effect significant change, or whether they might bill excessive fees to a corporation that has no choice but to pay. Some of the more recent corporate prosecution agreements include more specifics for how the process will work, instructing monitors to come up with a "work plan," describing the steps "reasonably necessary" to conduct a review, and asking the company and prosecutors to comment on the plan before it is carried out.[50] Such frameworks are sensible if they do not unduly narrow the scope of the monitor's work. But apart from statements in the agreements themselves, we know little about the work of monitors unless a dispute spills into public sight.

We do know that corporate monitors are expensive. The Government Accountability Office has described how some monitors charge rates from $290 to $895 per hour, which is typical for senior lawyers, but also have a total cost per month ranging from $8,000 to $2.1 million, as it is not just the monitor being hired but an entire team of lawyers and investigators.[51] Some corporations have included monitor costs in their SEC filings. The Willbros company reported that its monitor cost more than $8 million over two years.[52] Faro Corporation reported paying its monitor $1 million in one quarter, about the same amount as its fine for FCPA violations.[53] The AIG monitor was reportedly paid over $20 million from 2005 to 2009, after the company was prosecuted for securities fraud. (Of course, AIG approached bankruptcy during that time and received a federal bailout in 2008 after making risky bets in subprime mortgage securities, an area unrelated to the monitor's specific assignment.)[54] One judge said at a hearing regarding a corporate guilty plea that "it's an outrage, that people get $50 million to be a monitor . . . It's a boondoggle."[55] Such costs may be relatively small given the leniency companies receive in exchange for adopting compliance reforms, but there is too little information to judge if the money is being spent wisely.

Cronyism?

Corporate monitors became national news in 2008, but not because of their work or the nature of a particular corporate crime. A prosecutor in the U.S. Attorney's Office in New Jersey received an email from a lawyer at Zimmer, a company that would soon be under supervision, about "a potential issue with [our] monitor." The email, which would later become politically explosive, did not mince words: "I have to tell you that I was shocked by the proposed fee agreement." The agreement would require Zimmer to pay a "monthly flat fee of $270,000" for the monitor and two additional executives, plus further costs in hourly pay for others on their staff. Even at hourly rates of $1,000, this would mean working "750 hours per month for 18 months. I seriously doubt that such a level of effort will ever be required in this matter." With a flat fee, "Zimmer would be expected to pay the bill with no questions asked." Zimmer's lawyer added, "It also strikes me as highly ironic that the Monitor would be trying to avoid the type of transparency that it will be insisting on in Zimmer's relationships with other consultants."[56]

The monitor was to review payments to consultants in the artificial hip and knee joint replacement industry. Zimmer was one of five companies that collectively held over 94 percent of this market, and all five entered deferred prosecution agreements with the U.S. attorney of New Jersey in 2007. An indictment or conviction might have led to disbarment from participating in Medicare, which funds most hip and knee replacement procedures, meaning the companies likely would have gone out of business.

The U.S. attorney would later say that "negotiating these agreements was akin to landing five airplanes on the same runway at the same time."[57] We rarely hear anything about how deferred prosecution agreements are negotiated, but these particular negotiations would be described in hearings before a U.S. House of Representatives subcommittee. The U.S. attorney later recalled that the negotiations went on for four and a half months:

> We went through nearly a dozen drafts of that agreement which meant 60 copies of it because each was times five, with different negotiation requests. These were incredibly contentious negotiations that literally, sir, were not resolved until 9 A.M. on the morning that we announced these agreements at 11 A.M., is when the last issues were resolved.[58]

After all, this was an $80 billion industry, and each of these five companies was a competitor to the others. The U.S. attorney recalled always being asked, "Is everybody agreeing to exactly the same thing . . . because if they are not, I am not signing."[59]

The negotiations over the fees charged by the monitor would not last so long. The total charges might be $1.5 to $2.9 million per month. In his email, the lawyer for the company concluded: "At bottom, what we have here is a demand by the Monitor that Zimmer automatically transfer to it $13.5 million dollars . . . no matter how much or how little work they actually do."[60] The monitor's team responded that they had "substantial responsibilities" and had already been doing a great deal of work without an agreement for twenty-five days. They were "uncertain as to the issues that will be uncovered," so a flat fee was needed.[61] Ultimately, the U.S. attorney declined to intervene in the billing dispute, telling the sides to take "another stab" at resolving the matter.[62]

Who might command this kind of payment? The U.S. attorney had recommended a monitor for each firm, and each company accepted the proposed name.[63] Zimmer apparently "wanted someone with Midwestern sensibilities," and they received John Ashcroft, former U.S. senator from Missouri and former U.S. attorney general.[64]

The U.S. attorney in New Jersey who had proposed that Ashcroft take the job was Chris Christie, who had previously worked for Ashcroft at the Department of Justice. Ashcroft was called to testify before Congress, and in his brief testimony, he was asked whether there was anything wrong with an "employee hiring their former boss." He responded by saying, "There is not a conflict. There is not an appearance of a conflict."[65] The morning of those hearings, the DOJ announced new guidelines for the selection of corporate monitors, perhaps to head off further congressional scrutiny. (I testified at that hearing, but I was not in the hot seat.)

At the hearing, representatives repeatedly pressed Ashcroft about the money he charged as monitor. Records showed billings of more than $7.5 million for the first five months of the monitorship, with a fixed monthly bill of $750,000 and hourly billing for additional team members.[66] Ashcroft explained that the case involved an unusually complex job for the monitors, as "this investigation involves an entire industry," meaning that each of the monitors has "an additional responsibility of not only investigating their own companies, but also assisting in the investigations of the other orthopedic manufacturers and providers."[67]

When it was pointed out that other monitors provided itemized billing for their work, rather than demanding a fixed fee, Ashcroft responded: "We believe that the quality of the services is the important point and that we have agreed and provided information about our fees in advance."[68] Some legislators called Ashcroft's deal a "no-bid" contract. They asked him to supply documentation of his billing, which he agreed to provide.[69] One congressman commented: "In the Zimmer case, it is my understanding that Mr. Ashcroft's firm was paid $52 million. To me, that is outrageous. I don't care what you did. It is not worth $52 million. Even if you took steroids and hit 70 home runs, it is not worth $52 million."[70]

In response to the outcry, the Justice Department changed the rules to require central review of the hiring of corporate monitors. New guidelines required any monitor to be approved by both a separate standing committee in each U.S. Attorney's Office and the Office of the Deputy Attorney General at the Justice Department. Conflict-of-interest rules were to be carefully followed to avoid not just actual conflicts but also the appearance of them, as well as to ensure that each monitor was "highly qualified and respected."[71] The new rules added that three candidates should be selected, giving the company the ability to choose between them.[72] Some thought the result was that fewer monitors would be appointed, but monitors continue to be used as before, particularly in environmental, FCPA, and fraud cases. But even after the rule change, there remains no requirement for independent judicial review over the decision to require a monitor, the monitor's selection, the monitor's fees, or the work the monitor does.

Missing Monitors

Why do so many cases lack monitors? I am far less concerned with how much monitors are paid when actually used, given that the fees can be small compared to criminal fines. This is true even when those fines are substantially reduced in exchange for implementing compliance reforms. In the case of Sirchie Acquisitions, the company was even allowed to directly deduct costs of monitoring from its fine. The primary concern is whether monitors actually enact the meaningful reforms they are paid to oversee, and if so, why they are appointed so rarely.

In some cases, it is understandable there was no monitor, as the company hired someone else to supervise compliance. In over one-third of agreements (86 of 255), companies were required to create new positions to supervise the compliance program. However, those are employees of the company, not someone independent. In thirteen other cases, prosecutors required outside auditors or experts, but ones without the sweeping power of a monitor. They audited a specific area and did not report directly to prosecutors.

Often, prosecutors seemed satisfied that a company was adopting compliance on its own. A large number of cases cited compliance already performed by the corporation before prosecutors entered the agreement. The vast majority of companies hired auditors, accountants, and outside law firms, or they created new compliance officer positions. Of the more than 2,000 companies convicted since 2001, docket sheets and plea agreements indicate that more than 110 involved monitors. Those monitors report to a judge, not just to prosecutors. If a monitor reporting to a judge uncovers noncompliance or new violations, then the judge can sanction the company.

It is not only prosecutors who appoint monitors. Some regulators also use monitors to supervise corporations in civil enforcement proceedings. The Securities and Exchange Commission began doing this more often over the past decade, perhaps taking a cue from the Justice Department. The Environmental Protection Agency often requires corporations to retain monitors in environmental cases. And the Office of Inspector General at the Department of Health and Human Services requires monitors to supervise health care fraud cases, usually civil ones. Maybe regulators feel particularly comfortable supervising monitors since the regulators frequently oversee compliance.

To be sure, some cases involved misconduct a monitor might not be able to help fix. But it is very hard to see what is so different about the sixty-five deferred prosecution agreements or the more than 110 convictions that included monitors. Even where the company voluntarily creates new positions, those people could report to prosecutors and to the court. The lax approach toward monitoring suggests a need to require more judicial involvement in supervising prosecution agreements.

Improving Monitor Effectiveness

Our new corporate prosecution system works only if the tandem of carrot and stick—less punishment for more reform—results in changes that actually prevent future crimes. We do not know how successful these compliance programs really are or how well the monitors supervise them. Corporations may be getting off the hook based on adopting paper reforms, or "cosmetic compliance," that is not tested or implemented carefully. Monitors do everything from hands-off reviewing of paperwork to hands-on supervision of structural reforms. Unlike in criminal convictions or civil consent decrees, no judge reviews what the monitor is doing or whether the corporation actually complies.

The Government Accountability Office found that monitors were rarely required to provide a work plan detailing the steps they would take, something a judge could insist on.[73] Monitors are typically supposed to provide "periodic written reports" both to the company and to prosecutors, detailing what the monitor has been doing, company efforts to improve compliance, and whether additional measures are needed.[74] If judges supervise monitors, these reports could also be made public, at least in part.

Judges could step in when there is a breakdown. The DOJ guidelines suggest that monitors should tell the government if the company is not adopting recommendations "within a reasonable time." They should also report any new misconduct uncovered if the allegations are credible. Furthermore, the DOJ recommends extending agreements if the monitor cannot complete the job in time.[75] A judge might play a far more independent role in resolving disputes over monitor pay, the scope of the monitor's work, new crimes uncovered, or any other area of contention. A judge could make the final decision about whether the monitor's work is done and the agreement can end.

Within DOJ, the environmental crimes group has long asked for judges to approve court-appointed monitors to supervise environmental compliance; most of the convicted companies that had monitors were in environmental cases.[76] Many such plea agreements require monitors to make reports both to the judge and to the probation office.[77] Sometimes the monitor may recommend that the judge order an early end to the supervision if the company completed its work. In the Kassian Navigation case, the court-appointed monitor and the independent compliance consultant both recommended to the judge that probation be ended early, and the judge agreed, resulting in the first ruling of its kind in a prosecution for ocean dumping from a commercial ship.[78]

It is hard to understand why the Justice Department has avoided following a similar judge-supervised process in some of its highest-profile cases. The DOJ told Congress that it is looking into "performance measures," but it is not at all clear how well monitors are performing or how compliance is supervised where they are not required.

Cured?

Even after it arguably breached its deferred prosecution agreement, Bristol-Myers Squibb was declared cured. Do all recidivists receive such lenient consequences? Wright Medical Group was accused of breaching a deferred prosecution agreement with the U.S. attorney in New Jersey, which included a $7.9 million fine and a year of corporate monitoring. Despite this, the company reported that its general counsel and other executives left "without good reason" and that its board received a tip leading to an investigation that uncovered "credible evidence of serious wrongdoing."[79] The prosecutors concluded the company had "knowingly and willfully breached" the deferred prosecution agreement. What was the punishment? The prosecutors said they were "pleased" with the firm's new interim management, and they simply extended the deferred prosecution another year to allow for more oversight by the federal monitor. All's well that ends well.

This situation highlights the need to change corporate monitoring by requiring a judge to supervise its implementation. We do not know if monitors can effectively reform an entire company in just a few years, and the public should learn more about what the monitor actually does. Having a judge more involved is by no means a cure-all; we have seen some judges reluctant to supervise any deferred prosecutions, though others have been more active and demanded more information from both companies and the government alike. However, a judge is ideally impartial and independent—like a monitor. The complexity of structural reform and the importance of these cases to the public mean that judges must be involved in some manner. Even without new legislation, judges can insist that a deferred prosecution agreement on their docket means that they will supervise compliance. Judges should demand to approve monitors, supervise compliance, and decide whether an agreement was successfully concluded. This will ultimately benefit prosecutors and strengthen structural reforms by placing the authority of the judge behind them.

Compliance as Good Business

"One company alone isn't able to make a better world," Dr. Waigel notes. If judges make public more of what monitors do, then other companies can learn from success stories. Siemens decided to try to use the force of its own example by entering a new kind of agreement with competitors—not the sort that would raise antitrust issues, but a different type aimed at promoting ethical business practices. Siemens has entered into quite a few such "integrity pacts" with other companies, including in China and Russia, following an idea developed by Transparency International.[80]

Some companies may have been skeptical that Siemens, having just been caught and punished in a massive criminal case, was in a position to promote ethics. Yet Siemens has been persistent, acting like a religious proselytizer in pursuing agreements between companies with a common government customer to abide by ethical standards and practices. Siemens says that if employees violate the rules, the company will put a stop to it, and if Siemens hears about a competitor's employees violating the rules, it will let the competitor know right away. It plans to "intensify interaction" with outside stakeholders to combat corruption and promote responsible business practices; included in such "collective actions" are agreements among competitors to follow the rules. Siemens promotes industry-wide codes of conduct and reaches out to government integrity offices around the world to support anti-corruption efforts. U.S. monitor Joseph Warin recalled speaking to government regulators about these agreements, including officials in Egypt, India, and Russia, and finding them all to be very enthusiastic.

Siemens lauds the FCPA and similar anti-corruption laws, saying the concept of a "level playing field" began with the FCPA, and since "clean business" is necessary for "free enterprise," anti-corruption laws will help everyone. Siemens's new CEO noted, "Clearly, we have learned a lesson regarding business integrity." He described how compliance must be "inherent in a company's values" and asserted that today Siemens is a "role model."[81]

Siemens is also a role model in another way. Some ask whether complying with anti-bribery laws means losing business to less ethical competitors. The German business community had been skeptical that it was possible to work in the developing world without bribes, and some in the United States have expressed similar skepticism. Siemens answered this in the only way a business can: its earnings have risen since it adopted rigorous compliance measures. At his 2012 annual speech to shareholders, the CEO highlighted "an excellent year" and noted how "value-based culture is especially important to us in times when markets are volatile and trust in government institutions and authorities is diminished." The CEO cited a top score in the Dow Jones compliance category, specifically hailing the monitor: "Dr. Waigel, you deserve much of the credit for the fact that Siemens today is a role model of integrity. We extend our sincere gratitude to you."[82]

Making real compliance a valued part of Siemens' culture has apparently been good for its business. Making compliance more valued, through the rigorous use of monitors and judicial supervision, would be good for corporate prosecutions.

⚛ 8 ⚛

The Constitutional Rights of Corporations

Liquid mercury might seem as though it would be interesting to play with, since it looks like silver but accumulates into pools and scatters into little balls. This characteristic has given it another popular name, quicksilver. But liquid mercury, which evaporates rapidly and has no detectable odor, is very poisonous. Ingesting it, inhaling it, or absorbing it through the skin can result in hypertension, kidney disease, and a potentially fatal condition known as "pink disease." It also causes brain damage; in the past, milliners, who were exposed to mercury compounds during the production of felt for their products, were often victims of mercury-related dementia (giving rise to the phrase "mad as a hatter"). This chapter begins with a case in which a corporation was held responsible for environmental violations involving mercury in Rhode Island. But in a sense, quicksilver is a rather appropriate metaphor for corporate crime more generally—shape-shifting, hard to detect, and very dangerous.

A subsidiary of Southern Union Co., a natural gas company, stored old gas regulators in a dilapidated building in Pawtucket, Rhode Island. Mercury from those regulators was haphazardly kept in kiddie pools, plastic containers, and even a milk jug.[1] There were no warning signs posted about hazardous substances. The building had broken fences, windows, and doors, resulting in break-ins and homeless people living inside, but Southern Union decided to stop paying a security guard to monitor the premises. In 2004, three neighborhood kids who had played with the liquid mercury in the building took some back to the apartment complex where they lived. Other residents tracked it around. When Southern Union employees discovered what happened, they did not notify the fire department or the authorities. Only when the incident was discovered by residents weeks later was there a cleanup and community testing for mercury poisoning.[2]

The company went on trial in Rhode Island, and the jury returned its verdict on a written form:

> As to Count I of the indictment, on or about September 19, 2002 to October 19, 2004, knowingly storing a hazardous waste, liquid mercury, without a permit, we the jury find the Defendant, Southern Union Company GUILTY.[3]

Once Southern Union was found guilty, it had to be sentenced. The judge commented: "It is important to send a message to all companies who may be illegally storing hazardous waste that a serious price will be paid if you get caught. That's what deterrence is all about."[4] Recall from Chapter 6 that not all federal crimes involve sentences under the U.S. Sentencing Guidelines. The environmental statute that applied in this case, the Resource Conservation and Recovery Act of 1976, prescribed that that fines for knowingly storing hazardous waste without a permit should be calculated at a rate of $50,000 a day.[5]

While the jury was not specifically asked how many days the violations lasted, it concluded that there had been about 762 days of illegal storage of the mercury. Based on that figure, the judge could have imposed a maximum fine of $38,100,000. He instead ordered a $6 million fine, emphasizing that the company had already paid $6 million to clean up the site. The judge also ordered the company to pay $12 million in community service to the Rhode Island Red Cross, to other charities, and to fund grants for children's education and health. Finally, the judge ordered probation, requiring the company "to submit evidence of an existing and ongoing corporate-wide environmental compliance program."

Southern Union argued that these fines violated its Sixth Amendment right to a jury trial, since the jurors had not been asked to find "beyond a reasonable doubt" the specific number of days it had violated the environmental statutes. Could the company assert a constitutional right to have the jury determine the fine rather than the judge? As the previous chapters have explained, prosecutors target corporations largely in the shadow of the law, based on informal guidelines and practices. Judges and the sentencing guidelines play a role, as do outsiders such as monitors. The rights of victims and individual employees may also come into play, especially if prosecutors target the latter. One subject I have not yet discussed is whether the constitutional rights of corporations themselves affect their prosecution.

The trial judge rejected Southern Union's constitutional argument, citing "clear and essentially irrefutable" evidence that the mercury had been stored for over two years, and judges on appeal agreed. However, the Supreme Court reversed the lower courts in a 6–3 decision written by Justice Sonia Sotomayor.[6] The Court relied on its 2000 decision in *Apprendi v. New Jersey*, which held that the prosecution must prove beyond a reasonable doubt to the jury any facts that could result in the imposition of a sentence higher than the maximum penalty that would otherwise apply.[7] Cases such as *Apprendi* involved jail time rather than criminal fines, and the government argued that the role of the jury is crucial only where there is a "physical deprivation of liberty." Companies can be fined, but they cannot be jailed. The Court was unmoved by this argument, however.

As we have seen, corporations and other types of organizations are in many respects treated as legal persons, and they have some—but not all—of the same constitutional rights. The structure, rights, and obligations of corporations are largely defined by state law, but in criminal cases, their rights are also defined by the U.S. Constitution and its wide range of protections governing everything from initial police searches through a trial and the appeal process. The decision in *Southern Union* largely avoided the topic of corporate constitutional rights, mentioning that corporations have a right to a jury trial under prior rulings, at least if the company is facing fines that are not petty.

Corporations today can face massive fines, particularly under provisions that calculate the fine at up to twice the loss the crime caused others or the gain the company obtained. In *Southern Union*, the Supreme Court noted the record $448.5 million fine paid by Siemens and the then-record fine paid by Pfizer and Pharmacia & Upjohn of $1.195 billion as examples of the importance of fines. The *Southern Union* ruling would be particularly important since, as Justice Sotomayor noted, fines "are frequently imposed today, especially upon organizational defendants who cannot be imprisoned." In fiscal 2011, "a fine was imposed on 9.0% of individual defendants and on 70.6% of organizational defendants in the federal system."[8] There are also huge fines imposed in individual white-collar cases, and this decision means that more may be needed to prove their basis. Very few companies are prosecuted and even fewer are convicted, but the *Southern Union* ruling could require prosecutors to provide stronger evidence even when negotiating with companies. Justice Stephen Breyer, joined by two others, dissented and argued that modern federal sentencing statutes enhanced fines because there had been a history of judges imposing fines that were uneven and too low. He feared the majority opinion would undercut those reforms.

Some prosecutors had already treated the Sixth Amendment as applying to corporations. The biggest antitrust fine ever imposed was on Taiwan-based AU Optronics Corporation and its U.S. subsidiary after a jury trial in 2012. The case involved allegations of a worldwide conspiracy to fix prices for liquid crystal display panels, affecting what people paid for computers, laptops and flat screen televisions. The conspirators apparently fixed prices "during monthly meetings with their competitors secretly held in hotel conference rooms, karaoke bars, and tearooms around Taiwan."[9] The judge instructed the jury that it needed to specifically determine the size of the harm or loss that the price fixing conspiracy caused. Since AU Optronics took the case to trial, it did not get leniency, as other companies did. By this time, too, prosecutors had more information about the scope of the conspiracy and its effect on prices. As the jury concluded the companies involved had gained $500 million from the price fixing, the total fine could have been as much as $1 billion. The judge was reluctant to impose quite that much, however, and opted for $500 million.[10]

While this suggests serious consequences may still await a company at a trial, *Southern Union* may narrow the bargaining range, as Justice Breyer pointed out in his dissent. Major corporations can hire teams of lawyers to challenge fines all the way up to the Supreme Court. And while the issue of paying restitution to victims or community service did not come up in this case, civil payments such as the $12 million in community service the judge had ordered Southern Union to pay—twice the criminal fine—might someday also be covered by the Supreme Court's new rule, since they are not petty amounts. Still other questions include whether criminal forfeiture, such as the $1.7 billion JPMorgan forfeited for violations related to Bernie Madoff's

Ponzi scheme, could be covered by the reasoning of *Southern Union*. The *Southern Union* case may not be the last time the Court has to rule on how the Sixth Amendment affects the money corporate criminals are ordered to pay.

After the Supreme Court's ruling, the trial judge felt constrained to reduce Southern Union's penalty from the $18 million previously imposed to only $500,000 in community service and two years of probation. The judge called this result "manifestly unsatisfactory and even unjust."[11]

The Corporation and the Constitution

Southern Union dealt with the jury trial rights of corporations, and the Supreme Court avoided mentioning any general theory of when corporations have constitutional rights. However, the case naturally raises the question of what other constitutional rights corporations have and how they impact criminal prosecutions.

The word *corporation* does not appear in the Constitution; in the days of the Early Republic, corporations were not common, most of those that did exist were government entities, which played a minor role in the economy.[12] However, the Supreme Court soon had to grapple with the constitutional status of corporations and other organizations. Chief Justice John Marshall, writing for the Court in a 1809 case about the Bank of the United States, called corporations "a mere creature of the law, invisible, intangible, and incorporeal," but also said that they were "citizens" for purposes of federal jurisdiction, noting that "corporations have been included within terms of description appropriated to real persons."[13] That kind of pragmatic approach characterizes a fair amount of the Court's decisions on this subject—the justices focus on the reality of how organizations operate. The justices treat organizations as separate from their owners, officers, or employees, and as a result, companies can exercise some, but not all, constitutional rights.

Citizens United

When we think of corporations and constitutional rights, the first right that may come to mind is free speech. This is due to the high-profile nature of the Supreme Court's recent decision in *Citizens United*, which held that Congress could not pass laws barring corporations from certain types of spending during elections. The strategically named Citizens United, a nonprofit corporation, sought to release a documentary entitled *Hillary: The Movie* during the 2008 Democratic presidential primaries, which pitted Hillary Clinton against Barack Obama and other contenders. Federal campaign finance laws, notably the Bipartisan Campaign Reform Act of 2002, prohibited corporate expenditures of that sort. The 2002 act said that only political action committees (PACs) could spend in that way, since individuals could decide whether they wanted to donate to a PAC, whereas the shareholders of a corporation may not have a say in whether corporate money is spent on political speech.

The Supreme Court, in a lengthy opinion by Justice Anthony Kennedy, "rejected the argument that political speech of corporations or other associations should be treated differently under the First Amendment simply because such associations are not 'natural persons.'" He recognized corporations might speak in ways shareholders disapprove of but held that the "procedures of corporate democracy" could allow shareholders to exercise their voice or instead buy shares in a different company. At the oral arguments, Justice Sonia Sotomayor criticized the notion of imbuing "a creature of State law," the corporation, "with human characteristics."[14] In earlier First Amendment free speech rulings, the Court suggested that the Constitution's "purely personal" guarantees were unavailable to corporations "because the 'historic function' of the particular guarantee has been limited to the protection of individuals." However, the *Citizens United* ruling did not adopt any particular test for deciding whether a corporation has a constitutional right.

The ruling is less surprising given the long history of recognizing constitutional rights of corporations. The Court had assumed for decades that corporations have at least some First Amendment rights. In some of its earliest nineteenth-century rulings, the Court recognized that corporations have constitutional rights under the contracts clause,[15] and it later recognized corporate rights under other provisions of the Constitution as well.[16] Of course, the Court has not extended all of the constitutional rights that individuals may exercise to corporations or organizations. Corporations lack rights such as the Fifth Amendment right against self-incrimination[17] and the liberty right resulting from the due process clause.[18] Dissenting in *Citizens United*, Justice John Paul Stevens verged on sarcasm when discussing the idea of which rights should remain unavailable: "Under the majority's view, I suppose it may be a

First Amendment problem that corporations are not permitted to vote, given that voting is, among other things, a form of speech."[19] (Corporations cannot vote because the Court has ruled they are not citizens under the Fourteenth Amendment.)[20] The set of rights that protect criminal defendants are particularly helpful in understanding when corporations have constitutional rights and why they sometimes do not.

When Do Corporations Have Constitutional Criminal Procedure Rights?

There are many Bill of Rights provisions that apply to criminal prosecutions, and they have been interpreted to offer a wide range of protections. Corporations do not have a right against self-incrimination, as they have no will to be overborne by a psychologically or physically coercive inquisitor. But corporations are entitled to a jury trial under the "reasonable doubt" standard, even if few corporate defendants risk a trial as Arthur Andersen did. During criminal investigations, corporations have Fourth Amendment rights to be free from unreasonable searches and seizures, but government officials may broadly use subpoenas to obtain records from companies, and a more intrusive search might be "reasonable" for a corporation.

Is there any rhyme or reason to these varying protections? Focusing chiefly on First Amendment cases such as *Citizens United*, scholars have called the Court's approach "ad hoc," "right-by-right," "arbitrary," and inconsistent.[21] Criminal prosecutions may best show consistencies in the Court's approach, as there are so many different criminal procedure rights, and criminal cases most clearly raise the interest of the government in holding corporations and individuals accountable. Generally, the Supreme Court focuses on what the particular constitutional right is, examining "the nature, history and purpose of the particular constitutional provision."[22] Unless the organization is an association that represents the interests of its members and can sue on their behalf, an organization or corporation is considered legally separate from individuals. Whether it can assert a constitutional right is a separate question.[23] The Court has also long tried to ensure that individual wrongdoers cannot hide behind a corporation or use it to avoid responsibility for crimes. More generally, the Court also tries to keep organizations from using the corporate form to shield their business activities from government regulators or prosecutors.

Due Process Rights

A host of key constitutional rights in criminal cases flow from the due process clause, which protects against government actions that might arbitrarily deprive a person of life, liberty, or property. In a 1906 decision, the Supreme Court held that the due process clause does not protect liberty interests of corporations. The liberty protected "is the liberty of natural, not artificial persons."[24] The clause does protect the property interests of corporations, and corporations have long brought challenges to legislation that might affect their economic rights.[25] In criminal cases, the due process clause ensures that fair criminal procedures are used during investigations and trials, and a corporation can claim that unfair procedures would deprive it of property in the form of a criminal fine. One remarkable case illustrates the role of these due process rights in corporate prosecutions.

A husband and wife, directors of the Grupo Internacional de Asesores S.A., decided to purchase a Ferrari for $297,500 and a $1.8 million yacht named the *Dream Seeker*. These were not for their enjoyment but for that of officials in the Mexican state-owned utility company, the Comisión Federal de Electricidad (CFE). According to prosecutors, the two Grupo directors also paid more than $170,000 worth of American Express bills for a CFE official and sent $600,000 to relatives of another. Prosecutors had been following the money trail in another bribery case, one involving the Mexican utility and ABB Inc., the U.S. subsidiary of a Swiss and Swedish multinational company.[26] In that case, the government said ABB used a Mexican middleman to pay bribes, and after his 2009 arrest, he became a cooperator in the ABB case.

Federal prosecutors said the payments and luxury gifts were bribes to win contracts for an American company, Lindsey Manufacturing. Lindsey makes, among other things, towers for electric power lines and emergency systems to bring power back on after an outage. It is based in California and has about 100 employees. It received contracts from the Mexican utility, CFE, to supply both towers and emergency restoration systems. The Grupo directors had offered to represent companies seeking business with CFE, and in May 2002, Lindsey hired Grupo to be its sales representative in Mexico, subsequently entering into about ten contracts worth about $9 million.[27] Grupo would receive a percentage of Lindsey's sales in Mexico—a 30 percent commission—so this did not come cheap; Lindsey had to raise prices.[28] Prosecutors said these commissions were laundered and used to pay for the lavish bribes and gifts to CFE officials.[29] Mexican law makes it illegal for public servants to receive such gifts, and American law also prohibits such bribes to government officials. Lindsey Manufacturing, its president, and its vice president were all soon charged with violating the Foreign Corrupt Practices Act.

The defense lawyers said their clients had not been aware that any bribes were paid in connection with the contracts, and the company was willing to take the case to trial. "We've become a nation of cooperators," one of its lawyers said disapprovingly. "We approached this case from the beginning with the attitude that we were going to fight."[30] This was the first trial of a corporation for FCPA violations, and it was a closely watched event. Few corporations risk a trial, and while a host of criminal procedure rights have been interpreted to apply to criminal investigations and trials, they can usually only be tested if the defendant does not plead guilty. Due process entitles a criminal defendant to a fundamentally fair trial, one where its guilt needs to be proven beyond a reasonable doubt, where police and prosecutors turn over important exculpatory evidence, and where prosecutors are restricted from making overly inflammatory arguments.

After a five-week trial in 2011, the corporation and employees were all convicted. The company faced large fines, and the president and vice president also faced a maximum of five years in prison. One of the Mexican sales agents was also convicted and sentenced to time already served. Assistant Attorney General Lanny Breuer announced: "Lindsey Manufacturing is the first company to be tried and convicted on FCPA violations, but it will not be the last. Foreign corruption undermines the rule of law, stifling competition and the health of international markets and American businesses." Breuer touted how the Department of Justice remains "fiercely committed to bringing to justice all the players in these bribery schemes . . . Bribery has real consequences."[31]

But that was not the end of the story. The defense made motions to overturn the verdict, arguing the government had not produced key evidence until the trial. They were relying on a due process right. The Supreme Court held in *Brady v. Maryland* that the government may not hide from the defense important evidence showing innocence or undercutting its case. If it violates the *Brady* rule, the verdict may be reversed.

The focus of the complaint was on the grand jury proceedings. An FBI special agent told the grand jury that one of the defendants, when asked about the bribery, responded that he "didn't want to know." Yet the interview contained no such statement, and the agent had not even been present when the interview took place. The court later described the agent's testimony as "inept, evasive, self-serving and incomplete."[32] Grand jurors were understandably interested in whether Grupo paid bribes from the money it received from Lindsey, and the FBI agent told them "there were essentially no other funds" in Grupo's account or that Lindsey had supplied "90, 95 percent of the funds." Earlier sworn statements instead made clear that Lindsey's money accounted for only 70 percent of the funds. Indeed, there had been a major $433,000 deposit right around the time of the Ferrari purchase—a deposit that was not from Lindsey. The FBI agent was kept off the prosecutors' witness list, and the defense did not know if the agent would be called at trial. The defense also complained that the agent's grand jury testimony was only disclosed mid-trial when the judge ordered the defense be given a copy.[33]

That grand jury testimony had other inconsistencies. The agent had said Lindsey was no longer the lowest bidder on contracts yet still somehow got them. Lindsey countered that the government knew it had no competitors in Mexico at the time, since the only other company that made similar electric towers had stopped doing so.[34] In November 2008, two of Lindsey's buildings were apparently searched without a warrant. The affidavit supporting the warrant described large payments by Lindsey to a Panamanian corporation, an allegation that the prosecution later admitted to be false.[35] An inconsistency emerged in an affidavit by another FBI agent, but the prosecutors said this was because a prosecutor reviewing it was new to the case and had made a mistake.

The judge angrily concluded: "The government has acknowledged making many 'mistakes,' as it characterizes them. 'Many' indeed. So many, in fact, and so varied, and occurring over so lengthy a period (between 2008 and 2011) that they add up to an unusual and extreme picture of a prosecution gone badly awry."[36] The judge announced a tentative decision and then gave the sides a chance to weigh in on whether the conviction should be thrown out. After conducting hearings, the judge explained:

> In this Court's experience, almost all of the prosecutors in the
> Office of the United States Attorney for this district consistently

display admirable professionalism, integrity and fairness. So it is with deep regret that this Court is compelled to find that the Government team allowed a key FBI agent to testify untruthfully before the grand jury, inserted material falsehoods into affidavits . . . improperly reviewed e-mail communications between one Defendant and her lawyer, recklessly failed to comply with its discovery obligations, posed questions to certain witnesses in violation of the Court's rulings, engaged in questionable behavior during closing argument and even made misrepresentations to the Court.

The judge assumed the company had the due process right, under *Brady v. Maryland*, to have exculpatory evidence turned over to it by the prosecution. The Supreme Court has never addressed this question, but it would certainly be disturbing if the government could hide evidence of innocence in corporate trials. The judge finally concluded the misconduct was so "flagrant" and the need to deter prosecutorial misconduct so great that he had to take the "drastic step" of ordering the entire case dismissed with no retrial.[37]

Another high-profile corporate prosecution unraveled in 2009. W. R. Grace faced fines of up to $1 billion for environmental crimes regarding asbestos contamination of a small Montana town. At trial, the judge learned that prosecutors had failed to provide the defense with information about the government's relationship with its star witness. The judge instructed the jury that "the Department of Justice and the United States Attorney's Office have violated their constitutional obligations to the defendants, they have violated the Federal Rules of Criminal Procedure, and they have violated orders of the Court." Calling this an "inexcusable dereliction of duty," the judge struck part of the witnesses' testimony, and told the jury to view it with "great skepticism."[38] The jury ultimately acquitted W. R. Grace.[39]

The Department of Justice has had other scandals concerning failure to turn over exculpatory information, including in high-profile prosecutions such as that of the late U.S. senator Ted Stevens. Journalists uncovered how prosecutors had known for years that hundreds of cases were tainted by flawed forensic testimony of analysts working for the FBI. Several of those cases later came to light because DNA tests showed innocent people had spent decades in prison for crimes they did not commit. Prosecutors knew of the problem beginning in the mid-1990s, but they kept their investigation of the cases from the public and defense lawyers. In 2012, the FBI agreed to do an audit of hundreds and maybe thousands of affected cases.[40] The Justice Department has responded that such problems can be prevented by training and supervision within prosecutors' offices.[41] It is extremely important when well-resourced defendants bring prosecutorial misconduct to light, as there may be more such errors in everyday cases than we suppose. This is another reason it would be troubling if corporations could not protest if given an unfair trial. Both corporations and individuals alike may be harmed by arbitrary government action violating due process rights.

Fourth Amendment Rights

Corporations can protest against unreasonable searches and seizures—they have some privacy rights under the Fourth Amendment—but key Supreme Court rulings give the government extremely broad authority to search corporations. The Fourth Amendment protects "the right of the people to be secure in their persons, houses, papers, and effects, against unreasonable searches and seizures" and also requires that warrants be properly supported, including by "probable cause." Yet Fourth Amendment law is notoriously detailed, and the Court interprets it by balancing individual privacy interests against the interest of law enforcement in solving crimes. As a result, the same rules that apply when police seek to arrest a person or search a car do not apply to business records.

The Fourth Amendment law that applies to corporations, in a way, is incredibly simple. One key rule matters: the government can use official requests for documents, called subpoenas, very broadly. Government investigations of corporate conduct often involve searches designed to examine business premises and obtain business records. In white-collar prosecutions, as law professor William Stuntz put it, "the damning documents may be everything—there is no equivalent to crime scene evidence, and witnesses are typically involved in the crime."[42] For regulators, information is "the fuel without which the administrative engine could not operate."[43] A government investigation usually begins with sending subpoenas to request records; recall that when the Securities and Exchange Commission sent its subpoena to Arthur Andersen, the document shredding suddenly ground to a halt. Later, prosecutors themselves sent out subpoenas seeking additional information about who had done what at Andersen. The firm objected, arguing that the subpoenas were too broad, and that once the grand jury had indicted the company, prosecutors could not keep using the grand jury to send out more subpoenas. The trial judge disagreed, stating that the subpoena power is broad, and "as anyone following the news is fully aware, the collapse of Enron has spawned a complex and seemingly ever expanding investigation involving a wide range of parties."[44]

Such subpoenas seeking business records do not bring up the same privacy concerns as the search of a person on the street or a seizure from inside someone's home. A subpoena asks that the person or company do the search itself and provide officials with the documents requested. The Supreme Court has ruled on corporate challenges to regulatory subpoenas for over a century, when some of the first large federal regulatory agencies became active. In a very early decision in 1886, the Court ruled in *Boyd v. United States* that a subpoena for customs invoices need not be responded to at all since it sought "a man's private papers."[45] Yet those were not particularly "personal" or private papers; they were business invoices relevant to whether a company was illegally importing goods. With the rise of modern federal agencies designed to regulate commerce, the Court abandoned that rule in 1906, ruling in *Hale v. Henkel* that a corporation must comply with reasonable subpoena requests.[46]

Perhaps best known is the *Morton Salt* decision in 1950, in which the Federal Trade Commission was investigating salt producers, some of which challenged subpoena requests. The Court held that "corporations can claim no equality with individuals in the enjoyment of a right to privacy."[47] It has consistently said that a company must comply with a subpoena that is "not too indefinite" and seeks "reasonably relevant" information within the authority of the regulatory agency. This is true even if the subpoena was based on nothing more than "official curiosity." After all, companies have a "collective impact on society" and should not have "an unqualified right to conduct their affairs in secret."[48]

Agencies have very broad subpoena powers. The Administrative Procedure Act, which provides rules for all federal agencies, provides that any subpoena can be issued by an agency so long as it shows "general relevance" and a "reasonable scope of the evidence sought."[49] Individual agencies have a broad mandate to investigate. For example, the SEC has the power to investigate "as it deems necessary to determine whether any person has violated, is violating, or is about to violate" the securities laws or regulations.[50] Just sending out a subpoena can have a major impact. It signals the launch of an official inquiry, and failure to comply may be obstruction of justice. A subpoena can also affect the reputation of an individual or business. As one journalist commented, "In the minds of the reading public," a subpoena with your name on it "means that you're guilty."[51]

When government officials want to do a physical search, they must usually get a warrant from a judge first.[52] The context matters, including whether the company is already regulated and watched over by bureaucrats. If inspectors are already monitoring aspects of what the company does, then no warrant may be required to conduct a search; the Supreme Court has said "it is the pervasiveness and regularity of the federal regulation that ultimately determines whether a warrant is necessary to render an inspection program reasonable under the Fourth Amendment."[53] For example, mines or licensed liquor or gun dealers can be inspected without a warrant, but Occupational Safety and Health Administration inspectors need a warrant due to the huge number of workplaces the agency can inspect.[54]

The Dow Chemical Company brought a Fourth Amendment challenge to a search of a chemical manufacturing plant in Midland, Michigan, that sprawled over 2,000 acres.[55] Dow was concerned with secrecy at the plant and maintained "elaborate security" at the perimeter; it would even investigate any low aircraft flights above the factory. While Dow ensured the buildings were all covered, some of the manufacturing equipment between the buildings was not covered due to cost and safety—in the event of a malfunction or explosion, a cover would trap chemicals and harm employees. The Environmental Protection Agency was concerned with whether two power plants on the site complied with environmental rules. They asked to do an on-site inspection, and Dow agreed. However, Dow did not consent to a second inspection. Instead of seeking a warrant, the EPA hired an aerial photographer to fly over the site with a precision aerial mapping camera (these were the days before Google Earth).

When Dow learned that the EPA had ordered these flights, it sued in federal court, claiming that its Fourth Amendment rights had been violated. It argued that according to the common law as well as the Supreme Court's modern rulings, the "curtilage," or the land right around a house, is protected in its privacy. This means police cannot hide in the bushes right outside a window and say they are no longer in a private area. Dow argued that the machinery around its factory buildings deserved similar protection. The district court ruled for Dow, but the appeals court rejected Dow's arguments, noting "the peculiarly strong concepts of intimacy, personal autonomy and privacy associated with the home," whereas Dow's facility was a massive industrial complex.[56]

The Supreme Court also decided against Dow. It emphasized that corporations do have some Fourth Amendment privacy rights, saying, "Dow plainly has a reasonable, legitimate, and objective expectation of privacy within the interior of its covered buildings." But "the photographs here are not so revealing of intimate details as to raise constitutional concerns." Other situations may raise business privacy concerns, such as an "electronic device to penetrate walls or windows so as to hear and record confidential discussions of chemical formulae or other trade secrets." By contrast, Dow's outside facilities were more like an "open field" that could be seen by all, or at least from open airspace. The Court's decision appeared to offer less protection to a business, even one that was strenuous in trying to protect its facility from prying eyes.

Even the physical search protections mentioned in the *Dow* ruling do not help corporations much if officials can obtain a warrant. After immigration officials raided the Agriprocessors meat packing plant in Postville, Iowa, as discussed in Chapter 4, the company disputed the validity of the warrant that allowed authorities to search the plant and arrest hundreds of undocumented immigrant employees. The warrant said Immigrations and Customs Enforcement officials had permission "to enter the buildings and areas on the premises" and then "to make such search as is necessary to locate aliens present in the United States without legal authority and who are employed at present within Agriprocessors, Postville, Iowa." The judge rejected all of the company's Fourth Amendment arguments, pointing out that the Court "has made clear over the past 100 years that corporations do *not* enjoy the same right against unreasonable searches and seizures under the Fourth Amendment as natural persons enjoy." The company also argued that the warrant was not specific enough, but the judge said it was plenty specific.[57]

Fifth Amendment Rights

There is at least one constitutional right that corporations unquestionably do not have. One of the oldest lines of Supreme Court cases denies any type of company or organization constitutional rights under the Fifth Amendment's protection against a person being "compelled in any criminal case to be a witness against himself."[58] The Supreme Court first grappled with this issue in *Hale v. Henkel*, the same case that forced corporations to comply with subpoena requests. The government issued a subpoena to the MacAndrews & Forbes Company, a New Jersey corporation, as part of an antitrust investigation (the Sherman Antitrust Act had been passed in 1890). The request was broad: all documents or correspondence between the company and six other companies, and all letters it had received from a dozen other companies in seven states since it was incorporated.

The person serving as secretary and treasurer of the company refused to comply with this request. At the grand jury, he stated his name, residence, and job title, but "he declined to answer all other questions in regard to the business of the company, its officers, the location of its office, or its agreement or arrangements with other companies." He cited the corporation's Fourth Amendment and Fifth Amendment rights and said that the answers to the request would tend to incriminate him. The judge held him in contempt.

The Supreme Court ruled that the company had no Fifth Amendment right against self-incrimination and the corporate officer could not refuse to provide documents on Fifth Amendment grounds. The Court emphasized that if corporations had these rights, they would be able to hide crimes of employees, as corporations can never themselves be forced to testify in a courtroom. "Were the cloak of the privilege to be thrown around these impersonal records and documents, effective enforcement of many federal and state laws would be impossible," the Court noted. After all, "the corporation is a creature of the state." This allows the government to readily compel corporations to produce their records.

Companies cannot refuse to comply with document requests from officials or prosecutors, even if those documents might end up incriminating the individuals who must respond, with only narrow exceptions.[59] The Supreme

Court has emphasized its simple rule: "corporate records are not private." Any other approach "would have a detrimental effect on the Government's efforts to prosecute 'white-collar crime,' one of the most serious problems confronting law enforcement authorities."[60] The Supreme Court denies self-incrimination rights not just to corporations but also to any other type of "collective entity" or organization, even small firms such as a three-person partnership. So long as it is not a mere "loose, informal association of individuals," it lacks Fifth Amendment rights.[61]

The real reason for the lack of Fifth Amendment rights may be that the Fifth Amendment is about preventing individual people from being compelled to incriminate themselves, not to keep individuals or corporations from incriminating others. In the more recent case of *U.S. v. Hubbell*, the Court said the "act of production" defense does not apply to a corporate officer being asked to produce records. This defense allows individuals to avoid providing documents when doing so would incriminate them personally, but a corporation cannot hide documents by asserting the rights of employees.

For similar reasons, the Supreme Court in 2011 ruled that AT&T could not object to a Freedom of Information Act request for documents it had provided to the Federal Communications Commission Enforcement Bureau, since the statutes referred to "personal privacy, and corporations do not have privacy.[62] Chief Justice John Roberts explained, "We do not usually speak of personal characteristics, personal effects, personal correspondence, personal influence, or personal tragedy as referring to corporations or other artificial entities." He added, "This is not to say that corporations do not have correspondence, influence, or tragedies of their own, only that we do not use the word 'personal' to describe them." After all, the choice of the phrase "personal privacy" instead "suggests a type of privacy evocative of human concerns—not the sort usually associated with an entity like, say, AT&T."[63]

Sixth Amendment Rights

A corporation has the right to have a lawyer represent it; obviously a company or organization cannot appear except through a representative. But what if the entity lacks the funds for a lawyer? Must the court appoint one? The Sixth Amendment right to have a defense lawyer appointed in a felony case is one of our most fundamental protections and dates back the landmark 1963 ruling in *Gideon v. Wainwright*. However, Congress has not provided funds to appoint lawyers to defend corporations,[64] and judges have ruled that corporations lack a Sixth Amendment right to appointed counsel. For example, one federal court of appeals ruled that a corporation "cannot litigate in a federal court unless it is represented by a lawyer."[65] The court concluded: "Pro se litigation is a burden on the judiciary, and the burden is not to be borne when the litigant has chosen to do business in entity form. He must take the burdens with the benefits." In a few cases, judges have said that a company with one owner (a sole proprietorship) may have a court-appointed lawyer.[66] One court also indicated that pretrial seizure of assets can violate a corporation's Sixth Amendment right to obtain counsel with its own money.[67]

Can a corporation claim that its lawyer provided ineffective assistance? That is the most common claim by individuals in habeas proceedings, that the trial lawyer made blunders in the courtroom or failed to sufficiently investigate the case. In one case, a corporation claimed its lawyer never disclosed a conflict of interest—but the judge concluded that "the government has no responsibility to ensure that a corporation is represented by competent counsel."[68] The judge concluded that the two officers "jointly decided to plead the corporation guilty, and both fully understood the consequences. No one was in a better position to understand the unlawful ways in which they had utilized the corporation than they were." The judge said another lawyer would not have "insisted on going to trial rather than pleading guilty."[69]

The Sixth Amendment also provides a right to confront witnesses against the criminal defendant. Courts have suggested that corporations have this right as well, but the situation is complicated where the witness is an employee who may have committed the crime for which the company is being prosecuted. The Sixth Amendment confrontation right does not do much to help corporations in that context.[70] The employee may assert Fifth Amendment privilege against self-incrimination, but prosecutors can introduce prior statements by this employee, as they can for any admissions by employees of the corporation.

Eighth Amendment Rights

The Eighth Amendment states that "excessive bail shall not be required, nor excessive fines imposed, nor cruel and unusual punishments inflicted."[71]

Companies cannot be put in heinous prison conditions involving "unneces-sary and wanton infliction of pain," nor can they be sentenced to be drawn and quartered, tortured, or executed,[72] and while the Supreme Court has increasingly regulated punitive damages awards against corporations, it has rejected any "cruel and unusual punishment" basis for those decisions, rely-ing instead on the due process clause. The excessive fines clause of the Eighth Amendment has been of equally little value to corporations looking to chal-lenge fines.[73] The *Southern Union* case now regulates the calculation of fines in criminal trials, so perhaps the Court will have no reason to address whether very large criminal fines could violate due process or be "cruel and unusual" or excessive and violate the Eighth Amendment.

Double Jeopardy and Acquitted Corporations

When a jury acquits, it is a major blow to prosecutors, especially given the small number of criminal trials. When the jury acquitted Richard Scrushy, the CEO of HealthSouth, this was perceived as a major defeat. Corporations can also be acquitted, and like individual defendants, having been tried once, they cannot be criminally tried again for the same offense (at least not by fed-eral prosecutors). The Supreme Court has suggested in passing that corpora-tions benefit from double jeopardy, and judges have accepted this ever since.[74] Double jeopardy, however, does not bar the government from pursuing sepa-rate civil charges, and this explains why parallel proceedings are common.[75] Nor does double jeopardy prevent state and federal prosecutors from sepa-rately pursuing charges, or prevent both the parent company and a subsid-iary from facing charges if they are separate companies.[76]

As a result, double jeopardy provides little protection to most corpora-tions. Since there are only a handful of corporate trials annually, corporate acquittals are rare. Each year, though, a jury may acquit a corporation or two, and more corporate cases are dropped by prosecutors or dismissed by judges. The Sentencing Commission keeps no data on this, but I have found more than a dozen examples of corporate acquittals, including that of Stora Enso North America.

The Stora Enso trial was short, in some ways simple, and remarkable for happening at all. The case involved companies that made glossy coated paper for magazines and high-volume catalogues.[77] It is a multibillion-dollar industry. Stora Enso Oyj is a Finnish company and Stora Enso North America is its U.S. subsidiary. Along with its competitors, it raised prices beginning in August 2002. After being indicted in 2006 under antitrust law, it argued there was no evidence that the company and its competitors "made any commitments or promises to one another." The case went to trial in 2007 in Hartford, Connecticut, and the company faced a $10 million fine if convicted.[78]

The Sherman Antitrust Act forbids competitors from entering agreements to set their prices. It may be hard to find out if companies fix their prices, but in the Stora Enso case, the Antitrust Division had given leniency to a competing Finnish company, which reported the scheme and cooperated with prosecutors.[79] The president of Stora Enso was "old friends" with the president of the company that turned in Stora Enso in exchange for amnesty.[80] But Stora Enso would not admit guilt and decided to risk a trial.

The prosecutors began the trial by saying their evidence would come from two presidents: the president of the competing company's magazine division and a former president of Stora Enso North America.[81] Both had the final authority to set prices and both were receiving leniency in exchange for their cooperation and admissions of guilt. The prosecutors explained that "two presidents of two huge billion dollar corporations" would admit they had been "talking to each other at least six times within seven months" after not having "talked to each other about pricing for over 20 years."[82] This occurred just a few months before Stora Enso raised its prices.

The first witness was the president of the Finnish competitor, who described multiple conversations with the president of Stora Enso. They talked about how bad prices were for glossy paper. The best-selling type of paper, called "coated #5," was used in magazines such as *Time* and in ads for retailers such as Kmart and Target. Prices for this paper had fallen 20 percent that year and were still falling. The dot-com industry had collapsed and the economy was doing badly, so less advertising was being printed in magazines.[83] An American company named International Paper had the largest share in the market, and the two competitors talked about how International Paper had announced a price increase of $60 per ton and whether they should match the increase.[84] They had a "kind of a common understanding" that they would follow International Paper's lead.[85] However, the

competitor's president also said his company had decided on its own to follow the price increase even before calling the president at Stora Enso. On
the other hand, he admitted he hoped that his friend at Stora Enso would
raise prices too.[86]

The next day saw the second president testify, the former head of Stora
Enso North America. He described social get-togethers with his counterpart and complaining together about low prices. He also described a final
telephone call where he said Stora Enso "had decided to announce the price
increase." He recalled it was "comforting" to know a big competitor was increasing prices as well. He also admitted knowing it was "poor judgment" to
talk about prices with a competitor, and that it violated company policy—a
"Taboo Chart" of things not to do, which said, "Don't set prices or verify the
activities of our competitors by calling competitors."[87]

The trial was not long, and on the fourth day, the sides gave their closing
arguments. The defense lawyer argued this whole case put a "cloud" over
an innocent company.[88] There had been just a brief phone call—"less than
15 words" long—in which Stora Enso said it "already matched" the others'
prices. The defense emphasized that "there's a reason big companies and
smart companies do the same thing. Because it makes sense." After all,
prices were the "lowest in twenty years," and the prosecution theory was
"like saying two thirsty men in the desert would have to conspire to drink
water." The theme of the defense was "Price following is not price
fixing."[89]

The judge instructed the jury that a corporation is "entitled to the same
presumption of innocence as a private individual." A corporation can be
found guilty only "if the evidence establishes its guilt beyond a reasonable
doubt." The judge explained that competitors must have been "acting together" and not just engaged in similar conduct.[90] The jury knew the competitor had received amnesty—neither it nor its employees would be prosecuted if they cooperated.[91] The judge also instructed the jury that witnesses
who receive amnesty may have "a motive to testify falsely."[92]

The jury acquitted. Perhaps the jurors agreed there was not enough evidence of a mutual agreement to raise prices. This was not a case like Arthur
Andersen, in which the case was close because the evidence was so complex;
this was a case where the jury, with close evidence, decided there was not
enough to convict.

A Theory of Constitutional Rights of Corporations

Some argue that it is nonsensical for corporations to have constitutional rights, at least under amendments designed to protect individual liberty. The Supreme Court has recognized a wide range of constitutional rights that apply to organizations even as it has declined to recognize others. There *is* some reason to these rulings, and a look at the rights related to criminal procedure illustrates this well. In the past, the justices on the Court have been sensibly concerned with the purpose of each constitutional right and making sure that those rights do not, when exercised separately by corporations, allow them to undermine the rights of individuals or hide conduct from the government. That explains the Court's Fourth and Fifth Amendment rulings, as each ensures government officials have broad access to corporate records. The rulings jibe with the central purpose of corporate criminal liability: to make sure individual people are accountable and that corporations as a whole are accountable for the crimes of their employees. With corporate rights come responsibilities. However, the *Southern Union* decision suggests that the Court could be moving away from a view that constitutional rights ensure corporate accountability. The ruling helps corporations when calculating fines in both negotiations with prosecutors and in the rare cases that go to trial. We may see much more constitutional litigation by corporations in the years to come.

❧ 9 ❧

Foreign Corporate Criminals

British Airways Flight 195 landed at George Bush Intercontinental Airport in Houston, Texas, for a brief layover on its way to the United Kingdom. The feds were waiting.

On the plane were the CEO and directors of BAE Systems plc, the third-largest defense contractor in the world and the largest military contractor in Europe. When they disembarked, armed federal officers took the CEO to an interrogation room. For twenty minutes, he and the others were searched, their documents copied, and their laptops and cell phones downloaded. They got served with subpoenas to appear before federal grand juries.[1]

These searches stemmed from a sale of seventy-two Eurofighter jets in a massive $80 billion arms deal with Saudi Arabia, a deal known as Al Yamamah ("the dove" in Arabic).[2] The Saudis had signed this deal with BAE in the 1980s, and there were allegations that it was secured through bribes and lavish entertaining of visiting royalty in London. The allegations and criminal investigation would precipitate a diplomatic firestorm and would eventually lead the United Kingdom to adopt one of the toughest bribery laws in the world.

For years it had seemed like the authorities would quietly bury the Al Yamamah investigation. The United Kingdom made no arrests. British authorities at the Serious Fraud Office (SFO) long had had a hesitant approach toward corporate bribery; the SFO had investigated several matters but was not bringing prosecutions.[3] High-level officials had counseled against pursuing this particularly sensitive case, but U.S. prosecutors were now threatening to blow it wide open.

A Foreign Corporation

In the past, domestic prosecutions of foreign corporations were not noteworthy. Foreign nations did not complain that the United States inappropriately prosecuted their firms or questioned their criminal law or its enforcement. Foreign companies did not complain about being held accountable for crimes far outside their home county. All of this has changed. Federal prosecutors now advertise how they target foreign companies, with the Department of Justice publicizing its goal to "root out global corruption."[4] The U.S. attorney for the Southern District of New York, Preet Bharara, explained that "crime has gone global and national security threats are global."[5] In response, corporate prosecutions have gone global as well.

U.S. prosecutors target foreign corporations more than ever before, and the average fines levied against foreign corporations are far larger than for domestic ones. These prosecutions have had an outsized impact and are reshaping industries around the world. Foreign firms and their employees are increasingly convicted of a range of crimes including antitrust violations, violations of the Bank Secrecy Act, environmental crimes, violations of the Foreign Corrupt Practices Act, tax fraud, and wire fraud. Thirteen percent of the 2,262 corporate prosecutions between 2001 and 2012 that I studied were foreign corporations (13 percent, or 283 of 2,262 companies). Most of these foreign firms were convicted of just a few major crimes, which are the focus of this chapter: antitrust (78 companies), ocean pollution (73 companies), and FCPA violations (48 companies).

How do U.S. prosecutors even go about targeting foreign corporations? There are several ways for them to get jurisdiction over foreign companies whose foreign employees committed crimes in foreign countries. These include jurisdiction based on the company listing stock publicly in the United States, owning U.S. subsidiaries, or committing criminal acts in the territorial United States. But having jurisdiction does not make it easy to investigate foreign corporate crime. Take the BAE case: the key evidence was likely abroad, such as in BAE's London offices. Prosecutors also face serious diplomatic issues. I will describe how, despite the challenges, U.S. prosecutors have taken on significant prosecutions of foreign firms and even entire industries.

Foreign corporations often do not receive deferred prosecution or nonprosecution agreements. Only about one-fifth of the deferred prosecution and non-prosecution agreements involved foreign companies (21 percent, or 54 of 255 agreements). And of the foreign companies prosecuted between 2001 and 2012, less than one-fifth received deferred prosecution or non-prosecution agreements (19 percent, or 54 of 283 foreign companies). The rest of those foreign companies were convicted. Foreign corporations also were subject to much larger fines than domestic firms. A big part of the story of this book— the rise in the size of corporate fines over the past decade—is the rise in big prosecutions of foreign corporations. Figure 9.1 shows this rise, with a remarkable increase to over $3 billion in fines against foreign companies in 2012.

What explains the size of these foreign corporate fines? That is a puzzle. I did not expect to see such a big difference between domestic and foreign corporations, since very large companies in the United States are also prosecuted. But when I examined more than 2,250 corporate prosecutions over the past decade, I found foreign firms received an average fine of $35 million and made an average total payment of almost $66 million. The comparison with domestic firms is stark, as they received an average fine of $4.7 million and made an average total payment of $12 million.

I wondered whether the differences could have to do with other characteristics of the cases. I used regressions to control for the type of crime and whether the company was public or not, but even taking those factors into account, foreign corporations still paid larger fines on average. For otherwise comparable firms, foreign firms received fines that were on average over *seven times* larger and made total payments over *nine times* larger than was the case for domestic firms. The results of these regressions are detailed in the

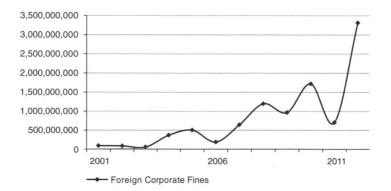

Figure 9.1 Foreign Corporate Fines, 2001–2012

Appendix. This raises the question of whether prosecutors single foreign companies out. Or could foreign firms be the worst violators? If so, why were they prosecuted so infrequently in the past? Perhaps something else accounts for why so many of the biggest corporate prosecutions now involve foreign companies. I will look at several possible explanations, but there are no definitive answers to this puzzle.

As with so many of the problems explored in this book, there is no single coordinated approach used by prosecutors when targeting foreign corporations. How prosecutors actually exercise their discretion is something of a black box, since we have so little information about why they make their decisions. The outsized role played by prosecutions of foreign corporations suggests we need to know far more about how prosecutors pick and choose their corporate cases. The success stories in these foreign prosecutions, which involve so many practical challenges, suggest something else: that domestic corporate prosecutions could be handled far more aggressively than they so often are.

To back up further: what is a foreign corporation? In my analysis of corporate prosecutions from 2001 to 2012, I focus on the 283 companies that were incorporated abroad. That does oversimplify matters. How about a multinational company listed on multiple stock exchanges around the world—where is its home? For example, seventy-three of these foreign companies had stock listed in the United States. What if such a firm has a wholly owned U.S. subsidiary? What if most of the shareholders or owners of a company are foreign? A law that was proposed but never passed, the DISCLOSE Act, would have defined a foreign corporation as one that was incorporated overseas or 20 percent owned or de facto controlled by foreign citizens.[6] I focus here on companies such as BAE that are incorporated abroad, but also include information about domestic companies owned by a foreign subsidiary. BAE is named for a merger of British Aerospace and Marconi Electronic Systems, both British companies. BAE's headquarters are in London, and it is listed on the London Stock Exchange, but it is a multinational firm, with stock traded in the United States using American Depositary Receipts (ADRs). It owns Lockheed Martin Aerospace Electronic Systems and Armor Holdings, both U.S. companies, and it does a fair amount of business in the United States, including defense contracting, for which, as a foreign corporation, it needs special security clearances.

Holding foreign corporations accountable for violating U.S. criminal laws can be difficult. It may be hard for prosecutors to get jurisdiction in the

United States over employees and documents, and sending agents to search foreign offices may be out of the question. Prosecutors increasingly convince foreign companies to turn themselves in or incentivize whistle-blower employees to do so.

The Travel Agent

The Travel Agent was no ordinary tour planner. He provided holidays that were "way beyond the life style of most film stars" for special BAE clients, including months-long vacations for Saudi royalty involved in the Al Yamamah arms deals.[7] The vacations were worth millions, but arms deals were worth billions. The Travel Agent also chartered an entire Boeing 747 cargo plan for a shopping spree of a Saudi prince's wife. Ever thoughtful, he sent another prince's wife a Rolls-Royce on her birthday. Saudi pilots visiting London were treated to nights on the town, while Saudi embassy employees received gold cutlery.

Uncovering corporate crimes committed by foreign companies in foreign countries is not easy. BAE was not paying lavish bribes out in the open. BAE apparently created a front corporation with a high-security vault in Switzerland, where it stored financial information. The front was registered in the British Virgin Islands, where there would be no need to show BAE owned it. BAE systems paid The Travel Agent and other such agents through Swiss bank accounts and offshore companies.[8] BAE used travel agents to distribute about $225 million in bribes, calling it "accommodation and support services." The bribes may have been paid elsewhere around the world, including the Czech Republic, Hungary, Tanzania, and others.[9]

In 2004, The Travel Agent leaked evidence of his dealings to a British newspaper, which passed it on to the SFO. In response, BAE called the allegations "ill-informed and wrong."[10] The documents from this whistle-blower, however, led the SFO to multiple slush funds and offshore businesses. They discovered how hundreds of millions of dollars had been diverted to Saudi Arabia's Prince Bandar, including through an account jointly used by BAE and the British Ministry of Defense, and revealed lurid allegations about how those funds were used to entertain Saudi royals visiting the United Kingdom.[11] Now the SFO wanted to see the Swiss banking records.

The British and Saudis each had a stake in any investigation of the matter. In 2005, BAE wrote a letter to the British attorney general suggesting that investigating further would jeopardize the Al Yamamah contract, which was still being negotiated. When the investigation continued, BAE wrote another memo, which was presented to the prime minister, foreign secretary, and defense secretary, emphasizing the need not to upset Saudi Arabia, "a key partner in the fight against Islamic terrorism." SFO investigators continued looking into Swiss bank accounts to follow the money trail, apparently prompting a more explicit threat of Saudi withdrawal from counterterrorism cooperation agreements and an end to Al Yamamah. In December 2006, the SFO ceased its investigation into Al Yamamah, explaining it was "necessary to balance the need to maintain the rule of law against the wider public interest."[12]

American Exceptionalism

In 1990, Justice William J. Brennan, Jr. deplored the extraterritorial expansion of federal criminal law, stating that "the enormous expansion of federal criminal jurisdiction outside our Nation's boundaries has led one commentator to suggest that our country's three largest exports are now rock music, blue jeans, and United States law."[13] Few foreign countries have anything like the broad standard for corporate criminal liability that the United States has long had in federal courts. Common law countries such as Australia, Canada, New Zealand, and the United Kingdom have some form of corporate criminal liability, but in England, for example, the concept remains quite narrow.[14] Most civil law countries in Europe, Latin America, and elsewhere had no corporate criminal liability for many years; they viewed holding an artificial entity criminally liable as odd and morally problematic. In the past few decades, more European countries have created corporate crimes, partially in response to calls from the European Union and Council of Europe for some form of corporate criminal accountability. Countries in Asia (including China, India, Japan, and Korea), the Middle East (including Israel, Qatar, and the United Arab Emirates), and Africa (including South Africa) have adopted some form of corporate criminal liability.

Although more countries have adopted corporate crimes, they are very limited compared to the strict federal standard in the United States. Countries usually limit criminal liability to conduct involving specific crimes or "leading persons" such as high-level officers.[15] Many other countries remain steadfastly opposed to any criminal liability for corporations; for example,

Brazil and Germany lack criminal liability, although they do have administrative penalties that can be imposed on corporations in cases involving criminal conduct.

Foreign companies may resent or simply misunderstand the U.S. approach due to unfamiliarity with strict corporate criminal liability and having never encountered before the broad power of federal prosecutors. When foreign companies have tried to push back, the consequences have not been good for them. Corporations have some incentive to cooperate with local regulators, but cooperating with U.S. prosecutors is imperative. Not only is there broad liability for corporations in the United States for the criminal acts of employees, but federal criminal law is also broader and far more punitive than that in other countries. Moreover, U.S. prosecutors are simply more powerful than most prosecutors elsewhere in the world. They possess extraordinarily wide discretion, and the adversarial system in the United States creates an unusually prosecution-friendly dynamic by placing great discretion in the hands of prosecutors—which also gives corporations more to gain by cooperating. In civil law countries, prosecutors lack the same leverage, as judges marshal the evidence, review charges, facts, and sentences, and exercise great discretion at each stage. Now that U.S. prosecutors have targeted more foreign corporations than ever before, foreign companies and governments must reckon with the new U.S. approach toward prosecuting corporations. The result can be a culture clash.

The British Drop It

The British did not want to pursue the salacious bribery allegations involving their biggest defense contractor. Another inquiry began in the Serious Fraud Office, but after two years, that investigation was dropped also, with Prime Minister Tony Blair explaining in 2007 that the investigation "would have been devastating for our relationship with an important country with whom we cooperate closely on terrorism, on security, [and] on the Middle East Peace process."[16] A legal challenge brought in the United Kingdom argued that the SFO ignored the public interest when dropping the case. The judge agreed, finding the SFO had effectively caved in to political pressure from the Saudis and that the rule of law had been damaged by "abject surrender" to a "blatant threat" from the Saudis. The head of the SFO admitted that dropping the investigation "went against my every instinct as a prosecutor." The case went to the House of Lords, which in its role as a final court of appeals upheld the authority of prosecutors to decide whether or not to bring a case, particularly where national security could be at risk.[17]

The U.S. State Department spoke out against the British failure to investigate BAE, and by then the Department of Justice had begun to investigate. British officials rebuffed a DOJ request for assistance.[18] Lacking any cooperation from BAE or the British government, the DOJ obtained testimony from a former BAE executive, who described hundreds of millions of dollars in bribe payments. This led to the episode in the Houston airport where BAE's CEO and directors were detained, searched, and issued subpoenas.

Hoping to ward off a U.S. prosecution, the SFO revived the case and planned a settlement. But the status of any such settlement was thrown into doubt by a ruling from a U.K. judge in another case that prosecutors had no authority to enter a plea bargain, as only a court could impose a sentence.[19] A conviction in the United Kingdom could have had dire consequences, because under European Union law, BAE could be debarred from government contracting. The impasse continued between U.S. and U.K. prosecutors.[20] Which country would budge?

The Babe Ruth of Whistle-blowers

The largest individual whistle-blower payment ever made by the U.S. government went to a man who had just spent two years in prison. Bradley Birkenfeld helped wealthy clients avoid U.S. taxes by using Swiss bank accounts, but by becoming a whistle-blower, he collected a $104 million whistle-blower award.[21] He told reporters: "I'm the most famous whistle-blower in the history of the world. It's a question of doing the right thing, and that's what I did." His lawyer called him "the Babe Ruth of whistle-blowers."[22]

Whistle-blowers are not usually welcomed with open arms by their bosses. "Usually, whistle blowers get fired. Sometimes, they may be reinstated. Almost always, their experiences are traumatic, and their careers and lives are profoundly affected."[23] The law can try to protect whistle-blowers or reward insiders who bring misconduct to light. Under long-standing statutes, persons known as qui tam plaintiffs can file actions reporting fraud against the federal government.[24] The Securities and Exchange Commission now has a dedicated Office of the Whistleblower because the Dodd-Frank legislation, passed in the wake of the last financial crisis, provides for a reward to anyone who brings to the SEC's attention "original" information leading to a penalty of more than $1 million, and the whistle-blower can file a lawsuit and recover 10–30 percent of the money.[25] The SEC can share whistle-blower information with prosecutors, and companies cannot retaliate against the employees who provided that information. Other agencies also have whistle-blower provisions; the Internal Revenue Service has long had them, and in 2006 the IRS rules were strengthened to provide enhanced cash rewards to whistle-blowers.[26]

The stereotypical image of bankers may be one of conservative number crunchers wearing green eyeshades, but Birkenfeld, living in Switzerland since the late 1990s, worked with a group of bankers more reminiscent of James Bond. Their version of special operations facilitated tax fraud. Birkenfeld was one of dozens of bankers of UBS AG, the largest bank in Switzerland, who traveled across the United States seeking out wealthy clients and advising them on how to hide their money from the IRS to avoid paying taxes. The bankers would travel anonymously, claiming on customs forms that they were traveling for pleasure. UBS agreed in 2001 to disclose to the IRS information about its clients moving income from the United States into offshore bank accounts. However, Birkenfeld was told to continue his work. UBS was managing over $20 billion of assets belonging to clients in the United States, euphemistically calling it "United States undeclared business."[27]

The bankers would host extravagant parties to lure rich potential clients. UBS sponsored events at the Art Basel festival in Miami, Florida, or at tennis tournaments. The bank later admitted to the widespread use of sham accounts to conceal assets of U.S. citizens seeking to evade taxes. It actively marketed the "Swiss Solution," assisting rich clients to hide assets in offshore dummy corporations set up in Panama, the British Virgin Islands, Hong Kong, Liechtenstein, and of course Switzerland. They would explain to their clients that they should store art, jewelry, and other valuables in safe deposit boxes in Switzerland, destroy all records of their offshore accounts, and use Swiss credit cards that the U.S. government would not track down.[28]

Birkenfeld personally took checks from clients to Switzerland. Most notoriously, he smuggled diamonds for a client by hiding them in a tube of toothpaste.[29] However, before resigning in 2005, he wrote memos to higher-ups telling them that they were violating U.S. tax laws. As he later put it:

When I put my concerns in writing to the UBS legal and compliance departments in Switzerland, they refused to address any of my concerns. So I proceeded to invoke my UBS rights to protect against retaliation and send my same written concerns to the general counsel of UBS.[30]

When no changes were made, he concluded there was a "cover-up," and he "was determined to contact the U.S. authorities to expose this scandal."[31] While his now former employer was sending him letters threatening him with prosecution if he divulged information, he decided to tell U.S. prosecutors what UBS was doing—in part because the new whistle-blower statute for tax fraud removed the $10 million cap on whistle-blower rewards, and provided for a maximum reward of 30 percent of the back taxes recovered.[32]

This left him in a bind. In Switzerland, where he lived, it was against the law to violate bank secrecy—"if I divulged any names without a subpoena I would go to jail." In 2008, he traveled to the United States to meet with the SEC and the U.S. Senate—and to go to a high school reunion. He was arrested when he exited his plane in Boston.[33] After his arrest, though, he agreed to continue cooperating with the government, and he met with prosecutors to describe in detail the tax fraud schemes, the amounts of money involved, and the activities of the bankers. He also provided names, internal procedures, emails, and other documents.

What he did not tell them was that he had also engaged in tax fraud, including with a wealthy Florida real estate developer who for a time was his biggest client of all. The bankers had helped the client set up offshore accounts, transfer ownership of his yacht to Gibraltar, and ultimately conceal $200 million in assets.[34] They helped him get UBS credit cards. After that real estate developer pleaded guilty (and paid over $50 million in back taxes), Birkenfeld was prosecuted for conspiracy to defraud the United States, and in particular the IRS, and he pleaded guilty.

Prosecutors asked for his sentence to be reduced, citing the "substantial assistance" he had given them: "Without Mr. Birkenfeld walking into the door of the Department of Justice in the summer of 2007, I doubt as of today that this massive fraud scheme would have been discovered." They would not have prosecuted him at all had he told them about his own criminal conduct.[35] While $104 million was a huge whistle-blower award, the U.S. government could use his information to collect billions in unpaid taxes from UBS—or at least it could try.

Would UBS Settle?

Swiss banks are known for their commitment to customer privacy. As Birkenfeld knew, it is a crime in Switzerland to violate client confidentiality, though it is not a crime to fail to disclose assets or income. Only what Swiss law terms tax fraud, which is defined as willful conduct, is illegal. UBS would either have to violate Swiss banking privacy laws or face prosecution in the United States. U.S. prosecutors said UBS had violated U.S. law—but to make it right, the company was being asked to violate Swiss law. UBS was now in the same bind as its banker. Which country's law would win out?

United States and Swiss law directly conflicted, but no court reviewed the case, as UBS settled on the eve of U.S. Senate hearings. The United States obtained only 150 names of U.S. citizens who were UBS clients, and those individuals promptly sued UBS in Switzerland for violating Swiss bank secrecy laws. In 2009, UBS signed a deferred prosecution agreement with federal prosecutors in the Southern District of Florida. The company paid prosecutors $780 million in fines and agreed to cooperate by divulging the names and accounts of the U.S. customers it assisted in avoiding taxes in the United States.

The IRS, meanwhile, continued to pursue a civil action seeking information on 52,000 account holders. UBS angrily responded that this request "simply ignores the existence of Swiss law and sovereignty." It added, "To the extent that the IRS is not satisfied with treaties that the U.S. government has negotiated, that concern should be remedied through diplomacy, not an enforcement action." A DOJ official responded that it was "not going head to head with the Swiss government." Yet the Swiss government was an integral part of negotiations with the IRS, the DOJ, and UBS. And they did go head to head.

In August 2010, the IRS finally received an agreement to obtain the names of 4,550 account holders from among the tens of thousands with such accounts. The Swiss government stated that it would only disclose accounts larger than 1 million Swiss francs or with certain types of false documents or account activity. The Swiss government would also allow taxpayers an opportunity to file administrative appeals of the decision to disclose their account information. Indeed, a special task force was set up to expedite appeals, and new judges were hired to help handle such appeals.

The IRS responded with another technique, declaring an amnesty program that allowed account holders who voluntarily disclosed offshore accounts and agreed to pay back taxes to avoid prosecution and higher penalties. More than 14,000 people came forward during the amnesty. Other Swiss banks asked clients to waive confidentiality requirements, fearing that they too might be prosecuted. The settlement did not provide all that either side desired. Most remarkable, though, was the degree to which it involved a diplomatic resolution. Such sensitive issues can be handled in a variety of ways when they come up. The DOJ has an Office of International Affairs that coordinates international agreements, among other foreign-policy-related efforts. In some areas, formal treaties or mutual assistance agreements provide for cooperation at the enforcement level, or more informally, prosecutors collaborate with international organizations or foreign law enforcement. Even in the area of corporate prosecutions, prosecutors are an eclectic bunch. Different types of prosecutions are handled by different groups of prosecutors within the DOJ working with different regulators and using different rules. One size does not fit all.

Magic Pipes

The M/T *Kriton* is a large oil tanker vessel, 600 feet long and weighing 42,000 deadweight tons. In March 2007, it was docked in New Haven, Connecticut, during a trip delivering fuel and diesel up and down the East Coast. The ship was flagged from the Bahamas and managed by a Greek company, Ionia Management, S.A., which operates a fleet of ocean vessels. There were twenty-three crewmembers on board.

On March 20, 2007, a Coast Guard officer received a phone call from The Electrician on the *Kriton*, reporting that the ship was dumping oily water illegally at sea. The Electrician was from the Philippines but spoke English; although the chief engineer and master of the ship were Greek, as were the owners, much of the crew were Filipino, and they all spoke English. The Coast Guard officer later explained that English "is the language of the sea, for the most part now."[36]

The Electrician had sent videos from his cell phone, but they did not clearly show the sought-after "magic pipe," or hose. A team of Coast Guard officers boarded the ship to inspect the records and conduct a search. They did not find a magic pipe, but they interviewed those on board the vessel.

What is a magic pipe? It is an improper way for ships to dispose of waste. Large ships create sludge when fuel oil is purified by oil filters, and this sludge is supposed to be stored in onboard tanks and deposited in large tanks at shore when the ship docks. Ships also create oily bilge water, which, as the prosecutor later explained at trial, "is created when water at the bottom of the vessel . . . is mixed in with oil that is leaked from the extensive piping throughout the ship and the machinery that is on board such a large oil tanker vessel like the Kriton."[37] Ships discharge bilge water from their engines and other piping, and that water may include oil, lubricants, cleaning fluids, and other waste. Ships are required to monitor, store, and process these oily wastes under an international treaty concerning oil pollution at sea. In the United States, the Act to Prevent Pollution from Ships (APPS), ratified in 1980, implements the treaty.[38] The law prohibits ships in international waters, an area more than twelve nautical miles from the coast, from discharging more than fifteen parts per million of oil in wastewater. However, if the ship's equipment is not working properly, or if the crew wants to hide the extent of leaks in their engine room, or if they simply do not care about environmental rules, the crew may use a "magic pipe" or hose to dump the oily wastes overboard rather than properly store them.

Upon docking at a U.S. port, ships are required to show the Coast Guard an Oil Record Book signed by the ship's chief engineer and make their documentation, as well as the ship itself, available to the Coast Guard for inspection.[39] If foreign vessels provide the Coast Guard with false records concerning oil discharges, they may be prosecuted—not for the polluting conduct itself, which occurs on the high seas, but for making false statements to federal officials. As a result, courts have rejected jurisdictional challenges to such prosecutions, since jurisdiction is premised on false reporting while at a U.S. port.[40] Few firms contest jurisdiction, with the overwhelming majority pleading guilty, but Ionia Management took the case to trial. They were charged with conspiracy, violations of the APPS, falsifying records in a federal investigation, and obstruction of justice.

Prosecutors argued at trial that "the chief engineer and the second engineer specifically directed the engine room crew to bypass these [pollution prevention] devices by the use of a bypass hose, or what became known as a magic hose." They would "remove some of the ship's piping and the flanges that connected these pipes together," and then connect "this magic hose, which you will hear was a black rubber hose, about four to five meters long, which is about 12 to 15 feet." They would then "pump out the waste oil tank directly overboard into the sea . . . bypassing the storage tanks and the pollution prevention equipment that was on board the vessel."[41] When they reached port, the prosecutors said, they would disconnect and hide the "magic pipe," replace the stripped piping and clean and repaint it, and not tell the Coast Guard. Because it occurs in international waters, this sort of dumping can be impossible to catch.

Why did The Electrician call the Coast Guard, then? He could potentially receive an enormous bounty under the whistle-blower provisions in the APPS, which reward seamen who report oily discharges to the United States. A crewmember may receive as much as half of a criminal fine that may amount to the millions of dollars.[42] Indeed, The Electrician said one reason he reported this to the Coast Guard was that he had read a magazine article about how crewmembers could get rewards for reporting ocean dumping.[43]

The engine room on a ship like the *Kriton* is a big place. It has multiple decks, and several people work in it. When Coast Guard officers boarded, they did not find a hose, but they did find worn-out bolts on the piping, which was unusual, since they are generally not removed (unless one is improperly masking a magic pipe). When they spoke to the crew, one was "extremely nervous," and admitted that "the discharge hose would be hooked up after the ship left port and that it had been disconnected a couple of days before the ship arrived in New Haven."[44]

The trial took place in federal court in Connecticut in fall 2007. The defense lawyer emphasized in the opening arguments that the employees who had reported the discharge were "looking to cash in and get a reward" and should not be trusted. For The Electrician in particular, "one of the first things he told the Coast Guard when he called was that he was ready to accept his reward for calling, that he hopes to become an instant millionaire."[45] Others, like the second engineer, may have cooperated when they were "charged and pressured," argued the defense.[46]

Four crewmembers from the *Kriton* testified they participated in the ocean dumping. A "wiper," a low-level crewmember, and a cadet engineer described how they were the ones who actually connected the magic pipe after leaving each port. They claimed they hooked up the pipe below the engine room floor, on the orders of the higher-up second engineer. They would reconnect the pipes and repaint everything before arriving at a port. An oiler, also a low-ranking crewmember, testified that he was asked to help with "pump outs" to the sea through the pipe. The chief engineer told him that "if the Coast Guard asks any questions that [he] should say only oily water separator," and that "the separator is the only thing that is used for pumping the bilges." The second engineer also testified and said that the chief engineer specifically told him they should keep using the magic pipe. The government had more evidence as well: the Dutch Coast Guard had flown a surveillance aircraft that on January 30, 2007, used radar to take an image of the *Kriton* with an 11.7-kilometer stream of discharge trailing behind it.

The defense lawyer asked whether this magic pipe might just be imaginary: "The magic hose, where is it?" In the closing arguments, he emphasized that it is "for you," the jury, to "decide if there ever really was a magic hose."[47] After all, the Coast Guard "searched the ship high and low" and didn't find the hose. He argued the hose the crew had described couldn't reach all the way to the bilge pump: "It just doesn't make sense, does it?"[48] The Coast Guard found no oil "dripping down the outside of the ship" nor "traces of oil" inside the ship. The only evidence of a hose were photos The Electrician had taken that "showed the hose lying on top of the engine room floor."[49]

The defense argued, "Ionia shore-side management is not accused of anything wrong itself or even having any knowledge anything was wrong." The jury was told that "they are a first-rate, environmentally-friendly ship management company." Ionia's crew were "well trained" and "well aware" of Ionia's pollution prevention measures.[50]

The prosecutors responded that the company did have something to gain. ConocoPhilips, Shell, and Chevron were "paying customers" of Ionia, and if the ship does not pass the inspections, then "they don't sail" and "don't get paid. This is all about money, money and convenience at the expense of the environment." Prosecutors also responded that it was nothing special that Ionia had training and practices on disposing of oily bilge water. After all, "the fact that these environmental policies were in place to begin with is because it's required by United States law." Regardless, the policy the company had was "not worth the paper it's written on because they weren't following it."[51] Moreover, Ionia had been prosecuted for similar conduct several years before and was under an EPA consent decree from 2004–2007, with a Coast Guard auditor. Employees testified that supervisors had told them to use the magic pipe and make false entries in their records book. This violated Ionia's probation.

The jury found Ionia guilty on all counts.[52] The company paid a $4.9 million fine and was required to have a special master report to the court every six months regarding the company's compliance. From that fine, The Electrician received an award of $550,000, and the oiler and engineer who also cooperated each received $350,000. The lawyer for the engineer said this would be "a life changing experience" for his client, since the cost of living is low in the Philippines, his home country.

In 1993, the Department of Justice's Environment and Natural Resources Division, the U.S. Coast Guard, and the Environmental Protection Agency's Criminal Investigation Division began a Vessel Pollution Initiative to "detect, investigate, and prosecute illegal vessel discharges of oily wastes, plastics, and other wastes that are in violation of U.S. environmental laws."[53] The prosecutions grew from a perception that illegal dumping was "rampant and so pervasive within the maritime community." Prosecutors warned the initiative would continue until the number of referrals "dwindle[s] to zero."[54]

Over the years, prosecutions accelerated and foreign firms operating vessels increasingly faced large fines. These ocean dumping cases typically have been brought against foreign ship owners. Only 8 percent (6 out of the 79) APPS convictions I was able to locate involved domestic firms; the 73 others, or 92 percent, were foreign. Maybe this should be no surprise. Few commercial shipping companies flag or register their vessels in the United States. Many of the ship management companies are based in Greece and Hong Kong.

The Department of Justice averages approximately two to four new vessel pollution cases per month.[55] Many DOJ vessel pollution prosecutions involve falsified oil record books in addition to magic pipe allegations.[56] Often whistle-blowers on the ship send photos and videos to the Coast Guard from their smartphones. In contrast to the whistle-blowers, senior crew who fail to report as required have been prosecuted and convicted. Practitioners also attribute the acceleration of prosecutions to improvements in technology used by the Coast Guard, greater media coverage of ocean dumping, and the DOJ's increased skill in litigating such cases. Like the Ionia case, these cases are resolved by convictions, not deferred prosecution agreements. Most such as cases are brought or led by the DOJ's Environmental Crimes Section or led by them, and those prosecutors do not tend to use deferred prosecution agreements—they pursue convictions.

Antitrust Prosecutions

The lysine cartel changed the world of antitrust prosecutions. Lysine is an amino acid, an important building block for protein in our bodies. Farmers give animals feed with extra lysine added to it, and several major agricultural companies manufacture it in large quantities, along with other food additives such as citric acid. Five companies dominated the market for lysine in the late 1990s: Archer Daniels Midland (ADM) in the United States, two Japanese companies, and two Korean companies. They all eventually pleaded guilty to participating in a price fixing cartel.

The Supreme Court has called such price-fixing cartels "the supreme evil of antitrust."[57] The five companies would meet around the world to discuss the prices they would charge. This kept any one company from undercutting its rivals, allowing all of the competitors to raise prices together and reap greater profits without fear of competition.

How could prosecutors know that these secret high-level conversations were occurring? Like in the ocean dumping cases and the UBS tax fraud case, a whistle-blower came forward, in this case an ADM employee. His involvement was dramatized in a book and the movie *The Informant*.[58] He wore a wire and provided prosecutors with taped conversations of international executives fixing prices. This was the very first prosecution of an international price-fixing conspiracy, and when the case settled, ADM paid what was then the largest-ever antitrust fine at the time, over $100 million. Today this would merely be a pretty big case. But after the record fines levied in this case, there were much greater incentives for whistle-blowers and companies to report new violations. This created momentum that brought new antitrust cases to prosecutors' attention.

Antitrust cases stand out for the vast size of the fines. British Airways paid $300 million in fines in 2007, and Air France/KLM paid $350 million in 2008. Yazaki Corporation paid $450 million in 2012, taking second place behind F. Hoffmann-La Roche, which paid $500 million in 2007, and AU Optronics Corporation, which paid $500 million in 2012.[59] All of these companies pleaded guilty except AU Optronics, which was convicted after a trial. There are not many antitrust prosecutions; the largest number in a year that I found was twenty-five cases in 2012, and the average was fifteen cases per year, most of which were guilty pleas. Yet the size of the fines make the cases stand out, as the average antitrust fine is over $34 million. Figure 9.2 displays these fines over the past decade.

The biggest recent antitrust case broke open a cartel to fix prices for the liquid crystal display (LCD) panels used in laptops, desktops, and television screens—the big bump in fines in 2012 comes in large part from LCD cartel prosecutions. For years, executives at the biggest manufacturers of LCD panels conspired to keep prices up, holding "crystal meetings" monthly in hotel rooms to plan their operations. When they later worried authorities had caught wind, they sent lower-level employees to meet in public places such as karaoke bars, restaurants, and cafes.[60]

This time U.S. prosecutors found out about such secretive conduct not from an individual whistle-blower but from one of the companies involved in the conspiracy. That first company was the ultimate corporate snitch. It turned in the other members of the LCD cartel, and in exchange it received a complete pass—outright amnesty from U.S. prosecutors. That company and its employees were not prosecuted, but seven of the other companies were, and most pleaded guilty, agreeing to pay over $890 million in fines.

One of the cartel members steadfastly refused to admit guilt. In 2012, AU Optronics Corporation, the largest LCD manufacturer in Taiwan, took its

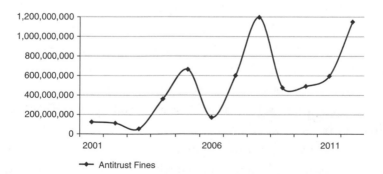

Figure 9.2 Total Fines in Antitrust Prosecutions, 2001–2012

case to a criminal trial, the first criminal trial in an antitrust case in a decade. AU Optronics lost. Three of its executives were sentenced to three years in prison, and the government asked for a $1 billion fine, which would have been the largest criminal fine ever in an antitrust case, "to underscore the seriousness of the matter."[61]

The judge noted that the defendants made "an extremely useful product" which "really has changed the world," but that this was a "serious and a far-reaching conspiracy." Further, it had "enormous" consequences for U.S. consumers. And while other companies and executives cooperated, "admitted their conduct and got out early," AU and its employees did not.[62] Yet the judge ultimately decided to reduce the fine to $500 million.

Prosecutors objected, arguing that these defendants "played pivotal roles in a global conspiracy that had an unprecedented impact on the pocketbooks of countless American consumers."[63] There were high-level executives who also had taken their cases to trial. They had not apologized. The company continued to say that what it did was not wrong or illegal; it argued that it was just exchanging market and pricing information with other companies. Prosecutors pointed out that the closest antitrust case to this one in seriousness was the ADM case that had started it all, the lysine and citric acid cartel case. But ADM had pleaded guilty and admitted responsibility—and had still been sentenced to "ten times the then statutory max." The prosecutors argued that "$500 million is not enough to deter cartels like this from forming."[64] They noted another company in the LCD cartel received a 50 percent reduction in its fine because it provided such substantial assistance to prosecutors— something that AU had refused to do. The defense lawyers countered that their client should not be punished for deciding to take its case to trial. They said that it was not fair that the first company to report was like "Clint Eastwood's empty chair in this case," receiving a complete pass.[65]

The judge concluded that a $1 billion fine, "although dramatic," was "simply substantially excessive." It just seemed like too much. The judge could have also fined AU Optronics America, the U.S. subsidiary, but that would "be piling on," as there were also civil lawsuits pending, which could result in hundreds of millions in additional fines.[66] On top of that, the judge sentenced the executives to relatively light sentences, noting that while they had made "poor choices," at the time they had felt they were "doing the right thing" for their company. These executives were not trying to take money "so that they could keep it and spend it."[67] Finally, the judge ordered AU Optronics to implement a compliance program and admit wrongdoing in "major trade publications" in the United States and in Taiwan.[68]

Price fixing cartels can be tough nuts to crack. As in the lysine and LCD cartels, high-level executives can operate in secret. There are very few deferred prosecutions in antitrust cases, as prosecutors do not reward compliance or best practices. Instead, they use leniency as a weapon. The way to penetrate those smoke filled rooms is to use the ultimate snitches: the cartel members themselves. The idea is simple, giving members of a price fixing cartel more incentive to defect and stop charging artificially high prices. The Antitrust Division at DOJ exclusively brings antitrust prosecutions, together with field offices specializing in antitrust. To harness those incentives between competitors, the Antitrust Division adopted a remarkable approach known as the "Corporate Leniency Program."[69] The first company to report on the others in the cartel can receive leniency in the form of complete amnesty for turning the others in. The Corporate Leniency Program was first created in 1978, and significantly revised in 1993 to make participating more attractive,[70] giving automatic and complete amnesty to the first reporting firm, if it cooperates. Having been turned in by one of their own, the other cartel members have every incentive to plead guilty and cooperate rather than face a trial. One may never publicly hear which that first reporting company was—it is the "empty chair" in the case—but the competitors are typically convicted of crimes and pay large fines. Indeed, to further encourage self-reporting antitrust crime, the DOJ now provides credit, though not full amnesty, to a "second-in" or subsequently reporting cartel member that cooperates fully after the first obtains amnesty.[71]

This is the clearest approach to corporate prosecutions that any group of prosecutors has devised. The goal is to break up cartels, not a vague desire to improve corporate compliance. Antitrust Division prosecutors do not impose corporate monitors. They do not normally impose detailed compliance requirements. They use a hammer to smash cartels. Unless self-reporting first, violators receive harsh penalties. Even if other crimes do not have the same incentive structure as a cartel, prosecutors could adopt a similarly clear policy of promoting self-reporting and effective compliance, while making the consequences of hiding violations severe. One lesson from these antitrust cases is that treating the cases as criminal and insisting on convictions has not discouraged self-reporting. Quite the contrary.

Over the past decade, enforcement against foreign firms has accelerated as the DOJ focused on prosecuting larger and international cartels. Of the antitrust prosecutions in my data, 45 percent were foreign companies (78 of 175 companies). International cartel cases account for more than 90 percent of fines imposed.[72] An Antitrust Division diagram displaying prosecutions with fines over $10 million, includes firms with household names: British Airways, DeBeers, and Samsung Electronics. Only 16 of the 112 firms fined over $10 million were domestic.[73] The result has been record fines at a level so threatening (or so desirable) that more foreign countries are trying to pass antitrust laws that mirror those in the United States. As the laws of other countries converge with those of the United States, there has been more cooperation among prosecutors globally, and corporations have more incentives to self-report both at home and to U.S. authorities.

Prosecutors have actively tried to spread their gospel. The Antitrust Division made a major priority of promoting international cooperation and convergence, including by working with the International Competition Network and the OECD. Such efforts have accompanied a "convergence in leniency programs," in which at least forty-eight other countries adopted such programs. This "made it easier and more attractive for companies to simultaneously seek and obtain amnesty in the United States, Europe, Canada and other jurisdictions."[74] Such programs allow a company to avoid the danger of others self-reporting and the firm then facing civil and criminal enforcement in multiple jurisdictions. The convergence of law enforcement has included cooperation agreements, coordinated and parallel investigations, and prosecutions. The United States informally cooperates and shares information with other jurisdictions so that a firm can make simultaneous amnesty applications to multiple authorities.

The leniency program also provides strong incentives for individual employees to defect and report. A company obtaining leniency also obtains it for employees, officers, and directors. In addition, a 1994 DOJ policy gave leniency to individuals who report cartel behavior.[75] Success builds on success, and each conviction reinforces the strength of these leniency policies. As other countries cooperate and adopt parallel approaches, convergence may encourage still additional self-reporting by foreign and domestic firms.

FCPA and Other Criminal Statutes

Federal prosecutors pursue charges of foreign bribery under the Foreign Corrupt Practices Act. These cases have been few in number but stand out for the size of their fines. Fewer than 100 companies have been prosecuted under the FCPA since 2001, but these cases have an average fine of $27 million. Recall the case that I began this book with, in which Siemens paid a $450 million criminal fine in the largest FCPA case of all time. Siemens is by no means the only major company to settle foreign bribery charges, as a mounting number of the biggest prosecutions of public companies are FCPA cases. I found that of the FCPA cases brought from 2001 to 2012, about half were foreign companies (49 percent, or 48 of 97 companies).

The FCPA makes it a crime to "corruptly" pay certain types of bribes to foreign officials. Its civil accounting provisions also oblige companies that issue stock in the United States to keep accurate books and records and maintain a system of internal accounting controls.[76] The SEC also has authority to enforce the FCPA civilly, a power shared with the DOJ, but only the DOJ can prosecute criminal FCPA violations.

Why prosecute bribery that occurs in other countries? Prosecutors argue that corruption is bad for business and undermines democracy and the rule of law. There is evidence that bribery and corruption are rampant in some parts of the world, although it is obviously difficult to measure such behavior. A 2011 survey by Dow Jones, for example, found that 40 percent of surveyed companies reported losing business to competitors that used corruption.[77] A study of reported bribery cases by public companies found that the median bribe was $2.5 million and that firms gained $11 for every dollar they spend in bribes.[78]

The FCPA is not a new law. It was passed in 1977, in the wake of the Watergate scandal and revelations that corporations regularly bribed government officials.[79] Yet only 25 corporations were prosecuted for violating the FCPA before 1998, when an international treaty on corruption was signed: the OECD Convention, now ratified by thirty-eight countries.[80] Parties are required to institute "effective, proportionate, and dissuasive" criminal penalties for the bribery of foreign officials.[81] In 1998, the FCPA was amended in part to comply with the OECD Convention.[82] The amendments made the FCPA much broader, expanding the coverage of the statute and providing for wider "alternative jurisdiction" over extraterritorial acts by domestic firms. The amendments require that a foreign company with stock listed in the United States "make use of the mails or any means or instrumentality of interstate commerce" in furtherance of the bribery acts, but that a foreign company that does not have stock listed in the United States must do so "while in the territory of the United States."[83]

With other major countries agreeing to enforce anti-corruption and anti-bribery laws, it became more palatable for the United States to get more aggressive. Siemens had been paying bribes around the world for decades, but once doing so was against the law in Germany, U.S. prosecutors eventually intervened. Not only are FCPA prosecutions a major DOJ priority, but the FBI and SEC created units dedicated to FCPA investigations.[84] There has also been a rise in prosecutions of individual employees for FCPA violations. As Figure 9.3 shows, the numbers of FCPA corporate prosecutions have increased from a handful each year to more than twenty.

More and more cases fall into the laps of U.S. prosecutors. Companies now frequently self-report to avoid the harsh consequences of a prosecution.[85] As DOJ deputy chief Mark Mendelsohn put it, "If we call them before they call us, it's not where they want to be."[86] The FCPA also has an unusual structural provision, pursuant to a 1988 amendment, that adds a different sort of deference to corporate actors. Unlike in typical criminal cases, potential violators can seek written opinions from the DOJ as to whether a

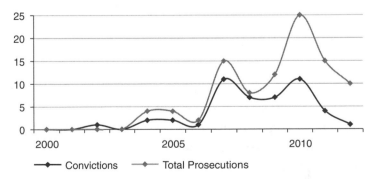

Figure 9.3 Numbers of FCPA Corporate Prosecutions, 2001–2012

transaction violates the FCPA.[87] The DOJ has thirty days to issue an opinion, and if the DOJ says the transaction is allowable, it is a binding decision that creates a presumption that the transaction complies with the FCPA. This notice procedure had been little used in the past, but opinions have been solicited more often in recent years. The DOJ and SEC have also offered guidelines on the FCPA to give more notice to companies. They emphasize that companies should adopt "risk based" compliance programs by dedicating more resources to compliance in high-risk countries.[88] As with antitrust and ocean dumping cases, success generates further success for prosecutors. More companies have incentives to self-report if they fear the consequences of employees (like The Banker at Siemens) or competitors reporting them first.

However, FCPA prosecutions are far more muddled affairs than antitrust or environmental prosecutions. The prosecutions sometimes resulted in a conviction (in 34 cases), but an increasing number resulted in a deferred prosecution or non-prosecution agreement (63 cases). There is no clear reason that explains whether a company receives a deferred prosecution agreement filed with a court, or a non-prosecution agreement not filed with a court, or a plea agreement resulting in a conviction. And many FCPA cases are just handled by the SEC as civil cases. From 2001–2012, the SEC brought 92 cases against companies, though in 61 of those cases, there was also a prosecution. Only a third of the SEC's FCPA cases (31 of the 92 cases) were unaccompanied by a criminal prosecution.

While the SEC can impose a fine, civil fines averaged less than half of the criminal penalty. For example, Baker Hughes was fined $11 million by prosecutors, but the SEC imposed no penalty. Syncor paid $2 million to prosecutors and only $500,000 to the SEC. The civil penalties were almost entirely disgorgement of profits and interest; the SEC is hamstrung by legislation that permits only fairly small penalties in most civil cases beyond disgorgement of profits.[89] That helps to explain why it may have so often been necessary to bring a criminal prosecution alongside the SEC case, as the SEC may feel it simply cannot impose adequate fines on its own. In criminal enforcement of the FCPA, with the far larger fines, 36 percent of the firms involved (35 of 97 firms) were foreign. In SEC civil enforcement, 28 percent (26 of 92 firms) were foreign.

Although the DOJ and SEC provided long-awaited guidance on the FCPA, they have not established clear guidelines on what kind of corporate prosecution agreements are appropriate and or on what types of compliance can best prevent foreign bribery. While deferred prosecution and non-prosecution agreements often talk about the need to audit compliance or assess the risk of corrupt practices in a given country, there is no detail normally provided about how to do that. There is not research or performance evaluation of how well these anti-corruption practices work. Yet prosecutors give substantial leniency when they impose fines in FCPA cases, often giving credit for work to implement new compliance remedies. The result is a lack of an adequately principled and clear approach to corporate FCPA prosecutions. Self-reporting and cooperation should be strongly rewarded, as in antitrust cases, but otherwise, egregious failures of compliance should result in serious structural reforms and fines.

Prosecutors enforce a range of other criminal statutes against foreign companies. Even in cases involving the FCPA or antitrust violations, more typical federal crimes (conspiracy, wire and mail fraud, or RICO charges) may accompany the primary charges. Another related family of statutes has to do with international commerce: crimes related to import and export violations, which may directly implicate foreign firms moving goods internationally. It is also a crime to violate international sanctions. Other statutes aim to prevent the use of financial institutions to transfer illegal funds, including transfers abroad, related to banking fraud, money laundering, and material support of terrorism, as well as illegal imports and exports. Adopting a still different approach in support of terrorism cases, the State Department designates organizations for which material support is forbidden, but only after a process that includes notice and consultation with the Attorney General, Department of the Treasury and Congress.[90]

Jurisdiction

Prosecutors have been able to get jurisdiction over foreign companies, even for conduct by foreign employees that primarily occurred in foreign countries. "Corporations are often present in many countries," as the Supreme Court has noted, yet the Court does not typically presume that a U.S. law reaches corporations that are active outside the United States or conduct that occurred abroad, nor does it presume even that "mere corporate presence" in the United States suffices.[91] However, the reach of U.S. criminal law is broad. Some criminal laws, such as the FCPA, explicitly apply to foreign companies

and conduct. Foreign firms that list securities in the United States are considered "present" in the United States, and they agree to be subject to SEC
disclosure requirements that can prompt self-reporting and then prosecutions. As the Court noted in a case involving securities listed in the United
States, harm to stockholders in the United States may be direct regardless
whether the company is domestic or foreign.[92] Jurisdiction is also straight-
forward if foreign companies commit crimes in U.S. territory. Cases involving reports of oil discharge made to U.S. authorities, cartels that fix
prices for goods bought by U.S. consumers, or failure to report bribes in
reports to the SEC all directly implicate U.S. jurisdiction. Absent direct
harm felt in the United States, jurisdiction may also be premised on a "pro-
tective principle" if there is a potential harm to U.S. interests or national
security.[93]

Nor is there any such thing as international double jeopardy. Federal prosecutors can proceed even if foreign prosecutors already prosecuted the company. Federal prosecutions may choose to abstain in this situation, but they
are not required to do so. As the Supreme Court has often emphasized, "the
very nature of executive decisions as to foreign policy is political, not judicial."[94] In civil antitrust prosecutions, for example, the Court ruled in *Hartford Fire Insurance Co. v. California* that a foreign firm may be prosecuted despite the fact that its home nation has different antitrust rules, unless the firm
would be held to completely incompatible norms of conduct.[95] Prosecutors
may take foreign prosecutions into account in other ways. A settlement in
the Akzo Nobel N.V. case imposed a fine, but just on the condition its subsidiary did not pay fines to the Dutch Public Prosecutor. Ultimately, the
DOJ imposed no additional penalty after the firm settled with Dutch authorities.[96] The Statoil case, however, saw a prosecution go forward against a
company majority-owned by the government of Norway that had already
been prosecuted and fined $3 million in Norway. A U.S. prosecutor empha-
sized that "the Department will not hesitate to enforce the FCPA against
foreign-owned companies."[97]

Prosecutions are a quintessential exercise of U.S. sovereign power. Some
commentators have argued that extraterritorial jurisdiction in the United
States can benefit countries that lack effective, fair judicial systems for resolving commercial disputes. Others decry the rising globalization of litigation
involving foreign plaintiffs and defendants in U.S. courts.[98] Criminal cases

are not like cases brought by private litigants, whose choice of a U.S. court might undermine foreign policy; it is prosecutors within the executive branch who choose to bring a criminal case. And given that most companies settle their criminal cases, a judge may not have an opportunity to answer questions of jurisdiction. Most important are the practical obstacles to investigating foreign corporate crimes, and the diplomatic issues a prosecution may raise.

Cooperation

Cooperating with foreign prosecutors can make actions against foreign corporations far more likely to go forward. The largest example of such cooperation is the investigation into oil companies that participated in the U.N. Iraq Oil for Food program. "Conceivably the largest international anti-corruption investigation ever," this inquiry, led by former Federal Reserve chairman Paul Volcker, "implicated 2253 companies worldwide and $1.8 billion in alleged 'kickbacks' to the Iraqi regime of Saddam Hussein," and involved the DOJ, the SEC, "two U.S. Attorney's Offices, four congressional committees, the Manhattan District Attorney's Office, the Department of Treasury's Office of Foreign Asset Control, the United Nations, and at least six foreign governments, to date."[99]

The Independent Inquiry Committee that initially led the investigation was convened by the United Nations with an international membership. Its findings led to investigations in a number of countries; DOJ investigations resulted in FCPA prosecutions and deferred prosecution agreements with firms that participated in the Iraq Oil for Food program. Additional non-FCPA prosecutions were brought by the Manhattan District Attorney's Office. Not all prosecutions of foreign firms are federal, but because of the diplomatic issues involved, foreign prosecutions by state or local prosecutors have typically been conducted in conjunction with federal counterparts.

Diplomacy and the Swiss Banks

The negotiations that finally resulted in a settlement with UBS, the largest bank in Switzerland, did not completely resolve matters. A Swiss federal administrative court ruled that UBS could not disclose the name of a U.S. taxpayer, reasoning that Swiss law does not prohibit tax evasion. The deferred prosecution agreement and IRS settlement suddenly appeared at risk. Prosecutors said they would renew their suits should UBS not comply. Negotiations continued. The result was an agreement between Switzerland and the United States, approved by the Swiss Parliament in June 2010, amending an earlier treaty to allow more exchange of information on potential tax evaders.[100] The prosecution was ultimately resolved not just through standard law enforcement but with a treaty.[101]

UBS still faced the wrath of wealthy former clients in the United States, some of whom sued UBS, arguing that they suffered because of the services UBS provided to help them avoid taxes. The appellate court threw out their lawsuit in 2012, calling it a "travesty" and saying, "It is very odd, to say the least, for tax cheats to seek to recover their penalties . . . from the source, in this case UBS, of the income concealed from the IRS."

Meanwhile, prosecutors are still using information from UBS clients to pursue other foreign banks. Deutsche Bank entered a non-prosecution agreement with the DOJ with a penalty of over $550 million, and Wegelin & Company, Switzerland's oldest private bank, pleaded guilty to tax fraud and paid $74 million.[102] Wegelin had even tried to lure some of UBS's clients after UBS was prosecuted; Wegelin's website had proclaimed, "Neither the Swiss government nor any other government can obtain information about your bank account." There had been few tax prosecutions of foreign firms in the past, but that is changing, and Credit Suisse and other Swiss banks or banks with branches in Switzerland are under investigation. In 2013, Liechtensteinische Landesbank AG, a bank based in Liechtenstein, entered a non-prosecution agreement and paid more than $23.8 million.[103] Tax prosecutors announced a settlement program that provided leniency in the form of non-prosecution agreements for banks that came forward before 2014, noting that any banks that did not disclose their role in helping individuals avoid U.S. taxes would be treated more harshly.[104] All of these prosecutions have placed pressure on the Swiss government to allow Swiss banks to give more information about their clients to U.S. authorities. A new tax treaty is in the works, and total fines paid by the Swiss government for tolerating tax evasion could total $10 billion.[105]

Global Fallout: Siemens and BAE

What about Siemens, the case that I began this book with? Did the company enjoy "global peace" once it settled with U.S. prosecutors, as I described in the introduction to the book? It seems Pax Americana may not be enough for a multinational firm: Siemens now faces prosecutions in other countries, and it has already settled an action in Greece.[106] Apparently the United States and German governments, after the Siemens bribery case came to light, sent information uncovered in their investigation to officials in China. Chinese authorities then prosecuted two executives at state-owned telecommunications firms, with one sentenced to death.[107] Authorities in Brazil settled a potential prosecution after Siemens self-reported evidence concerning bribery in that country.[108] Siemens's compliance program also uncovered and reported a new bribery case in its Kuwaiti unit.[109] Perhaps this is no surprise. The legacy of years of global bribery does not disappear with one U.S. prosecution agreement, even a massive one.

As for BAE, after years of stalled investigations its case came to a swift conclusion in February 2010. BAE Systems PLC, the U.S. subsidiary of BAE, entered a guilty plea with the DOJ and admitted to violating the Arms Export Control Act and making false statements to the government concerning FCPA compliance. BAE Systems agreed to pay $400 million in fines, create a compliance program to detect FCPA violations, hire a corporate monitor, and enter three years of corporate probation. With the U.S. subsidiary pleading guilty, however, the parent avoided a conviction entirely. As in the Siemens agreement, the BAE agreement provides that the monitor be a U.K. citizen, approved by the United Kingdom and with appropriate security clearance as required by Her Majesty's Government.[110]

The United States is the leading exporter of corporate criminal law. Countries influence each other's criminal law by example, cooperation, and diplomatic pressure. The United States applies soft forms of pressure by sharing resources and training with foreign prosecutors as well as wielding the hard threat of a U.S. prosecution. U.S. prosecutors also sometimes face diplomatic pressure from other countries in high-profile cases, and we may see more pressure from other countries as the criminal law policy and practice of nations becomes increasingly connected. After all, the United States depends on cooperation of other nations in a host of enforcement efforts. Prosecutors increasingly collaborate on international work, assisted by treaties cementing norms against corruption and fraud. There may then be more prosecutions by foreign prosecutors, including of U.S. companies. For example, Nigeria brought criminal charges against the U.S.-based Halliburton for bribery, which ended with a $35 million settlement.[111]

We may see more foreign corporate monitors as well. In addition to the Siemens case, the Alcatel-Lucent case also involved a foreign monitor, this one appointed in France. France has a "blocking statute" that prohibits sharing confidential economic information outside the country, so a monitor reporting to the DOJ and the SEC in the United States might have violated French law. High-level meetings with French Ministry of Justice officials and judges were needed to work out how the monitor would be able to function effectively.[112]

I began this chapter by noting that foreign companies received larger fines than comparable domestic firms. There is not one single explanation for this. A central problem with data in cases that prosecutors decided to bring is that we do not know what types of cases prosecutors declined to bring. I do not want to suggest that foreign firms are somehow being singled out unfairly, as they could be selected for good reasons, including because they are the worst violators. Perhaps many thought they could avoid U.S. criminal law in the past, and U.S. prosecutors have now sent a message that this has changed. Prosecutors may simply not bother to go after a foreign firm except in a very serious case, due to the practical obstacles in targeting foreign corporations. As noted, one obstacle can be jurisdiction, but since it may be premised on the foreign firm having stock listed in the United States, as a result, prosecutors may more easily target the largest public foreign companies. U.S. prosecutors may also view foreign civil penalties as an inadequate punishment in the most serious cases, resulting in larger average fines. Domestic companies may better understand how to garner leniency by cooperating with U.S. prosecutors than their foreign competitors. This may be changing, and perhaps criminal fines against foreign companies will no longer be so prominent in the future. After all, international cooperation was a big part of the story I have told, in which treaties and cooperation helped pave the way for prosecutors to take on more foreign companies.

If you can't beat them, join them—that may be the thinking of prosecutors in other countries. The United Kingdom changed much about its approach in response to the BAE case, and in late 2012, it decided to permit deferred prosecution agreements. Perhaps had that tool been available earlier, it could have prosecuted BAE without seeking a conviction and remained sensitive to Saudi interests. Other countries are considering using deferred prosecutions as well.

In July 2011, the United Kingdom put into effect a far tougher Bribery Act regulating payments to foreign officials.[113] The Serious Fraud Office adopted guidelines that mirror Department of Justice guidelines for corporate prosecutions, including rewards for self-reporting and the use of monitors—a British equivalent of deferred prosecutions. In the foreword to the new Bribery Act, Justice Secretary Jack Straw emphasized that "the UK is determined to work closely with its international partners to tackle bribery."[114] Perhaps a sign of things to come, rather than prosecute Innospec Inc. for foreign bribery in 2007, the DOJ referred the case to the United Kingdom's SFO, which obtained a guilty plea.

Now that the United States and United Kingdom share a similar approach, fewer tensions may result from corporate prosecutions. If other countries adopt the U.S. approach to corporate prosecutions, there may be more room for collaboration, less work for U.S. prosecutors, and stronger incentives for corporations around the world to adopt compliance programs and governance reforms.

The U.S. approach to negotiating corporate prosecutions is fairly new and much of it remains untested. All of the problems described earlier in this book should give us more pause, especially once we realize that while the new non-prosecution approach to corporations has taken hold, corporate prosecutions by federal prosecutors have gone global. As a global leader, the United States now bears a special responsibility to lead by example by ensuring we all get corporate prosecutions right.

That said, not only are foreign prosecutions some of the largest ones, with ambitious goals to reform entire industries, but they are brought in areas in which prosecutors seek stringent punishments. For example, antitrust cases tend to involve corporate convictions, while environmental cases tend to require judicially supervised monitors, and FCPA cases tend to specify that compliance be audited. The areas dominated by foreign corporate prosecutions show how prosecutors can insist on convictions and court-monitored compliance, perhaps without overly discouraging corporations from reporting their crimes and cooperating. There are real lessons to be learned for domestic prosecutions from the ways that against all odds, U.S. prosecutors have successfully targeted companies around the globe.

❧ 10 ❧

The Future of Corporate Prosecutions

"It could potentially cost a fortune. Would really appreciate any help . . ."

During the previous week, a trader at a major international bank had emailed a coworker who submitted interest rate estimates, telling him, "We have an unbelievably large set on Monday . . . We need a really low fix."

When Monday came, the trader sent a reminder that "the big day has arrived" and his New York counterparts "were screaming at me about an unchanged" rate. The submitter duly altered his estimate, acknowledging that it wasn't "what I should be posting."

The trader was appreciative: "I agree with you and totally understand. Remember, when I retire and write a book about this business your name will be in golden letters."

"I would prefer this not be in any books!"[1]

Now it is in a book. Before, during, and after the global financial crisis that began in 2007, a group of major banks were gaming the system. The trader sending those messages worked at Barclays Bank PLC, a financial services firm headquartered in London. He and others asked their counterparts at other banks to manipulate an important banking rate known as the London InterBank Offered Rate, or LIBOR.

LIBOR, a measure of how costly it is for banks to borrow money from each other, is used in hundreds of trillions of dollars' worth of transactions each year. Other rates, such as the Euro Interbank Offered Rate (EURIBOR), are related to it. Banks use LIBOR to set interest rates for futures and options, including three-month Eurodollar contracts sold on the Chicago Mercantile

Exchange—the largest futures market in the world, with a value of over $550 trillion in 2011.[2] Everything from commodity trades to student loans, mortgages, and credit cards relies on those benchmark rates as a reference. LIBOR is like a barometer that measures changes in pressure on the global money markets. It may be the "world's most important number."[3]

The British Bankers Association set LIBOR rates daily by asking a group of sixteen banks to estimate what they would pay to borrow funds from another bank. The association would exclude the highest and lowest estimates, and the rate was set based on the average of the rest.[4] The banks were supposed to submit a rate based on their own fair estimates, but emails and texts captured how the submissions were anything but fair.

In another email exchange in 2006, the same Barclays trader said (referencing the three-month Eurodollar contracts): "We're getting killed on our 3m resets, we need them to be up this week before we roll out of our positions. Consensus for 3m today is 4.78–4.7825, it would be amazing if we could go for 4.79 . . . Really appreciate ur help mate."

"Happy to help," emailed the other banker in response. That day, Barclays submitted a rate of 4.79 percent, the rate its traders were hoping for.

Other emails and instant messages said it was "very important that the setting comes as high as possible. . . . thanks," and "I . . . dont [sic] want to loose [sic] money on that one," and "Seriously, thanks a million dude." Always friendly, one banker responded to a request for a lower EURIBOR submission by noting, "We always try and do our best to help out . . ." Another responded, "Done . . . for you big boy . . ." More formally, another responded, "Always happy to help, leave it with me, Sir." The mood could even be celebratory, as in 2006, when a Barclays trader told a counterpart banker, "Dude I owe you big time! Come over one day after work and I'm opening a bottle of Bollinger! Thanks for the libor." The other trader replied, "Know [sic] worries!!!"[5]

Despite their poor spelling and grammar, the bankers gamed rates high and low to make profits. The goal changed after the worldwide financial crisis hit in 2007, as bankers made efforts to push rates lower to appear more stable and not admit to higher borrowing costs than other banks. Apparently management wanted Barclays to remain "within the pack" and keep its "head below the parapet" so it would not get shot off. In early 2008, for example, one Barclays banker admitted that the "honest truth" about Barclays' actual borrowing rates could be a "can of worms."[6]

A senior Barclays employee raised concerns in December 2007:

> My worry is that we are being seen to be contributing patently
> false rates. We are therefore being dishonest by definition and
> are at risk of damaging our reputation in the market and with
> the regulators. Can we discuss urgently please?

A meeting was called with a senior compliance officer and someone from management, which was followed by a report to the U.K. Financial Services Authority that tough market conditions might be altering the LIBOR submissions, and that there might be "problematic actions" by other banks as well. They later told regulators, "We're clean, but we're dirty-clean, rather than clean-clean." Barclays would continue to tell the press it had submitted "accurate and fair" LIBOR rates.[7] Would Barclays ever get caught, and if so, would the company be punished? Or, as a megabank, was it "too big to jail"?

Too Big to Fail or Jail

The phrase "too big to fail" has been widely used in the wake of the last financial crisis. Some fear the government may have encouraged what economists call a "moral hazard"—the biggest banks know they are so vital to the global financial system that the government will save them if they are in trouble, knowledge that encourages them to take risks that can push them to the brink. This dynamic may also be affecting how prosecutors target corporations. The "too big to jail" concern is that some companies may be so valuable to the economy that prosecutors will not hold them accountable for crimes. That concern is very real, and prosecutors, including at the very top, have expressed it. In March 2013, Attorney General Eric Holder told the Senate Judiciary Committee:

> I am concerned that the size of some of these institutions becomes so large that it does become difficult for us to prosecute them when we are hit with indications that if we do prosecute—if we do bring a criminal charge—it will have a negative impact on the national economy, perhaps even the world economy.[8]

Those comments touched off renewed questioning of whether prosecutors had held Wall Street sufficiently accountable.[9] One group of critics asked: "During the Global Financial Crisis that began in 2007, we became accustomed to the phrase 'too big to fail.' Is it possible that some financial executives are 'too big for jail'?"[10] The Financial Crisis Inquiry Commission's report described what criminologists call "crime-facilitative environments" among lenders, an environment ripe for mortgage fraud leading up to the crisis.[11] Others, such as federal judge Jed Rakoff, ask why more top executives have not been prosecuted; if there was in fact "fraudulent misconduct," then "the failure of the government to bring to justice those responsible for such colossal fraud bespeaks weaknesses in our prosecutorial system that need to be addressed."[12] Of course, one more reason for a lack of prosecutions may have been the government's own involvement in the deregulation of banking and encouraging risky mortgage practices, and then reshaping the major banks in the wake of the crisis.[13] Criminologists Henry N. Pontell, William K. Black, and Gilbert Geis asked whether the government was more interested in "damage control" than crime control.[14] And in a sarcastic response to Holder's comments, the House Financial Services Committee issued its own version of Monopoly's "get out of jail free" card (see Figure 10.1).

"There is no such thing as too big to jail," Attorney General Holder announced in a stern video message in May 2014, underscoring that no financial institution "should be considered immune from prosecution," and having

Figure 10.1 A "Too Big to Jail" Card

described his prior remarks as "misconstrued."[15] I have argued in this book that there is such a thing as "too big to jail." Moreover, the "too big to jail" concern is not just about big banks not being prosecuted due to "sheer size" and "influence on the economy." That is just one "too big to jail" concern, but I have described several others that are equally important. The "too big to jail" concern also extends to whether officers or employees are held account-able; they can literally be put in jail. The "too big to jail" concern extends be-yond banks, and it applies to many other types of large corporations that may commit a wide range of crimes, but obtain non-prosecution deals. The "too big to jail" concern extends to whether those corporate prosecution agree-ments are too lenient. And the "too big to jail" concern extends to whether corporate settlements effectively punish or reform a company.

To start with just the first "too big to jail" criticism, the concern that fi-nancial institutions are not prosecuted, it is important to focus on the cases prosecutors bring, but also the ones that they do not bring. We simply do not have good data on such cases. Prosecutors sometimes say that they are very careful about deciding to prosecute a company and note that they often de-cline to do so. But there is usually no public record of a decision by a prosecu-tor to decline a case, including for the good reason that one would not want to make an investigation public if a person is cleared of wrongdoing. Even in the highest-profile corporate cases, prosecutors generally avoid transparency in their decision making. We do not know whether they made a sound deci-sion not to prosecute or a poor one, and we know even less about how many corporate crimes never come to the attention of prosecutors.

We do know about public agreements not to prosecute, and they show that prosecutors do not treat all companies alike. Banks are prime beneficia-ries of the new leniency approach toward companies, as they generally receive deferred prosecution or non-prosecution agreements rather than convictions, including on charges related to fraud, money laundering, and other crimes. The list of companies receiving deferred prosecution or non-prosecution agreements includes many major banks, and several had multiple agreements in recent years, including Barclays, HSBC, JPMorgan, UBS, and Wachovia. Why were recidivist banks not treated more severely the second time around? Fifty-seven deferred prosecution and non-prosecution agreements between 2001 and 2012 involved financial institutions, ranging from banks to invest-ment advisors and trading firms. Only a handful of major banks have ever been convicted. Moreover, the major Wall Street banks have typically received non-prosecution agreements, rather than deferred prosecution agreements filed in a court.[16]

The "too big to jail" concern extends to individuals and employees who are not prosecuted, in cases involving financial institutions, but also in deferred and non-prosecution agreements generally, as I described in Chapter 4. Few higher-ups, such as CEOs, are ever prosecuted when a company settles its case. The "too big to jail" concern also runs beyond Wall Street. Other large companies, such as accounting firms, hospitals, military contractors, and pharmaceutical companies, all reach agreements to avoid a prosecution, by arguing that the collateral consequences of a conviction would be too great. There is nothing wrong with trying to minimize collateral consequences to a corporation. Prosecuting a corporation can impact officers, employees, shareholders, and others who committed no crime. However, a careful balance must be struck between minimizing collateral consequences and adequately punishing wrongdoers. A corporation provides a setting that can incentivize crime and magnify its consequences. Corporate prosecutions should prevent corporations from becoming crime scenes again, but we have little assurance that leniency is being offered in exchange for effective structural reforms.

In this chapter, I explore how we could put to rest all of these "too big to jail" concerns. I look more broadly at each of the concerns with how prosecutors approach corporate crime, beginning with investigations of the major banks. In the second part of this chapter, I evaluate corporate prosecutions, examining what we know about corporate crime rates, comparing what prosecutors do in corporate cases to what happens in individual cases, looking at what prosecutors do as compared to regulators who bring civil cases, and responding to those who argue corporations should not be criminally liable at all. In the third part of the chapter, I explore how to address "too big to jail" concerns, not by simply denying that any company is "too big to jail," but by actually making corporate prosecutions more effective, with reforms including (1) convicting corporations and lessening reliance on deferred prosecution agreements, (2) judicial oversight of any deferred prosecution agreements, (3) carefully audited compliance and structural reforms, (4) more serious fines, and (5) greater transparency and public information about corporate prosecutions.

Leniency for Barclays

It took years for investigations to uncover the misconduct at Barclays and the other banks involved in setting the LIBOR and similar rates. The Commodities Futures Trading Commission (CFTC) fined Barclays $200 million and required a series of reforms, including firewalls to make sure LIBOR submitters do not receive improper communications from others at the bank, and documentation of all factors relied upon to make submissions.[17] In the summer of 2012, Barclays received a deal rewarding its "extraordinary" and "extensive" cooperation. In addition to committing to future cooperation with authorities in the United States and the United Kingdom, Barclays paid a $160 million penalty to prosecutors and a $93 million fine to U.K. regulators. Barclays admitted and acknowledged responsibility for its conduct, but not for any particular crime.

Was this bank being treated as "too big to jail"? Barclays avoided a prosecution entirely, instead receiving a non-prosecution agreement. Prosecutors noted that Barclays "was the first bank to cooperate in a meaningful way." The bank was also arguably a recidivist, having previously entered a 2010 deferred prosecution agreement for "knowing" and "willful" violations of economic sanctions against countries such as Burma, Cuba, and Iran. In that 2010 agreement, Barclays agreed not to violate any U.S. federal law and paid an almost $300 million fine. Now the judge from that earlier case issued an order asking Barclays to explain why its additional crimes had not violated the 2010 deferred prosecution agreement; the judge was apparently satisfied with the explanation, as the deferred prosecution agreement was allowed to expire in 2012.[18] It is hard to understand why Barclays did not receive at least a more serious result than its earlier deferred prosecution agreement, but perhaps prosecutors were rewarding its cooperation as they built cases against other banks involved in LIBOR misconduct.

In the United Kingdom, there was a different type of accountability: the Barclays CEO was called in for a grilling by Parliament. He apologized: "It was wrong. I am sorry. I am disappointed, and I am also angry. There is absolutely no excuse for the behaviour that was exhibited in those activities and the types of e-mails that were written."

He also said, "It is a sign of the culture of Barclays that we were willing to be first, we were willing to be fast and we were willing to come out with it."[19]

He emphasized that with 140,000 employees, the actions of the fourteen or so involved in LIBOR manipulation did not represent the entire firm. However, his questioners pressed him on the corporate culture:

> I can understand a hot-headed idiot sitting in the New York swaps desk, thinking it would be cool to send a bottle of champagne around to the bloke in London and say, "Can you fix LIBOR for me?" But here is the reality: why weren't those LIBOR setters turning round to these traders and saying, "Guys, you can't do this. You're not allowed to do this. Stop sending me e-mails; otherwise I will tell my boss"?

The CEO responded, "Some were and some weren't."

Pushing harder, a legislator asked:

> The LIBOR setters, I would imagine, are not hot-headed 25 to 35-year-olds who like drinking Bollinger at the weekends. They are probably slightly boffin-like people. So what has gone wrong there? Why has that department got it so fundamentally wrong?

The CEO could only say:

> I'm trying to disagree with your characterisations of people, but I know what you mean, because the rate setters . . . they were some of our most senior staff.[20]

Moreover, U.K. regulators had found that "Barclays had no specific systems and controls in place relating to its LIBOR and EURIBOR submissions processes" until late 2009. Another legislator noted Barclays' previous violation of international sanctions. The CEO responded, "In each and every one of those cases, we have been open with the authorities and worked to get the solution and the changes in place."[21]

The Barclays CEO resigned after the hearings.[22] Should "I'm sorry" have been good enough? U.S. prosecutors could have demanded more serious monitoring and perhaps a more serious public inquiry, as in the United Kingdom.

Prosecuting with Convictions

In 2013, perhaps responding to the "too big to jail" concerns, prosecutors announced a welcome change in the approach toward targeting banks: convictions. Japanese subsidiaries of UBS and the Royal Bank of Scotland became the first big banks convicted in years. The head of DOJ's criminal division said: "I want financial institutions to know that this department will absolutely hold them to account."[23] Royal Bank of Scotland and UBS traders had also manipulated LIBOR, sending damning emails much like those at Barclays. For example, as prosecutors closed in, one of the traders warned others at UBS not to talk to investigators: "The U.S. Department of Justice, mate, you know," they are the "dudes who . . . put people in jail. Why . . . would you talk to them?"[24] Yet although their Japanese subsidiaries pleaded guilty and were convicted, UBS and Royal Bank of Scotland themselves entered deferred prosecution agreements, as have other banks, such as Dutch lender Rabobank. The head of the criminal division at the DOJ hinted at "too big to fail" and "too big to jail" concerns, stating that "our goal here is not to destroy a major financial institution."[25] Having foreign subsidiaries rather than the parent bank take a conviction was not exactly newfound resolve to hold banks fully criminally accountable. That said, insisting on a criminal conviction of a subsidiary, as has often occurred in pharmaceutical cases as well, is far preferable to deferred prosecution and non-prosecution agreements that avoid convictions entirely. Companies can be convicted through subsidiaries without the collateral consequences of convicting the parent, and without forgoing prosecution.

Prosecutors can also point to the 2013 conviction of major hedge fund SAC Capital for insider trading as a sign that financial institutions are not "too big to jail." No comparable Wall Street firm had been convicted since Drexel Burnham Lambert pleaded guilty to securities fraud in the late 1980s. Rather than receive a deferred prosecution, SAC pleaded guilty and paid $1.8 billion: the largest-ever penalty in an insider trading case. However, the SAC case does not mean we should forget our "too big to jail" concerns. SAC was not a public company and had largely lost outside investors by the time it pleaded guilty. Prosecutors knew when they convicted SAC that there was no risk of hurting innocent investors or the financial system more generally.

Perhaps a change in Wall Street prosecutions is finally coming. In April 2014, prosecutors announced convictions for Credit Suisse for offshore tax

evasion, and France's largest bank, BNP Paribas, for Bank Secrecy Act violations. Prosecutors sought convictions, having obtained assurances from regulators that convictions will not result in charter revocations preventing the
banks from doing business in the United States.[26] The "too big to jail" concerns raised by critics may have encouraged prosecutors to make felony convictions of financial institutions more feasible and more common.

Has LIBOR itself been reformed, making it harder for banks to game the
system? LIBOR will now be overseen by a new entity, the company that
owns the New York Stock Exchange, but questions remain whether sufficient
changes have been made.[27] Meanwhile, the LIBOR cases raise questions
of whether other major financial benchmark rates have been manipulated.
Regulators are looking into possible misconduct and collusion concerning
interest rate swaps, for example, another massive market in the hundreds of
trillions of dollars.[28] More investigations and possible prosecutions of major
banks are coming.[29]

Banks Not Prosecuted

Despite its size, LIBOR fraud was not a main cause of the global financial
crisis. Were other banks "too big to jail" for conduct more closely related to
subprime mortgages, mortgage-backed securities, and credit default swaps?
In 2010, the SEC began to investigate Goldman Sachs, filing civil charges
concerning a group of transactions known as Abacus, after the premodern
calculator that involved shuffling beads to count sums. This group of transactions involved shuffling the risk of bets on the subprime mortgage market
before the crisis hit.[30]

A U.S. Senate committee issued a report calling for a prosecution, but in
2012, prosecutors announced no charges would be pursued and the case was
closed, as the "burden of proof to bring a criminal case could not be met based
on the law and facts as they exist at this time."[31] Goldman paid $550 million
in a civil settlement with the SEC, admitting "incomplete information" in
Abacus marketing materials and agreeing to change how future marketing
materials would be reviewed.[32] It may have been unlikely criminal charges
would be brought, given the difficulty of showing that anyone was misled in
complex deals between sophisticated industry players. "Whether the decision
by the Department of Justice is the product of weak laws or weak enforcement,

Goldman Sachs' actions were deceptive and immoral," said Sen. Carl Levin, who called for more stringent regulations.[33] Maybe they were deceptive— but regulators in other cases have been unable to show banks deceived sophisticated investors.[34]

Ratings agencies were also central players in the collapse of the housing market. Firms such as Standard & Poor's, Moody's, and others earned hundreds of millions in fees for rating subprime mortgage-related investments as sound. Did they put their stamp of approval on subprime mortgage investments they knew were risky? In early 2007, before the subprime market collapse caused a global financial crisis, an employee at Standard & Poor's Financial Services LLC known only as "Analyst D" composed song lyrics describing how the subprime market was in trouble. To the tune of "Burning down the House" by the Talking Heads, the song described how "subprime is boiling over" and was "bringing down the house." Thinking better of the lyrics, Analyst D followed up the email saying, "For obvious professional reasons, please do not forward this song. If you are interested, I can sing it in your cube;-)." A few days later, getting over his stage fright, he sent another email with a video of him "singing and dancing" the first verse to laughing coworkers.[35]

Five years later, DOJ filed a multibillion-dollar suit against Standard & Poor's, but not a criminal prosecution. The case would be covered by a reduced civil standard of proof under the Financial Institutions Reform, Recovery, and Enforcement Act of 1989 (FIRREA), a previously little-used law allowing prosecutors to file civil charges for fraud affecting financial institutions.[36] In 2013, prosecutors won a jury trial involving FIRREA charges against Bank of America for fast-paced sales of mortgage-backed securities by its Countrywide unit before the financial crisis.[37] FIRREA is being used against Wells Fargo and the Bank of New York and was part of the case against JPMorgan, which entered a record $13 billion civil settlement in 2013. Prosecutors announced that JPMorgan had admitted to conduct that "contributed to the wreckage of the financial crisis," and the company would therefore "pay the largest FIRREA penalty in history." As the associate attorney general put it, "We are demanding accountability and requiring remediation from those who helped create a financial storm that devastated millions of Americans."[38]

The results in these civil actions do not fully alleviate "too big to jail" concerns either. In bringing FIRREA cases, prosecutors presumably thought they lacked the evidence for a criminal case. Some of these civil resolutions raise real questions about whether prosecutors were adequately "demanding accountability and requiring remediation." The JPMorgan settlement was not nearly so large as it appeared. The $13 billion included prior settlements, such as $4 billion paid to the Federal Housing Finance Agency. There was no explanation of where the fine amounts came from. The deal did not include clear admissions of wrongdoing or detailed descriptions of facts. Indeed, prosecutors did not clearly explain what violations had occurred. The deal was completed out of court and not approved by a judge. Still more troubling, the deal did not purport to demand structural or compliance reforms. Such opaque out-of-court civil deals make it all the more imperative that serious penalties result in the cases meriting criminal prosecution.

The Corporate Crime Rate

"Too big to jail" concerns with bank prosecutions are just a part of the story; I have described "too big to jail" concerns with corporate prosecutions generally. If we had a better sense of the underlying corporate crime rates, we would know what to make of decisions whether to bring corporate prosecutions. Police and prosecutors face public pressure when the murder rate goes up and too many murder cases remain unsolved. However, there are no statistics on how many corporations commit crimes. The FBI keeps statistics on street crimes in its Uniform Crime Reports, but there is no corporate equivalent. Unlike street crime and violent crime, people who are the victims of a financial fraud, for example, may not know it. Nor are the definitions of what constitutes many business crimes always so clear-cut. And some corporations may never get caught.

In fact, there are not good statistics on how many companies even exist, much less how many commit crimes. We do know that about half of U.S. businesses are incorporated in just five states—California, Delaware, Florida, New York, and Texas.[39] Delaware reported almost 1 million active companies in 2011, including over half of all public companies.[40] The IRS reported about 12 million companies in 2011.[41] A government study in 2006 concerning shell companies, those used to hide assets or identities of owners, found about two million firms created each year in the United States.[42] That is half as many companies as people born each year.[43]

How many of those companies are born to be criminals? Only a tiny fraction are convicted. In federal courts, almost 3,800 organizations have been

convicted since the Sentencing Guidelines were put in place in late 1991 (a
total of 3,780 through fiscal 2012). More than 300 firms have obtained deferred prosecution and non-prosecution agreements. In addition, several
dozen companies were acquitted at a trial and many more had charges dismissed by a judge or dropped by a prosecutor. This is not much more than
4,000 prosecuted companies (see Figure 10.2).

Does that mean corporate crime is rare—a few thousand companies out
of millions—or does it just mean corporate prosecutions are rare?

The picture is different for public companies. Of those with stock listed
on exchanges in the United States, 273 were prosecuted between 2001 and
2012, according to my data.[44] That is not trivial and represents about 5 percent of 5,000 total public companies (a very rough estimate, since numbers of
public companies change and some companies had more than one conviction).
Of those prosecuted, 46 percent were convicted (125 of 273 firms) and 54
percent received deferred prosecution or non-prosecution agreements (148 of
273 firms). Just over a quarter were foreign companies (73 of 273 firms). Public companies paid an average fine of $45 million, a larger amount than other
companies prosecuted for the same crimes, but minuscule compared to their
value—the fines averaged 0.04 percent of the market capitalization, or the
total dollar value of their outstanding shares, at the time of settlement.[45]
That prompted complaints by the victims in the BP Texas Refinery explosion; the fine of $50 million in that case was just 0.07 percent of BP's market
capitalization of over $70 billion. As discussed, the fines are calculated not

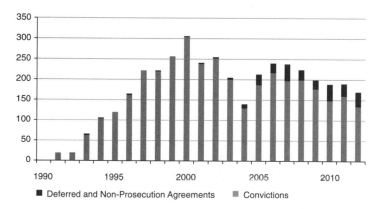

Figure 10.2 Numbers of Convictions and Deferred Prosecution and
Non-Prosecution Agreements with Organizations, 1991–2012

based on the size of the company but based on sentencing guidelines, stat-utes, or, alternatively, the gains and losses caused by the crime. But the fines actually imposed were often at or below what the guidelines or statutes rec-ommended. The results were fines the companies could readily afford to pay.

Some scholars have tried to estimate the occurrence of different types of white-collar and corporate crime. According to one estimate, about 14.5 per-cent of large publicly traded firms commit fraud.[46] Such evidence cannot tell us if there should be more corporate prosecutions. We know that little effort has been put into assessing how much corporate crime there is, and few cor-porations are prosecuted. Looking at what happened in cases where corpora-tions were prosecuted can tell us something more, though, about how well prosecutors target corporations when they do decide to bring a criminal case.

Mass Incarceration and Corporate Leniency

A second way to evaluate corporate prosecutions is to compare them to pros-ecutions of individuals. To be sure, one of my goals in this book has been to describe how different the two worlds are. For corporations, which cannot literally be jailed, a prosecutor's goal is to single out those that seriously violate criminal laws, in order to punish, deter, and reform them. Without offering some leniency, corporations would have little incentive to report crimes or adopt compliance measures, so prosecutors use both the carrot and the stick to deter and rehabilitate.

Prosecutors rarely offer leniency to encourage individuals to rehabilitate. We are the mass incarceration nation. Beginning in the 1970s, the United States has had the largest prison population in the world and the highest in-carceration rate.[47] Our criminal justice system is highly punitive, and only recently has there been any thaw in our attitude toward mass incarceration. The U.S. Sentencing Guidelines were notorious for not even mentioning the rehabilitative potential of the defendant, calling it "not ordinarily rele-vant."[48] It took the Supreme Court to assert that "self-motivated rehabilita-tion" was very much a relevant factor and may carry "great weight."[49] Federal prosecutors are now taking baby steps in the use of deferred prosecutions for nonviolent and addicted defendants, in order to give them drug or mental health treatment rather than prison, but these efforts have taken place on a very small scale so far.[50]

While corporate crimes often involve serious violations of regulatory offenses rather than violence, that does not explain why corporations so often receive alternatives to punishment even in the most serious cases, while individuals typically do not. Most of the federal criminal docket consists of nonviolent crimes. In some areas, the difference in priorities for corporations versus individuals is particularly stark. More than a third of the federal docket now consists of prosecutions of noncitizens who violated immigration rules, including by entering the country without permission. Federal efforts such as Operation Streamline use fast-track procedures for the vast numbers of people detained for illegally entering the country, offering leniency to most convicts in order to process convictions quickly.[51] These are not cases involving prosecution of immigrants for committing other crimes. Illegal entry or reentry does not require much of a criminal state of mind; judges tend to presume that immigrants know whether they are in compliance with technical immigration rules. Most countries treat immigration matters as civil and not criminal, as the United States largely did until recent decades. Why vast numbers of immigrants are being labeled as criminal is a troubling question.

Few employers are prosecuted for immigration crimes. Employers may face charges for knowingly bringing in or harboring noncitizens unlawfully present in the United States, but this is difficult to prove.[52] Ten companies have entered deferred prosecution agreements for immigration violations. In 2006, for example, federal agents conducted raids at forty factories operated by IFCO Systems manufacturing pallets for shipping. They detained more than a thousand noncitizens and estimated there were thousands more—more than half of IFCO employees had false Social Security numbers.[53] Several managers were charged with immigration violations.[54] IFCO paid almost $21 million in fines, including back wages and civil penalties, and agreed to take compliance measures, including joining the E-Verify system allowing instant checks on employee social security numbers. In another case, WesternGeco paid $19.6 million in fines for submitting fraudulent visa applications for workers on Gulf of Mexico oil vessels. Out of the more than 2,000 corporate convictions I examined, 107 were for immigration violations.[55] These pale in comparison to the nearly 40,000 individuals prosecuted each year for immigration violations, few of which were employers.[56]

Drug prosecutions are another example in which highly punitive prosecution policies have led to a high rate of incarceration, despite crimes that are usually nonviolent. Federal drug crimes chiefly involve possession or distribution of controlled substances. More than a quarter of federal prosecutions of individuals were for distribution or conspiracy to distribute controlled substances, and half of inmates in federal prisons are serving time for drug offenses.[57] The crimes are designed to shut down a business—the illegal drug trade—but jailing low-level dealers does little to make that happen. A small proportion of the vast numbers prosecuted for drug offenses had any significant criminal history or used a weapon in the offense. Less than 6 percent were managers or leaders of a drug operation.[58] As federal judge John Gleeson put it, "anyone who believes that the federal system deals only with 'the most serious drug and violent' offenders isn't familiar with the federal criminal docket."[59] Even low-level and nonviolent offenders get lengthy federal sentences, while in contrast the guidelines offer flexible sentencing for organizations.

In addition, the overwhelming majority of crack cocaine offenders singled out for heightened punishment were black.[60] There was no leniency program for these offenders. It was the opposite: a "severity" program. There were no prosecution guidelines for drug cases as there are for corporate prosecutions. In 1997, the DOJ got rid of guidelines that offered some guidance for when to bring a federal drug case and when to leave a case to state authorities.[61] Congress and the Sentencing Commission did eventually reduce the crack sentencing disparity, but it took more than fifteen years before Attorney General Eric Holder announced that this approach toward drug prosecutions was "counterproductive" and that new guidelines would permit leniency, nonprosecution, and alternatives to prosecution for low-level drug offenders.[62]

The war on drugs has not affected corporations much—I found just a handful of corporations prosecuted for illegal sales of controlled substances, failing to track sales of Sudafed (which can be used to manufacture methamphetamine), or distributing drug paraphernalia. Prosecutors have decided not to try to prosecute the hundreds or thousands of sales employees at major pharmaceutical companies who were involved in paying kickbacks to doctors or promoting off-label sales of drugs. They thought it better to simply prosecute the corporation rather than hold individuals accountable; indeed, as described, prosecutors may prosecute a subsidiary and not hold the parent company accountable for pharmaceutical violations. HSBC was given leniency for money laundering on a grand scale that benefited, among others, major drug cartels, and in such cases, employees at banks are rarely prosecuted. Yet when fighting a different war on drugs, prosecutors have been willing to jail tens of thousands of participants in the drug trade, including low-level participants.

The failure to insist on serious punishments for corporate offenders seems especially indefensible when we strictly prosecute low-level crimes by individuals. Nor is it so easy to say that white-collar or corporate crimes are "not really crimes" because they are regulatory, since much of what federal prosecutors do involves nonviolent and regulatory crimes. A corporation should not be prosecuted for a trivial civil violation, but if serious violations warrant a criminal case, then serious criminal punishment and structural reforms should follow.

A Tale of Two Regulators

A third way to evaluate criminal prosecutions of corporations is to compare them to the civil alternative: enforcement by regulatory agencies. Some argue that corporations, since they cannot be held morally accountable for crimes, should only face civil liability from regulators or private plaintiffs. However, I view prosecutors as crucial to filling the gap left by regulators who may lack adequate resources to punish the most severe corporate violators. Two federal regulatory agencies provide a study in contrasting enforcement resources and patterns: the Environmental Protection Agency and the Securities and Exchange Commission. The EPA does far more enforcement than the SEC. Comparing the two sheds light on why big banks face few prosecutions, while prosecutors bring many environmental cases each year. If we want to get the relationship between corporate criminal punishment and civil enforcement right, we may need more resources for both prosecutors and regulators.

The prosecution following the *Deepwater Horizon* spill in the Gulf of Mexico resulted in the largest criminal fine ($1.2 billion) and the largest community service award ($4 billion) of all time, but those pale in comparison to the more than $17 billion BP may have to pay in civil fines to the EPA and state regulators. In fiscal 2011 the EPA described 249 environmental crime cases, resulting in $35 million in fines and restitution.[63] Those criminal cases were just the tip of the iceberg; the EPA also brought civil and administrative actions, which secured $104 million in penalties.[64] In turn, those were dwarfed by administrative proceedings, in which the EPA resolved 1,760 administrative penalty orders (with another $48 million in fines) and 1,324 administrative compliance orders. Less formally, the EPA did 19,000 inspections and received 3.5 million voluntary commitments to reduce pollution. The EPA also brings cases in conjunction with state regulators. Environmental prosecutions were the biggest category of criminal prosecutions in my data. From 2011 through 2012, I found more than 500 environmental prosecutions (not including wildlife offenses), only six of which were deferred prosecution or non-prosecution agreements. To be sure, many of those EPA cases involved smaller companies, and a conviction in an environmental case may not have the same consequences for a company. But federal environmental prosecutors believe that cases should normally either be civil or result in a criminal conviction.

By contrast, the SEC brings very few enforcement actions against companies. In 2012, they brought 813 total civil actions, but most of these were against individuals—for example, of 106 civil cases having to do with reporting or disclosure, fewer than twenty were against companies.[65] This may explain why there have been just twenty-three deferred prosecution agreements from 2001 to 2012 involving securities fraud charges and just three corporations convicted of securities fraud. While antitrust, environmental, FCPA, and other federal criminal violations were associated with higher average fines, securities fraud cases were not.

What explains this? In part, the SEC is hamstrung by Congress. Current laws limit the SEC to obtaining disgorgement of profits rather than fines in most cases.[66] The SEC has pushed for legislation to permit civil penalties that are far larger.[67] Moreover, as a *New York Times* reporter noted in 2007: "It's no secret that the Securities and Exchange Commission is terrifically understaffed and wildly underfunded compared with the populous and wealthy Wall Street world it is supposed to police."[68] Shortly thereafter, three former SEC chairmen echoed those sentiments with this statement: "The problem with the S.E.C. today is that it lacks the money, manpower and tools it needs to do its job."[69] The SEC has since added enforcement resources and a dedicated FCPA group and has started to use corporate monitors.[70] One of the goals of the Dodd-Frank legislation was to give the SEC "more power, assistance and money at its disposal to be an effective securities markets regulator."[71] But in 2011, the SEC noted that its budget was "already forcing the agency to delay or cut back enforcement and market oversight efforts."[72] There was mounting criticism of how the SEC settled cases, allowing companies to "neither admit nor deny" wrongdoing. One judge approved an SEC agreement, but wrote:

> In this age when the notion labeled "too big to fail" (or jail, as the case may be) has gained currency throughout commercial markets, some cynics read the concept as code words meant as encouragement by an accommodating public—a free pass to evade or ignore the rules, a wink and a nod as cover for grand fraud, a license to deceive unsuspecting customers.[73]

The SEC changed its policy to discourage such use of "neither admit nor deny" language, but concerns remain that regulators treat major companies too leniently.

If regulators cannot always enforce adequately, then prosecutors may be a crucial backstop. Indeed, prosecutions may be symptoms of regulatory failures. Recall the massive money laundering case brought against HSBC, discussed in Chapter 4. The Senate issued a report calling the culture at the bank "pervasively polluted," highlighting how the Office of the Comptroller of the Currency had "failed to take any enforcement" action until 2010, despite the bank having been cited for problems as early as 2003.[74] It took a "jolt from law enforcement" for the regulators to realize how important the problems were.[75] We cannot expect prosecutors to completely fill in the void left by inadequate regulatory enforcement, though we can expect prosecutors to take up the most serious violations and impose more serious consequences, such as admissions of guilt, deterrent fines, and strict structural reforms.

The Abolitionists

Some believe that each of the comparisons I have just made point to one conclusion: that corporate prosecutions are unjust and it would be preferable to prosecute individuals instead and bring civil regulatory actions. These abolitionists argue that since corporations cannot be jailed, prosecutors should not try to punish them. For example, law professor Albert Alschuler calls blaming "mindless legal entities" for crimes a "mistake" and similar to the ancient legal practice of deodand: "the punishment of an animal or inanimate object that has killed a person."[76] Professor Alschuler does find somewhat more justified the use of corporate prosecutions to induce employees to monitor each other, which is my view of their purpose. Other scholars argue that criminal liability should be replaced with civil enforcement or with a form of insurance.[77] Corporate groups, for good reasons, may wholeheartedly agree with those proposals to limit or do away with corporate criminal liability.

A case about dumping oily bilge water became the focus of an unlikely set of allies bent on limiting corporate criminal liability, if not abolishing it. Recall the case of Ionia Management, the Greek shipping company that took its case to trial when it was accused of using a "magic pipe" to illegally dump oily water overboard. The company lost at trial, as described in the last chapter, but appealed and was joined by a diverse group of allies. The Association of Corporate Counsel, the Chamber of Commerce, the National Association of Manufacturers, and the Washington Legal Foundation represented corporate interests opposed to tough standards for corporate liability. But the National Association of Criminal Defense Lawyers and the New York State Association of Criminal Defense lawyers, which argue for fairer criminal procedure generally, also joined them.[78] They did not argue for abolition of corporate crime, but asked the federal appeals court to recognize good compliance as a defense to corporate criminal liability.

Companies have also lobbied for a compliance defense to the FCPA. Compliance, of course, is already a reason sentences are reduced under the guidelines and in deferred prosecution and non-prosecution agreements. Perhaps, as law professor Peter Henning points out, companies should be careful what they wish for.[79] Few cases go to trial, and with a compliance defense, prosecutors could dig deep into the effectiveness of the company's policies. Would the defense really help companies if the commission of a crime by an employee meant that the compliance program had failed? In the Ionia case, the company was found in violation of a prior EPA consent agreement, so that information was not helpful for the company.

Some scholars, such as Professor Alschuler, have also argued that federal corporate criminal liability should be limited—that companies should have a "good faith" compliance defense if they are prosecuted, allowing the company to argue that a good compliance program overrides an employee's failure to comply with it.[80] Still others argue that corporate criminal liability should be limited to cases where upper management encouraged agents to commit crimes.[81] The Model Penal Code, adopted by some states, takes that approach, and adds that a company may be prosecuted only with clear legislative intent that a crime should apply to corporations.[82] Regardless, in the Ionia case, the federal court of appeals rejected the company's arguments, citing long-standing federal law permitting corporate criminal liability for actions of employees acting in the scope of their employment.[83]

One federal appeals court has approved an even broader standard for corporate criminal liability—a "collective knowledge" theory in which no one employee needs to have the full criminal intent, so long as multiple employees had the required intent collectively. The rationale is that since a corporation can "compartmentalize knowledge," the corporation can be liable for the "totality of what all of the employees know within the scope of their employment." However, no criminal case since has held a corporation liable under such a theory.[84]

As I have described in this book, despite the broad federal standard for corporate criminal liability, prosecutors impose criminal liability in practice only in a limited group of cases. Prosecutors say they select companies for prosecution based on factors that focus on compliance and on whether civil liability or individual prosecutions would be adequate. I have suggested throughout that prosecutors have not adequately followed those already unclear principles. If prosecutors have a weak case or the underlying law or regulation is based on unsound policy, then criminal enforcement is not a good idea. Most violations of regulations are not and should not be treated as crimes—but serious criminal violations should, including cases in which a company was engaging in misconduct that was repeated, concealed, or tolerated. Defining what constitutes a serious violator or an egregious failure of compliance is not easy, but prosecutors could adopt more concrete measures, such as whether the company is a recidivist, the number of employees involved, the size of the violation, or whether higher-ups played a role. Nor have prosecutors made clear that a different, more serious category of criminal penalties results when there has been corporate toleration of misconduct. Still more serious penalties should flow from recidivism.

Prosecutors as David

It is very hard to see prosecutors as the little guy in any fight. In 1940, Attorney General Robert Jackson said that a prosecutor "has more control over life, liberty, and reputation than any other person in America."[85] And although federal prosecutors are already the most powerful prosecutors in the country, with broad federal criminal law, tough federal sentencing guidelines, and both the FBI and federal regulatory agencies at their disposal, they need more resources to tackle large companies, which can outgun prosecutors with massive spending. One goal in this book has been to explain why it is understandable that prosecutors adopted a compromise approach with corporations.

Prosecutors are highly dedicated to their jobs, and there is no evidence corporations have "captured" or influenced prosecutors. Corporations have been unsuccessful in opposing stricter criminal laws, although complaints have resulted in some changes to the DOJ's corporate prosecution guidelines. We do know companies appeal their cases to the highest levels, even to the attorney general—recall the high-level meetings in Washington, D.C., that KPMG's legal team arranged. Federal prosecutors have prestigious jobs and strong incentives to prosecute vigorously, but they know they must keep supervisors advised, because ultimately the attorney general may hear about the case from the company's lawyers, even if management just wants to be able to assure its board that it has done everything possible to get the best deal.

There is also a revolving door concern. Many prosecutors leave for lucrative work in private firms or in the private sector. There has been an explosion in white-collar practice at big law firms, and companies may want to hire former prosecutors who can get them access to those meetings at the Justice Department.[86] As noted, many corporate monitors were themselves former prosecutors. Still, that probably gives prosecutors an incentive to be tough on corporations—to show that they know how to handle big cases.

What can level the playing field? Prosecutors depend on investigators to uncover corporate crime and build solid cases. The FBI is supposed to be the lead agency investigating corporate fraud, but it assigned fewer agents to white-collar matters after the September 11, 2001, attacks. After the global financial crisis hit, the FBI reversed this trend, assigning more agents to investigate mortgage fraud and securities and reporting growing numbers of fraud investigations each year from 2007 to 2011.[87] This is the pipeline for prosecutions, and if Congress wants to take corporate crime seriously, it could fund far more agents and investigations.

Prosecutors also depend on regulators to uncover violations, as regulatory agencies may have far more access to corporate records. Regulators uncovered false hospital billing in the WakeMed case in North Carolina because data mining uncovered abnormal patterns in the billing records. The FBI and regulators are promoting such sophisticated data-mining techniques as a way to identify patterns of fraud, systemic problems, and unusual billing activity. The FBI is also using data mining to detect mortgage fraud. And in 2009, the FBI created the Financial Intelligence Center to provide "tactical analysis" of financial intelligence data and uncover securities fraud, money laundering, and other financial fraud.

Federal prosecutors are the focus of this book, but state and local prosecutors are far more numerous. Few have the resources to take on major corporate cases, although some of those offices, such as the Manhattan District Attorney's Office and the New York Attorney General's Office, have long done so. States have also brought important cases regarding environmental violations, workplace injuries, and consumer fraud, and state and local prosecutors have increasingly sought to bring major financial fraud cases as well, with some creating regional task forces and focusing on specific issues, such as fraud that targets seniors.[88] Prosecutors at all levels have begun to cooperate in fraud investigations, including through a partnership of state attorneys general.[89] Such coalitions may prove unwieldy, or perhaps they will prove effective.

Compare the response to most recent financial crisis to the savings and loan scandal in the 1980s. Congress, having deregulated S&Ls in the first place, passed legislation providing for tens of millions of dollars to investigate and prosecute banking crimes. Congress extended the statute of limitations for bank fraud to give prosecutors five more years to bring cases, and it funded the creation of strike forces and a Financial Institutions Fraud Unit at DOJ to bring the cases.[90] As a result, many hundreds of bank executives who ran failed S&Ls were convicted. The S&L prosecutions show how prosecutors can be tougher if given the resources. Still, some of the frauds in those cases were fairly easy to prove—some executives lavishly lent themselves money from bank assets—and the prosecutions still could not make victims whole: only $130 million in restitution was recovered.[91]

The S&L cases were what criminologist William K. Black terms "control frauds," where those who control a company use it to defraud others and as a shield to conceal their schemes.[92] Particularly strong outside oversight is needed to prevent those at the very top from corrupting internal controls. However, a totally corrupted company may not be worth saving, or, like Enron, it may be defunct and not available to prosecute. For a viable company not wholly engaged in crimes, strong internal controls are needed to prevent officers and employees at lower levels from breaking the law. Ideally, the threat of prosecutions would prevent corporate crime in the first place, but it is not clear that the non-prosecution approach so often used can accomplish this.

A Road Map for Reform

Sen. Jeff Merkley objected to the deferred prosecution agreement HSBC received by citing a larger problem: "four years after the financial crisis, the Department appears to have firmly set the precedent that no bank, bank employee, or bank executive can be prosecuted." Senator Merkley called it a "'too big to jail' approach."[93] No HSBC employees were prosecuted. Sen. Elizabeth Warren voiced concern that, "evidently, if you launder nearly a billion dollars for drug cartels and violate our international sanctions, your company pays a fine and you go home and sleep in your own bed at night."[94] On the other hand, the DOJ did require top-to-bottom compliance reforms at HSBC, and the company switched leadership, spent hundreds of millions of dollars on compliance, and agreed to change executive compensation so that bonuses were based on compliance. The terms of that agreement are actually far more rigorous than most. The question is whether the agreement will accomplish lasting reforms. We should also ask whether other corporate prosecution agreements result in structural reform, and why there is no evaluation of whether these reforms are working in practice.

The distinctive purpose of the criminal law is lost when prosecutors fail to impose effective consequences on the most serious corporate violators. This is particularly so where an egregious lack of compliance is the reason the case merited criminal prosecution in the first place. When prosecutors do target corporations, compliance is too much of a defense—prosecutors should not be so quick to credit cosmetic compliance when they offer leniency. Federal judge Jed Rakoff has argued that prosecutors are too inclined to settle corporate cases on lenient terms after hasty investigations, and that prosecuting only individuals would be far more effective than "imposing internal compliance measures that are often little more than window-dressing."[95] It would require substantial resources to prosecute more upper-level officers and to more rigorously supervise corporate prosecutions. My view is that both are important. Neither individuals nor corporations should be left off the hook.

When the corporation is targeted, prosecutors should seek to do far more than impose cosmetic compliance. Such lenient settlements raise the question of why the case is being criminally prosecuted in the first place. The standards for corporate criminal settlements and sentences should be made tougher, not weaker. Fortunately, some corporate prosecutions described in this book provide real models for an approach that treats corporate criminal behavior more seriously. Each of the chapters in this book sought to answer a different question about how we prosecute corporations and to suggest how corporate prosecutions can be made more effective. In the concluding sections, I focus on those concrete proposals to reduce "too big to jail" concerns with how corporations are prosecuted.

Rethinking the Punishment of Corporations

A central purpose of criminal law is to send a message of blame. As law professor Henry M. Hart Jr. famously put it, "What distinguishes a criminal from a civil sanction . . . is the judgment of community condemnation which accompanies and justifies its imposition."[96] Criminal prosecutions can hurt the reputations of companies more than a noncriminal settlement, and that is part of the point. The "too big to jail" concern, though, is that corporate punishments are too light. What would a system look like that more sharply distinguished between civil and criminal enforcement against companies? It would look more like what environmental and antitrust prosecutors now do: cases would be either criminal or civil, without so many settlements occupying a gray zone in between. In my view, a conviction should be pursued far more often, with the option to convict a subsidiary if the collateral consequences of a conviction of the parent would be too great. If the collateral consequences of any type of plea agreement are still too great, a deferred prosecution should be an option, but only with careful monitoring supervised by a judge. Non-prosecution agreements should simply not be used.

In addition, fines should be imposed within the sentencing range. The only reason lenient fines should be offered is to reward voluntary and prompt self-reporting and cooperation, as well to promote documented and audited compliance. Compliance programs that are mere window-dressing should not be rewarded. Prosecutors should also be far more transparent about how fines are calculated. Judges could scrutinize corporate sentencing more closely if corporations were required to plead guilty more often. Prosecutors should also seek far stricter penalties for a recidivist company.

Apart from the blaming function of criminal law, the collateral consequences that companies may most want to avoid—and why they may most fear a prosecution—is the risk of suspension or debarment. Such regulatory consequences may result in what is effectively a death penalty for a company, and in many cases prosecutors and regulators are right to want to avoid such severe consequences for the entire company. Yet the rules for both suspension and debarment from doing work in an industry or with the government can be quite vague. The federal government may suspend a company from government work until the company corrects the conditions that led to the violations (the government suspended BP in the wake of the Gulf spill, but only as to new contracts). Or the government may debar the firm outright, typically for a fixed period up to three years.[97] Some debarments are for fraud or misconduct in government contracting—about 16 percent as of 2011—but the vast majority, 84 percent, were for other violations, such as health care fraud or illegal exports.[98] A government study of debarment found most were by the Department of Health and Human Services.[99] For corporate prosecutions to have real teeth, debarment and suspension should be exercised more clearly and forcefully, particularly for recidivists, to ensure that they implement meaningful compliance.[100]

Corporate crime can be deterred not just by stricter penalties but by improving detection of wrongdoing. As discussed, Congress could provide far greater investigative resources to prosecutors. In addition, greater rewards for self-reporting by companies can help, as can incentivizing competitors to report on each other and giving whistle-blowers incentives to report from within a company. International prosecutions highlight the role whistle-blowers can play. The main response to the global financial crisis, the Dodd-Frank Wall Street Reform and Consumer Protection Act, includes a whistle-blower provision that received very little attention at the time, but empowers whistle-blowers that report possible violations to regulators—by giving them more protection from retaliation and greater rewards.[101] This may ultimately make enforcement by regulators and prosecutors stronger, although it also might discourage internal reporting and compliance.[102]

Taking Structural Reform Seriously

The "too big to jail" catchphrase is somewhat tongue in cheek, since a company literally cannot be jailed. A company can be punished, however, and also reformed, but it is not clear that prosecutors take compliance seriously. What makes a corporate prosecution distinctly criminal is the focus on punishment and not merely imposing fines. A big fine may not harm the corporate officers, as shareholders, customers, or the public may absorb the cost of the fine. A corporate prosecution can condemn criminal behavior, impose punishment, deter future crime, and rehabilitate a company to prevent future crime. A prosecution serves a specific purpose if the company itself is to blame for egregious violations, such as serious deviations from accepted business practices, gross failures to comply, or repeat violations. And prosecutors say that a lack of effective compliance is a primary consideration in prosecuting a corporation.

This makes it yet another great "too big to jail" concern that so many corporate prosecution agreements do not impose serious structural reforms. In contrast, the most successful corporate prosecutions are those based on a firm picture of what the prohibited conduct is and how preventing that conduct through compliance is supposed to work. Internal structures should build compliance into the everyday work of employees, since responding to problems after the fact is not enough if the wrong incentives exist. We do not want prosecutors to act as "superregulators" and make ill-considered changes in corporate governance.[103] But effective compliance with existing regulations and criminal statutes must be secured. Yet only in a few specialized areas do prosecutors seem to know what compliance they want. The federal prosecution guidelines should address this subject in detail.

The biggest and most complex organizations can carry out the most damaging crimes. In my data, record fines are concentrated among public companies, foreign companies, and multinational companies, along with companies in large concentrated industries, such as pharmaceuticals. A Yale University study of federal white-collar offenses in the late 1970s found a close relationship between complex organizations, crimes that require "a high level of planning and organization," and large numbers of victims across local, state, and national borders.[104] Organizational complexity itself enables more complex and damaging crimes. But complex organizations can also be more challenging to reform, making it especially important to take compliance seriously.

Many of the chapters in this book describe failures: Chapter 2 described the Arthur Andersen case and the potential costs of overly strict corporate crime enforcement; Chapter 3 described the failure to require careful structural reforms; Chapter 4 described failures to prosecute individual employees; Chapter 5 described the failure to adequately vindicate victim interests; Chapter 6 described the failures of the sentencing guidelines; Chapter 7 described the failures to hire corporate monitors in most cases; Chapter 8 described failures of incentives created by criminal procedure rules. But I have also highlighted a number of bright spots. Prosecutors have successfully prosecuted more large-scale corporate crimes, including the pharmaceutical cases described in Chapter 4 and the foreign corporate prosecutions described in Chapter 9, including cases handled under the long-standing corporate leniency program of the Justice Department's Antitrust Division. That program is not so lenient at all compared to the deferred prosecution approach the DOJ follows in other areas. Prosecutors seek to break up cartels and punish with convictions the companies that do not report themselves first.

In other areas, prosecutors appear uncertain of their ultimate goal. Prosecutors offer leniency in agreements that do not require any detailed description of the structural reforms or careful auditing or testing of compliance. For example, there has been a rise in large FCPA prosecutions. Many companies self-report FCPA violations to prosecutors. However, the agreements rarely describe FCPA compliance in any detail; we do not know how many companies have built compliance into their business, as Siemens says it has done. Similarly, in Big Pharma settlements, the question is whether the changes imposed, such as modifying the way sales representatives are compensated, will really impact industry practices.

Agreements with prosecutors typically do not alter terms of compensation or promotion. Instead they rely on hiring new compliance staffers or on new codes of ethics, training, or other procedures. That may simply not be enough if employees still are rewarded for conduct that bends the rules. In other areas, agreements do not describe what compliance is expected. Telling a company to just adopt "best practices" does not give real guidance; prosecutors should impose provisions explaining how compliance should be implemented. Serious violations demand serious structural reforms.

Prosecutors could also use fines to punish noncompliance while delegating the assessment of future compliance to monitors, judges, or even regulators. Law professor Jennifer Arlen has recommended that prosecutors use fines to incentivize compliance but give civil regulators sole authority to impose and assess structural reforms.[105] So long as meaningful structural reforms follow from egregious corporate criminal violations and a regulator exists to handle the job, such delegation can be productive. That kind of delegation occurs in practice—in the KPMG case, the IRS supervised compliance throughout and for two years past the date the deferred prosecution agreement concluded.

Assessing Compliance

When Sen. Edward Kennedy, a sponsor of the legislation that gave birth to the sentencing guidelines, spoke about the guidelines for organizations in 1995, he pointed out that the key was that law enforcement "must be able to tell the difference between sincere and cosmetic compliance efforts."[106] The carrot-and-stick approach of the sentencing guidelines sparked a corporate compliance revolution. However, prosecutors offer too much carrot and too little stick. They often do not formally evaluate a company's compliance program, say whether it gets credit for being effective, or explain how effective compliance will be ensured after an agreement ends.[107]

A compliance program must be evaluated. The sentencing guidelines for organizations insist that an effective compliance program must not be just a checklist of written policies, yet the DOJ prosecution guidelines do not require follow-up evaluation, and as a result, neither do most deferred prosecution and non-prosecution agreements. Nor do many companies assess their compliance routinely; according to one industry survey in 2013, less than half conduct periodic compliance assessments.[108] And nobody evaluates whether corporate prosecution agreements are working in general. The Government Accountability Office found that the DOJ "cannot evaluate and demonstrate the extent to which" deferred prosecution and non-prosecution agreements "contribute to the department's efforts to combat corporate crime" without any "measures to assess their effectiveness." DOJ has so far responded that it will examine corporate prosecutions to develop "performance measures."[109] We do not know what "performance measures" exist, if any, or how prosecutors are trained, if at all, on how to be sure that structural reforms are really working.

Prosecutors do not seem to have a concrete idea how to measure effective compliance. The American Bar Association is working on a set of best practices for corporate monitors, but none currently exist.[110] There is little evidence that compliance is assessed in most cases. Some agreements say that the company should evaluate and improve its effectiveness, or receive monitor reports on the subject, but there is rarely detail about how auditing should be done. At best, there is generic language.

In some areas, statutes or regulations lay out best practices. For example, laws require banks to have an anti-money-laundering program that meets minimum requirements and to undergo independent testing for compliance.[111] That is why the HSBC agreement required adoption of a customer risk-rating methodology. Similarly, pharmaceutical agreements have detailed provisions for how to prevent off-label promotion of drugs. In contrast, even when the DOJ released a book-length guide to the FCPA, it said little about what makes for a "strong compliance program" aside from stating that risk assessment is "fundamental" and noting how "targeted audits" can be used to test compliance procedure.[112] There are sources of data on public corruption that could be used, and a company can generate its own data. Anonymous compliance and reports of ethics violations can be tracked to inform risk-based analysis. Particular groups or employees can be red-flagged for additional training or supervision. Prosecutions should impose clear best practices and require careful auditing of corporate compliance.

Punishing and Rewarding Individuals

We can take the "too big to jail" concern quite literally if individuals avoid jail time when the company settles its criminal case. We should ask whether corporate prosecution deals are distorting justice for white-collar defendants. Prosecutions of individual officers or employees accompanied just over one-third of the deferred prosecution and non-prosecution agreements, and just one-quarter of convictions of public companies.

Good corporate prosecutions can create incentives for companies to themselves hold individuals accountable. It is troubling when the officers and employees involved in criminal acts receive promotions, bonuses, or raises, rather than suffer professional consequences. The most detailed agreements with prosecutors use structural reforms to change the incentives of individuals to report misconduct and of companies to punish wrongdoers. Those agreements require a company to create internal whistle-blower hotlines, new corporate codes of conduct, and discipline for employees who violate the rules. Some agreements change the ways that employees are paid, to encourage them to comply with criminal laws. Cases against financial institutions provide an example, as some blamed the global financial crisis in part on compensation plans that rewarded executives for taking excessive risks to gain short-term rewards.[113] Bear Stearns and Lehman Brothers each paid over $1 billion in bonuses to executives in the years before the crisis.[114] The Dodd-Frank legislation required companies to claw back compensation from executives who engage in certain types of misconduct, but the SEC had often failed to enforce earlier clawback provisions, and whether new rules will be enforced remains to be seen.[115] Prosecutors have gone farther in agreements like that with HSBC and the Big Pharma settlements, calling not only for clawbacks but also for changing the structure of compensation going forward. Such terms, if actually taken seriously, might create conditions for better internal accountability of both higher-ups and lower-level employees.

There are other ways to hold employees and higher-ups accountable. Sarbanes-Oxley requires that CEOs and CFOs certify corporate financial reports and internal controls, and if they knowingly sign false reports, they face jail time.[116] As with other legislation enacted in response to corporate scandals, it has rarely been enforced, and the high-profile prosecution of Health-South's CEO ended in an acquittal.[117] Executives have insulated themselves by requiring certifications from subordinates so they can defend themselves by showing how they relied on reviews by others: the ostrich problem again. Certification provisions could be made broader. The SEC has sometimes demanded that executives certify compliance; when Goldman Sachs entered an SEC consent decree, it agreed that the general counsel or head of compliance would certify compliance annually.[118] Similarly, Health and Human Services demands that executives certify compliance in pharmaceutical cases.[119] A few deferred prosecution and non-prosecution agreements include terms like that; for example, the Credit Suisse agreement requires the company's CEO to personally certify that all relevant employees received new training by 2010 and that new policies were in place. Prosecutors could demand certifications routinely and make clear that executives will be personally liable if certifications turn out to be false and the company violates the law.

The top-to-bottom reforms adopted at Siemens integrate compliance into the everyday jobs of employees at all levels. Prosecutors may be leery of imposing comprehensive reforms, but to go beyond mere window-dressing, such structural reforms may be necessary. These can make more information about compliance available to outsiders such as shareholders, increasing accountability. Far more must be done to study what makes compliance effective.

Why Come to Court?

"Why are you coming to court if you tell me you don't need me?" asked one federal judge in North Carolina. "I'm just window dressing in this case."[120]

Prosecutors had spent two years negotiating a deferred prosecution agreement with WakeMed, a large nonprofit hospital, for false Medicare billing. The judge refused to sign the deal: "It's very difficult for society and the court to differentiate between the everyday working Joe or Jane who goes to prison and the nonprofit corporate giant who doesn't go to jail, who gets a slap on the hand and doesn't miss a beat."

If this was a slap on the wrist, what was the alternative? Pleading guilty was not a good choice, since the judge acknowledged that a felony conviction might make WakeMed ineligible for Medicare and Medicaid billing, possibly resulting in the death of the nonprofit hospital. That could hurt the community. And the agreement already required the hospital to pay millions in fines, hire a corporate monitor, and report to prosecutors and the Department of Health and Human Services. What the agreement did not do was permit supervision by the judge to make sure that the hospital was taking compliance seriously.

Judges have been almost entirely left out of these corporate settlements, and it is not surprising that they have started to raise alarms. The judge in the WakeMed case noted that "every American wage earner and every American citizen" was a victim in the case. As discussed, victims have intervened to stand for the public interest, but judges rarely respond to victim objections. The problem lies with how a judge's role is defined: it is hard for a judge to protect the public interest if prosecutors design agreements to avoid judicial oversight. In the WakeMed case, the judge ordered the terms of the agreement changed so that the corporate monitor and parties would have to periodically report to him.[121] Why is this not standard practice? Prosecutors have done what they do best in negotiating settlements, but they are not accustomed to long-term supervision. Corporate prosecution settlements that provide for probation or deferral average just over two years in length. Can a company be reformed in just a year or two?

There is another model for handling cases that raise important issues of public interest: the structural reform model. When regulators or prosecutors seek a civil consent decree to reform an institution, they must do it in court, with notice and a chance for the public to participate, and where the judge must explicitly consider the public interest. The same standards should govern corporate prosecutions. A few judges have refused to approve corporate plea agreements, finding them not in the public interest. Judges should consider the public interest when reviewing both plea agreements and deferred prosecution agreements. Formal rules for ensuring participation of victims and the public should be put into place. Judges should insist on full and open hearings before approving corporate prosecution agreements. Congress could pass legislation laying out clear standards for approving corporate criminal settlements.

It is unclear how well corporate prosecution agreements are being implemented, but what we do know is alarming. There is very little information about what high-paid corporate monitors are doing and whether it is effective. Prosecutors may have scaled back the use of monitors after being faced with criticism regarding cronyism in hiring and complaints about monitors overcharging. The vast majority of agreements rely on voluntary compliance by companies rather than monitoring. At best, they may recognize that regulators are already monitoring the company, but often they simply ask companies to hire consultants to review their books and records. How independent are these consultants? Concerns have been raised in cases involving major banks; HSBC had hired Deloitte & Touche to review transactions for money laundering during the period for which it was later prosecuted for massive violations. During U.S. Senate hearings, Sen. Jack Reed asked, "How can you be independent if you're hired by the entity you're reviewing?"[122] That is all the more reason for judges, regulators, and prosecutors to ensure independent supervision of corporate prosecution agreements.

One judge asked why prosecutors entered a "sweetheart deal" with Barclays Bank in a 2010 prosecution. The prosecutor emphasized "the serious nature of the criminal conduct," which included helping "Cuba, Iran, Sudan, Libya, and Burma to illegally move more than $500 million."[123] Although regulators required Barclays to hire a third party to improve compliance, the agreement did not require a monitor. The judge raised the "too big to jail" concern:

> It's proceedings like this that raise concerns in the public's mind about fairness and justice and why are financial institutions being treated the way in which they're being treated when everyone else who is charged criminally has to acknowledge criminal responsibility.

The judge pointed out that monitors "have been appointed in other cases but not this case," and insisted on "status hearings every three months so I can also monitor what's going on."[124] Judges should indeed fill this gap and supervise corporate prosecutions through both their oversight of deferred prosecutions and supervision of probation when companies plead guilty.

Further, prosecutors should ban or sharply limit the use of corporate non-prosecution agreements not filed with a judge, as whether Congress could pass a law to do so raises questions of constitutional separation of powers between the legislature and the executive branches. Non-prosecution agreements are nearly as common as deferred prosecution agreements, but corporate agreements are far too important to avoid judicial review entirely. Nor does a criminal prosecution system work if companies do not know whether they might receive a non-prosecution or deferred prosecution agreement depending on their clout or other invisible factors.

In the HSBC case, federal judge John Gleeson waited months before approving the deferred prosecution agreement. The judge ultimately concluded that he had supervisory authority over such a case—he was not, "to borrow a famous phrase, a potted plant." The judge asked to receive quarterly reports to monitor the implementation of an agreement, noting that all sorts of situations might call for his intervention, such as a possible breach of the agreement and selecting a replacement monitor.[125] Perhaps more judges will insist on supervising corporate agreements. Judges could also do more in plea agreements by imposing special conditions of probation, similarly making monitors' reports transparent if not public, and stating specific reasons why probation supervision should end or continue.

Judges should select monitors, allaying concerns that prosecutors offer these plum positions mostly to former colleagues, by supervising a competitive process for bidding on the positions. Judges could review the fees charged and ensure that monitors or special masters are appointed when needed. The overwhelming majority of deferred prosecution and non-prosecution agreements now reached do not include a monitor. Judges should also review the decision to conclude an agreement and should ask whether a company has sufficiently reformed. A company should not be let off the hook until a judge has reviewed the monitor reports, heard from regulators and prosecutors, and decided it is in the public interest to conclude the case.

We should feel uneasy about the fact that some firms get convicted and others get a better deal for similar crimes. While the reasons for this are usually unknown, such disparities can have a corrosive effect on companies who see others let off the hook for doing basically the same thing they did. The DOJ has adopted no guidance on what compliance to require or how to ensure it is effective. Still more problematic, however one defines them, are recidivist companies, which typically face no additional punishment. I have described how prosecutors agree to fines much lower that what the guidelines recommend. Lenient fines may become a merely a minor cost of doing business, and judges should outright reject settlements that fail to adequately punish. Federal judge William Young rejected a proposed plea agreement with APTx Vehicle Systems Ltd. for defrauding the federal government to the tune of $5.7 million by failing to deliver to Iraq Jeeps the army had paid for. The prosecution deal called for a $1 million fine and a $2 million civil settlement. Judge Young rejected the deal as against the public interest and emphasized that a judge's role is to "ensure that justice is done." The judge called the fine "meager" and "strikingly low," given that according to the guidelines the company could be fined up to $11.4 million. A great many of these corporate settlements include fines well below the limits set by statute and the guidelines, and judges should intervene if prosecutors agree to a fine so "paltry" as to result in a "denigration of criminal law."[126]

Judicial review is no panacea. If prosecutors decide not to pursue a conviction, there is nothing a judge can do, and placing a straitjacket on the types of terms that agreements can include is not a good idea, either. Nor will all judges supervise these complex cases carefully. Still, greater involvement of judges and the public would be a real improvement.

Conclusion

Judge Gerard Lynch has described federal prosecutors as playing "the role of God."[127] Prosecutors are the most powerful actors in our criminal justice system, but in corporate prosecutions the tables are turned. Large organizations create complex environments ripe for commission of crimes on a massive scale, and that complexity makes crime difficult to uncover and punish. In this book I have described the many challenges of prosecuting corporations, both in order to make it understandable why prosecutors tend to compromise in the ways that they do and to underscore how important it is to get corporate prosecutions right.

Corporations have "no soul to damn," as the Lord Chancellor in England famously remarked.[128] Some critics call it nonsensical to hold corporations criminally accountable, while critics on the other side argue that corporations should be punished especially severely.[129] There is a middle ground. The great pragmatist philosopher John Dewey famously argued we should stop using the word *person* to apply to corporations, since the term is distracting—what matters are the "concrete facts" concerning how an organization actually operates and whether it needs to be regulated or given legal rights.[130] The current view held by most prosecutors is also pragmatic. Prosecutors say that only serious violations of regulations and criminal statutes, such as involvement by upper management or tolerance of misconduct, deserve a distinctly criminal punishment. However, prosecutors are also too pragmatic in the negative sense of that word, sacrificing principle to expediency. Serious criminal violations demand imposition of serious structural reforms and not just window-dressing. Prosecutors should demand companies pay full statutory fines, typically up to twice the gain or loss to victims, and not the slap-on-the-wrist penalties that are all too common. Prosecutors should normally seek a conviction if a corporation deserves criminal punishment and the collateral consequences are not inappropriate. After all, major companies are routinely convicted without suffering Arthur Andersen's fate: BP, SAC Capital Advisors, and Siemens received criminal convictions.

Each of the "too big to jail" concerns could be addressed by a new set of guidelines for prosecuting companies, designed to strengthen the use of criminal prosecutions as a distinct punishment for companies that engage in the most serious violations. The overall theme of these reforms is that egregious

lack of compliance should be treated as criminal and result in serious punishment and an effective overall of compliance. Prosecutions should (1) require
a conviction, except in the unusual cases in which collateral consequences
would be severe, and convictions of subsidiaries should be preferred in those
cases, but if that is not possible, then (2) a deferred prosecution should be
supervised by a judge, through either a statute or supervisory authority, typically relying on regulators or monitors reporting to the judge. Prosecutors,
having determined that a criminal prosecution is justified, should (3) insist on
detailed structural reforms to ensure that effective compliance is put into
place and supervised by prosecutors, regulators, or a monitor, and (4) impose
fines intended to be a deterrent, mitigated only by voluntary self-reporting
and carefully documented efforts to create compliance. The Organizational
Sentencing Guidelines could also be revised to provide far greater punishment for recidivists and companies that do not self-report, while more clearly
requiring that compliance be audited. Corporation prosecutions deserve
more sunlight: (5) the public and the shareholders should know more about
corporate crime, including through release of all prosecution agreements,
detailed accounting of how fines are calculated, and publicly available progress reports describing compliance.

The problem of corporate prosecutions is double-edged. Under the current system, corporate prosecutions are both over- and underused. It is troubling if prosecutors offer a company an alternative to prosecution because
they think they have a weak case—in such circumstances, prosecutors should
not be bringing a criminal case at all. But it is also troubling if prosecutors
bring strong cases against egregious corporate violators, only to then settle
for reduced fines and superficial compliance. Overly lenient settlements of corporate prosecution undermine the legitimacy of the criminal law. They send
a corrosive "too big to jail" message to industry and to the public.

To be sure, none of these are silver-bullet solutions to the set of "too big to
jail" concerns raised by corporate prosecutions. Even with clearer guidelines,
prosecutors retain enormous discretion in making decisions about whom to
prosecute and how, and they decide whether a breakdown in compliance occurred or rogue employees were responsible. Prosecutors will still largely depend on corporations for information about what actually happened and must
offer leniency in exchange for cooperation and self-reporting. The ability of
judges to supervise prosecution decisions is limited, and the ability of judges,

prosecutors, and others to structurally reform corporations using a criminal case is also limited. Lastly, and most fundamentally, we do not know enough about how complex organizations work or what compliance systems are the most effective. If anything, the current approach toward settling corporate prosecutions keeps both compliance failures and success stories in the dark.

My goal in this book has been to describe the intricate hidden world of corporate prosecutions. No longer is it an unusual practice for the largest corporations to receive criminal punishments. Blockbuster corporate prosecutions are the largest-scale criminal prosecutions of all time, in terms of their economic stakes, and they deserve closer attention. The sheer size and complexity of some corporate crime makes it troubling and fascinating. Indeed, corporate crime can overwhelm the limited resources of the criminal justice system.[131] Whether and how to provide more resources to prosecutors and regulators who investigate corporate conduct is a larger social, political, and policy question. Meaningful regulation of corporations must come from sustained political and regulatory involvement, but prosecutors provide a last line of defense against the most serious violations.

Corporate prosecutions have been transformed in recent years, but also compromised. While the world of corporate prosecutions has dramatically changed, we should be troubled both by what we know and how much we do not.[132] Although the data I present here provide a rich picture of the current practice, we lack sufficient knowledge about how prosecutors exercise their discretion when targeting corporations. Much remains hidden, including how agreements are carried out, whether compliance is carefully supervised, how fines are calculated, why so few individuals are prosecuted, and what explains the wide range in fines. The apparent success stories, such as in the Siemens case that I began this book with, suggest how large corporations and even entire industries can be reformed. However, far more needs to be done to investigate when and whether compliance programs are effective—currently, very little is made public about how they are implemented in practice. The globalization of corporate prosecutions raises still more questions; we should be careful to evaluate a new corporate prosecution approach before encouraging its spread around the world. We want other countries to insist on accountability and not just adopt new ways to compromise with corporations.

Even the biggest corporate prosecutions lack the courtroom drama of individual criminal cases. Corporations understandably try to settle criminal cases quietly and outside the public eye. However, corporate prosecutions can succeed only if judges, prosecutors, lawyers, regulators, lawmakers, shareholders, and ultimately the public stay informed and involved. Prosecutors have made some changes already in response to the "too big to jail" concerns that people have raised, but much more needs to be done. It is crucial that we get corporate prosecutions right, given the size, seriousness, and complexity of the crimes that can occur in the corporate setting. Corporate prosecutions are themselves too big to fail.

APPENDIX

NOTES

ACKNOWLEDGMENTS

INDEX

APPENDIX

This book began with a problem: I wondered what happens to companies that are prosecuted, but there was no good source for data on corporate prosecutions. While the U.S. Sentencing Commission keeps data on prosecutions of organizations, those data were incomplete, and the problem was growing worse, since prosecutors had started to enter into more deferred prosecution and non-prosecution agreements that were not being tracked by the commission or anyone else. Since there was no official national corporate offender registry, I created one, building a database of more than 300 deferred prosecution or non-prosecution agreements with companies, with invaluable help over the years from Jon Ashley and the University of Virginia Law Library. I made these data available online as a public resource, and the database remains the most authoritative and complete source for information about those agreements.[1] Next, I amassed a second, larger archive of federal corporate convictions from the past decade, more than 2,000, mostly guilty pleas by corporations, and I placed these data online as well.[2] We intend to continue to update these data.

Each chapter in this book tells a different part of the story of how corporate prosecutions have evolved. In this appendix, I describe the methods used to collect and analyze these data. Chapter 1 of this book began by describing the new leniency approach used by federal prosecutions. I noted that an overall decline in convictions of companies beginning in 2000 accompanied an expansion in the use of deferred prosecution agreements. What was missing from that picture? We do not know what the underlying corporate crime rate is. Nor do we know how many corporate crimes come to the attention of prosecutors but that they choose not to bring. I collected data on formalized non-prosecution agreements, but other non-prosecutions may never be formalized in an agreement not to prosecute. Prosecutors may simply decline to pursue charges, including because they lack sufficient evidence that a crime occurred or conclude that no crime occurred, or because they view a civil enforcement action as sufficient. These data do not include leniency agreements in the Antitrust Division's leniency program, which are kept confidential. Nor do these data include convictions overturned on appeal, such as the Arthur Andersen conviction. Nor do these data include cases in which the indictment was dismissed or the company was acquitted at trial, discussed in Chapter 8. In Chapter 1, I displayed total corporate fines from 1994 through 2012. The commission's data are useful since they go back to the early 1990s, but as I found when I collected data on corporate prosecutions from 2001 to 2012, and as others have found when examining 1990s data, the commission underreports total fines, perhaps because of incomplete reporting by the federal courts.

Not only have total fines gone up over the last decade in particular, but average fines have also gone up steadily, as Figure A.1 shows. This could reflect prosecutors focusing on the most serious offenders. I note that there are growing discrepancies between what I found in dockets and the commission data, which suggest their information is incomplete. In the period from 2001 to 2005, discrepancies may also be due to the fact that it was not always possible to separate the commission's data into calendar years (they use fiscal years). There may be discrepancies in dates reported to the commission re-

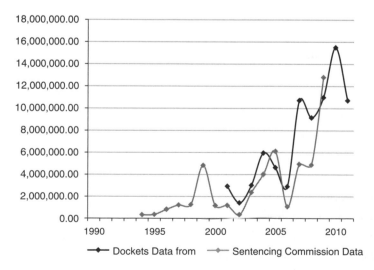

Figure A.1 Average Corporate Fines, 1994–2012

Table A.1 The Top Twenty Corporate Fines, 2001–2012				
	Company	Fine	Year	Crime
1	Pharmacia & Upjohn	$1.195 billion	2007	Pharmaceuticals
2	GlaxoSmithKline, LLC	$957 million	2012	Pharmaceuticals
3	Eli Lilly	$515 million	2009	Pharmaceuticals
4	Abbott Laboratories	$500 million	2012	Pharmaceuticals
5	AU Optronics Corp.	$500 million	2012	Antitrust
6	Yazaki Corp.	$470 million	2012	Antitrust
7	Siemens Aktiengesellschaft	$448.5 million	2009	FCPA
8	Kellogg Brown & Root LLC	$402 million	2009	FCPA
9	BAE Systems plc	$400 million	2010	FCPA
10	LG Display Co., Ltd.	$400 million	2008	Antitrust
11	UBS AG	$400 million	2012	Fraud
12	Air France/KLM	$350 million	2008	Antitrust
13	Allergan	$350 million	2010	Pharmaceuticals
14	Prudential Equity Group, LLC	$325 million	2008	Securities fraud
15	Merck Sharp & Dohme Corp.	$322 million	2012	Pharmaceuticals
16	British Airways	$300 million	2007	Antitrust
17	Korean Airlines	$300 million	2007	Antitrust
18	Samsung Electronics Company	$300 million	2005	Antitrust
19	TAP Pharmaceutical Products, Inc.	$290 million	2001	Pharmaceuticals
20	Guidant LLC	$254 million	2004	Pharmaceuticals

garding when sentencing occurred versus when the judgment was entered. There may also be cases the commission reported that were not available in docket sheets, including, perhaps if a case was sealed.

Table A.1 lists the top twenty corporate fines from 2001 to 2012 to give a sense of the small number of very large blockbuster cases that have pushed up the fines in recent years. The largest fine is now the $1.256 billion fine paid by BP in 2013. These cases were dominated by pharmaceutical-related and antitrust prosecutions, with more FCPA prosecutions in recent years.

Figure A.2 displays the fines each year in deferred prosecution and non-prosecution agreements from 2001 to 2012, when added to the fines in cases of corporate convictions (displaying data collected from dockets and not commission data). While fines have gone up in deferred prosecution and non-prosecution agreements, the bulk of the fines each year are in cases of convictions.

In Chapter 3, I explore how fines are just a part of the total payments made by prosecuted organizations, which may also be sued by private plaintiffs, they may make disgorgement, forfeiture, restitution, and community service payments to prosecutors, and they may pay fines and make other payments to regulators. As noted in Chapter 3, information on civil suits reflects what could be learned from reported cases or media accounts; many civil settlements are kept confidential. The figures on total payments do not include expenses for legal defense, accountants, compliance, media, and other expenses companies incur when prosecuted. The average fines and total payments varied quite a bit depending on the crime. Figure A.3 shows the variation in average fines and total payments, broken down by type of crime. The largest average fines and total payments were in securities fraud cases, pharmaceutical cases, and Bank Secrecy Act cases, followed by antitrust and FCPA cases.

In Chapter 3, I also discussed characteristics of deferred prosecution and non-prosecution agreements, focusing on what types of compliance was required. The figure presented in Chapter 3 showed that compliance reforms are generally required, but fewer agreements required corporate monitors or specific governance changes. In many agreements, regulators required compliance, not just prosecutors. The charts below display the mixture of crimes that companies were prosecuted for that received deferred prosecution and

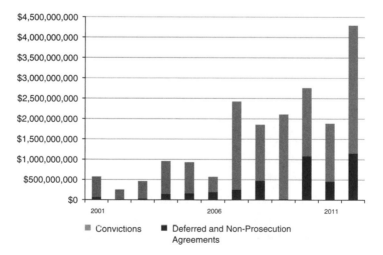

Figure A.2 Added Fines in Organizational Deferred Prosecution and Non-Prosecution Agreements and Convictions, 2001–2012

non-prosecution agreements, in Figure A.4, versus the crimes in cases in which the companies were convicted, in Figure A.5. As discussed in Chapters 3 and 9, the deferred prosecution and non-prosecution agreements were dominated by fraud and FCPA cases. The convictions were dominated by antitrust, environmental, and fraud statements convictions. These data reflect the most specific "lead" charges against the companies; often, the lead offenses charged are also accompanied by more general charges such as fraud or false statements.

Chapter 4 focuses on prosecutions of employees. As noted, in about one-third (35 percent, or 89 of 255) deferred prosecution or non-prosecution agreements, corporate officers or employees were prosecuted for related crimes, based on information available from prosecutors' press releases, docket searches, and news searches for reports of such individual prosecutions. In about two-thirds of those agreements, no employees were prosecuted. Of course, even if employees were indicted and a prosecution was initiated, the case might not result in a conviction.

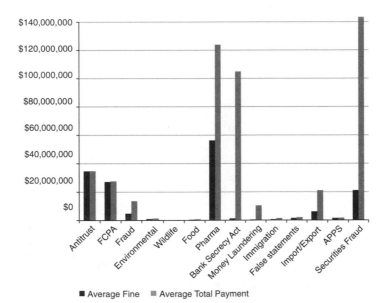

Figure A.3 Average Fines and Payments in Corporate Prosecutions, 2001–2012, by Crime

Chapter 5 focuses on the role of victims in corporate prosecutions, and presented data on rising amounts of restitution paid by convicted organizations. I included Sentencing Commission data for the period before 2001, but found that the data were missing restitution information collected from docket sheets and deferred prosecutions from 2001 to 2012. Chapter 6 discussed sentencing of corporations, and noted how few of the deferred prosecution and non-prosecution agreements provided a sentencing guidelines

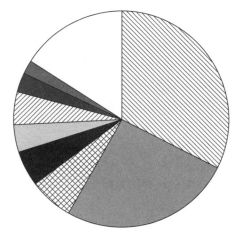

Fraud (79)
FCPA (63)
Kickbacks (16)
Bank Secrecy Act (13)
Immigration (10)
Import/Export (12)
Antitrust (7)
Environmental (5)
Other (39)

Figure A.4 Crimes and Organizational Deferred Prosecution and Non-Prosecution Agreements, 2001–2012

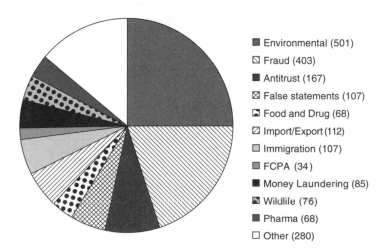

Environmental (501)
Fraud (403)
Antitrust (167)
False statements (107)
Food and Drug (68)
Import/Export (112)
Immigration (107)
FCPA (34)
Money Laundering (85)
Wildlife (76)
Pharma (68)
Other (280)

Figure A.5 Crimes and Organizational Convictions, 2001–2012

calculation; when that did occur, the sentence was at or below the bottom of the guidelines. In that chapter, I also discussed Sentencing Commission data, which provide information on judges' sentencing calculations far richer than what can be gathered from docket sheets, such as, for example, when they did or did not credit for corporate compliance and the like. Chapter 7 focuses on the role of corporate monitors, and described how 25 percent (65 of 255) deferred prosecution and non-prosecution agreements from 2001 to 2012 require a monitor to provide independent supervision of that compliance.

Chapter 9 focuses on prosecutions of foreign corporations. Figure A.6 displays the types of crimes that foreign corporations were convicted of; Chapter 9 explains why in these areas in particular, corporate prosecutions have taken off, and it presents data concerning rising fines in foreign corporate prosecutions and in antitrust and FCPA cases in particular.

Data Collection

I have tried to gather all of the available information about organizational prosecutions in federal courts, focusing on the period 2001–2012. I have not gathered information about state court prosecutions of organizations. I could not find any large states that keep data on organizations separate from sentencing information on individual defendants. From reading reported cases and news reports, I gather that state and local prosecutors do not bring

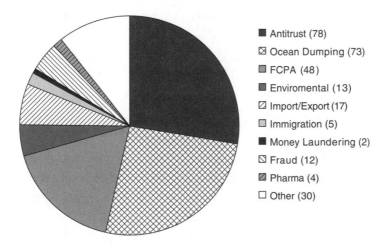

- Antitrust (78)
- Ocean Dumping (73)
- FCPA (48)
- Enviromental (13)
- Import/Export (17)
- Immigration (5)
- Money Laundering (2)
- Fraud (12)
- Pharma (4)
- Other (30)

Figure A.6 Foreign Corporate Crimes of Prosecution

major corporate cases nearly to the degree that federal prosecutors do. The notable exceptions are the Manhattan District Attorney's Office and the New York Attorney General's Office, which have long stood watch over Wall Street, and a few other more active state attorneys general. They sometimes cooperate with federal prosecutors in important cases, but they may also sometimes pick up cases that federal prosecutors decide not to bring.

The Sentencing Commission began keeping data on prosecutions of organizations, including corporations, partnerships, limited liability companies, and other entities, after the Organizational Sentencing Guidelines took effect in 1991. The commission relies on information provided by federal judges. I include in several tables data from the commission for purposes of comparison and to provide some information about organizational prosecutions before 2001. However, their data were apparently quite spotty in the 1990s, and they remain incomplete to this day.[3] The commission does report several hundred more corporate convictions during the period 2001–2009 than I was able to locate. However, the commission does not report deferred prosecution and non-prosecution agreements. For conviction of organizations, the commission is missing quite a bit of fine and restitution information. This may be due to their dependence on reporting by courthouses, or it may be because they have less information in cases in which sentencing is not done under the guidelines. The commission does not publish names of convicted organizations (or individuals). They do not follow up and add information not supplied by the judge and not used to sentence a particular firm; as a result, they often do not note whether a convicted company is public or not, for example, although that information should be readily available.[4]

To gather far more complete data, I decided to hand-collect data on all corporate prosecutions from 2001 to 2012 resulting in a conviction or a deferred prosecution or non-prosecution agreement. These data are available online as a resource, including the text of prosecution agreements themselves (and we will continue updating it; 2013 agreements are available, for example). I identified 255 deferred prosecution and non-prosecution agreements with organizations from 2001 to 2012, as well as 14 such agreements from 1992 to 2000. The deferred prosecution agreements were brought across the country, but almost half were brought by the Department of Justice itself (119 cases), particularly the Fraud Section (75 cases), and other departments such as the Antitrust Division (8 cases). Other agreements were brought by

U.S. Attorney's Offices around the country, led by the Southern District of New York (32 cases), which, due to its proximity to Wall Street, has traditionally brought corporate and white-collar prosecutions, but also other offices such as the District of Massachusetts (17 cases) and the District of New Jersey (11 cases), and U.S. attorneys in California (23 total).

These data on deferred prosecution and non-prosecution agreements was collected starting in 2005, by identifying agreements through news searches, press releases by the Department of Justice and U.S. Attorney's Office, and also when practitioners brought agreements to our attention. The Government Accountability Office conducted a study of federal deferred prosecution and non-prosecution agreements with organizations, and in August 2010, the GAO provided a list of those agreements in response to an information request, which added several additional agreements that had not previously been known. Finally, searches of the Bloomberg dockets database located a handful of additional deferred prosecution agreements with companies that had not previously been known. Some of these agreements have been reported in the news, but the text of the agreements themselves have not made public. Jon Ashley has contacted each of the U.S. Attorney's Offices to request those agreements, and they have not been disclosed; some were said to be under seal by agreement between the parties, while others could not be located by the relevant office. An effort by the First Amendment Clinic at the University of Virginia School of Law to litigate Freedom of Information Act requests for missing agreements is under way.

I did not treat as a separate case a deferred prosecution or non-prosecution agreement that additionally named a subsidiary, unless prosecutors entered a separate agreement with the subsidiary. Since plea agreements, in contrast to deferred prosecution and non-prosecution agreements, sometimes formally included a separate conviction and agreement with the subsidiary, the set of corporate convictions contained more separate but related cases.

The collection of corporate convictions was a much larger project. I identified 2,008 federal corporate convictions entered from January 1, 2001, through December 31, 2012. These data on corporate prosecutions came from several sources. First, we collected large numbers of plea agreements, as well as identifying a small number of cases in which a company was convicted at a trial. These were identified with substantial help from Jon Ashley and a team of law student research assistants. Those agreements were identified in several stages. First, plea agreements were located using searches of DOJ and U.S. Attorney's Office websites, which post press releases and sometimes the agreements themselves online (a more common practice in recent years), and by contacting such offices. SEC database searches located additional agreements reported by corporations to the SEC. News searches and Westlaw searches were also used to identify additional agreements. Plea agreements were obtained and have been made available online, along with a spreadsheet detailing these data. The agreements that we did not locate, if any, were likely mostly small firms not listed or required to report convictions to the SEC. I excluded corporate convictions for petty offenses such as traffic tickets, of which there were a fair number in a few district courts.

Second, we searched and collected docket sheets. Jon Ashley and I searched both the dockets database on WestlawNext and the Bloomberg dockets database and ran multiple searches specifying terms such as "corp." and "inc." and "incorporated" and "LLC." We eliminated cases in which the firm had the charges dismissed or was acquitted at trial. The docket sheets were very useful as a supplement to plea agreements, since docket sheets typically noted the final sentence and fine imposed, while plea agreements might only specify a sentence range for the judge to consider. I also thank David Uhlmann and the Michigan Environmental Crimes Project for sharing preliminary environmental prosecution data from 2005 to 2010.

Data Analysis

A range of information was coded concerning these corporate prosecutions. As displayed above, the deferred prosecution and non-prosecution agreements had more detailed information coded concerning the various compliance-related terms in the agreements. The deferred prosecution and non-prosecution agreements also had information coded concerning agreements and penalties by regulators as well as any available public information about settlements in private suits. Only for the deferred prosecution and non-prosecution agreements, I collected information regarding whether the prosecution of the corporation was accompanied by a prosecution of employees.

For just the FCPA cases, I coded information concerning the SEC enforcement cases and prosecutions and enforcement actions against employees, to compare outcomes in criminal prosecutions with civil enforcement, as described in Chapter 9. For all of the corporate prosecutions, however, information was coded concerning the crime, the prosecuting office, the fines, restitution, and other penalties, probation, and whether a corporate monitor was appointed, as well as characteristics of the companies, including whether they were publicly listed in the United States and whether they were incorporated in the United States or abroad.

To examine whether larger fines were correlated with certain types of companies or crimes, I analyzed that information using two regressions. For these regressions, cases with zero fine had one dollar added to them (and in fact, there was a nominal fine in such cases, since I did not include in the fine calculations the several hundred dollar special assessments imposed by federal courts). I thank Vahid Gholampour for his invaluable assistance in conducting these analyses of these data. Tables A.2 and A.3 present results of log regressions run on the independent variable of the fines imposed, in all 2,262 corporate prosecutions studied from 2001–2012, as well as on the total payments made by those firms.

I wondered whether larger fines were correlated with certain types of crimes, or companies, specifically, whether firms were foreign or domestic, and public or not public (defined as whether the company had stock listed in the United States, and include subsidiaries, and firms with American depositary receipts listed in the United States). Of the 2,262 cases examined from 2001 to 2012, only about 80 were dropped from the analysis because they were missing fine information. The first table shows a regression of just the criminal fine. The second displays an otherwise identical regression, but with the total payment by the firm, including restitution or forfeiture as well as the fine. For the second regression, only about forty cases were dropped from the analysis due to missing payment information.

The regression selected as the most informative and the best fit was a log regression, because there was such a wide range of fines, with many firms receiving nominal fines and, at the other end of the spectrum, firms with fines in the hundreds of millions of dollars. Using a linear regression and other types of regressions suggested that the effects were not uniform among these data. The tables above also present exponentials of the coefficients to show how many times larger, within a 95 percent confidence interval, the fines were when controlling for the other factors.

Table A.2 Regression of Logfines					
Crime Code	Variables	(1) Logfine	Exp. of Coefficients	95% Interval	
	foreign	2.000*** (0.431)	7.39	3.17	17.20
	public	1.456*** (0.384)	4.29	2.02	9.10
1	antiT	4.624*** (0.493)	101.90	38.77	267.81
4	env	2.427*** (0.349)	11.32	5.71	22.44
2	FCPA	4.336*** (0.659)	76.40	21.00	278.01
3	fraud	−1.346*** (0.363)	0.26	0.13	0.53
10	immig	0.206 (0.602)	1.23	0.38	4.00
9	money	−2.870*** (0.753)	0.06	0.01	0.25
6	food	0.895 (0.684)	2.45	0.64	9.35
7	pharma	3.973*** (0.647)	53.14	14.95	188.88
8	bankSecrecy	−5.166*** (0.886)	0.01	0.00	0.03
12	impExp	1.250** (0.535)	3.49	1.22	9.96
13	Apps	3.399*** (0.734)	29.93	7.10	126.17
14	secFraud	−3.221*** (1.090)	0.04	0.00	0.34
15	bribery	2.926** (1.477)	18.65	1.03	337.28
18	healthFraud	−3.372*** (0.698)	0.03	0.01	0.13
19	accFraud	−9.349*** (2.652)	0.00	0.00	0.02
	Constant	7.757*** (0.237)			
	Observations R-squared	2,180 0.222			

Standard errors in parentheses
* $p < 0.1$
** $p < 0.05$
*** $p < 0.01$

Table A.3 Regression of Log on Total Payment					
Crime Code	Variables	(1) logAdjPay	Exp. of Coefficients	95% Interval	
	foreign	2.209*** (0.372)	9.11	4.39	18.88
	public	2.362*** (0.332)	10.61	5.54	20.34
1	antiT	3.409*** (0.425)	30.23	13.14	69.55
4	env	1.670*** (0.301)	5.31	2.94	9.58
2	FCPA	2.064*** (0.569)	7.88	2.58	24.03
3	fraud	1.728*** (0.312)	5.63	3.05	10.38
10	immig	0.500 (0.520)	1.65	0.59	4.57
9	money	−0.101 (0.649)	0.90	0.25	3.23
6	food	0.0953 (0.594)	1.10	0.34	3.52
7	pharma	2.900*** (0.559)	18.17	6.08	54.36
8	bankSecrecy	0.831 (0.752)	2.30	0.53	10.02
12	impExp	0.813* (0.463)	2.25	0.91	5.59
13	Apps	2.086*** (0.631)	8.05	2.34	27.74
14	secFraud	0.433 (0.931)	1.54	0.25	9.56
15	bribery	1.232 (1.284)	3.43	0.28	42.46
18	healthFraud	0.944 (0.598)	2.57	0.80	8.30
19	accFraud	−2.923 (2.307)	0.05	0.00	4.95
	Constant	9.440*** (0.203)			
	Observations R-squared	2,218 0.132			

Standard errors in parentheses

* $p < 0.1$

** $p < 0.05$

*** $p < 0.01$

What the tables show is that that among all of these prosecutions, the public companies received fines that were on average over four times larger than the other companies, even controlling for the type of crime and other characteristics of the cases. That was not surprising; public companies are far larger and might tend to commit more substantial offenses that impact more victims or result in more gains to the company. I also found that foreign companies paid fines that were on average over seven times larger, even controlling for some other characteristics of the cases. In addition, several crimes stood out as associated with far larger fines on average: antitrust, FCPA, and pharmaceutical prosecutions in particular. Antitrust cases had fines on average over a hundred times larger, FCPA cases over seventy-five times larger, and pharmaceutical cases on average over fifty times larger than other cases.

The results taking into account total payments by companies, and not just the criminal fine, were similar, but with even larger average payments by public companies (nine times larger payments on average) and public companies (over ten times larger payments on average), while someone more modest crime-related increases. Total payments for prosecuted companies were on average thirty times larger in antitrust cases, almost eight times larger on average for FCPA cases, and eighteen times larger for pharmaceutical cases.

I emphasize, however, that those averages should not be taken as an overly precise measure of the relative size of the effect, since the confidence intervals in these regressions were quite wide, and therefore reflect wide ranges in estimates. Another important qualification is that these results only show associations among cases obtained, in which prosecutors successfully brought cases against organizations in federal court during that time period. These data do not reflect cases not brought by prosecutors, dismissed by the judge, or dropped by prosecutors, or rare corporate trial acquittals or reversals on appeal. Most important, these data do not show that prosecutors are necessarily more aggressive when they pursue, for example, foreign firms or public firms or antitrust cases. These data could reflect that more very substantial and serious cases involving foreign firms or public firms or antitrust violations happened to come to prosecutors' attention. Or, as to foreign firms, it may be that prosecutors simply decide to pursue cases against foreign firms only when they are very serious and involve large firms and substantial harm or egregious violations.

The descriptions in this book of what prosecutors say their priorities are, including bringing antitrust and FCPA cases, suggest that the biggest cases do reflect prosecutors' goals to be "aggressive" in these areas. To be sure, prosecutors may simply have more low-hanging fruit, or big serious cases, come their way in those areas. For example, the pharmaceutical cases involve very large criminal and civil fines, but as discussed, they are often initially brought by *qui tam* whistle-blowers. How prosecutors exercise their discretion cannot be known just from observing the outcomes in cases they do decide to bring. These data, while detailed, provide only a first step. There are rich and complex explanations for how prosecutors use their discretion in corporate prosecutions. My goal in this book has been to situate these data by using examples from cases, describing the changes in prosecutors' practices, and exploring the dynamics at work in legislatures, regulatory agencies, courts, the defense bar, and the business world.

NOTES

1. United States vs. Goliath

1. Siri Schubert and T. Christian Miller, "At Siemens, Bribery Was Just a Line Item," *New York Times*, December 20, 2008.
2. *Frontline*, "Black Money," PBS, April 7, 2009, www.pbs.org/wgbh/pages/frontline/black money/etc/script.html.
3. Carter Dougherty, "Ex-Manager at Siemens Convicted in Bribery Scandal," *New York Times*, July 28, 2008.
4. *Frontline*, "Black Money."
5. John C. Coffee, "'No Soul to Damn: No Body to Kick': An Unscandalized Inquiry into the Problem of Corporate Punishment," *Michigan Law Review* 79 (1981): 386.
6. 212 U.S. 481 (1909).
7. Ibid., 494–496.
8. 558 U.S. 310 (2010).
9. 1 U.S.C. § 1.
10. More than 95 percent of felonies are prosecuted at the local level. Bureau of Justice Statistics, U.S. Dept. of Justice, Office of Justice Programs, *Felony Sentences in State Courts 2010* (2011). In contrast, while few states keep data on organizational prosecutions, reported cases suggest state and local prosecutors do not bring major corporate cases to the degree federal prosecutors do, with some notable exceptions, such as the Manhattan District Attorney's Office and New York Attorney General's Office, which have long stood watch over Wall Street. For an exploration of corporate prosecutions brought by local prosecutors, particularly in smaller cases, see Michael L. Benson and Francis T. Cullen, *Combating Corporate Crime: Local Prosecutors at Work* (Boston: Northeastern University Press, 1998).
11. Mark A. Cohen, "Theories of Punishment and Empirical Trends in Corporate Criminal Sanctions," *Managerial and Decision Economics* 17 (1996): 401.
12. U.S. Department of Justice, Office of the Deputy Attorney General, Corporate Fraud Task Force, *First Year Report to the President*, July 22, 2003, 2.2.
13. Brandon L. Garrett and Jon Ashley, Federal Organizational Prosecution Agreements, University of Virginia School of Law, http://lib.law.virginia.edu/Garrett/prosecution _agreements/home.suphp. All deferred prosecution and non-prosecution agreements cited in this book by name of company can be read at that website.
14. Brandon L. Garrett and Jon Ashley, Federal Organizational Plea Agreements, University of Virginia School of Law, http://lib.law.virginia.edu/Garrett/plea_agreements/home

.php. All corporate plea agreements with judgments entered between 2001 and 2012 cited in this book by name of company can be read at that website, while any 2013–2014 agreements are cited in full.

15. David Crawford and Mike Esterl, "Inside Bribery Probe of Siemens: Liechtenstein Bank Triggered an International Hunt," *Wall Street Journal*, December 28, 2007.

16. *United States v. Siemens Aktiengesellschaft*, No. CR-8-367 (December 15, 2008), Plea Agreement, ¶ 98, www.usdoj.gov/opa/documents/siemens.pdf.

17. *Frontline*, "Black Money."

18. U.S. Dept. of Justice, "Siemens AG and Three Subsidiaries Plead Guilty to Foreign Corrupt Practices Act Violations and Agree to Pay $450 Million in Combined Criminal Fines," press release, December 15, 2008.

19. Nathan Vardi, "The Bribery Racket," *Forbes*, May 28, 2010.

20. Mike Esterl et al., "Siemens Internal Review Hits Hurdles," *Wall Street Journal*, January 23, 2008; David Crawford and Mike Esterl, "Siemens Ruling Details Bribery across the Globe," *Wall Street Journal*, November 16, 2007.

21. Siemens Plea Agreement, ¶ 4.

22. Schubert and Miller, "Where Bribery Was Just a Line Item."

23. Catherine Hickley, "Siemens Bribes Leave Von Pierer Unbowed in CEO Memoir," *Bloomberg News*, January 26, 2011.

24. U.S. Dept. of Justice, "Siemens AG and Three Subsidiaries Plead Guilty."

25. "Ex-Siemens Execs Found Guilty in Bribery Case," Reuters, April 20, 2010.

26. Honoré de Balzac, *Le Père Goriot* (New York: W. W. Norton, 1835), 124, 131.

27. *Frontline*, "Black Money."

2. The Company in the Courtroom

1. *U.S. v. Arthur Andersen, LLP*, No. H-02-121 (S.D.Tx. May 13, 2002), Trial Transcript, 1663–1665.

2. Ibid., 1665.

3. Ibid., 1672.

4. Ibid., 1973.

5. Ibid., 1676.

6. Barbara Ley Toffler, *Final Accounting* (New York: Broadway Books, 2003), 20, 27.

7. Ibid., 78–79, 83–84.

8. Ibid., 92–98.

9. Andersen Trial Transcript, 1683, 1688–1689.

10. Julie Mason, "Andersen Fires Enron Auditor," *Houston Chronicle*, January 16, 2002.

11. Andersen Trial Transcript, 664.

12. Ibid., 1800–1806, 2922–2923.

13. Complaint, *SEC v. Bergonzi*, No. 1: CV02-1084 (E.D.P.A. 2002).

14. Leslie Wayne, "How Delaware Thrives as a Corporate Tax Haven," *New York Times*, June 30, 2012.

15. Alix Stuart, "Is Going Public Going Out of Style," *CFO Magazine*, May 1, 2011.

16. SEC Rules of Practice, 17 C.F.R. § 201.102(e) (2006).

17. Andersen Trial Transcript, 667–668.

18. Ibid., 4603.

19. Ibid., 1874–1879.

20. Ibid., 6394.

21. Joe Berardino, "Enron: A Wake-Up Call," *Wall Street Journal*, December 4, 2001.

22. 18 U.S.C. 1512(b)(a)(A)–(B).

23. For example, the generic obstruction statute, 18 U.S.C. § 1503, did not require a persuasion theory, but it required a pending judicial proceeding; similarly, 18 U.S.C. § 1505 required a pending administrative proceeding.

24. For fiscal 2000–2012, 8 percent, or 210, of 2,592 firms found guilty were convicted at a trial. U.S. Sentencing Commission, *Sourcebook of Federal Sentencing Statistics*, various editions, 2000–2012.

25. Todd Ackerman, "Andersen Verdict, Case Turns on Counsel's Note," *Houston Chronicle*, June 10, 2002.

26. Karen Hosler, "Andersen Puts Blame on Auditor," *Baltimore Sun*, January 25, 2002.

27. Delroy Alexander and Stephen J. Hedges, "Andersen Charged in Shredding," *Chicago Tribune*, March 15, 2002.

28. Jonathan Weil, Richard B. Schmitt, and Devon Spurgeon, "Arthur Andersen Met with U.S., Hoping to Strike Agreement," *Wall Street Journal*, April 8, 2002.

29. Richard B. Schmitt et al., "Behind Andersen's Tug of War with U.S. Prosecutors," *Wall Street Journal*, April 19, 2002.

30. Gil Rudawsky, "Goldman Sachs Legal Bills Could Top $100 Million," *Daily Finance*, April 30, 2010.

31. Andersen Trial Transcript, 15.

32. Ibid., 2523.

33. Ibid., 65, 68.

34. Ibid., 29.

35. Ibid., 31–32.

36. Ibid., 32.

37. Joel Bakan, *The Corporation* (New York: Free Press, 2004), 17–18.

38. Richard W. Stevenson and Richard A. Oppel Jr., "Enron's Many Strands: The Overview; U.S. to Reconsider Agency Contracts in Enron Scandal," *New York Times*, January 26, 2002.

39. Andersen Trial Transcript, 339.

40. Ibid., 347–348, 351–355.

41. Ibid., 372.

42. Ibid., 356, 258.

43. Ibid., 369.

44. Ibid., 382, 392.

45. Ibid., 644.

46. Jt. Appendix at 2613, Athur Andersen LLP v. United States, 2005 WL 474013 *133.

47. Ibid., 2756–2760.

48. Andersen Trial Transcript, 5724.

49. Ibid., 2063.

50. Ibid., 1734.

51. Ibid., 1885 (the memo was introduced as exhibit 1012A at trial).

52. Ibid., 1850.

53. Ibid., 1891–1893.

54. Ibid., 1896–1897.

55. Ibid., 1904, 1909.

56. Ibid., 2262.

57. Ibid., 1976.

58. Mason, "Andersen Fires Enron Auditor."

59. Andersen Trial Transcript, 2001–2005.

60. Ibid., 2003.

61. Ibid., 2007, 2020, 2033–2035, 2302.

62. Ibid., 2135–2136.

63. Ibid., 2689.

64. Ibid., 2433.

65. Ibid., 2773.

66. Jonathan D. Glater, "Witness Cites Confusion in Shredding at Andersen," *New York Times*, May 23, 2002.

67. Andersen Trial Transcript, 480–481.

68. Ibid., 2786.

69. Ibid., 1884–1885.

70. Ibid., 4965–4966, 5018–5021.

71. Ibid., 5498.

72. Ibid., 5714, 5715.

73. Ibid., 3670.

74. Stephen Landsman, "Death of an Accountant," *Chicago-Kent Law Review* 78 (2003): 1222.

75. 212 U.S. 481 (1909).

76. Paul Halliday, *Dismembering the Body Politic: Partisan Politics in England's Towns, 1650–1730* (Cambridge: Cambridge University Press, 1998).

77. Eng. Rep., vol. 77, 9. 973 (10 Co. Rep. 32b). The quotation comes from Coke's report of the Case of Sutton's Hospital, "the single most influential writing on corporations in the seventeenth and eighteenth centuries." Halliday, *Dismembering the Body Politic*, 31.

78. William Blackstone, *Commentaries on the Laws of England*, 15th ed. (London, 1809).

79. E.g., *People v. Corporation of Albany*, 11 Wed. 539 (N.Y. Sup. Ct. 1834).

80. *Bissell v. Mich. S. R.R. Co.*, 22 N.Y. 258, 263–264 (N.Y. 1860).

81. *State v. Morris & Essex Railroad*, 23 N.J.L. 360 (1852); *Commonwealth v. Proprietors of New Bedford Bridge*, 68 Mass. 339 (1854). For a wonderful discussion of the evolution of these cases, see Kathleen Brickey, *Corporate Criminal Liability* (Deerfield, Illinois: Clark Boardman Callaghan 1992), § 2.08.

82. *United States v. Nearing*, 252 F. 223, 231 (S.D.N.Y. 1918).

83. Model Penal Code § 2.07(1).

84. Gary Fields and John R. Emshwiller, "Many Failed Efforts to Count Nation's Federal Criminal Laws," *Wall Street Journal*, July 22, 2011.

85. For example, official extortion comes from the phrase "under color of right" in the Hobbs Act.

86. John C. Coffee Jr., "Paradigms Lost: The Blurring of the Criminal Law Models—and What Can Be Done About It," *Yale Law Journal* 101 (1992): 1880.

87. *Watergate Special Prosecution Report* (1975), 72–77; 15 U.S.C. §§ 78a, 78(m), 78dd-1–3, 78ff.; *Report of the Securities and Exchange Commission on Questionable and Illegal Corporate Payments and Practices* (May 12, 1976).
88. Andersen Trial Transcript, 6331.
89. Ibid., 6332–6333.
90. Ibid., 6344.
91. Ibid., 6289–6316.
92. Ibid., 6313.
93. Ibid., 6310, 6316.
94. Ibid., 6485.
95. Ibid., 6340.
96. Ibid., 6371, 6373.
97. Ibid., 6354–6356, 6444.
98. Ibid., 6668.
99. Ibid., 6482, 6618.
100. Ibid., 6638.
101. Ibid., 1732.
102. Ibid., 6638.
103. Ibid., 6686–6689.
104. Mary Flood, "The Andersen Verdict, Decision by Jurors Hinged on Memo," *Houston Chronicle*, June 16, 2002.
105. Andersen Trial Transcript, 6702, 6710–6711, 6720.
106. Ibid., 6784.
107. Ibid., 6813–6815, 6928, 6995.
108. Ibid., 6890.
109. Ibid., 6891, 6901.
110. Ibid., 6893.
111. Ibid., 6925.
112. Luisa Beltran, Brett Gering, and Alice Martin, "Andersen Guilty," CNN, June 13, 2002.
113. Ibid.
114. Flood, "The Andersen Verdict."
115. See Linda Tucci, "Andersen Clears Out Office but Leaves Some Ex-Staffers Behind," *St. Louis Post-Dispatch*, August 29, 2002.
116. *U.S. v. Arthur Andersen, LLP*, 374 F.3d 281, 299 (5th Cir. 2004).
117. Brief of Amici Curiae Washington Legal Foundation and Chamber of Commerce of the United States in Support of Petitioner, *U.S. v. Arthur Andersen*, No. 04–368, February 22, 2005.
118. *U.S. v. Arthur Andersen*, 2005 WL 1106590 (April 27, 2005).
119. 18 U.S.C. 1512(b)(2)(A)–(B); *U.S. v. Doss* (9th Cir. 2011); *United States v. Farrell*, 126 F.3d 484, 488 (3d Cir. 1997); *United States v. Thompson*, 76 F.3d 442, 452 (2d Cir. 1996).
120. Mary Flood, "Supreme Court Overturns Arthur Andersen's Enron Conviction," *Houston Chronicle*, May 31, 2005.
121. Ibid.
122. Elizabeth K. Ainslie, "Essay: Indicting Corporations Revisited: Lessons of the Arthur Andersen Prosecution," *American Criminal Law Review* 43 (Winter 2006): 110.

123. *United States v. Stein* (Stein I), 435 F. Supp. 2d 330, 336, 381 (S.D.N.Y. 2006).

124. U.S. Gen. Accounting Office, Report to the Chairman, Committee on Banking, Housing and Urban Affairs, U.S. Senate, *Financial Statement Restatements: Trends, Market Impacts, Regulatory Responses and Remaining Challenges* (2002), 4.

125. Floyd Norris, "The Markets: Market Place: Yes, He Can Top That," *New York Times*, July 17, 2002.

126. Public Company Accounting Reform and Investor Protection Act of 2002. 107 Pub. L. No. 204, 116 Stat. 745 (2002) (codified at 15 U.S.C. § 7201).

127. 18 U.S.C. § 1519.

128. Pub. L. No. 110–197, § 4, 121 Sta. 2557 (January 7, 2008); 18 U.S.C. § 1341.

129. 18 U.S.C. § 1349.

130. 18 U.S.C. § 1513.

131. 18 U.S.C. § 905.

132. *U.S. Sentencing Guidelines Manual* (2003), §§ 2B1.1(a)(1), (b)(2)(C), 2J1.2–3.

133. Dodd-Frank Wall Street Reform and Consumer Protection Act, Pub. L. No. 111–203, 124 Stat. 1376 (2010); 7 U.S.C. § 13(a)(5) (new insider trading crimes).

134. David A. Skeel Jr. and William J. Stuntz, "Christianity and the (Modest) Rule of Law," *University of Pennsylvania Journal of Constitutional Law* 8 (2006): 826–827.

135. Vikramaditya S. Khanna, "Corporate Crime Legislation: A Political Economy Analysis," *Washington University Law Quarterly* 82 (2004): 97.

136. John C. Roper, "Feds Won't Retry Andersen," *Houston Chronicle*, November 23, 2005.

3. What Happens to a Prosecution Deferred?

1. Google Inc., Code of Conduct, ¶ 1, http://investor.google.com/corporate/code-of-conduct.html.

2. U.S. Department of Justice, "Google Forfeits $500 Million Generated by Online Ads and Prescription Drug Sales by Canadian Online Pharmacies," press release, August 24, 2001.

3. Senate Permanent Subcommittee on Investigations of the Committee on Homeland Security and Governmental Affairs, *U.S. Tax Shelter Industry: The Role of Accountants, Lawyers, and Financial Professionals*, Senate Hearing 108-473 (November 18 and 20, 2003), 1:32.

4. Ibid., 1:39–44.

5. *Frontline*, "Tax Me if You Can: KPMG's Senate Testimony," PBS, February 19, 2004.

6. *United States v. KPMG*, No. 1:05-CR-00903-LAP (S.D.N.Y., August 29, 2005), Statement of Facts, ¶ 34.

7. George W. Bush, "Remarks by the President at Malcolm Baldrige National Quality Award Ceremony," March 7, 2002.

8. Larry D. Thompson, Deputy Attorney General, U.S. Department of Justice, "Remarks at Michigan Federal Bar Association," October 5, 2002.

9. *Frontline*, "Tax Me if You Can: Interview with Carl Levin," PBS, February 19, 2004.

10. IRS, "KPMG to Pay $456 Million for Criminal Violations in Relation to Largest-Ever Tax Shelter Fraud Case," press release, August 29, 2005.

11. KPMG History, KPMG, www.kpmg.com/Global/en/about/Overview/Pages/History.aspx.

12. KPMG, "Why KPMG? Culture," www.kpmg.com/global/en/careers/whykpmg/culture/pages/default.aspx.

13. KPMG, www.kpmg.com.

14. Senate Hearing 108-473. Appendix A provides a case-study description of BLIPS.

15. Senate Hearing 108-473, opening statement of Sen. Carl Levin.

16. Ibid., 129.

17. The government noted that "only two of the almost 200 BLIPS clients stayed in BLIPS somewhat longer than 60 days, both exiting before year-end to get their tax loss." The government quoted an email from two participants stating, "It would be a nice idea if we could find a client to stay in beyond 60 days" because it otherwise "looks terrible." *U.S. v. Pfaff et al.*, 2010 WL 8939963 *16 (January 15, 2010), Appellate Brief.

18. *Frontline,* "Tax Me if You Can: KPMG Exhibits, KPMG Email: Simon Says," *PBS,* February 19, 2004.

19. KPMG Agreement, Statement of Facts, ¶ 6.

20. Senate Hearing 108-473; KPMG Agreement, Statement of Facts, ¶¶ 6–7.

21. Senate Permanent Subcommittee on Investigations of the Committee on Homeland Security and Governmental Affairs, *The Role of Professional Firms in the U.S. Tax Shelter Industry,* S. Rep. No. 109-54, April 13, 2005, 13 ("Senate Report").

22. Senate Hearing 108-473, 19–20.

23. Ibid., 31.

24. Ibid., 151.

25. Ibid., 37, 46.

26. KPMG Agreement, Statement of Facts, ¶¶ 29–30; Senate Hearing 108-473, 157.

27. Senate Report, 22, 148.

28. Ibid., 22.

29. KPMG Agreement, Statement of Facts, ¶ 7.

30. Senate Hearing 108-473, 159.

31. KPMG Agreement, Statement of Facts, ¶ 19.

32. IRS Notice 2000-44.

33. Treasury Regulation § 1.752–756; see also Testimony of Calvin H. Johnson, Senate Hearing 108-473, 15. See *United States v. Home Concrete & Supply LLC,* 132 S. Ct. 1836 (2012) (holding IRS audit violated three-year statute of limitations when it sought in 2006 to enforce 2000 filings using Son of Boss tax shelter).

34. *United States v. Morton Salt,* 338 U.S. 632, 642–643 (1950).

35. Internal Revenue Act of 1864, § 14, 13 Stat. 226 (1864) (current version at 26 U.S.C. § 7602 (1988)).

36. *United States v. KPMG,* 316 F. Supp. 2d 30, 31–32 (D.D.C. 2004); KPMG Agreement, Statement of Facts, ¶¶ 28–33.

37. KPMG Agreement, Statement of Facts, ¶ 33.

38. Ibid., ¶ 30.

39. Senate Hearing 108-473, 9–10.

40. See, e.g., David Cay Johnston, "Corporate Risk of Tax Audit Is Still Shrinking, I.R.S. Data Show," *New York Times,* April 12, 2004; IRS Oversight Board, *Annual Report 2007* (2008), 9.

41. U.S. Securities and Exchange Commission, *Address of William O. Douglas before the Bond Club of Hartford,* 1938.

42. U.S. Department of Justice, *United States Attorneys' Manual* (2008), § 9-28.400, "Principles of Federal Prosecution of Business Organizations: Special Policy Concerns."

43. *United States v. Stein*, 435 F. Supp. 2d 330, 339 (S.D.N.Y. 2006).

44. IRS Announcement IR 2004-64, May 5, 2004.

45. Lynnley Browning, "Court Case Gives Rare Look at Tax Shelter Clients," *New York Times*, June 11, 2005.

46. Executive Order No. 13,271.

47. See, e.g., Stephen J. Rackmill, "Printzlien's Legacy, the 'Brooklyn Plan,' A.K.A. Deferred Prosecution," *Federal Probation*, June 1996, 8.

48. *U.S. Sentencing Guidelines Manual* (2011), § 8B2.1(a)(3).

49. Defense Industry Initiative on Business Ethics and Conduct, "Who We Are," www.dii.org /about-us.

50. Michele DeStefano, "Creating a Culture of Compliance: Why Departmentalization May Not Be the Answer," *Hastings Business Law Journal* 10 (2014): 155.

51. Memorandum from Eric Holder, Deputy Attorney General, Department of Justice, to Component Heads and United States Attorneys, "Bringing Criminal Charges against Corporations," June 16, 1999.

52. Memorandum from Deputy Attorney General Larry D. Thompson, U.S. Department of Justice, to Heads of Department Components and U.S. Attorneys, "Principles of Federal Prosecution of Business Organizations," January 20, 2003.

53. Jennifer Arlen, "Corporate Crime Liability: Theory and Evidence," in *Research Handbook on the Economics of Criminal Law*, ed. A. Harel and K. Hylton (Northampton, MA: Edward Elgar, 2012).

54. Thompson, Principles, § I.A.

55. Vanessa Blum, "Justice Deferred: The Feds' New Weapon of Choice Makes Companies Turn Snitch to Save Themselves," *Legal Times*, March 21, 2005, 1 (quoting prosecutor in Computer Associates case).

56. Terrence E. Deal and Allan A. Kennedy, *Corporate Cultures: The Rites and Rituals of Corporate Life*, 2nd ed. (Cambridge, MA: Perseus Books, 2000), 109–154.

57. Kim S. Cameron and Robert E. Quinn, *Diagnosing and Changing Organizational Culture*, 3rd ed. (San Francisco: Jossey-Bass, 2011).

58. Edgar H. Schein, *The Corporate Culture Survival Guide*, rev. ed. (Hoboken, NJ: John Wiley and Sons, 2009), describes methodologies for determining the current state of corporate culture and presenting models for changing those cultures.

59. Brent Fisse and John Braithwaite, *The Impact of Publicity on Corporate Offenders* (Albany: State University of New York Press, 1983), 232–235.

60. Barry D. Baysinger, "Organizational Theory and the Criminal Liability of Organizations," *Boston University Law Review* 71 (1991): 367.

61. Lauren B. Edelman et al., "Legal Ambiguity and the Politics of Compliance: Affirmative Action Officer's Dilemma," *Law and Policy* 13 (1991): 71.

62. *U.S. v. Stein*, 435 F.Supp. 2d 330, 339, 345 (S.D.N.Y. 2006).

63. Ibid., 348.

64. Ibid., 348–349.

65. Alberto R. Gonzales, U.S. Attorney General, U.S. Department of Justice, "Prepared Remarks at the Press Conference Regarding KPMG Corporate Fraud Case," August 29, 2005.

66. Fed. R. Crim. P. 6(e)(3)(A); see also *United States v. Procter & Gamble*, 356 U.S. 677 682–683 (1958).

67. *United States v. KPMG LLP*, No. 1:05-CR-00903-LAP (S.D.N.Y., August 29, 2005).

68. KPMG Agreement, Statement of Facts, ¶ 2.

69. *U.S. Sentencing Guidelines Manual* (2004), § 8C2.5(g).

70. The agreements with Adelphia Communications, Collins & Aikman, Elan Corp., Hitachi, MCI, NEC Corporation, NetVersant, Omega Advisors, Royal Ahold, Stryker Orthopedics, and Tommy Hilfiger lack such admissions. The Elan Corp. agreement notes, "This Agreement is made in compromise of disputed claims" and states the firm did not admit guilt. Elan Corp. Agreement, 3.

71. Edward Wyatt, "Judge Blocks Citigroup Settlement with S.E.C.," *New York Times*, November 28, 2011.

72. James B. Stewart, "S.E.C. to Require Admissions of Guilt," *New York Times*, June 21, 2013.

73. Russell Mokhiber, "Raman Defends Deferred and Non Prosecution Agreements for Major Corporate Crime Cases," *Corporate Crime Reporter*, May 22, 2013.

74. In earlier agreements in the Southern District of New York and the District of New Jersey, prosecutors did not always insist on acceptance of responsibility. Antitrust agreements often do not include acceptance of responsibility or such statements of facts.

75. Roger Williams Medical Center Agreement, ¶ 2.

76. Barclays Bank PLC Agreement, 1.

77. Officer's Certificate, Deferred Prosecution Agreement, *United States v. Ingersoll-Rand*, 1:07-CR-00294-RJL (October 31, 2007).

78. Letter from Michael J. Sullivan, U.S. Attorney, U.S. Department of Justice, to Ethan M. Posner, Partner, Covington & Burling LLP, March 27, 2007.

79. Peter J. Henning, "Sending a Message for Backpedaling on Settlements," *New York Times*, March 25, 2013.

80. This figure includes cases in which the subsidiary of a Fortune 500 firm entered an agreement.

81. ABB Ltd. Agreement, 4-5.

82. Beazer Homes Agreement, 3.

83. Example include the agreement with Bixby Energy Systems, Inc., in which the government cited its "financial condition." Bixby Energy Agreement, 10. Collins & Aikman paid no fine or restitution in light of its "dire" financial situation. Collins & Aikman Agreement, 3. CommunityOne Bank was "on the verge of failure" and its holding company had negative net worth. CommunityOne Bank Agreement, 2. The Diamondback Capital Management agreement cited "the negative effect . . . on Diamondback's financial condition and its remaining employees and investors." Diamondback Capital Management Agreement, 1.

84. Brandon L. Garrett and Jon Ashley, Federal Organizational Prosecution Agreements, University of Virginia School of Law, http://lib.law.virginia.edu/Garrett/prosecution _agreements/home.suphp.

85. The First Amendment Clinic at the University of Virginia School of Law is currently litigating FOIA requests for thirty prosecution agreements. Ben Protess, "Your Homework Assignment: Sue the Federal Government," *New York Times*, April 8, 2014.

86. Mary Jacoby, "Grassley Grills DOJ National Security Chief about Secret Settlement with Islamic Bank," *Main Justice*, September 21, 2011.

87. 18 U.S.C. §§ 1341, 1343; *Neder v. United States*, 527 U.S. 1, 22–23, 25 (1999) (discussing "materiality" requirement).

88. *McNally v. United States*, 483 U.S. 350, 356 (1987) (quoting *Congressional Globe*, 41st Cong., 3rd Sess. 35 (1870) (remarks of Rep. Farnsworth)).
89. 18 U.S.C. §§ 1343 (wire fraud), 1344 (bank fraud), 1346 (honest services), 1347 (health care fraud), 1348 (securities and commodities fraud), 1351 (foreign labor contracting fraud).
90. 18 U.S.C. § 287 (false claims); 18 U.S.C. § 371 (conspiracy to defraud the United States).
91. U.S. Department of Justice, "Bank of America Agrees to Pay $137.3 Million in Restitution to Federal and State Agencies as a Condition of the Justice Department's Antitrust Corporate Leniency Program," press release, December 7, 2010.
92. N. Richard Janis, "Deputizing Company Counsel as Agents of the Federal Government: How Our Adversary System of Justice Is Being Destroyed," *Washington Lawyer*, March 2005, 34.
93. Richard A. Epstein, "The Deferred Prosecution Racket," *Wall Street Journal*, November 28, 2006.
94. Letter from Ralph Nader and Robert Weissman to Alberto Gonzales, Attorney General, June 5, 2006, *Multinational Monitor Editors Blog*, July 6, 2006, www.multinationalmonitor.org/editorsblog/?p=30.
95. Government Accountability Office, *Preliminary Observations on the DOJ's Use and Oversight of Deferred Prosecution and Non-Prosecution Agreements*, June 25, 2009, 41.
96. Ibid., Table 52.
97. KPMG Agreement, ¶ 21.
98. Office of the Inspector General, U.S. Department of Justice, Audit Report 06-17, *Office of Justice Programs Annual Financial Statement: Fiscal Year 2005* (2006).
99. On the 1980s trend toward larger fines and more prosecutions of large public firms, see Marc A. Cohen, "Corporate Crime and Punishment: An Update on Sentencing Practice in the Federal Courts, 1988–1990," *Boston University Law Review* 71 (1991): 252–253.
100. Cf. 18 U.S.C. § 3663A (mandatory restitution to victims in certain federal criminal cases, including fraud cases) with 18 U.S.C. § 3663 (restitution discretionary in cases not covered by 18 U.S.C. § 3663A).
101. The companies are Prudential Equity Group, LLC ($325 million), Technip S.A. ($240 million), Snaprogetti Netherlands ($240 million), JGC ($218.8 million), Barclays Bank PLC ($160 million), Forest Laboratories ($150 million), GlaxoSmithKline ($140 million), Serono Holding, Inc. ($137 million), Science Applications International Corp. ($130 million), and KPMG ($128 million), for a total of $1,738,736,000.
102. KPMG Agreement, ¶ 18.
103. Gonzales, "Prepared Remarks at the Press Conference Regarding KPMG Corporate Fraud Case."
104. Report of Investigation Pursuant to Section 21(a) of the Securities Exchange Act of 1934 and Commission Statement on the Relationship of Cooperation to Agency Enforcement Decisions, Exchange Act Release No. 44,969, 76 SEC Docket 296, October 23, 2001, www.sec.gov/litigation/investreport/34-44969.htm (asking, among factors informing SEC discretion, "Did the company adopt and ensure enforcement of new and more effective internal controls and procedures designed to prevent a recurrence of the misconduct?"); EPA Incentives for Self-Policing: Discovery, Disclosure, Correction and Prevention of Violations, 65 *Federal Register* 19,618, April 11, 2000; FAR Contractor Business Ethics

Compliance Program and Disclosure Requirements, 73 *Federal Register* 67064, 67091–67092, November 12, 2008; Enforcement Advisory, Division of Enforcement, U.S. Commodity Futures Trading Commission, *Cooperation Factors in Enforcement Division Sanction Recommendations*, August 11, 2004; Office of Foreign Assets Control, Department of the Treasury, 31 C.F.R. §§ 501.601–606 (2006).

105. Patient Protection and Affordable Care Act of 2010, Pub. L. No. 111–148, § 6102 (2010).

106. OECD, Recommendation of the Council for Further Combating Bribery of Foreign Public Officials in International Business Transactions, Annex II, 2009.

107. Orthofix International N.V. Agreement, C-3.

108. MoneyGram International Agreement, C-2.

109. GlaxoSmithKline Plea Agreement, Addendum A.1.

110. Abt Associates Agreement, 5.

111. On the question of whether it is a good thing for prosecutors and regulators to encourage the separation of the compliance and legal functions, see DeStefano, "Creating a Culture of Compliance."

112. Aibel Group Agreement, 9.

113. Aurora Foods Agreement, 4.

114. P.P. List Management Agreement, 5–6.

115. Academi LLC Agreement, 5.

116. Governor's Independent Investigation Panel, *Report to the Governor: Upper Big Branch*, May 2011, 4.

117. David M. Uhlmann, "For 29 Dead Miners, No Justice," *New York Times*, December 10, 2011.

118. See, e.g., Kimberly D. Krawiec, "Cosmetic Compliance and the Failure of Negotiated Governance," *Washington University Law Quarterly* 81 (2003): 504–505.

119. Vikramaditya S. Khanna, "Corporate Crime Legislation: A Political Economy Analysis," *Washington University Law Quarterly* 82 (2003): 108; Daniel Fischel and Alan O. Sykes, "Corporate Crime," *Journal of Legal Studies* 25 (1996): 348; Jonathan R. Macey, "Agency Theory and the Criminal Liability of Organizations," *Boston University Law Review* 71 (1991): 316.

120. U.S. Sentencing Guidelines § 8B2.1(b)(5)(B).

121. The Computer Associates case is one such example. Computer Associates, "CA Announces That Term of Independent Examiner Extended to May 1, 2007," press release, September 16, 2006.

122. 18 U.S.C. § 3161(h)(2) (2008). The legislative history is not informative. See H.R. Rep. No. 93–1508 (1974), 1, reprinted in *U.S. Code Congressional and Administrative News*, 1974, 7401.

123. U.S. Government Accountability Office, GAO-10-110, *DOJ Has Taken Steps to Better Track Its Use of Deferred and Non-Prosecution Agreements, but Should Evaluate Effectiveness*, 2009, 25.

124. *United States v. Meyer*, 157 F.3d 1067, 1076 (7th Cir. 1998); *United States v. Miller*, 406 F.3d 323, 334 (5th Cir. 2005).

125. *Stolt-Nielson, S.A. v. United States*, 442 F.3d 177, 187 (3d Cir. 2006).

126. *Stolt-Nielsen, S.A. v. United States*, No. 06-cr-466 (E.D. Pa. November 29, 2007).

127. New York Racing Association Agreement, ¶ 10.

128. James M. Odato, "NYRA Deal in the Works," *Albany Times Union*, December 6, 2003; Associated Press, "Video Slot Machines Starting Up at NYC's First 'Racino,'" NJ.com, October 27, 2011.

129. Roger Williams Medical Center Agreement, 5; Office of Governor Donald L. Carcieri, State of Rhode Island, "Health Department to Renew Hospital License with Increased Oversight," press release, April 7, 2006.

130. Bristol-Myers Squibb Agreement, ¶ 20.

131. House Subcommittee Hearing 111-52, June 25, 2009 ("It was not my idea, it was not my suggestion, I did not suggest Seton Hall").

132. "Prosecutor to Corporation: Endow a Chair at My Law School, or Else," *Corporate Crime Reporter*, August 3, 2005, 32.

133. *U.S. Attorney's Manual*, § 9–16.325.

134. "Justice Department Letter Vindicates Former American Express Bank International Chairman," Reuters, June 30, 2010.

135. U.S. Attorney's Office, S.D.N.Y., "Statement on the Dismissal of Charges against KPMG," press release, January 3, 2007.

136. *United States v. KPMG LLP*, No. 1:05-CR-00903-LAP, 2007 WL 541956 (S.D.N.Y., February 14, 2007).

137. This is the Aibel Group case, discussed along with other recidivist firms in Chapter 6.

138. Edward Iwata, "Ernst & Young Partners Indicted," *USA Today*, May 30, 2007.

139. Letter from Michael J. Garcia, U.S. Attorney, U.S. Department of Justice, to Robert B. Fiske Jr. and James P. Rouhandeh, Partners, Davis Polk & Wardwell, March 26, 2007, 2.

140. "Sidley Austin LLP Pays IRS $39.4 Million Penalty," press release, May 13, 2007; Lynnley Browning, "Big Law Firm Won't Face Criminal Charges in Tax Case," *New York Times*, May 24, 2007.

141. Rebecca Leung, "Gimme Shelter," *60 Minutes*, February 11, 2009.

142. BDO USA, LLP, Deferred Prosecution Agreement, 3.

143. Ibid., 2.

144. Lynnley Browning, "7 Indicted on Charges of Selling Tax Shelters," *New York Times*, June 9, 2009.

145. Chad Bray, "Tax-Shelter Case Brings Convictions," *Wall Street Journal*, May 25, 2011; *United States v. Daugerdas et al.*, 2012 WL 2149238 (S.D.N.Y. June 4, 2012); Christie Smythe and Bob Van Voris, "Former Lawyer Daugerdas Convicted in Tax-Fraud Scheme Retrial," *Bloomberg News*, November 1, 2013.

146. HVB Bank Agreement.

4. The Ostriches

1. C. Plinius Secundus, *Pliny's Natural History in Thirty-Seven Books*, Trans. Dr. Philemon Holland (London: George Barclay, 1601).

2. Dr. Karl S. Kruszelnicki, "Ostrich Head in Sand," *ABC Science*, November 2, 2006.

3. *U.S. v. Black*, 530 F.3d 596, 604 (7th Cir. 2008). But even Judge Posner could not resist including the image above in one of his decisions: *Gonzalez-Servin v. Ford Motor Co.*, 662 F.3d 931, 934 (7th Cir. 2011). Judge Posner was criticizing a litigant, not the instruction. He also included an image of a lawyer with his head in the sand.

4. *United States v. Ramsey*, 785 F.2d 184, 189 (7th Cir. 1986).

5. E.g., Justin C. From, "Avoiding Not-So-Harmless Errors: The Appropriate Standards for Appellate Review of Willful-Blindness Jury Instructions," *Iowa Law Review* 97 (2011): 275.

6. Francis T. Cullen, *Corporate Crime under Attack: The Ford Pinto Case and Beyond* (Cincinnati, OH: Anderson Publishing, 1987), 352.

7. William K. Black, *The Best Way to Rob a Bank Is to Own One* (Austin: University of Texas Press, 2005), xiii–xv.

8. U.S. Sentencing Commission, *2011 Sourcebook of Federal Sentencing Statistics* (2012), Table 3 (8,632 offenders; over 10 percent of the federal criminal docket consisted of fraud convicts). For a study of individual white-collar prosecutions in the federal system, see David Weisburd et al., *Crimes of the Middle Classes: White-Collar Offenders in the Federal Courts* (New Haven, CT: Yale University Press, 1991), 104–106.

9. "Mendelsohn Says Criminal Bribery Prosecutions Doubled in 2007," *Corporate Crime Reporter* 36, no. 1 (September 16, 2008): 22.

10. Kurt Eichenwald, "Economy and Business; After a Boom, There Will Be Scandal," *New York Times*, December 16, 2002.

11. John C. Danford, "When Enforcement Becomes Harassment," *New York Times*, May 6, 2003; Joel Cohen, "No More 'Perp Walks,'" *National Law Journal*, August 5, 2002.

12. *Lauro v. Charles*, 219 F.3d 202, 204 (2d Cir. 2000).

13. *U.S. v. Arthur Andersen, LLP.*, No. H-02-121 (S.D.T.X. June 6, 2002), Trial Transcript, 6278.

14. *United States v. Duncan*, Defendant David Duncan's Memorandum of Law in Support of His Unopposed Motion to Withdraw His Guilty Plea and to Dismiss the Information, No. 02-209 (2005), Exhibit C, Rearraignment (April 9, 2005), 18.

15. Fed. R. Crim. P. 11(d)(2)(B) (2012).

16. Ibid., 3.

17. Stephen Taub, "Enron Auditor Withdraws Guilty Plea," CFO.com, November 28, 2005.

18. Docket entry, *SEC v. Duncan*, 4:08-cv-00314 (2008).

19. Charles E. Ramirez, "Andersen Workers Settle into New Careers," *Detroit News*, December 1, 2002.

20. Linda Tucci, "Andersen Clears out Office but Leaves Some Ex-Staffers Behind," *St. Louis Post-Dispatch*, August 29, 2002.

21. Edwin H. Sutherland, *White Collar Crime* (New York: Dryden Press, 1949), 29; Edwin H. Sutherland, "White-Collar Criminality," *American Sociological Review* 1 (1940): 5.

22. Gilbert Geis, "White-Collar Crime: What Is It?" in *Reflecting on White-Collar and Corporate Crime*, ed. David Shichor, Larry Gaines, and Andrea Schoepfer (Long Grove, IL: Waveland Press, 2012).

23. C. S. Lewis, *The Screwtape Letters and Screwtape Purposes* (New York: Macmillan, 1961), viii.

24. E.g., John Braithwaite, "White Collar Crime," *Annual Review of Sociology* 11 (1985): 1–21; Marshall B. Clinard, *Corporate Ethics and Crime: The Role of Middle Management* (Beverly Hills, CA: Sage, 1983).

25. James William Coleman, *The Criminal Elite: Understanding White Collar Crime* (New York: St. Martin's Press, 1998), 206–207.

26. Kristen Hays, "Skilling Maintains Innocence, Vows Appeal," *Houston Chronicle*, October 24, 2006.

27. *Skilling v. United States,* 130 S.Ct. 2896 (2010).

28. Weisburd et al., *Crimes of the Middle Classes,* 85, 172.

29. Sridhar Ramamoorti, "The Psychology and Sociology of Fraud," *Issues in Accounting Education* 23 (2008): 529.

30. Coleman, *The Criminal Elite,* 196.

31. Ramamoorti, "The Psychology and Sociology of Fraud," 527.

32. For a careful study of the role of cooperating defendants in white-collar investigations, see Weisburd et al., *Crimes of the Middle Classes,* 104–106.

33. Brandon L. Garrett, *Convicting the Innocent: Where Criminal Prosecutions Go Wrong* (Cambridge, MA: Harvard University Press, 2011), 118–144.

34. *United States v. Stein,* 495 F. Supp. 2d 390, 417–418 (S.D.N.Y 2007) (*Stein* II).

35. Ibid., 395, 402–403.

36. *United States v. Stein,* 541 F.3d 130, 137 (2d Cir. 2008).

37. Ibid., 408–409.

38. *Stein* II, 495 F. Supp. 2d at 401–402.

39. Ibid., 402.

40. Memorandum from Deputy Attorney General Larry D. Thompson, U.S. Department of Justice, to Heads of Department Components and U.S. Attorneys, U.S. Department of Justice, January 20, 2003.

41. Ibid., II.A.

42. *Upjohn Co. v. United States,* 449 U.S. 383, 394–395 (1981).

43. Charles Gasparino, "Merrill Fires Two Linked to Enron," *Wall Street Journal,* September 19, 2002.

44. Dennis J. Block and Nancy F. Barton, "Implications of the Attorney-Client Privilege and Work-Product Doctrine, in Barry F. McNeil and Brad D. Brian, eds., Internal Corporate Investigations," 17, 37 (Chicago, Illinois: American Bar Association 2007) (quoting Frederick B. Lacey).

45. George M. Cohen, "Of Coerced Waiver, Government Leverage, and Corporate Loyalty: The Holder, Thompson, and McNulty Memos and Their Critics," *Virginia Law Review in Brief* 93 (2007): 160.

46. ABA Task Force on Attorney-Client Privilege, Report to the House of Delegates, August 2006, 17.

47. *United States v. KPMG,* 316 F. Supp. 2d 42–44 (D.D.C. 2004); KPMG Agreement, Statement of Facts, at ¶¶ 28–33.

48. KPMG Agreement, ¶¶ 35–36. KPMG did not offer to waive privilege regarding communications about the prosecution agreement itself or civil matters, or as to third parties, including employees. KPMG agreed to cooperate in pending investigations and prosecutions.

49. See, e.g., Lance Cole, "Revoking Our Privileges: Federal Law Enforcement's Multi-Front Assault on the Attorney-Client Privilege (and Why It Is Misguided)," *Villanova Law Review* 48 (2003): 469; William R. McLucas et al., "The Decline of the Attorney-Client Privilege in the Corporate Setting," *Journal of Criminal Law and Criminology* 96 (2006): 621.

50. Mary Beth Buchanan, "Effective Cooperation by Business Organizations and the Impact of Privilege Waivers," *Wake Forest Law Review* 39 (2004): 598.

51. United States Chamber of Commerce, Testimony before the American Bar Association Task Force on Attorney-Client Privilege, February 22, 2005.

52. Memorandum from Robert D. McCallum Jr., Acting Deputy Attorney General, to Heads of Department Components and U.S. Attorneys, October 21, 2005.

53. Daniel Richman, "Decisions about Coercion: The Corporate Attorney-Client Privilege Waiver Problem," *DePaul Law Review* 57 (2008): 299–300.

54. In one additional case, of Symbol Technologies, privilege had previously been waived.

55. *Braswell v. United States*, 487 U.S. 99, 105, 115 (1988).

56. Lisa Kern Griffin, "Compelled Cooperation and the New Corporate Criminal Procedure," *New York University Law Review* 82 (2007): 311; Samuel W. Buell, "Criminal Procedure within the Firm," *Stanford Law Review* 59 (2007): 1613; Preet Bharara, "Corporations Cry Uncle and Their Employees Cry Foul: Rethinking Prosecutorial Pressure on Corporate Defendants," *American Criminal Law Review* 44 (2007): 53.

57. 385 U.S. 493, 497, 500 (1967); see also Brandon L. Garrett, "Corporate Confessions," *Cardozo Law Review* 30 (2008): 930–931.

58. *Stein* II, 440 F.Supp. 2d at 322.

59. Ibid., 322, 330.

60. *United States v. Stein*, 435 F. Supp. 2d 330, 338–39 (S.D.N.Y. 2006) (*Stein* I).

61. Brandon L. Garrett, "The Substance of False Confessions," *Stanford Law Review* 62 (2010): 1051.

62. *Stein* I, 435 F.Supp. 2d 330 (S.D.N.Y. 2006).

63. *U.S. v. Stein*, 495 F.Supp. 2d 390, 420–424 (S.D.N.Y. July 16, 2007).

64. Attorney-Client Privilege Protection Act of 2007, S. 186, 110th Cong. § 3 (2007).

65. Christopher M. Matthews, "Senators Question Enforcement Policies in Hearing," *Main Justice*, November 30, 2010.

66. FBI, "Eight Former Senior Executives and Agents of Siemens Charged in Alleged $100 Million Foreign Bribe Scheme," press release, December 13, 2011.

67. Joe Palazzolo, "Specter Salutes Justice Dept, Slams Republicans," *Wall Street Journal*, December 14, 2011.

68. Douglas Gillison, "Facing Extradition, Siemens Argentina Defendant Settles with SEC," *CNN Money*, December 3, 2013.

69. Scott D. Hammond, "Measuring the Value of Second-in Cooperation in Corporate Plea Negotiations," American Bar Association Section of Antitrust Law Spring Meeting, March 29, 2006. The Antitrust Division has altered its approach toward "carve-outs" to focus on potential targets rather than employees who do not cooperate. See Department of Justice, Office of Public Affairs, "Statement of Assistant Attorney General Bill Baer on Changes to Antitrust Division's Carve-Out Practice Regarding Corporate Plea Agreements," April 12, 2013.

70. Amsouth Deferred Prosecution Agreement, 7 (October 13, 2005).

71. 31 C.F.R. § 1020.320.

72. Marshall B. Clinard and Peter C. Yeager, *Illegal Corporate Behavior* (Washington, DC: U.S. Government Printing Office, 1979).

73. Mark A. Cohen, "Corporate Crime and Punishment: An Update on Sentencing Practice in the Federal Courts," *Boston University Law Review* 71 (1991): 268.

74. "Greenpeace, Climate Activists Convicted of Climbing Mt. Rushmore, Sending Critical Message," press release, January 5, 2010; Docket, *U.S. v. Greenpeace, Inc.*, 5:09-cr-50058-KES-1 (D.S.D. February 3, 2010).

75. Department of Justice, "Former Morgan Stanley Managing Director Pleas Guilty for Role in Evading Internal Controls Required by FCPA," press release, April 25, 2012.

76. Securities and Exchange Commission, "SEC Charges Former Morgan Stanley Executive with FCPA Violations and Investment Adviser Fraud," press release, April 25, 2012.

77. Julia Preston, "270 Immigrants Sent to Prison in Federal Push," *New York Times*, May 24, 2008.

78. Ingrid V. Eagly, "Prosecuting Immigration," *Northwestern University Law Review* 104 (2010): 1302–1303; Immigration Raids: Postville and Beyond: Hearing Before the Subcommittee. on Immigration, Citizenship, Refugees, Border Security, and International Law of the House Committee on the Judiciary, 110th Cong. 106 (July 24, 2008).

79. Spencer S. Hsu, "Immigration Raid Jars a Small Town," *Washington Post*, May 18, 2008.

80. *U.S. v. Agriprocessors, Inc.*, No. 2:08-cr-01324-LRR (N.D. Iowa, November 19, 2009).

81. Department of Justice, "Rochester Asbestos Contractor and Company Sentenced for Violating Clean Air Act and Lying to OHSA," press release, September 22, 2011.

82. "Mendelsohn Says Criminal Bribery Prosecutions Doubled in 2007," *Corporate Crime Reporter* 36, no. 1 (September 16, 2008): 22.

83. 31 U.S.C. § 5331–5332.

84. 18 U.S.C. § 1956–1957.

85. 18 U.S.C. § 5324.

86. 18 U.S.C. § 1957(a).

87. 31 U.S.C. § 5318(I). The USA PATRIOT Act of 2012 strengthened controls over foreign accounts. See, e.g., 31 U.S.C. § 5331.

88. 31 U.S.C. 5311–5314e.

89. Douglas Gillison, "We Didn't Protect HSBC, Treasury Officials Tell Senate Committee," *Main Justice*, March 7, 2013.

90. 12 USC § 93(d)(1).

91. Ibid., § 93(d)(1)(B), (d)(2).

92. 31 U.S.C. § 5318(h)(l) and 12 C.F.R. § 563.177(c).

93. U.S. Senate, Permanent Subcommittee on Investigations, Committee on Homeland Security and Governmental Affairs, *U.S. Vulnerabilities to Money Laundering, Drugs, and Terrorism Financing: HSBC Case History*, July 17, 2012, 2–3.

94. Ibid., 4–6.

95. See, e.g., "2000 International Narcotics Control Strategy Report," U.S. Department of State, V-27–28.

96. HSBC Case Study, 35, 49.

97. "Sigue Confirms Resolution of Compliance Issues," January 28, 2008, www.globenewswire.com/newsroom/news.html?d=135137.

98. HSBC Case Study, 7.

99. Carrick Mollenkamp and Brett Wolf, "Special Report: HSBC'S Money-Laundering Crackdown Riddled with Lapses," Reuters, July 13, 2012.

100. Christopher M. Matthews, "HSBC Says It's Sorry: Highlights from the Bank's Senate Hearing," *Wall Street Journal*, July 17, 2012.

101. HSBC Case Study, 26–27, 30–32.

102. Ben Protess and Jessica Silver-Greenberg, "HSBC to Pay 1.92 Billion to Settle Charges of Money Laundering," *New York Times*, December 10, 2012.

103. HSBC Deferred Prosecution Agreement, December 11, 2012, ¶ 6.

104. Ibid., Statement of Facts, ¶ 81.

105. MoneyGram Int'l Deferred Prosecution Agreement, 14.

106. Hearing, *U.S. v. Barclays*, No. CR 10–218 (D.D.C. August 17, 2010), 5–6.

107. Ibid., 12.

108. 21 U.S.C. §§ 331, 333.

109. Food and Drug Modernization Act of 1997, 21 U.S.C. § 36aaa(b)–(c).

110. 42 U.S.C. § 1320a–7b(b)(2)(A) (2006).

111. Federal Bureau of Investigations, *Financial Crimes Report to the Public 2011* (2011).

112. Scott Hensley, "Pfizer Whistleblower Tells His Story," National Public Radio, September 3, 2009.

113. Bill Berkrot, "Pfizer Whistleblowers Ordeal Reaps Big Rewards," Reuters, September 2, 2009.

114. Ibid.

115. Eric Holder, U.S. Attorney General, "Speech at Press Conference on Medicare Fraud Strike Force Actions," February 17, 2011; U.S. Department of Justice, "Health Care Fraud Prevention and Enforcement Efforts Result in Record-Breaking Recoveries Totaling Nearly $4.1 Billion," press release, February 14, 2012.

116. 42 U.S.C. § 1320a-7 (2006).

117. Health Care Programs: Fraud and Abuse; Revised OIG Exclusion Authorities Resulting from Public Law 104–191, 63 *Fed. Reg.* 46,676, 46,680 (September 2, 1998) (codified at 42 C.F.R. pts. 1000, 1001, 1002, 1005).

118. Duff Wilson, "Side Effects May Include Lawsuits," *New York Times*, October 3, 2010.

119. Department of Justice, "Abbott Labs to Pay $1.5 Billion to Resolve Criminal and Civil Investigation of Off-Label Promotion of Depakote," press release, May 7 2012.

120. Duff Wilson, "For $520 Million, AstraZeneca Will Settle Case over Marketing of a Drug," *New York Times*, April 26, 2010.

121. Department of Justice, "GlaxoSmithKline to Plead Guilty and Pay $3 Billion to Resolve Fraud Allegations and Failure to Report Safety Data," press release, July 2, 2012.

122. Ibid., ¶¶ 71, 80, 82.

123. *U.S. v. GlaxoSmithKline*, Criminal Information, ¶ 70, July 2, 2012, www.justice.gov/opa/documents/gsk/gsk-criminal-info.pdf.

124. Alex Wayne, "Glaxo Case Pushes U.S. Health Settlements to $6.6 Billion," *Bloomberg Businessweek*, September 27, 2012.

125. GlaxoSmithKline Plea Agreement Addendum, 1, 8.

126. Abbott Labs Corporate Integrity Agreement, 52–54, www.justice.gov/opa/abbott-court-docs-2012/CorporateIntegrityStatement.pdf.

127. Katie Thomas, "Glaxo Says It Will Stop Paying Doctors to Promote Drugs," *New York Times*, December 16, 2013.

128. Eric Holder, U.S. Attorney General, "Speech at Press Conference on Medicare Fraud Strike Force Actions," February 17, 2011.

129. Corporate Fraud Task Force, "Report to the President," 2008, iii, at www.justice.gov/ar chive/dag/cftf/corporate-fraud2008.pdf.

130. Department of Justice, "Former Officer and Director of Global Engineering and Construction Company Pleads Guilty to Foreign Bribery and Kickback Charges," press release, September 3, 2008.

131. Stanley Plea Agreement, 14–17.

132. Laurel Brubaker Calkins, "Ex-KBR CEO Stanley Gets 2½ Years in Prison for Foreign Bribes," *Bloomberg*, February 24, 2012.

133. Stanley Plea Agreement, 14–18.

134. James B. Stewart, "Bribes without Jail Time," *New York Times*, April 27, 2012.

135. *U.S. v. Ebbers*, 458 F.3d 110, 113–115 (2d Cir. 2006).

136. Ibid., 124.

137. Jury Instructions, 19, *U.S. v. Ebbers*, 02-cr-1144 (BSJ) (S.D.N.Y. March 4, 2005).

138. Ibid., 19–20.

139. *Ebbers*, 458 F.3d at 129.

140. Dan Ackman, "Bernie Ebbers Guilty," *Forbes*, March 15, 2005.

141. *U.S. v. Ebbers*, 458 F.3d 110, 125 (2nd Cir. 2006).

142. FDA, *Regulatory Procedures Manual*, March 2007, § 6-5-1.

143. *Friedman v. Sebelius*, 686 F.3d 813, 816 (D.C. Cir 2012).

144. "HHS-OIG Drops Potential Action against Forest CEO," press release, August 5, 2011.

145. *Friedman v. Sebelius*, 686 F.3d at 828.

146. David M. Uhlmann, "For 29 Dead Miners, No Justice," *New York Times*, December. 9, 2011; Howard Berkes, "Massey Mine Boss Pleads Guilty as Feds Target Execs," National Public Radio, March 29, 2012; John Raby, "Ex-CEO Implicated in Massey Coal Mine Case," *USA Today*, February 28, 2013.

147. *United States v. Stevens*, 909 F.2d 431 (11th Cir. 1990).

148. 18 U.S.C. § 371.

149. *United States v. Hughes Aircraft Co.*, 20 F.3d 974 (9th Cir. 1994).

150. E.g., *United States v. Philip Morris USA Inc.*, 449 F.Supp. 2d 1 (D.D.C. 2006).

151. Jeffrey M. Kaplan and Joseph E. Murphy, *Compliance Programs and the Corporate Sentencing Guidelines* (New York: Clark Boardman Callaghan 2012), § 22:11.

152. Jeffrey T. Frederick, *Mastering Voir Dire and Jury Selection: Gain an Edge in Questioning Your Jury* (Chicago: American Bar Association 2012).

153. *Stein I*, 435 F. Supp. 2d at 380–382.

154. *Stein II*, 495 F. Supp. 2d at 410–417.

155. *United States v. Stein*, 541 F.3d 130 (2d Cir. 2008).

156. *Stein v. KPMG, LLP*, 486 F.3d 753, 756 (2d Cir. 2007).

157. *United States v. Pfaff*, 407 Fed. Appx. 506, 508 (2d Cir. 2010).

158. 26 U.S.C. §7201; 18 U.S.C. §371 (conspiracy to commit offense against the U.S.).

159. *Pfaff*, 407 Fed. Appx. at 509.

160. Larson Certiorari Petition at 7.

161. Appellate Brief, *United States v. Pfaff et al.*, 2010 WL 8939963 *30, 45–46, 129 (January 15, 2010).

162. Ibid., 61, 118.

163. *United States v. Pfaff*, 619 F.3d 172, 175 (2d Cir. 2010) (per curiam).

164. *United States v. Coplan*, 703 F.3d 45 (2d Cir. 2012).

165. *United States v. Rosen*, 487 F.Supp. 2d 721, 737 (E.D.Va. 2007).

166. Memorandum from Deputy Attorney Gen. Paul J. McNulty, U.S. Department of Justice, to Heads of Department Components and U.S. Attorneys, U.S. Department of Justice, December 12, 2006, 8–11 n. 3.

167. Ibid., 11–12.

168. Memorandum from Deputy Attorney General Mark R. Filip, U.S. Department of Justice, to Heads of Department Components and U.S. Attorneys, U.S. Department of Justice, August 28, 2008, 13.

169. Alicia Mundy, "U.S. Effort to Remove Drug CEO Jolts Firms," *Wall Street Journal*, April 26, 2011; Henry N. Pontell, William K. Black, and Gilbert Geis, "Too Big to Fail, Too Powerful to Jail? On the Absence of Criminal Prosecutions after the 2008 Financial Meltdown," *Crime Law Social Change*, 2013.

170. Zachery Kouwe, "Bear Stearns Managers Acquitted of Fraud Charges," *New York Times*, November 10, 2009.

171. Sam Buell, "Is the White Collar Offender Privileged?" *Duke Law Journal* 63 (2013): 823; U.S. Sentencing Commission, "Final Report on the Impact of *United States v. Booker* on Federal Sentencing," 2006, 75; U.S. Sentencing Commission, *Report on the Continuing Impact of* United States v. Booker *on Federal Sentencing* (2012), 6, 67.

5. The Victims

1. Statement of Ralph Dean, February 4, 2008, *United States v. BP Products North America*, No. 4:07-cr-00434 (S.D.Tex Feb. 4, 2008), 3.

2. Ibid., 3–4.

3. Abraham Lustgarten, *Run to Failure: BP and the Making of the Deepwater Horizon Disaster* (New York: W. W. Norton, 2012), 123.

4. U.S. Chemical Safety and Hazard Board Investigation Report, *Refinery Explosion and Fire*, March 20, 2007, 31 (CSHBI Report).

5. Lustgarten, *Run to Failure*, 123.

6. CSHBI Report, 23, 52.

7. Ibid., 21–22, 24.

8. Ibid., 21–22; Victims' Joint Memorandum in Opposition to Plea Agreement, 9–10, *United States v. BP Products North America*, No. 4:07-cr-00434 (S.D.Tex. Dec. 19, 2007).

9. CSHBI Report, 17.

10. Dean Statement, 6.

11. Lustgarten, *Run to Failure*, 129–131.

12. Ibid.

13. Ibid., 155.

14. Ibid., 160.

15. Dean Statement, 8–9.

16. 42 U.S.C. §§ 7412(r)(7), 7413(c)(1).

17. U.S. Department of Justice, "British Petroleum to Pay More than $370 Million in Envtl. Crimes, Fraud Cases," press release, October 25, 2007.

18. *Kenna v. U.S. Dist. Ct. for the Cent. Dist. of Cal.*, 435 F.3d 1011, 1013 (9th Cir. 2006).

19. Wayne R. LaFave et al., 1 Criminal Procedure § 1.4(k) (West 2d ed. 2004).

20. 18 U.S.C. § 3663; 18 U.S.C. § 3663A. On the history of the victim's rights movement, see Douglas E. Beloof, Paul G. Cassell, and Steven J. Twist, *Victims in Criminal Procedure*, 3rd ed. (Durham, North Carolina: Carolina Academic Press, 2010), 5–17.

21. U.S.S.G. § 8B1.1(a).

22. 18 U.S.C. § 3664(f)(2).

23. 18 U.S.C. § 3664(i), (j).

24. 18 U.S.C. § 3664(j).

25. 28 C.F.R. §§ 9.4, 9.8(b).

26. 28 C.F.R. § 9; Department of Justice, *Returning Forfeited Assets to Crime Victims: An Overview of Remission and Restoration* (2008).

27. See U.S. Department of Justice, "FY 2011 Summary of Justice Assets Placed into Official Use by Federal Agency by Type," 2011 (describing over $5.6 million in forfeiture to federal agencies in 2011). In contrast, hundreds of millions of dollars are distributed to state and local agencies. See U.S. Department of Justice, "Equitable Sharing Payments of Cash and sale Proceeds Executed during Fiscal Year 2011, by Recipient Agency."

28. JPMorgan Deferred Prosecution Agreement, January 6, 2014, Exhibit D, 1.

29. 18 U.S.C. § 3663A(3). The legislative history does not speak to white-collar matters or fraud prosecutions in particular, but notes concern with overly complex restitution determinations. Victim Restitution Act of 1995, S. Rep. 104–179, 104th Congress at 19 (Dec. 6, 1995).

30. 28 C.F.R. § 9.9(c).

31. Kenneth N. Gilpin, "Republic New York Pleads Guilty to Securities Fraud," *New York Times*, December 18, 2001. I note the docket sheet shows a different amount, $569 million in restitution for Republic Securities. Omitted were apparently erroneous entries of $9,999,999,999 or $9,999,999,997 that the commission apparently intended to use in neighboring columns to denote missing or indeterminate data or remedial orders not specified.

32. I include the commission data, because they have data from before 2001. For 2002–2009, commission data were adjusted to report it in calendar years, rather than fiscal years. For years before 2002, the commission does not provide month or calendar year of sentence, so it was not possible to adjust the data.

33. Receiver's Final Report and Agreed Motion to Close Receivership, 4–5, *SEC v. KL Group, LLC*, No. 9:05-cv-80186 (S.D. Fla. Dec. 10, 2008).

34. Ibid., 4.

35. *SEC v. Cioffi*, 866 F.2d 65, 66, 72 (E.D.N.Y. 2012).

36. 18 U.S.C. § 3771.

37. U.S.S.G. § 5F1.4; 18 U.S.C. § 3555.

38. 18 U.S.C. § 3771(e).

39. See, e.g., *In re McNulty*, 597 F.3d 344 (6th Cir. 2010).

40. According to the Sentencing Commission, only one organization was ordered to give victims notice in a federal criminal case in 2009; none were required to do so in 2008.

41. Hearing on BP Plea Agreement, 100, *U.S. v. BP Products North America, Inc.*, No. 4:07-cr-00434 (S.D. Tex. Oct. 7, 2008).

42. U.S. Department of Justice, "Attorney General Guidelines for Victim and Witness Assistance," May 29, 2005.

43. For a discussion of the frustration victims feel when prosecutors keep them in the dark, see Stephanos Bibas, "Transparency and Participation in Criminal Procedure," *New York University Law Review* 81 (2006): 922–923, 924.

44. *U.S. v. BP Products of North America Inc.*, No. H-07-434, 2008 WL 501321 at *1 (S.D. Tex. Feb. 21, 2008).

45. Dean Statement, 9.

46. 33 U.S.C. § 1319(c)(1) (negligent Clean Water Act violations); § 1319(2)(A) (prohibiting knowingly violating requirements imposed in a pretreatment program approved under the Clean Water Act).

47. U.S. Department of Justice, "Factors in Decisions on Criminal Prosecutions for Environmental Violations in the Context of Significant Voluntary Compliance or Disclosure Efforts by the Violator," July 1, 1991.

48. David Uhlmann, "The Erosion of Corporate Criminal Liability," *Maryland Law Review* 72 (2013): 1295.

49. Fed. R. Crim. Pro. R. 11(c); *In re Morgan*, 506 F.3d 705, 712 (9th Cir. 2007) (a judge must make an "individualized assessment" of the plea agreement); *U.S. v. Smith*, 417 F.3d 483, 487 (5th Cir. 2005) (a judge may reject a plea agreement "based on the court's belief that the defendant would receive too light of a sentence").

50. *U.S. v. Crowell*, 60 F.3d 199, 205–206 (5th Cir. 1995).

51. Victims Joint Memorandum, 2, *United States v. B.P. Products North America Inc.*, 4:07-cr-00434 (S.D. Tex. Dec. 19, 2007).

52. Alice Gomstyn, "BP Texas City Refinery Blast Victim: BP Keeps 'Killing People,'" ABC News, July 7, 2010.

53. *United States v. Van Schaick*, 134 F. 592, 602 (C.C.S.D.N.Y. 1904).

54. James W. Harlow, "Corporate Criminal Liability for Homicide: A Statutory Framework," *Duke Law Journal* 6 (2011): 123.

55. *Rochester Ry. & Light*, 88 N.E. at 24 (quoting N.Y. Penal Code § 179 (1908)).

56. Lee Strobel, *Reckless Homicide? Ford's Pinto Trial* (South Bend, IN: AND Books, 1980), 20.

57. Ibid., 20–22.

58. Ibid., 24–25.

59. *State v. Ford Motor Co.*, 47 U.S.L.W. 2514, 2515 (Ind. Super. Ct. 1979).

60. Strobel, *Reckless Homicide?*, 265, 270–271.

61. Francis T. Cullen, *Corporate Crime under Attack: The Ford Pinto Case and Beyond* (Cincinnati, OH: Anderson, 1987), 292–293.

62. Ibid., 293.

63. See, e.g., *People v. O'Neil*, 550 N.E.2d 1090, 1098 (Ill. App. Ct. 1990); *United States v. Van Schaick*, 134 F. 592, 602–605 (C.C.S.D.N.Y. 1904). See also Patrick J. Schott, "Comment, Corporate Criminal Liability for Work-Site Deaths: Old Law Used a New Way," *Marquette Law Review* 71 (1988): 805. Many of those cases are quite dated. For a New York case dismissing a second-degree manslaughter indictment against a company, see *People v. Warner-Lambert Co.*, 414 N.E.2d 660 (N.Y. 1980).

64. The prosecutors could have pursued convictions under 29 U.S.C. § 666(e), for willful violations of the Occupational Safety and Health Act, resulting in a worker's death, although, perhaps surprisingly, that is a misdemeanor and penalties are quite low (not more than $10,000).

65. "Text: Victim Impact Statement," *New York Times*, August 11, 2005.

66. Jennifer Bayot, "Ebbers Sentenced to 25 Years in Prison for $11 Billion Fraud," *New York Times*, July 13, 2005.

67. *In re Dean*, 527 F.3d 391, 396 (5th Cir. 2008).

68. Hearing on Plea Agreement, *United States v. BP Products North America*, 4:07-cr-00434 (S.D. Tex. Oct. 7, 2008).

69. Ibid., 18–19.

70. Ibid., 23.

71. Ibid., 67.

72. CSHBI Report, 20.

73. Ibid., 60, 64.

74. Ibid., 38.

75. Ibid., 60.

76. Transcript of Sentencing, 8, *United States v. BP Products North America, Inc.*, No. 4:07-cr-434 (S.D.Tex. March 26, 2009).

77. BP Products North America Inc.'s Sentencing Memorandum at 6, 11, *United States v. BP*, No. 4:07-cr-434 (S.D.Tex. Nov. 20, 2007).

78. Ibid., 10–11.

79. 18 U.S.C. § 2571(c)(3).

80. Victims' Joint Memorandum in Opposition to Plea Agreement at 35, BP Products North America, Inc., CR. No. 4:07-cr-434 (S.D.Tex. Dec. 19, 2007).

81. Ibid., 8.

82. Marilee Enge and David Postman, "Judge Rejects Exxon Deal," *Anchorage Daily News*, April 25, 1991.

83. However, the judge ultimately required Exxon to pay only $25 million, and credited $100 million based on cooperation and cleanup costs. Exxon did pay a total of $100 million in restitution. *United States v. Exxon Corporation (Alaska)*, www.justice.gov/enrd/3499.htm.

84. Hearing on Plea Agreement, 163, *United States v. BP Products North America*, 4:07-cr-00434 (S.D. Tex. Oct. 7, 2008).

85. Dean Statement, 10.

86. Victim's Joint Memorandum in Opposition to Plea Agreement, 12.

87. Brad Heath, Paul Davidson, and Chris Woodyard, "Hearings to Open on Alaska Oil Field Woes," *USA Today*, September 6, 2006.

88. Victims' Joint Memorandum in Opposition to Plea Agreement, 11.

89. BP Deferred Prosecution Agreement, *United States v. BP America, Inc.*, No. 07-cr-00683, (N.D. Ill. Oct. 25, 2007); U.S. Commodity Futures Trading Commission, "BP Agrees to Pay a Total of $303 Million in Sanctions to Settle Charges of Manipulation and Attempted Manipulation in the Propane Market," October 25, 2007.

90. Victims' Joint Memorandum in Opposition to Plea Agreement, 27.

91. Press Release, "What Experts Say about the Criminal Penalties in the BP Texas City Refinery Explosion," Texans for Public Justice, http://info.tpj.org/press_releases/BP/experts.pdf.

92. U.S. Department of Labor, "US Department of Labor's OSHA Issues Record-Breaking Fines to BP," news release, October 30, 2009.

93. Richard Mauer and Anna M. Tinsley, "Gulf Oil Spill: BP Has a Long Record of Legal, Ethical Violations," McClatchy, May 8, 2010.

94. Order Granting United States' Unopposed Motion to Enter Consent Decree, *U.S. v. BP Products North America*, No. 4:10-cv-3569 (S.D. Tex. Dec. 30, 2010).

95. United States Memorandum in Support of Its Unopposed Motion to Enter Consent Decree at 7, *United States v. BP Products North America*, No. 4:10-cv-03569 (S.D. Tex. Dec. 9, 2010).

96. Ibid., 11.

97. Ibid., 11 n. 7.

98. Ibid., 14.

99. Marian Wang, "Despite Safety Concerns at Texas Refinery, U.S. Won't Revoke BP Probation," ProPublica, September 28, 2010.

100. Tom Fowler and Lise Olsen, "Throw Out 2007 BP Plea Deal, Blast Victims Tell Feds," *Houston Chronicle*, July 5, 2010.

101. 18 U.S.C. § 3771(a)(2), (e).

102. Memorandum Opinion and Order, 2, *United States v. CITGO Petroleum Corp.*, No. C-06-563 (S.D. Tex., Sept. 14, 2012).

103. Ibid., 3.

104. Ibid., 7.

105. Memorandum Opinion and Order, 20, *United States v. CITGO Petroleum Corp.*, No. C-06-563 (S.D. Tex., April 30, 2014).

106. For examples of civil suits in which admissions made in prior criminal litigation were relied upon by courts in permitting the civil litigation to go forward, see, e.g., *Davis v. Beazer Homes, U.S.A., Inc.*, No. 1:08CV247, 2009 WL 3855935 *7 (M.D.N.C. Nov. 17, 2009) (finding admissions "a significant factor in assessing the plausibility" of plaintiffs' claims.); *Somerville v. Stryker Orthopaedics*, No. C 08–02443 JSW, 2009 WL 2901591 *3 (N.D.Cal., Sept. 4, 2009) (citing to non-prosecution agreement attached to complaint). For a judge finding a non-prosecution agreement inadmissible in civil litigation, *see* Andrew Keshner, "Non-Prosecution Agreement Ruled Inadmissible in Suit," *New York Law Journal*, September 17, 2011.

107. Barbara Black, "Should the SEC Be a Collection Agency for Defrauded Investors?" *Business Lawyer* 63 (2008): 330–331.

108. 15 U.S.C. § 7246.

109. Plan of Allocation for the Restitution Fund, 2 n. 2, *United States v. Computer Assocs. Int'l, Inc.*, No. 04–0837 (E.D.N.Y. June 28, 2005).

110. Gretchen Morgenson, "Giving Away Lots of Money Is Easy, Right?" *New York Times*, Feb. 13, 2005.

111. Notice of Claims Process for Distribution of the Restitution Fund, In Re: *United States v. Computer Associates International*, No. 04–0837 (E.D.N.Y. 2005), www.computerassociatesrestitutionfund.com/pdf/carf1not.pdf.

112. Order of Judge I. Leo Glasser, *United States v. Computer Assocs. Int'l, Inc.*, No. 04–0837, (E.D.N.Y. Mar. 27, 2008).

113. Notice of Claims Process for Distribution of the Restitution Fund, *United States v. Computer Assocs. Int'l, Inc.*, No. 04–0837 (E.D.N.Y. 2005), www.computerassociatesrestitutionfund.co/pdf/carf1not.pdf. For a detailed discussion of this problem, see Adam S. Zimmerman and David M. Jaros, "The Criminal Class Action," *University of Pennsylvania Law Review* 159 (2011): 1398.

114. In re: Bristol-Myers Squibb Derivative Litigation, No. 02 Civ. 8571(LAP), 2007 WL 959081 (S.D.N.Y. 2007).

115. Ibid., *5.

116. Alex Berenson, "Lilly Settles with 18,000 over Zyprexa," *New York Times*, January 5, 2007.

117. *Hood v. Eli Lilly & Co.* (In re Zyprexa Prods. Liab. Litig.), 671 F. Supp. 2d 397, 404–405 (E.D.N.Y. 2009).

118. Agreement between Newsday, Inc., Hoy Publications LLC, & the U.S. Attorney's Office for the Eastern Dist. of N.Y. at 4, 6, In re Newsday Litig., No. 08–0096 (E.D.N.Y. Dec. 17, 2007).

119. *United States v. Brennan* (In re Newsday Litig.), No. 08–0096, 2008 WL 4279570, at *1–3 (E.D.N.Y. Sept. 18, 2008).

120. Letter to Hon. Jack B. Weinstein, 3, In re Newsday Litigation, Criminal Action No. Misc.-08-0096, Civil Action No. CV-08-5280 (E.D.N.Y. Jan. 28, 2009).

121. *SEC v. Bear, Stearns & Co.*, 626 F. Supp. 2d 402, 416–417, 420 (S.D.N.Y. 2009) (ruling unclaimed money in the Distribution Funds transferred to the U.S. Department of the Treasury); 28 U.S.C. §§ 2041–2042.

122. 18 U.S.C. § 3771(d)(2).

123. Zimmerman and Jaros, "The Criminal Class Action," 1385.

124. Transcript of Change of Plea and Sentencing Hearing, 17, 22, *United States v. Alcatel-Lucent*, Case No. 1:10-cr-20907-MGC (S.D. Fla. June 1, 2011).

125. Ibid., 23–24.

126. Ibid., 27–28.

127. Ibid., 49.

128. Ibid., 52.

129. Transcript of Change of Plea and Sentencing Hearing at 52, *United States v. Alcatel-Lucent*, Case No. 1:10-cr-20907-MGC (S.D. Fla. June 1, 2011).

130. In re: Instituto Costarricense de Electricidad, No. 11–12708-G (11th Cir. 2011) (unpublished decision).

131. U.S. Attorney's Office, "Chevron Corp. Agrees to Pay $30 Million in Oil-for-Food Settlement," press release, November 14, 2007.

132. Plea Agreement at Exhibit B, *U.S. v. Style Craft Furniture Co., Ltd*, No. 1:08-cr-00279 (D.N.J., May 1, 2009).

133. *United States v. Urciuoli*, 613 F.3d 11, 18 (1st Cir. 2010).

134. See Memorandum from Mark Filip, Deputy Attorney General, to Holders of the *U.S. Attorneys' Manual*, May 14, 2008; *United States Attorneys' Manual* §9–16.325 (2010).

135. Jef Feeley and Janelle Lawrence, "Merck Unit's Plea over Vioxx Investigation Accepted by Judge," *Bloomberg Businessweek*, April 19, 2012.

136. Ibid.

137. Jef Feeley and Janelle Lawrence, "Orthofix's Settlement of Medicare Probe Rejected by Judge," *Bloomberg Businessweek*, September 6, 2012.

138. Jef Feeley and Janelle Lawrence, "Orthofix Medicare Fraud Probe Is Rejected Again by Judge," *Bloomberg Businessweek*, December 13, 2012.

139. Richard A. Bierschbach and Stephanos Bibas, "Notice-and-Comment Sentencing," *Minnesota Law Review* 97 (2012): 1.

140. Peter Maas, "What Happened at the Macondo Well?" *New York Review of Books*, September 29, 2011, 38–41.

141. *Deepwater Horizon* Study Group, "Final Report on the investigation of the Macondo Well Blowout," March 1, 2011, 6–7.

142. National Commission on the BP *Deepwater Horizon* Oil Spill & Offshore Drilling, *Deep Water: The Gulf Oil Disaster and the Future of Offshore Drilling*, 2011 (National Commission Report)., vii, 122.

143. Ibid., ix, 221.

144. *Deepwater Horizon* Study Group, 5, 6; see also National Commission Report, 221.

145. Clifford Krauss, "Engineer Arrested in BP Oil Spill Case," *New York Times*, April 24, 2012.

146. Affidavit of Barbara O'Donnell, *U.S. v. Mix* (E.D.L.A. April 23, 2012).

147. "BP Must Pay $400M for Indiana Refinery Emissions Controls," ENS Newswire, May 24, 2012.

148. 18 U.S.C. § 1115.

149. Steven Mufson, "BP Agrees to Criminal Plea, $4 Billion Settlement in Gulf Oil Spill Case," *Washington Post*, November 15, 2012.

150. News Release, "EPA to Lift Suspension and Debarment of BP from Federal Government Contracts/Agreement contains strong provisions to continue safety and ethics improvements in order to comply," Environmental Protection Agency, March 13, 2014.

151. "BP Texas Lawsuit: Texas City Resident Sue Oil Company," *Associated Press*, June 14, 2012; Harvey Rice, "Jury Absolves BP in Gas Leak Trial," *Houston Chronicle*, October 10, 2013.

152. Erwin Seba, "BP Texas City Refinery Not Profitable for Years—Report," Reuters, June 6, 2012; BP "BP Completes Sale of Texas City Refinery and Related Assets to Marathon Petroleum," press release, February 1, 2013.

153. Alice Gomstyn, "BP Texas City Refinery Blast Victim: BP Keeps 'Killing People,'" ABC News, July 7, 2010.

6. The Carrot and the Stick

1. Mary Flood and Tom Fowler, "Enron's Auditor Is Given the Max," *Houston Chronicle*, October 17, 2002.

2. *United States v. Booker*, 543 U.S. 220 (2005).

3. U.S.S.G. Chapter 5, Pt. A (Sentencing Table).

4. Jennifer Arlen, "The Failure of the Organizational Sentencing Guidelines," *Miami Law Review* 66 (2012): 231.

5. Compare 18 U.S.C. § 3571(c) with § 3571(d), which provides for fines up to twice the loss to victims or the gain to the firm.

6. Order, *United States v. Andersen, LLP*, Docket No. 4:02-cr-00121 (S.D. Tex. Mar 07, 2002).

7. Johnson & Johnson Deferred Prosecution Agreement at ¶ 4.

8. *U.S. v. Siemens A.G.*, Case 1:08-cr-00267-RJL (D.D.C. Feb. 4, 2009), Plea Hearing and Sentencing, 5.

9. Ibid., 6–7.

10. Ibid., 9.

11. Fed. R. Crim. P. 4(a), Fed. R. Crim. P. 43(b); see Christopher Jackson, "When a Company Confesses," *Michigan Law Review* 109 (2010): 387.

12. Siemens Plea Hearing, 10–12, 20–21.

13. Ibid., 15, 24, 30.

14. Ibid., 17–19.

15. Siemens Plea Agreement, 4; Mike Esterl et al., "Siemens Internal Review Hits Hurdles," *Wall Street Journal*, January 23, 2008; David Crawford and Mike Esterl, "Siemens Ruling Details Bribery across the Globe," *Wall Street Journal*, November 16, 2007.

16. 18 U.S.C. §3571.

17. Ibid., 31, 34.

18. *U.S. v. Guidant*, Crim. No. 10-mj-67 (D.MN. 2010), Memorandum Opinion and Order, 16–19.

19. A judge is not obligated to accept a Type C agreement that is involuntary, unfair, or contrary to the interests of justice. See, e.g., *U.S. v. Kling*, 516 F.3d 702, 704 (8th Cir. 2008).

20. Ibid., 22.

21. Letter to Hon. Donavan W. Frank, *U.S. v. Guidant*, Crim. No. 10-mj-67 (D.MN. April 12, 2010).

22. Ibid., 26.

23. *U.S. v. Guidant LLC*, No. 10-mj-67, 708 F.Supp. 2d 903, 921 (D.MN. 2010).

24. "Judge Accepts Guilty Plea by Guidant," *Bloomberg News*, January 13, 2011; "Judge Adds Probation to Guidant Plea Deal," Associated Press, January 12, 2011.

25. John C. Coffee Jr., "No Soul to Damn: No Body to Kick: An Unscandalized Inquiry into the Problem of Corporate Punishment," *Michigan Law Review* 79 (1981): 388; Mark A. Cohen, "Theories of Punishment and Empirical Trends in Corporate Criminal Sanctions," *Managerial and Decision Economics* 17 (1996): 399, 401; Ilene H. Nagel and John L. Hagan, "The Sentencing of White-Collar Criminals in Federal Courts: A Socio-Legal Exploration of Disparity," *Michigan Law Review* 80 (1982): 1427.

26. *Southern Union Co. v. U.S.*, 132 S.Ct. 2344 (Breyer, J., dissenting).

27. Richard S. Gruner, "Towards an Organizational Jurisprudence: Transforming Corporate Criminal Law through Federal Sentencing Reform," *Arizona Law Review* 36 (1994): 408; Ilene H. Nagel and Winthrop M. Swenson, "Federal Sentencing Guidelines for Corporations: Their Development, Theoretical Underpinnings, and Some Thoughts about Their Future," *Washington University Law Quarterly* 71 (1993): 215.

28. Criminal Fine Enforcement Act of 1984, Pub. L. No. 98–596, 98 Stat. 3134 (1984); Criminal Fines Improvement Act of 1987, Pub. L. No. 100–185, 101 Stat. 1279 (1987).

29. Mark A. Cohen et al., "Report on Sentencing of Organizations in the Federal Courts, 1984–1987," in United States Sentencing Commission, Discussion Materials on Organizational Sanctions, 1988, 7–11.

30. Cindy R. Alexander et al., "Regulating Corporate Criminal Sanctions: Federal Guidelines and the Sentencing of Public Firms," *Journal of Law and Economics* 42 (1999): 416, 419–420.

31. *United States v. Booker*, 543 U.S. 220 (2005).

32. For discussion of deterrence approach, see, e.g., Jeffrey S. Parker, "Criminal Sentencing Policy for Organizations: The Unifying Approach of Optimal Penalties," *American Criminal Law Review* 26 (1989): 554–561.

33. Jennifer Arlen, "The Potentially Perverse Effects of Corporate Criminal Liability," *Journal of Legal Studies* 23 (1994): 833; Jennifer Arlen and Reinier Kraakman, "Controlling Corporate Misconduct: An Analysis of Corporate Liability Regimes," *New York University Law Review* 72 (1997): 699.

34. In re Caremark Int'l., Inc. Derivative Litigation, 698 A.2d 959, 970 (Del. Ch. 1996).

35. U.S.S.G. § 8C.1.1 (2010).

36. Department of Justice, "Nexus Technologies Inc. and Three Employees Plead Guilty to Paying Bribes to Vietnamese Officials," press release, March 16, 2010.

37. *U.S. v. Nguyen et al.*, 2:08-cr-00522 (Sept. 8, 2010 E.D.P.A.), Government's Sentencing Memorandum, 1–3.

38. Ibid., 9.

39. Judgment, *U.S. v. Nguyen et al.*, 2:08-cr-00522 (Sept. 15, 2010 E.D.P.A.).

40. U.S.S.G. §8C2.2.

41. 2008 Commission Datafile.

42. *U.S. v. Barclays*, No. CR 10–218 (D.D.C. August 18, 2010), Hearing, 18.

43. Ibid., 15.

44. U.S.S.G. § 8B1.1 (in a case with an "identifiable victim" the court shall "enter a restitution order for the full amount of the victim's loss").

45. 18 USC § 3571(d).

46. U.S.S.G. § 2B1.1; *United States v. Parris*, 573 F. Supp. 2d 744, 754 (E.D.N.Y. 2008); *U.S. v. Adelson*, 441 F.Supp. 2d 506, 510 (S.D.N.Y. 2006).

47. U.S.S.G. § 2B1.1 Application Note 3(A)(ii).

48. U.S.S.G. §8C2.9.

49. Ibid., §8C2.5.

50. Ibid., §8C2.6.

51. Ibid., §8C2.5(b).

52. Ibid., §8C2.6 (table of minimum and maximum multipliers).

53. U.S. Sentencing Commission, "2009–2012 Sourcebook," 2012, Table 54. Five companies received credit for effective compliance from 1992 through 2012.

54. USSG §8B2.1(b)(2), USSG §8B2.1(a)(2); "Report of the Ad Hoc Advisory Group on the Organizational Guidelines," October 7, 2003.

55. USSG §8C2.5(3).

56. Mei Lin Kwan-Gett and Dane A. Lund, "Crediting Corporate Compliance but Withholding the Corporate Compliance Guideline's Credit," *Federal Sentencing Reporter* 26 (2013): 49.

57. 2008 Datafile, ICPSR, Organizations Convicted in Federal Criminal Courts Series, www.icpsr.umich.edu/icpsrweb/ICPSR/series/85.

58. Arlen, "The Failure of the Organizational Sentencing Guidelines," supra.

59. U.S.S.G. §8C2.5(g)(1).

60. 2012 Sourcebook, Table 54 (28.6% accepted responsibility).

61. U.S.S.G. §8C2.5(g)(2).

62. U.S.S.G. §8C2.5(g)(3); 2012 Sourcebook, table 54.

63. Ibid.

64. U.S.S.G. §8C4.1.

65. Motion to Depart, 3–4, *U.S. v. Panalpina*, No. 10-cr-765 (S.D.Tx. Dec. 7, 2010).

66. Ibid., 4–5.

67. USSG § 2B1.1.

68. *U.S. v. Bernard L. Madoff,* 09 CR 213 (DC) (S.D.N.Y. June 29, 2009), Sentencing Hearing, 40, 43.

69. Ibid., 3–30.

70. Ibid., 20.

71. Ibid., 34.

72. Ibid., 36, 38.

73. Diana B. Henriques, "Madoff Is Sentenced to 150 Years for Ponzi Scheme," *New York Times,* June 29, 2009.

74. *U.S. v. Madoff,* Sentencing Hearing, 46–47.

75. Sam Buell, "Is the White Collar Offender Privileged?" *Duke Law Journal* 63 (2013): 823.

76. Susan Pulliam and Chad Bray, "Trader Draws Record Sentence," *Wall Street Journal,* October 13, 2011; *United States v. Rajaratnam,* No. 09 Cr. 1184, slip op. at 1 (S.D.N.Y. Jan. 31, 2012).

77. U.S. Sentencing Commission, 2000–2012 Sourcebooks of Federal Sentencing Statistics.

78. Fed. R. Crim. P. 11(c)(1)(B) (plea agreement may "recommend" that "a particular sentence or sentencing range is appropriate"), Fed. R. Crim. P. 11 (c)(1)(C) (plea agreement may "agree that a specific sentence or sentencing range is the appropriate disposition of the case"); Fed. R. Crim. P. 11(c)(5) (procedure for rejecting a (c)(1)(A) or (C) plea agreement); see, e.g., In re Morgan, 506 F.3d 705, 712 (9th Cir. 2007) (court must make an "individualized assessment" of the plea agreement); *United States v. Smith,* 417 F.3d 483, 487 (5th Cir. 2005) ("A district court may properly reject a plea agreement based on the court's belief that the defendant would receive too light of a sentence.").

79. *U.S. v. Wampler,* 624 F.3d 1330, 1332–33 (10th Cir. 2010) (describing how the court rejected a plea agreement because it "unjustly let the company's principals off the hook").

80. Pamela MacLean and Karen Gullo, "Samsung SDI's Plea Deal in Price Fixing Case Blocked," *Bloomberg,* April 20, 2011.

81. U.S.A.M. § 9–28.1300.

82. See, e.g., 2011 Sourcebook, Table 53 (69.4 percent placed on probation); 2010 Sourcebook at Tbl.53 (70.5 percent placed on probation).

83. U.S.S.G. § 8D1.1(a)(3). This rule applies only to firms with more than 50 employees. U.S.S.G. § 8D1.3(a)(1)–(6).

84. Ibid., § 8D1.3(a)(1).

85. Nagel & Swenson, 216, 234; see, e.g., *United States v. Missouri Valley Constr. Co.,* 741 F.2d 1542 (8th Cir.1984); *United States v. John Scher Presents, Inc.,* 746 F.2d 959 (3d Cir.1984).

86. Michael B. Gerrard, "Corporate Probation: The Con Edison Sentence," *New York Law Journal,* May 26, 1995.

87. 42 USC §§11001 et seq.

88. U.S.S.G. § 8D1.4, Application Note 1.

89. U.S.S.G. § 8D1.4(5).

90. 2012 Sourcebook, Table 53.

91. Andrew Weissmann and Joshua A. Block, "White-Collar Defendants and White-Collar Crimes," *Yale Law Journal Pocket Part* 116 (2007): 286; U.S. Sentencing Commission,

"Measuring Recidivism: The Criminal History Computation of the Federal Sentencing Guidelines," 2004, 13.

92. 2011 Sourcebook, Table 54 (1.4 percent had a prior conviction in the past ten years). In 2009 and 2010, it was zero percent. 2009–2010 Sourcebook, Table 54.

93. For example, in 2008 the one recidivist company violated a probation order. 2008 Sourcebook, Table 54.

94. U.S.S.G. § 8C2.5(c); see also U.S.S.G. §2.8.

95. ABB Vetco Gray (UK) Ltd. Plea Agreement.

96. Ibid., Statement of Facts, 1.

97. Department of Justice, "Aibel Group Ltd. Pleads Guilty to Foreign Bribery and Agrees to Pay $4.2 Million in Criminal Fines," press release, November 21, 2008.

98. Ibid.

99. Department of Justice, "ABB Ltd and Two Subsidiaries Resolve Foreign Corrupt Practices Act Investigation and Will Pay $19 Million in Criminal Penalties," press release, September 29, 2010.

100. Deferred Prosecution Hearing, *U.S. v. ABB Ltd.*, Cr. No. H-10-665 (S.D.Tex. Sept. 29, 2010).

101. Ibid., 13.

102. Ibid., 10.

103. Department of Justice, "Agencies Listed by Size Categories," www.justice.gov/crt/508 /report2/agencies.php.

104. Transcript of Deferred Prosecution Hearing, *U.S. v. ABB Ltd.*, 10–11.

105. Ibid., 12.

106. USSG §8C2.5(c).

107. Ibid., 14.

108. Ibid., 20.

109. Samuel W. Buell, "The Blaming Function of Entity Criminal Liability," *Indiana Law Journal* 81 (2006): 501. John C. Coffee Jr. developed shortcomings of a reputation-focused approach towards corporate crime. Coffee, "No Soul to Damn," 424–434.

110. Gilbert Geis and Joseph DiMento, "Should We Prosecute Corporations and/or Individuals?" in *Corporate Crime: Contemporary Debates*, ed. Frank Pearce and Laureen Snider (Toronto, Ontario: University of Toronto Press, 1995), 79 (describing 1983 study).

111. Cindy R. Alexander, "On the Nature of the Reputational Penalty for Corporate Crime: Evidence," *Journal of Law and Economics* 42 (1999): 493.

112. Alpha Natural Resources, December 6, 2011 ("SPX five day big winners [include] Alpha Natural Resources (ANR) 24.05% . . .").

113. Dan M. Kahan, "What Do Alternative Sanctions Mean?" *University of Chicago Law Review* 63 (1996): 643.

114. See U.S.S.G. § 8C2.5, commentary (n. 14).

115. Jayne W. Barnard, "Reintegrative Shaming in Corporate Sentencing," *Southern California Law Review* 72 (1999): 961–962.

116. U.S.S.G. § 8D1.4(a); Andrew Cowan, "Scarlet Letters for Corporations? Punishment by Publicity under the New Sentencing Guidelines," *Southern California Law Review* 65 (1992): 2387.

117. Griffin Industries Agreement.

118. See EMI-SAR Trucking Plea Agreement.
119. Drew Griffin and Andy Segal, "Feds Found Pfizer Too Big to Nail," CNN.com, April 2, 2010.
120. See, e.g. In re Catfish Antitrust Litigation, 908 F. Supp. 400 (N.D. Miss. 1995) (a civil antitrust case).
121. Associated Press, "Lockheed Drops Titan Merger after Delays by Bribery Probe," *Los Angeles Times*, June 27, 2004.
122. Plea Agreement, *U.S. v. Abbott Labs*, Case No. 1:12-cr-00026-SGW (May 7, 2012).
123. Lloyds Deferred Prosecution Agreement, ¶ 15.
124. *U.S. v. BP Products North America, Inc.*, No. 4:07-cr-434 (S.D. Tex. March 26, 2009), Transcript of Sentencing, 10.

7. Enter the Monitors

1. *Plutarch's Lives and Writings: The Translation Called Dryden's*, ed. A. H. Clough (1905), 1:21.
2. Sentencing Memorandum, *U.S. v. Siemens Aktiengesellschaft* (D.D.C. December 12, 2008).
3. Siemens, "Sustaining Business Integrity," (2011), www.siemens.com/sustainability/pool/compliance/integrity_initiative/sustaining-business-integrity.pdf.
4. Sentencing Memo, 22.
5. Siemens Plea Agreement,11–12.
6. Securities and Exchange Commission, "Bristol-Myers Squibb Company Agrees to Pay $150 Million to Settle Fraud Charges," press release, August 4, 2004.
7. U.S. Department of Justice, "Statement from U.S. Attorney Christopher J. Christie on Expiration of Deferred Prosecution Agreement with Bristol-Myers Squibb," June 14, 2007.
8. U.S. Department of Justice, Office of the Deputy Attorney General, "Selection and Use of Monitors in Deferred Prosecution Agreements and Non-Prosecution Agreements with Corporations," March 7, 2008 ("Morford Memo").
9. The Aurora Foods agreement refers to an "outside consultant." Aurora Foods Non-Prosecution Agreement, 4. The Bank of New York agreement refers to an "independent examiner." Bank of New York Non-Prosecution Agreement, 11–12. The Boeing Agreement refers to a "Special Compliance Officer." Boeing Non-Prosecution Agreement, 6. The G.E. agreement refers to an "Independent Consultant." G.E. Non-Prosecution Agreement, 3.
10. Morford Memo, 2.
11. Ibid.
12. James B. Jacobs et al., "The RICO Trusteeships after Twenty Years: A Progress Report," *Labor Law* 19 (2004): 419.
13. *U.S. v. Int'l Bhd. of Teamsters*, 742 F.Supp. 94, 102 (S.D.N.Y. 1990).
14. I first explored the connection between structural reform litigation and corporate prosecution agreements in a law review article. Brandon L. Garrett, "Structural Reform Prosecution," *Virginia Law Review* 93 (2007): 853.
15. Abram Chayes, "The Role of the Judge in Public Law Litigation," *Harvard Law Review* 89 (1976): 1281, 1284, 1298.

16. For example, in a series of controversial decisions, the Supreme Court found remedies in certain desegregation cases too intrusive. *Missouri v. Jenkins*, 515 U.S. 70, 112–113 (1983); *Frew v. Hawkins*, 540 U.S. 431, 442 (2004).

17. E.g., William Fletcher, "The Discretionary Constitution: Institutional Remedies and Judicial Legitimacy," *Yale Law Journal* 91 (1982): 625; Paul J. Mishkin, "Federal Courts as State Reformers," *Washington and Lee Law Review* 35 (1978): 951; Charles F. Sabel and William H. Simon, "Destabilization Rights: How Public Law Litigation Succeeds," *Harvard Law Review* 117 (2004): 1019–1020; John C. Jeffries Jr. and George A. Rutherglen, "Structural Reform Revisited," *California Law Review* 95 (2007): 1387.

18. One set of monitor reports that were made public were in the University of Medicine and Dentistry of New Jersey case.

19. One cannot always tell from docket sheets whether the judge added special conditions, like a special master, to probation, but this appears to be fairly uncommon outside of FCPA and environmental cases.

20. Those three are the B.P., Computer Associates, and N.Y. Racing Association agreements.

21. Russell Mokhiber, "Morford Memo Morphed: Who Picks the Corporate Monitors?" *Corporate Crime Reporter*, January 1, 2013.

22. *Lincoln Savings & Loan Association v. Wall*, 743 F. Supp. 901, 920 (D.D.C. 1990); Donald C. Langevoort, "Where Were the Lawyers? A Behavioral Inquiry into Lawyers' Responsibility for Clients' Fraud," *Vanderbilt Law Review* 46 (1993): 76 ("Where were the lawyers? Perhaps rhetorical, even sarcastic, this question is being asked all too frequently after large financial frauds").

23. Jill E. Fisch and Kenneth M. Rosen, "Is There a Role for Lawyers in Preventing Future Enrons?" *Villanova Law Review* 48 (2003): 1097.

24. 148 Cong. Rec. S6524 (daily ed. July 10, 2002) (statement of Sen. Corzine).

25. Preliminary Report of the American Bar Association's Task Force on Corporate Responsibility, July 16, 2002, 47–50.

26. Sarbanes-Oxley Act, § 307, 15 U.S.C. § 7245 (2002). The SEC also gave firms the option of establishing a Qualified Legal Compliance Committee (QLCC) to receive reports of misconduct from attorneys. 17 C.F.R. § 205.3.

27. John C. Coffee Jr., "Gatekeeper Failure and Reform: The Challenge of Fashioning Relevant Reforms," *Boston University Law Review* 84 (2004): 360–363.

28. Barry F. McNeil and Brad D. Dian, *Internal Corporate Investigations* (Chicago: American Bar Association, 2007), 18.

29. Peter J. Henning, "The Mounting Costs of Internal Investigations," *New York Times*, March 5, 2012.

30. David S. Hilzenrath, "Justice Department, SEC Investigations Often Rely on Companies' Internal Probes," *Washington Post*, May 22, 2011.

31. Nathan Vardi, "The Bribery Racket," *Forbes*, May 28, 2010.

32. Jenkins Gilchrist Agreement, 2 (March 26, 2007); IRS news release IR-2007-71 (March 29, 2007), www.irs.gov/pub/irs-news/ir-07-071.pdf.

33. BMS Deferred Prosecution Agreement, ¶5.

34. Ibid., ¶5, 12, 14.

35. Ibid., Attachment B, 3, 5.

36. U.S. Department of Justice, "Bristol-Myers Squibb Charged with Conspiring to Commit Securities Fraud; Prosecution Deferred for Two Years," press release, June 15, 2005.

37. In re Bristol-Myers Squibb Securities Litigation, Master File No. 02-CV-2251 (LAP) (S,D.N.Y.).

38. BMS DPA, ¶8.

39. Ibid., ¶31, 34.

40. Brooke A. Masters, "Bristol-Myers Outs Its Chief at Monitor's Urging," *Washington Post*, September 13, 2006.

41. Form 10-Q, Bristol-Myers Squibb Company, Quarterly Report under Section 13 or 15 of the Securities Exchange Act of 1934 for the Quarterly Period Ended March 31, 2007.

42. The passages that discuss Dr. Waigel's work are based on an October 2, 2012, phone interview with him, and any quotations attributed to him come from that interview. I am very grateful that Dr. Waigel was willing to share his recollections and views concerning the monitorship.

43. Siemens Plea Agreement, 11–12; see also Siemens, Continuous Improvement.

44. Siemens, Index According to the Reporting Guidance on the 10th Principle by the UN Global Compact and Transparency International, April 2012, www.siemens.com/sustain ability/pool/en/core_topics/compliance/siemens-acrg-index-2011-en.pdf.

45. Ibid., 74–75.

46. I am grateful to Joseph Warin for discussing the monitoring work in a phone conversation on March 22, 2013.

47. Siemens, 2011 Annual Report, www.siemens.com/investor/pool/en/investor_relations /siemens_ar_2011.pdf.

48. Siemens, Annual Shareholders Meeting of Siemens AG, "Speech by Peter Löscher, President and CEO," January 24, 2012, www.siemens.com/press/pool/de/events/2012/corpo rate/2012-q1/2012-hv-speech-loescher.pdf.

49. Vikramaditya Khanna and Timothy L. Dickinson, "The Corporate Monitor: The New Corporate Czar?," *Michigan Law Review* 105 (2007): 1713.

50. E.g., Weatherford Int'l Inc. Deferred Prosecution Agreement (November 26, 2013), D-8.

51. Government Accountability Office, "Preliminary Observations on the DOJ's Use and Oversight of Deferred Prosecution and Non-Prosecution Agreements," June 25, 2009, 41.

52. New Release, "Willbros Reports Results from Continuing Operations for the Fourth Quarter and 2011 and Filing of Annual Report on Form 10-K," http://phx.corporate-ir .net/phoenix.zhtml?c=95816&p=irol-newsArticle&ID=1681131.

53. Faro Technologies, Inc., "SEC Filings," www.faro.com/contentv2.aspx?ct=us&content=misc &item=8.

54. Sue Reisinger, "Attorney General Holder Welcomes James Cole as Deputy AG," *Corporate Counsel*, January 5, 2011.

55. Nathan Vardi, "How Federal Crackdown on Bribery Hurts Business and Enriches Insiders," Forbes.com, May 24, 2010.

56. Email, "Monitor Agreement," October 15, 2007, http://judiciary.house.gov/hearings /pdf/Zimmer090625.pdf.

57. Prepared Statement by Christopher J. Christie, 53, Hearing before the Subcommittee on Commercial and Administrative Law of the Committee on the Judiciary, "Account-

ability, Transparency, and Uniformity in Corporate Deferred and Non-Prosecution Agreements," June 25, 2009, http://judiciary.house.gov/hearings/printers/111th/111-52 _50593.PDF.

58. Ibid., 119.

59. Ibid.

60. Christopher Dela Cruz, "Chris Christie Faces Questions about U.S. Attorney Contracts amid Release of Documents," *The Star Ledger*, June 25, 2009.

61. Hearing Testimony, October 22, 2007, email.

62. Ibid., October 19, 2007, email; see also David Kocieniewski, "In Testy Exchange in Congress, Christie Defends His Record as a Prosecutor," *New York Times*, June 26, 2009.

63. Statement by Christie, 54.

64. Ibid., 114.

65. Hearing before the Subcommittee on Commercial and Administrative Law of the Committee on the Judiciary, "Deferred Prosecution: Should Corporate Settlement Agreements Be without Guidelines," March 11, 2008, 290, http://judiciary.house.gov/hearings/print ers/110th/41190.PDF.

66. Ibid., 294; see also Testimony of the Honorable John Ashcroft, Former United States Attorney General, Chairman, The Ashcroft Group, LLC and Monitor for Zimmer, Inc., http://judiciary.house.gov/hearings/pdf/Ashcroft080311.pdf.

67. March 11, 2008, Hearing, 294.

68. Ibid.

69. Ibid.; Philip Shenon, "New Guidelines ahead of Ashcroft Testimony," *New York Times*, March 11, 2008.

70. June 25, 2009, Hearing, 5.

71. Morford Memo, 3.

72. Ibid., 4.

73. Government Accountability Office, "Preliminary Observations on the DOJ's Use and Oversight of Deferred Prosecution and Non-Prosecution Agreements," June 25, 2009, 41 (noting that in only two of twenty-six agreements reviewed was the monitor required provided a work plan in advance).

74. Morford Memo, 5.

75. Ibid., 5–7, 8.

76. Examples include the Aksat Denizcilik Ve Ticaret A.S., B. Navi Ship Management Services, Hiong Guan Navegacion Japan Co. Ltd., and Fleet Management Ltd. plea agreements.

77. For example, the Capital Data Management agreement notes, "Defendant will employ an independent corporate monitor, acceptable to the USAO and the Probation Office, to ensure compliance pursuant to the compliance program, and the corporate monitor shall submit quarterly reports to the United States Probation Office."

78. Chalos & Co., P.C., "Kassian Navigation's Probation Terminated Early for Extraordinary Environmental Compliance Measures," www.chaloslaw.com/kassian-navigation.html.

79. Sue Reisinger, "U.S. Attorney Accuses Wright Medical Group of Breaching Deferred Prosecution Agreement," *Corporate Counsel*, September 15, 2011; David Voreacos, "Wright Medical Stays under U.S. Oversight in Kickback Case," Bloomberg, September 15, 2011.

80. Siemens, "Problem-Specific Methods—Integrity Pacts," www.siemens.com/sustainability /en/core-topics/collective-action/our-approach.htm.

81. Siemens, Sustaining Business Integrity.

82. Speech by Peter Löscher.

8. The Constitutional Rights of Corporations

1. Petitioner's Appendix 3a–4a, *Southern Union Co. v. United States*, No. 11–94 (D.Ct. Oct. 19, 2011); *Southern Union Co. v. United States*, Court of Appeals Appendix 445–450, 569, 574–575 (2d Cir. 2012).

2. *Southern Union Co. v. United States*, No. 11–94, 132 S.Ct. 2344 (Oct. 19, 2011), Brief for the United States in Opposition, 4.

3. Petioner's Appendix, 42a.

4. Joint Appendix, 152.

5. 42 U.S.C. 6928(d).

6. 132 S.Ct. 2344 (2012).

7. 530 U.S. 466 (2000).

8. Ibid., n. 2.

9. FBI, "Taiwan-Based AU Optronics Corporation Sentenced to Pay $500 Million Criminal Fine for Role in LCD Price Fixing Conspiracy," press release, September 20, 2012.

10. Department of Justice, "Taiwan-Based AU Optronics Corporation, Its Houston-Based Subsidiary and Former Top Executives Convicted for Role in LCD Price-Fixing Conspiracy," press release, March 13, 2012; Department of Justice, "Taiwan-Based AU Optronics Corporation Sentenced to Pay $500 Million Criminal Fine for Role in LCD Price-Fixing Conspiracy," press release, September 20, 2012.

11. David Debold and Matthew Benjamin, "The Best to Be Done in a Bad Situation: *Southern Union* on Remand," *Criminal Law Reporter* 91 (November 13, 2013): 91.

12. Jonathan A. Marcantel, "The Corporation as a 'Real' Constitutional Person," *U.C. Davis Business Law Journal*, 2011.

13. *Bank of the United States v. Deveaux*, 9 U.S. (5 Cranch) 61 (1809).

14. *Citizens United v. Federal Election Commission*, 130 S. Ct. 876 (2010), Transcript of Oral Argument, 7.

15. *Trustees of Dartmouth College v. Woodard*, 17 U.S. (1 Wheat.) 518 (1819).

16. *Santa Clara County v. S. Pac. R.R.*, 118 U.S. 394, 396 (1886) (assuming in a preliminary note that corporations have Fourteenth Amendment equal protection clause rights).

17. *Hale v. Henkel*, 201 U.S. 43, 74–75 (1906).

18. *Northwestern National Life Insurance Co. v. Riggs*, 203 U.S. 243, 255 (1906).

19. *Citizens United v. FEC*, 130 S. Ct. 876, 948 (2010) (Stevens, J., dissenting).

20. *Paul v. Virginia*, 75 U.S. (8 Wall.) 168, 177 (1869) ("The term citizens . . . [as used in the Fourteenth Amendment] applies only to natural persons . . . not to artificial persons created by the legislature").

21. See, e.g., Jess M. Krannich, "The Corporate 'Person': A New Analytical Approach to a Flawed Method of Constitutional Interpretation," *Loyola University Chicago Law Journal* 37 (2005): 62; Carl J. Mayer, "Personalizing the Impersonal: Corporations and the Bill of Rights," *Hastings Law Journal* 41 (1990): 650.

22. *First National Bank v. Bellotti*, 435 U.S. 765, 765 n. 14 (1978).

23. *NAACP v. Alabama*, 357 U.S. 449 (1958); *Hunt v. Washington State Apple Advertising Commission*, 432 U.S. 333, 343–344 (1977); *UAW v. Brock*, 477 U.S. 274, 288–290 (1986).

24. *Northwestern National Life Insurance Co. v. Riggs*, 203 U.S. 243, 255 (1906).

25. *Smyth v. Ames*, 169 U.S. 466, 522 (1898).

26. *United States v. ABB Inc.*, No. 10-CR-664 (S.D. Tex.), *United States v. ABB Ltd.-Jordan*, No. 10-CR-665 (S.D. Tex.), and *United States v. O'Shea*, No. 09 CR-629 (S.D. Tex.).

27. Defendants' Motion to Dismiss the Indictment with Prejudice Due to Repeated and Intentional Government Misconduct, *United States v. Aguilar*, 831 F.Supp. 2d 1180 (C.D. Cal. 2011) (No. 10–1031).

28. Ibid., 13.

29. U.S. Department of Justice, "California Company and Two Executives Indicted for Their Alleged Participation in Scheme to Bribe Officials at State-owned Electrical Utility in Mexico," press release, October 21, 2010.

30. Alison Frankel, "What FCPA defendants Can Learn from Blockbuster Lindsey Win," Thompson Reuters, December 2, 2011.

31. U.S. Department of Justice, "Southern California Company, Two Executives and Intermediary Convicted in Scheme to Bribe Officials at State-Owned Electrical Utility in Mexico," press release, May 10, 2011.

32. *U.S. v. Aguilar*, 831 F.Supp. 2d 1180, 1189 (C.D.Cal. 2011); Order Granting Motion to Dismiss, 12; Supplemental Brief in Support of Motion to Dismiss the Indictment with Prejudice Due to Repeated and Intentional Government Misconduct, 10, *United States v. Aguilar*, No. 10–1031 (C.D. Cal. September 8, 2011).

33. Defendants' Motion to Dismiss the Indictment with Prejudice Due to Repeated and Intentional Government Misconduct, 9–10; *Aguilar*, 831 F.Supp. 2d at 1190–1193.

34. Defendants' Motion, 13.

35. Ibid., 21.

36. *Aguilar*, 831 F.Supp. 2d at 1185.

37. Ibid., 1182.

38. "Fiery Jury Instructions," *Inside Counsel*, July 1, 2009.

39. Steven Andersen, "Asbestos Acquittal: W. R. Grace Unexpectedly Wins Environmental Crimes Trial," *Inside Counsel*, July 1, 2009.

40. Brad Heath and Kevin McCoy, "Federal prosecutors Likely to Keep Jobs after Cases Collapse," *USA Today*, December 10, 2010; Spencer S. Hsu, Jennifer Jenkins, and Ted Mellnik, "DOJ Review of Flawed FBI Forensics Processes Lacked Transparency," *Washington Post*, April 17, 2012; Spencer S. Hsu, "Justice Dept., FBI to Review Use of Forensic Evidence in Thousands of Cases," *Washington Post*, July 10, 2012.

41. E.g., U.S.A.M. 9–5.001(E).

42. William J. Stuntz, "Commentary, O. J. Simpson, Bill Clinton, and the Transsubstantive Fourth Amendment," *Harvard Law Review* 114 (2001): 858–861.

43. Bernard Schwartz, *Administrative Law*, 3rd ed. (Boston: Little, Brown, 1991), § 3.1.

44. Order, *U.S. v. Arthur Andersen*, No. H-02-0121 (S.D.T.X. April 9, 2002).

45. *Boyd v. U.S.*, 116 U.S. 616 (1886).

46. 201 U.S. 43, 70 (1906).

47. *United States v. Morton Salt*, 338 U.S. 632, 652 (1950).

48. Ibid.

49. Administrative Procedure Act, 5 U.S.C. § 555(d) (2006).

50. 15 U.S.C. § 78u(a)(1).

51. Michele Galen, "When the Subpoena Has Your Name on It," *Business Week*, October 7, 1991.

52. *See v. City of Seattle*, 387 U.S. 541 (1967); *Camara v. Municipal Court*, 387 U.S. 523 (1967).

53. *Donovan v. Dewey*, 452 U.S. 594 (1981).

54. *Marshall v. Barlow*, 436 U.S. 307 (1978), *Colonnade Catering Corp. v. U.S.*, 397 U.S. 72 (1970), *U.S. v. Biswell*, 406 U.S. 311 (1972).

55. *Dow Chemical Co. v. United States*, 476 U.S. 227 (1986).

56. *Dow Chemical Co. v. United States*, 749 F.2d 307, 314 (6th Cir. 1984).

57. *United States v. Agriprocessors, Inc.*, 2009 WL 2255729 *2 (N.D.Iowa 2009).

58. *Wilson v. United States*, 221 U.S. 361, 383–384 (1911); *Hale v. Henkel*, 201 U.S. 43, 74–75 (1906); *United States v. White*, 322 U.S. 694 (1944).

59. *Shapiro v. United States*, 335 U.S. 1 (1948).

60. *Braswell v. United States*, 487 U.S. 99 (1988).

61. Ibid.; *Bellis v. United States*, 417 U.S. 85, 92–93 (1974).

62. *FCC v. AT&T Inc.*, 131 S.Ct. 1177 (2011).

63. Ibid., 1182, 1184.

64. *United States v. Hartsell*, 127 F.3d 343, 350 (4th Cir.1997) (agreeing with the Ninth Circuit "that neither the Sixth Amendment to the United States Constitution nor the Criminal Justice Act [18 U.S.C. § 3006A] provides that counsel must be appointed, at public expense, to represent a corporation in criminal proceedings.")

65. *United States v. Hagerman*, 545 F.3d 579, 581–582 (7th Cir.2008).

66. E.g., *RZS Holdings AVV v. PDVSA Petroleo S.A.*, 506 F.3d 350, 354 n. 4 (4th Cir.2007); *U.S. v. Unimex*, 991F.3d 546, 549 (11th Cir. 1993); *Lowery v. Hoffman*, 188 F.R.D. 651, 653–654 (M.D.Ala.1999); *Eagle Associates v. Bank of Montreal*, 926 F.2d 1305, 1309–1310 (2d Cir.1991); *First Amendment Foundation v. Village of Brookfield*, 575 F.Supp. 1207 (N.D.Ill.1983); but see *United States v. Reeves*, 431 F.2d 1187 (9th Cir.1970).

67. *United States v. Unimex, Inc.*, 991 F.2d 546, 550 (9th Cir.1993).

68. *United States v. Rocky Mountain Corp.*, 746 F.Supp. 2d 790, 801 (W.D.Va 2010).

69. Ibid., 802.

70. *United States v. Follin*, 979 F.2d 369, 374 (5th Cir. 1992); *United States v. King*, 134 F.3d 1173 (2d Cir. 1998).

71. U.S. Constitution, Eighth Amendment.

72. *Rhodes v. Chapman*, 452 U.S. 337, 345–346 (1981).

73. *United States v. Bajakajian*, 524 U.S. 321, 322 (1998) (fines must be "grossly disproportionate" to the offense).

74. *United States v. Martin Linen Supply Corp.*, 430 U.S. 564 (1977); *Fong Foo v. U.S.*, 369 U.S. 142 (1962); see also Peter J. Henning, "The Conundrum of Corporate Criminal Liability: Seeking a Consistent Approach to the Constitutional Rights of Corporations in Criminal Prosecutions," *Tennessee Law Review* 63 (1996): 845–849.

75. For a time, corporations could pursue the theory that a prior civil proceedings was sufficiently punitive that double jeopardy attached, following *United States v. Halper*, 490 U.S. 435 (1989). The Supreme Court then rejected that rule. *Hudson v. United States*, 522 U.S. 93, 99 (1997).

76. See, e.g., *United States v. Cotton Baking Co., Inc.*, 513 F.Supp. 223, 224 (M.D. La. 1981); *United States v. Ashland Oil*, Inc., 537 F.Supp. 427, 429 (M.D. Tenn. 1982).

77. Trial Transcript, *S.A. v. Stora Enso North America*, 3:06-cr-00323-CFD (D.Ct. July 18, 2007), 29, 621.

78. Motion for Judgment of Acquittal Pursuant to Federal Rule of Criminal Procedure 29, *U.S.A. v. Stora Enso North America*, 3:06-cr-00323-CFD (D.Ct. July 18, 2007), 5.

79. Jeffrey May, "Paper Maker's Subsidiary Acquitted of Price Fixing, Despite Evidence from Corporate Leniency Applicant," *Trade Regulation Talk* (blog), July 23, 2007, at http://traderegulation.blogspot.com/2007/07/paper-makers-north-american-subsid iary.html.

80. Stora Enso Trial Transcript, 13, 34.

81. Ibid., 37.

82. Ibid., 605.

83. Ibid., 68, 89–90.

84. Ibid., 66–69.

85. Ibid., 87.

86. Ibid., 117, 119.

87. Ibid., 277, 286, 299–302.

88. Ibid., 604.

89. Ibid., 576, 578, 580.

90. Ibid., 616–617, 629.

91. Ibid., 380–383.

92. Ibid., 644.

9. Foreign Corporate Criminals

1. "Transcript: Black Money," *Frontline*, PBS, 2009, www.pbs.org/wgbh/pages/frontline /blackmoney/etc/script.html.

2. David Pallister, "The Arms Deal They Called the Dove: How Britain Grasped the Biggest Prize," *Guardian*, December 14, 2006.

3. Neil Roland, "Japan and Canada Failing to Crack Down on Bribes Says Watchdog Group," *Financial Week*, June 25, 2008.

4. Alice Fisher, Assistant Attorney General, U.S. Department of Justice, "Address at the American Bar Review National Institute on the Foreign Corrupt Practices Act," October 16, 2006.

5. See Benjamin Weiser, "For Prosecutor in New York, A Global Beat," *New York Times*, March 28, 2011.

6. H.R. 5175, S. 3295 (111th Cong. Sess. 2), § 102.

7. Michael Robinson, "BBC Lifts the Lid on Secret BAE Slush Fund," BBC News, October 5, 2004.

8. David Leigh and Rob Evans, "BAE's Secret Money Machine," *Guardian*, www.guardian.co .uk/baefiles/page/0,,2095840,00.html.

9. Christopher Drew and Nicola Clark, "BAE Settles Corruption Charges," *New York Times*, February 5, 2010.

10. Robinson, "BBC Lifts the Lid."

11. Josh Meyer, "U.S. Probing BAE Payoff Allegations," *Los Angeles Times*, June 15, 2007; Kevin Sullivan, "Saudi Reportedly Got $2 Billion for British Arms Deal," *Washington Post*, June 8, 2007, A15.

12. On the Application of Corner House Research and Others v. Director of the Serious Fraud Office, 2008 UKHL 60, www.publications.parliament.uk/pa/ld200708/ldjudgmt/jd080730/corner-1.htm.

13. *United States v. Verdugo-Urquidez*, 494 U.S. 259, 281–282 (1990) (Brennan, J., dissenting) (internal quotation and citation omitted).

14. Mark Pieth and Radha Ivory, eds., *Corporate Criminal Liability: Emergency, Convergence, and Risk* (Heidelberg: Springer Dordrecht, 2011).

15. Ibid., 9–13; Allens Arthur Robinson, "'Corporate Culture' as a Basis for the Criminal Liability of Corporations," for the United Nations Special Representative of the Secretary-General on Human Rights and Business (February 2008); Sara Sun Beale and Adam G. Safwat, "What Developments in Western Europe Tell Us about American Critiques of Corporate Criminal Liability," *Buffalo Criminal Law Review* 8 (2004): 110, 160.

16. Nelson D. Schwartz and Lowell Bergman, "Payload: Taking Aim at Corporate Bribery," *New York Times*, November 25, 2007; David Howarth, "Mystery of the Saudi 'Threat,'" *Guardian*, August 1, 2008.

17. Christopher Hope and James Kirkup, "BAE Bribery Case Could Be Reopened," *Telegraph*, April 11, 2008; Christoper Hope, "SFO Was Right to Call Off Saudi Corruption Inquiry, Say Law Lords," *Telegraph*, July 30, 2008.

18. David Leigh and Rob Evans, "U.S. Obtains Swiss Records and Flies in British Witness in BAE Investigation," *Guardian*, November 26, 2007.

19. Helen Power, "Fraud Office to Re-interview BAE Chiefs as Legal Adviser Says It Has a Strong Case," *Times*, December 18, 2009; Alex Spence, "Judge's Comments Throw into Doubt BAE's £30m Pact over Fraud Inquiry," *Times*, March 27, 2010.

20. U.S. Sentencing Memorandum, *United States v. BAE Systems PLC*, No. 1:10-cr-035, 15 (D.D.C. Feb. 22, 2010).

21. Tom Schoenberg and David Voreacos, "UBS Whistle-Blower Secures $104 Million Award from IRS," Bloomberg, September 12, 2012.

22. Alan Fram, "IRS Pays Whistleblower $104 Million," Associated Press, September 11, 2012.

23. A. Westin et al., *Whistleblowing! Loyalty and Dissent in the Corporation* (New York: McGraw-Hill, 1981).

24. 31 U.S.C. §§ 3729–3733.

25. SEC Office of the Whistleblower, "Claim a Reward," www.sec.gov/about/offices/owb/owb-awards.shtml; 15 U.S.C. 78u-6, 6(h)(1)(B).

26. Tax Relief and Health Care Act of 2006, Pub. L. No. 109–432, § 406, 120 Stat. 2958 (2006) (amending I.R.C. § 7623); IRS, *2008 Report to Congress on the Whistleblower Program* (June 24, 2008).

27. Statement of Facts p. *1–3, *U.S. v. Bradley Birkenfeld*, No. 08-cr-60099-ZLOCH (S.D.Fla filed June 18, 2008).

28. Ibid., 2–3.

29. Ibid., 4.

30. Transcript of Sentencing, *30, *U.S. v. Birkenfeld*, No. 08-60099-cr-ZLOCH (S.D.Fla. filed Aug. 26, 2009).

31. Ibid., 31.

32. I.R.C. § 7623(b)(1).

33. Sentencing Memo, 7 (Aug. 18, 2009).

34. Ibid., 4–7.

35. Plea Colloquy, 12–13.

36. Trial Transcript, 123, *U.S. v. Ionia Management*, S.A, No. 07CR134 (JBA) (D.Ct. August 22, 2007).

37. Ibid., 28.

38. The Act to Prevent Pollution from Ships, 33 U.S.C. §§ 1901–15 (2006); International Convention for the Prevention of Pollution from Ships, Nov. 2, 1973, 12 I.L.M. 1319, amended by Protocol, Feb. 17, 1978, 17 I.L.M. 546 (also known as MARPOL); see also H.R. Rep. No. 96–1224, at 1–2 (1980).

39. Oil Record Book, 33 C.F.R. § 151.25(a) (2009); id. § 151.23(a).

40. *United States v. Jho*, 534 F.3d 398, 401 (5th Cir. 2008); *United States v. Ionia Mgmt. S.A.*, 555 F.3d 303, 309 (2d Cir. 2009). Many such cases also involve charges of false statements. U.S. authorities may refer a matter to the home country if it is a treaty signatory. 33 U.S.C. § 1908(f) (2006).

41. Ionia Trial Transcript, 29.

42. 33 U.S.C. § 51908(b) (2006) ("An amount equal to not more than 1/2 of such penalties may be paid by the Secretary, or the Administrator as provided for in this chapter, to the person giving information leading to the assessment of such penalties.").

43. John Christoffersen, "Workers Rewarded for Cooperation in Oil Dump Case," *Huffington Post*, May 11, 2011.

44. Ionia Trial Transcript, 145.

45. Ibid., 36.

46. Ibid., 41.

47. Ibid., 1838–1839 (September 5, 1733).

48. Ibid., 1836.

49. Ibid., 1850.

50. Ibid., 1868.

51. Ibid., 1875.

52. *U.S. v. Ionia Management S.A.*, 555 F.3d 303, 305 (2d Cir. 2009).

53. U.S. Envtl. Prot. Agency, Cruise Ship Discharge Assessment Report, E.P.A. Doc. No. 842-R-07-005, § 1.4 (2008).

54. Jeanne M. Grasso and Allison L. Barlotta, "Presentation at the 2005 International Oil Spill Conference: Criminal Prosecutions and the Maritime Industry: A Worldwide Trend" (May 15, 2005).

55. Nicholas H. Berg, "Bringing It All Back Home: The Fifth and Second Circuits Allow Domestic Prosecutions for Oil Record Book Violations on Foreign-Flagged Vessels," *Tulane Maritime Law Journal* 34 (2009): 277.

56. Richard A. Udell, Senior Trial Attorney, Environmental Crimes Section, U.S. Department of Justice, "Presentation before INTERTANKO: Criminal Vessel Enforcement," March 21, 2005.

57. *Verizon Communications Inc. v. Law Offices of Curtis V. Trinko, LLP*, 540 U.S. 398, 408 (2004).

58. Kurt Eichenwald, *The Informant: A True Story* (New York: Broadway Books, 2000).

59. U.S. Department of Justice, "Division Update Spring 2012: Criminal Program," www.justice.gov/atr/public/division-update/2012/criminal-program.html.

60. FBI, "LCD Price Fixing Conspiracy: Taiwanese Company, Execs Sentenced," press release, November 16, 2012.

61. Transcript of Proceedings, *15, *U.S. v. Lin et al.*, No. 3:09-cr-00110-SI (N.D.C.A., filed September 20, 2012).

62. Ibid., 14–16.

63. Ibid., 21.

64. Ibid., 23.

65. Ibid., 27.

66. Karen Freifeld, "LCD Makers Settle Price-Fixing Case for $553 Million," Reuters, December 7, 2011.

67. Transcript of Proceedings, 18.

68. Ibid., 37–38.

69. U.S. Department of Justice, "Antitrust Division Corporate Leniency Policy," August 10, 1993, www.justice.gov/atr/public/guidelines/0091.pdf.

70. Ibid.; D. Daniel Sokol, "Cartels, Corporate Compliance and What Practitioners Really Think about Enforcement," *Antitrust Law Journal* 77 (2011): 201.

71. Scott D. Hammond, Deputy Assistant Attorney General for Criminal Enforcement, Antitrust Division, U.S. Department of Justice, "Address at the 54th Annual American Bar Association Section of Antitrust Law Spring Meeting: Measuring the Value of Second In Cooperation in Corporate Plea Negotiations," March 29, 2006, 5.

72. Thomas O. Barnett, Assistant Attorney General, Antitrust Division, U.S. Department of Justice, "Presentation at the Georgetown Law Global Antitrust Enforcement Symposium: Global Antitrust Enforcement," September 26, 2007, 2.

73. Antitrust Division, U.S. Department of Justice, "Sherman Act Violations Yielding a Corporate Fine of $10 Million or More," December 5, 2013.

74. Barnett, "Presentation," 2; Gary R. Spratling and D. Jarrett Arp, American Bar Association Section of Antitrust Law 2003 Annual Meeting, *The International Leniency Revolution* (2003), 8–9. On endemic delays in European Union antitrust investigations and prosecutions, see James Kanter, "An Old Chip Cartel Case Is Brought to a Swift End," *New York Times*, May 20, 2010.

75. Antitrust Division, U.S. Department of Justice, "Individual Leniency Policy," August 10, 1994.

76. Foreign Corrupt Practices Act of 1977, Pub. L. No. 95–213, 91 Stat. 1494 (1977) (codified as amended at 15 U.S.C. § 78m, et. Seq. (2006)).

77. Dow Jones State of Anti-Corruption Survey (2011).

78. Yan Leung Cheung, P. Raghavendra Rau, and Aris Stouraitis, "How Much Do Firms Pay as Bribes and What Benefits Do They Get? Evidence from Corruption Cases Worldwide," National Bureau of Economic Research working paper, 2012.

79. Foreign Corrupt Practices Act of 1977, Pub. L. No. 95–213, 91 Stat. 1494 (1977) (codified as amended at 15 U.S.C. §§ 78a, 78m, 78dd-1 to dd-3, 78ff (2006)).

80. OECD Convention on Combating Bribery of Foreign Public Officials in International Business Transactions: Ratification Status as of March 2009 (2009).

81. Convention on Combating Bribery of Foreign Public Officials in International Business Transactions, December 17, 1997, S. Treaty Doc. No. 105–143 (1998), 37 I.L.M. 1.

82. International Anti-Bribery and Fair Competition Act of 1998, Pub. L. No. 105–366, 112 Stat. 3302 (1998) (codified at 15 U.S.C. §§ 78dd-1 to 78dd-3, 78ff (2006)). Earlier 1988 amendments added an affirmative defense permitting a showing that the payment "was lawful under the written laws and regulations" of the foreign county or a "reasonable and bona fide expenditure" incurred by the foreign official. 15 U.S.C. § 78dd-1(c) (2006).

83. 15 U.S.C. § 78dd-1(a), dd-2(i), dd-3(a) (2006) ("alternative jurisdiction" over domestic "person[s]" "irrespective of whether such United States person makes use of the mails or any means or instrumentality of interstate commerce").

84. Robert Khuzami, Director, Division of Enforcement, U.S. Securities and Exchange Commission, "Remarks before the New York City Bar: My First 100 Days as Director of Enforcement," August 5, 2009.

85. Mike Koehler, "An Examination of Foreign Corrupt Practices Act Issues," *Richmond Journal of Global Law and Business* 12 (2013): 317 (noting majority of 2012 FCPA prosecution agreements cited voluntary disclosure).

86. Dionne Searcey, "U.S. Cracks Down on Corporate Bribes," *Wall Street Journal*, May 26, 2009.

87. See 28 C.F.R. §§80.1–80.2 (1994); 15 U.S.C. §§78dd-1(e), 78dd-2(f) (2006).

88. Department of Justice and the Securities Exchange Commission, "A Resource Guide to the U.S. Foreign Corrupt Practices Act," November 14, 2012, 11.

89. 15 U.S.C. § 78u-2.

90. 8 U.S.C. §§1189(c), 1189(a)(2)(A)(i) (2006); *National Council of Resistance v. Department of State*, 251 F.3d 192, 208 (D.C. Cir. 2001).

91. *Kiobel v. Royal Dutch Petroleum*, 133 S.Ct. 1659 (2013).

92. *Morrison v. National Australia Bank*, 130 S. Ct. 2869, 2884–85 (2010).

93. Barry E. Carter et al., *International Law* 649–654 (4th ed. 2003).

94. *Chicago & S. Air Lines, Inc. v. Waterman Steamship Corp.*, 333 U.S. 103, 111 (1948).

95. 509 U.S. 764, 798–799 (1993); Restatement (Third) of the Foreign Relations Law of the United States § 403 (1987).

96. Press Release, Department of Justice, "Akzo Nobel Acknowledges Payments Made by Its Subsidiaries to Iraqi Government under the U.N. Oil for Food Program, Enters Agreement with the Department of Justice," December, 20, 2007.

97. Prepared Remarks of U.S. Asst. Attorney General Alice S. Fisher, ABA Institute on the FCPA, October 16, 2006, 4.

98. Jens Dammann and Henry Hansmann, "Globalizing Commercial Litigation," *Cornell Law Review* 94 (2008): 3.

99. Independent Inquiry Committee, "Report on the Manipulation of the Oil-for-Food Programme by the Iraqi Regime," October 27, 2005.

100. Lynnley Browning, "Swiss Approve Deal for UBS to Reveal U.S. Clients Suspected of Tax Evasion," *New York Times*, June 17, 2010.

101. Ibid.

102. Memorandum from Preet Bharara, U.S. Attorney, S.D.N.Y., U.S. Department of Justice, to Mark F. Pomerantz, Paul, Weiss, Rifkind, Wharton & Garrison LLP, December 21, 2010, 3.

103. Editor, "Liechtenstein Bank Gets Non Prosecution Agreement, to Pay $23.8 Million," *Corporate Crime Reporter*, July 30, 2013.

104. Joint Statement between the U.S. Department of Justice and the Swiss Federal Department of Finance, August 29, 2013.

105. Lynnley Browning and Julia Wedigier, "Switzerland to Allow Its Banks to Disclose Hidden Client Accounts," *New York Times*, May 29, 2013.

106. Reuters, "Greece Says to Settle Siemens Bribery Row," March 9, 2012.

107. Stan Abrams, "What the Siemens Bribery Case Says about the Future of Corruption in China," *Business Insider*, June 30, 2011.

108. Bryan Gibel and Matheus Leitao, "Whistleblower, Politicians Drive Siemens Corruption Probes in Brazil," *Main Justice*, January 9, 2012.

109. Daniel Schäfer, "Siemens Uncovers Bribery Case at Kuwait unit," FT.com, June 10, 2011.

110. Letter from Paul E. Pelletier, Acting Chief, and Mark F. Mendelsohn, Deputy Chief, Criminal Division, Fraud Section, U.S. Department of Justice, to Lawrence Byrne, Linklaters LLP, February 4, 2010, 2, 9.

111. John Collins Rudolf, "Nigeria Drops Bribery Charges against Cheney," *New York Times Green Blog*, December 4, 2010.

112. *US v. Alcatel-Lucent*, Case No. 1:10-cr-20907-MGC (S.D.Fla. filed June 10, 2011), Transcript of Change of Plea and Sentencing Hearing, *43–44.

113. Margaret Ryznar and Samer Korkor, "Anti-Bribery Legislation in the United States and United Kingdom: A Comparative Analysis of Scope and Sentencing," *Missouri Law Review* 76 (2010): 415.

114. Bribery Act, 2010, c. 23, § 6 (Eng.); Bribery: Draft Legislation, U.K. Ministry of Justice 4 (March 25, 2009).

10. The Future of Corporate Prosecutions

1. Barclays Prosecution Agreement, Statement of Facts, ¶13.

2. Barclays CFTC Agreement, 5, www.cftc.gov/ucm/groups/public/@lrenforcementactions/documents/legalpleading/enfbarclaysorder062712.pdf.

3. "LIBOR: The World's Most Important Number," *Moneyweek*, October 10, 2008.

4. Barclays Prosecution Agreement, Statement of Facts, ¶3–4.

5. Ibid., ¶ ¶26; CFTC Agreement, 10.

6. Barclays Prosecution Agreement, ¶¶ 40, 46.

7. CFTC Agreement, 22–23.

8. Andrew Ross Sorkin, "Realities Behind Prosecuting Big Banks," *New York Times*, March 11, 2013.

9. See, e.g., Matt Taibbi, "Gangster Bankers: Too Big to Jail," *Rolling Stone*, February 14, 2013; Victoria Finkle, "Are Some Banks 'Too Big to Jail,'" *American Banker*, January 22, 2013; Jason S. Breslow, "Senators Bash DOJ for 'Evasive' Response on 'Too Big to Jail,'" *PBS.com*, March 5, 2013; *Frontline*, "The Untouchables," PBS, January 22, 2013; Susan Will, Stephen Handelman, and David C. Brotherton, eds., *How They Got Away with It: White Collar Criminals and the Financial Meltdown* (New York: Columbia University Press, 2013).

10. Government Accountability Institute, "Justice Inaction: The Department of Justice's Unprecedented Failure to Prosecute Big Finance," 2012, 16.

11. *The Financial Crisis Inquiry Report: Final Report of the National Commission on the Causes of the Financial and Economic Crisis in the United States*, 2011, 160. A dissenting statement asked whether fraud was "quantitatively significant enough" to be an "essential cause" of the crisis. Ibid., 425.

12. Jed S. Rakoff, "The Financial Crisis: Why Have No High-Level Executives Been Prosecuted?" *New York Review of Books*, January 9, 2014.

13. Ibid., 12–13.

14. Henry N. Pontell, William K. Black, and Gilbert Geis, "Too Big to Fail, Too Powerful to Jail? On the Absence of Criminal Prosecutions after the 2008 Financial Meltdown," *Crime Law Social Change*, 2013.

15. Jonathan Weil, "There is Still Such a Thing as 'Too Big to Jail,'" *BloombergView*, May 6, 2014.

16. Credit Lyonnais, Delta National Bank & Trust Co., Pamrapo Savings Bank, and Riggs Bank were the bank convictions located from 2001–2012. Among the over 2,000 organizational convictions in the dataset, only a dozen additional small financial services or other financial firms were convicted. In January 2014, JPMorgan entered a deferred prosecution agreement for Bank Secrecy Act violations.

17. CFTC Agreement, 34.

18. Nate Raymond, "U.S. Judge Asks if Barclays' Libor Deal Affects 2010 Settlement," Thompson Reuters, June 29, 2012; Aruna Viswanatha, "Judge Dismisses Sanctions Case against Barclays," Thompson Reuters, December 4, 2012.

19. House of Commons Oral Evidence Taken before the Treasury Committee Evidence from Bob Diamond, HC 481-I, 20, 23 (July 4, 2012).

20. Ibid., 35.

21. Ibid., 42.

22. Ben Protess and Mark Scott, "Barclay's C.E.O. Resigns as Bank Frames a Defense," *New York Times*, July 3, 2012.

23. Ben Protess and Mark Scott, "Guilty Plea and Big Fine for Bank in Rate Case," *New York Times*, February 6, 2013.

24. Ben Protess, "Leniency Denied, UBS Unit Admits Guilt in Rate Case," *New York Times*, December 19, 2012.

25. Jim Puzzanghera, "U.S. Says UBS Was Motivated by 'Sheer Greed' in LIBOR Rigging," *Los Angeles Times*, December 19, 2012.

26. Ben Protess and Jessica Silver-Greenberg, "Giant Banks, Seen as Immune, Become Targets," *New York Times*, April 29, 2014.

27. Gabriel Rauterberg and Andrew Verstein, "Index Theory: The Law, Promise and Failure of Financial Indices," *Yale Journal on Regulation* 30 (2013): 1; Nathaniel Popper, "NYSE Euronext to Take over LIBOR," *New York Times*, July 9, 2013.

28. Matt Taibbi, "Everything Is Rigged: The Biggest Price-Fixing Scandal Ever," *Rolling Stone*, April 25, 2013.

29. Ben Protess and Mark Scott, "Barclays Settles Regulators' Claims over Manipulation of Key Rates," *New York Times*, June 27, 2012.

30. *SEC Plaintiff v. Goldman Sachs and Co. and Fabrice Tourre, Defendants,* 2010 WL 1508202 (S.D.N.Y. 2010).

31. US Senate Permanent Subcommittee on Investigations, "Wall Street and the Financial Crisis," April 13, 2011; Pete Yost, "Government Won't Prosecute Goldman Sachs in Probe," *AP Financial Wire,* August 10, 2012.

32. SEC, "Goldman Sachs to Pay Record $550 Million to Settle SEC Charges Related to Subprime Mortgage CDO," July 15, 2010; Consent of Defendant Goldman, Sachs & Co., *SEC v. Goldman, Sachs, & Co.,* No. 10-CV-3229, 2010 WL 2779309 ¶3 (S.D.N.Y. 2010).

33. Peter Lattman, "U.S. Goldman Disclosure a Rare Break in Secrecy," *New York Times,* August 11, 2012.

34. James B. Stewart, "Few Avenues for Justice in the Case against Citi," *New York Times,* December 3, 2011.

35. *U.S. v. McGraw-Hill Companies Inc., and Standard & Poor's Financial Services LLC,* CV13–00779 (C.D.C.A. 2013), Complaint, 72–75.

36. 12 U.S.C. § 1833a.

37. Landon Thomas Jr., "Jury Finds Bank of America Liable in Mortgage Fraud Case," *New York Times,* October 23, 2013.

38. U.S. Department of Justice, "Federal and State Partners Secure Record $13 Billion Global Settlement with JPMorgan for Misleading Investors about Securities Containing Toxic Mortgages," press release, November 17, 2013.

39. Report to the Permanent Subcommittee on Investigations, Committee on Homeland Security and Government Affairs, U.S. Senate, Yvonne Jones, Director, Financial Markets and Community Investment, U.S. Government Accountability Office, *Company Formations: Minimal Information Is Collected and Available,* November 14, 2006, 10.

40. Jeffrey W. Bullock, Delaware Secretary of State, "2011 Annual Report, Delaware Division of Corporations" (2011); Mark Roe, "Delaware's Shrinking Half-Life," *Stanford Law Review* 62 (2009): 137.

41. Internal Revenue Service, Data Book, Table 2 (2011) (reporting 2,313,000 corporations, 4,545,000 S corporations, 3,574,000 partnerships, and 1,385 tax-exempt organizations); see also Annual Jurisdictional Reports, International Association of Commerical Administrators, www.iaca.org/node/80; Daniel M. Häusermann, "For a Few Dollars Less: Explaining State to State Variation in Limited Liability Company Popularity," *University of Miami Business Law Review* 20 (2011): 1. The Census Bureau reports over 27 million businesses, but only about 6 million have employees. U.S. Census Bureau, "Statistics about Business Size (Including Small Businesses)," 2007.

42. Jones, *Company Formations,* 3 (concluding that in 2004, 869,693 corporations were created and 1,068,989 LLCs were formed).

43. Centers for Disease Control and Prevention, "FastStats: Births and Natality," www.cdc.gov/nchs/fastats/births.htm.

44. These include firms that trade American Depository Receipts (ADRs) and subsidiaries of public companies.

45. The total payments made averaged just 0.09 percent of the market capitalization of these public companies.

46. Alexander Dyck, Adair Morse, and Luigi Zingales, "How Pervasive Is Corporate Fraud?" February 2013.

47. Adam Liptak, "U.S. Prison Population Dwarfs That of Other Nations," *New York Times*, April 23, 2008.

48. 18 U.S.C. § 3553(a).

49. *Gall v. United States*, 552 U.S. 38 (2007).

50. U.S. Department of Justice, "Deputy Attorney General James M. Cole Speaks on Alternatives to Incarceration Program: the Use of 'Drug Courts' in the Federal and State Systems," May 21, 2012 ("Any given federal drug court graduation may involve only 10–15 offenders annually—which is clearly small-scale when considering our current prosecution and imprisonment statistics.").

51. See Statistics Div., Admin. Office of the U.S. Courts, *Federal Judicial Caseload Statistics* (2011) (Table D-2, Cases Commenced in Federal Court in a 12-Month Period); 8 U.S.C. § 1325–1326 (illegal entry and reentry); see generally Ingrid V. Eagly, "Prosecuting Immigration," *Northwestern University Law Review* 104 (2010): 1281; Jennifer M. Chacón, "Managing Migration through Crime," *Columbia Law Review Sidebar* 109 (2009): 135; Juliet Stumpf, "The Crimmigration Crisis: Immigrants, Crime, and Sovereign Power," *American University Law Review* 56 (2006): 367.

52. 8 U.S.C. § 1324(a)(1)(A)(iii); *United States v. De Jesus-Batres*, 410 F.3d 154, 160 (5th Cir.2005). It may be hard to show the employer was concealing the illegal status of employees from the government and acting to "facilitate" the person remaining in the United States illegally; there are lesser penalties for failing to verify employee identification documents. 8 U.S.C. § 1324a.

53. "Conspiracy Charges against IFCO Systems," www.visalaw.com/print/13may106.html (last visited April 9, 2013).

54. IFCO Systems Deferred Prosecution Agreement at 2–3 (N.D.N.Y. 2008).

55. The Sentencing Commission reports seventy firms convicted of immigration violations from fiscal 2001 through 2012. U.S. Sentencing Commission, *2001–2012 Sourcebooks of Federal Sentencing Statistics*, Table 52.

56. TRAC Immigration, Syracuse University, "Illegal Reentry Becomes Top Criminal Charge," June 10, 2011; Memorandum from Marcy M. Forman, Director, Office of Investigations, U.S. Department of Homeland Security, to Assistant Director, Deputy Assistant Directors, and Special Agents in Charge, U.S. Immigration Customs and Enforcement, April 30, 2009.

57. Federal Bureau of Prisons, "Quick Facts About the Bureau of Prisons," 2013, www.bop.gov /news/quick.jsp (50 percent of federal prisoners were convicted of drug offenses); Sourcebook of Criminal Justice Statistics Online, Table 6.0023.2011 (2011) (50.7 percent of federal prisoners were convicted of drug offenses); U.S. Department of Justice, Bureau of Justice Statistics, *Prisoners in 2011* (2012), Table 12.

58. U.S. Sentencing Commission, *2012 Sourcebook of Federal Sentencing Statistics* (2013), Tables 37, 39 (in fiscal 2012, about 85 percent of federal drug convicts had no weapon involved in offense, and 53 percent had minor or no criminal history). A 2004 study found 37.5 percent of drug offenders had no criminal history, and of those who did, about 16 percent were violent recidivists. U.S. Department of Justice, Bureau of Justice Statistics, *Drug Use and Dependence, State and Federal Prisoners, 2004* (2006), 4.

59. *U.S. v. Leitch*, No. 11-CR-00609 JG, 2013 WL 753445 (E.D.N.Y., February 28, 2013).

60. U.S. Sentencing Commission, "Special Report to the Congress: Cocaine and Federal Sentencing Policy," B-7 (May 2007).

61. U.S.A.M. § 9–101.200 (1997); U.S.A.M. § 9–100 (the current section does not contain charging guidelines).

62. "Attorney General Eric Holder Delivers Remarks at the Annual Meeting of the American Bar Association's House of Delegates," press release, August 12, 2013.

63. Environmental Protection Agency, "Fiscal Year 2011: Enforcement and Compliance Assurance Accomplishments," 2010; U.S. Sentencing Commission, *2010 Annual Sourcebook* (2011), Table 13.

64. Environmental Protection Agency, "Fiscal Year 2011." The DOJ ENRD reports its results separately; in 2010, it reported $1.3 billion in civil enforcement and $104 million in criminal fines, restitution, community service funds, and special assessments. Department of Justice, "ENRD Accomplishments Reports: Fiscal Year 2010," April 28, 2011.

65. Securities and Exchange Commission, "Select SEC and Market Data," Fiscal Year 2012 (2013), Table 2, www.sec.gov/about/secstats2012.pdf. Similarly, in 2010, of 681 total actions brought by the SEC, only 126 had to do with issuer reporting or disclosure and less than 40 of those involved corporations. Securities and Exchange Commission, "Select SEC and Market Data," Fiscal 2010 (2011), Table 2, www.sec.gov/about/secstats2010.pdf.

66. 15 U.S.C. § 78u-2.

67. U.S. Securities and Exchange Commission, Chair Mary Jo White, "Deploying the Full Enforcement Arsenal," Sept. 26, 2013. The Stronger Enforcement of Civil Penalties Act of 2012 would have permitted the SEC to obtain up to triple the ill-gotten gains or amount of investor losses. Such penalties are currently available in insider trading cases. 15 U.S.C. § 78u-1(a)(2).

68. Gretchen Morgenson, "Quick, Call Tech Support for the S.E.C.," *New York Times*, December 16, 2007.

69. William Donaldson et al., "Muzzling the Watchdog," *New York Times*, April 29, 2008.

70. E.g., UBS Sec. LLC, Exchange Act Release No. 65,733, 2011 WL 5444407, *5 (Nov.10, 2011).

71. The Restoring American Financial Stability Act of 2010, 111 S. Rept. 176 (April 30, 2010).

72. Charles Riley, "SEC Starved for Reform Funds," CNNMoney.com, January 11, 2011.

73. Peter Lattman, "Judge Approves SAC Settlement in Insider Trading Case, with Reservation," *New York Times*, April 16, 2013.

74. United States Senate, Permanent Subcommittee on Investigations, Committee on Homeland Security and Governmental Affairs, "U.S. Vulnerabilities to Money Laundering, Drugs, and Terrorist Financing: HSBC Case History," July 17, 2012, 22–23.

75. Ibid., 327.

76. Albert W. Alschuler, "Two Ways to Think about Punishment of Corporations," *American Criminal Law Review* 46 (2009): 1336.

77. Vikramaditya Khanna, "Corporate Criminal Liability: What Purpose Does It Serve?" *Harvard Law Review* 109 (1996): 1477; Pamela H. Bucy, "Organizational Sentencing Guidelines: The Cart before the Horse," *Washington University Law Quarterly* 71 (1993): 339–340; Gerhard Muller, "Mens Rea and the Corporation," *University of Pittsburgh Law Review* 19 (1957): 21; but see, e.g., Lawrence Friedman, "In Defense of Corporate Criminal Liability," *Harvard Journal Law and Public Policy* 23 (2000): 833.

78. Brief for the Association of Corporate Counsel et al., as Amici Curiae in Support of Appellant Urging Reversal, *United States v. Ionia*, 07-5081-CR, June 6, 2008; see also James

R. Copland, "Regulation by Prosecution: The Problems with Treating Corporations as Criminals," Manhattan Institute Civil Justice Report, December 2010, 13.

79. Peter J. Henning, "Be Careful What You Wish For: Thoughts on a Compliance Defense under the Foreign Corrupt Practices Act," *Ohio State Law Journal* 73 (2012): 883.

80. Ellen S. Podgor, "A New Corporate World Mandates a 'Good Faith' Affirmative Defense," 44 *American Criminal Law Review* 1537 (2007).

81. William S. Laufer, "Corporate Bodies and Guilty Minds," *Emory Law Journal* 43 (1994): 677; Pamela H. Bucy, "Corporate Ethos: A Standard for Imposing Corporate Criminal Liability," *Minnesota Law Review* 75 (1991): 1103.

82. MPC § 2.07.

83. *U.S. v. Ionia Management S.A.*, 555 F.3d 303 (2d Cir. 2009).

84. *United States v. Bank of New England*, 821 F.2d 844, 855 (1st Cir. 1987). For a court adopting such a theory in a civil case, see In re WorldCom, Inc. Sec. Litig., 352 F. Supp. 2d 472, 497 (S.D.N.Y. 2005); but see *Southland Sec. Corp. v. INSpire Ins. Solutions, Inc.*, 365 F.3d 353, 366 (5th Cir. 2004).

85. Robert Jackson, "The Federal Prosecutor," *Journal of Criminal Law amd Criminology* 31 (1940): 3–6.

86. Charles D. Weisselberg and Su Li, "Big Law's Sixth Amendment: The Rise of Corporate White-Collar Practices in Large U.S. Law Firms," *Arizona Law Review* 53 (2011): 1221.

87. Office of the Inspector General, Department of Justice, "The Internal Effects of the Federal Bureau of Investigation's Reprioritization," September 2004; FBI, Financial Crimes Report to the Public, Fiscal Years 2010–2011.

88. E.g., North Carolina Division of Aging and Adult Services, "Senior Consumer Fraud Task Force," www.ncdhhs.gov/aging/fraud/alert.htm.

89. Financial Fraud Enforcement Task Force, "About the Task Force," www.stopfraud.gov/about .html (describing work with state and local partners); National Association of Attorneys General, "Combating Financial Fraud," 2013, www.naag.org/combating-financial-fraud.php.

90. Bruce A. Green, "After the Fall: The Criminal Law Enforcement Response to the S&L Crisis," *Fordham Law Review* 59 (1991): 155.

91. Anton R. Valukas, "White-Collar Crime and Economic Recession," *University of Chicago Legal Forum*, 2010, 14 n. 27.

92. William K. Black, *The Best Way to Rob a Bank Is to Own One* (Austin: University of Texas Press, 2005), xiii–xv.

93. Senator Jeff Merkley, "Merkley Blasts 'Too Big to Jail' Policy for Lawbreaking Banks," press release, December 13, 2012.

94. Chris Good, "Elizabeth Warren Wants HSBC Bankers Jailed for Money Laundering," ABC News, May 7, 2013.

95. Rakoff, "The Financial Crisis," 17.

96. Henry M. Hart Jr., "The Aims of the Criminal Law," *Law and Contemporary Problems* 23 (1958): 404.

97. Federal Acquisitions Regulations (FAR) §§ 9.406–2 and 9.407–2 (listing causes for debarment).

98. U.S. Government Accountability Office, "Suspension and Debarment: Some Agency Programs Need Greater Attention, and Governmentwide Oversight Could Be Improved," August 2011, 1, 9, 18.

99. Ibid., 9, 18.

100. Kyle Noonan, "The Case for a Federal Corporate Charter Revocation Penalty," *George Washington Law Review* 80 (2012): 602.

101. "Congress Expands Incentives for Whistleblowers to Report Suspected Violations to the SEC," *Harvard Law Review* 124 (2011): 1829 (quoting Bruce Carton).

102. 17 C.F.R. § 240.21F-5 (2011) (providing whistle-blowers may obtain 10–30 percent of award).

103. Sensible criticisms of such efforts have been made by scholars, including myself. See, e.g., Rachel E. Barkow, "The Prosecutor as Regulatory Agency," in *Prosecutors in the Boardroom*, ed. Anthony S. Barkow and Rachel E. Barkow, 181 (New York: New York University Press, 2011); Brandon L. Garrett, "Collaborative Organization Prosecution," in *Prosecutors in the Boardroom*, ed. Barkow and Barkow, 170–171.

104. David Weisburd et al., *Crimes of the Middle Classes: White-Collar Offenders in the Federal Courts* (New Haven, CT: Yale University Press, 1991), 40–43, 85.

105. Jennifer Arlen, "Removing Prosecutors from the Boardroom," in *Prosecutors in the Boardroom*, ed. Barkow and Barkow, 78–79.

106. Remarks of the Honorable Edward M. Kennedy, U.S. Sentencing Commission, Symposium Proceedings: "Corporate Crime in America: Strengthening the 'Good Citizen' Corporation," 1995, 120.

107. Report of the Ethics Resource Center's Independent Advisory Group, "The Federal Sentencing Guidelines for Organizations at Twenty Years, a Call to Action for More Effective Promotion and Recognition of Effective Compliance and Ethics Programs," 2012, 4.

108. Tony Chapelle, "Boards Beef Up Compliance Expenditures," *Agenda*, December 16, 2013 (reporting results of Association of Corporate Counsel survey).

109. U.S. Government Accountability Office, "DOJ Has Taken Steps to Better Track Its Use of Deferred and Non-Prosecution Agreements, but Should Evaluate Effectiveness," December 2009, 20.

110. I served as a reporter on an American Bar Association Task Force subcommittee making initial recommendations regarding practices for corporate monitors.

111. 12 C.F.R. §21.21; 31 U.S.C. § 5318(h)(1)(D).

112. Criminal Division of the U.S. Department of Justice and Enforcement Division of the U.S. Securities and Exchange Commission, *A Resource Guide to the U.S. Foreign Corrupt Practices Act* 58, 62 (2012).

113. Financial Crisis Inquiry Report, xvii–xix.

114. Lucian Bebchuk et al., "The Wages of Failure: Executive Compensation at Bear Stearns and Lehman 2000–2008," *Yale Journal on Regulation* 27 (2010): 259.

115. Dodd-Frank Wall Street Reform and Consumer Protection Act § 954, 124 Stat. at 1904; Sarbanes-Oxley Act of 2002 § 304, 15 U.S.C. § 7243 (2006); 15 U.S.C. § 78u-3(c)(3) (2006); Terrance Gallogly, "Enforcing the Clawback Provision: Preventing the Evasion of Liability under Section 954 of the Dodd-Frank Act," *Seton Hall Law Review* 42 (2012): 1245.

116. 17 CFR § 240.13a-14(a); 17 CFR § 240.15d-14(a); Securities Exchange Act of 1934, 15 U.S.C. § 78u.

117. Alison Frankel, "Sarbanes-Oxley's Lost Promise: Why CEOs Haven't Been Prosecuted," Thompson Reuters, July 27, 2012; Robert J. A. Zito, "SOX 302 Certifications: What Are They Good For?" *New York Law Journal*, November 19, 2007.

118. *SEC v. Goldman, Sachs, & Co.*, No. 10-CV-3229, 2010 WL 2779309 ¶3 (S.D.N.Y. 2010).

119. U.S. Department of Justice, "Amgen Inc. Pleads Guilty to Federal Charge in Brooklyn; Pays $762 Million to Resolve Criminal Liability and False Claims Act Allegations," December 19, 2012.

120. Anne Blythe and Joseph Neff, "Judge Refuses to Accept WakeMed Settlement with Federal Prosecutors," *News and Observer*, January 17, 2013.

121. Order, *U.S. v. WakeMed*, No. 5:12-CR-398-BO (E.D.N.C. February 8, 2013).

122. Jessica Silver-Greenberg and Ben Protess, "Doubt Is Cast on Firms Hired to Help Banks," *New York Times*, January 31, 2013.

123. Hearing at 5–6, *U.S. v. Barclays*, No. CR 10–218 (D.D.C. August 18, 2010).

124. Ibid., 24, 36, 39; Status Hearing, *U.S. v. Barclays*, No. CR 10–218 (D.D.C. November 23, 2010).

125. Memorandum and Order, *U.S. v. HSBC Bank USA, N.A.*, 12-CR-763 (E.D.N.Y. July 1, 2003).

126. Memorandum and Order 28, 45, *U.S. v. APTx Vehicle Systems Ltd.*, No. 12-10374-WGY (D.Ma. July 26, 2013).

127. Gerard E. Lynch, "Panel Discussion: The Expanding Prosecutorial Role from Trial Counsel to Investigator and Administrator," *Fordham Urban Law Journal* 26 (1999): 682.

128. John C. Coffee, "'No Soul to Damn: No Body to Kick': An Unscandalized Inquiry into the Problem of Corporate Punishment," *Michigan Law Review* 79 (1981): 386.

129. E.g., Joel Bakan, *The Corporation: The Pathological Pursuit of Profit and Power* (New York: Free Press, 2004), 79.

130. John Dewey, "The Historic Background of Corporate Legal Personality," *Yale Law Journal* 35 (1926): 666–667.

131. Henry Pontell, *A Capacity to Punish: The Ecology of Crime and Punishment* (Bloomington: Indiana University Press, 1982), 33–36.

132. On the need for further white-collar research generally, see Sally S. Simpson, "White-Collar Crime: A Review of Recent Developments and Promising Directions for Future Research," *Annual Review of Sociology* 39 (2013): 309.

Appendix

1. Brandon L. Garrett and Jon Ashley, Federal Organizational Prosecution Agreements, University of Virginia School of Law, http://lib.law.virginia.edu/Garrett/prosecution_agreements/home.suphp.

2. Brandon L. Garrett and Jon Ashley, Federal Organizational Plea Agreements, University of Virginia School of Law, http://lib.law.virginia.edu/Garrett/plea_agreements/home.php.

3. Letter from L. Ralph Mecham, Director, Administrative Office of the U.S. Courts, to the Honorable William W. Wilkins Jr., Chairman, United States Sentencing Commission, June 22, 1988, 2. The commission collects data on firms sentenced under the Organizational Sentencing Guidelines, but some firms are sentenced under other provisions, such as the alternative fines statute. Cindy R. Alexander, Jennifer Arlen, and Mark A. Cohen, "Regulating Corporate Criminal Sanctions: Federal Guidelines and the Sentencing of Public Firms," *Journal of Law and Economics* 42 (1999): 416, 419–420; Cindy R. Alexander, Jennifer Arlen, and Mark A Cohen, "Evaluating Trends in Corporate Sentencing: How

Reliable Are the U.S. Sentencing Commission's Data?" *Federal Sentencing Reporter* 13 (2000): 109–110.

4. The commission did not respond to several requests asking them to make available data for research purposes. I also asked the Office of Probation and Pretrial Services to share data with me, and in early 2013 it denied the request, suggesting that I contact the commission.

ACKNOWLEDGMENTS

This book benefited from invaluable comments on the manuscript by Kerry Abrams, Richard Abrams, Jennifer Arlen, Richard Bonnie, Andrew Boutros, Stephen Braga, Sam Buell, Joshua Fischman, Trevor Garmey, Bonnie Garrett, Amy Halliday, Mark Johnson, Ed Kitch, Lee Kovarsky, John McGlothlin, JJ Prescott, Brian Sawers, David Uhlmann, Urska Velikonja, Ethan Yale, and David Zaring. I thank Elizabeth Knoll, my editor at Harvard University Press, for her expert guidance in helping to shape this project from beginning to end. I am grateful for the useful comments from the anonymous reviewers, and to all of those at Harvard University Press whose work improved the manuscript. I thank my agent, Chris Calhoun, for his assistance and encouragement.

The research grew out of two law review articles studying aspects of corporate prosecutions: "Globalized Corporate Prosecutions," *Virginia Law Review* 97 (2011), and "Structural Reform Prosecution," *Virginia Law Review* 93 (2007). Shorter works exploring corporation prosecutions include: "Corporate Confessions," *Cardozo Law Review* 30 (2009), and "Collaborative Organizational Prosecution," a chapter in *Prosecutors in the Boardroom*, ed. Rachel Barkow and Anthony Barkow (New York: New York University Press, 2011). I thank for their helpful comments on that earlier research, Kenneth Abraham, Jennifer Arlen, Miriam Baer, Rachel Barkow, Tony Barkow, Josh Beaton, Richard Bierschbach, Darryl Brown, Albert Choi, George Cohen, Anne Coughlin, Quinn Curtis, Viet Dihn, Chris Elmendorf, Lisa Griffin, Paul Halliday, Toby Heytens, Richard Hynes, Jim Jacobs, Mike Koehler, Jody Kraus, Paul Mahoney, Greg Mitchell, John Monahan, Jed Purdy, Dan Richman, Jonathan Rusch, George Rutherglen, Richard Schragger, Molly Shadell, David Sklansky, Daniel Sokol, Paul Stephan, Susan Sturm, Mila Versteeg, and George Yin. The book benefited from several presentations at UVA law school, as well as at the University of Maryland School of Law and the University of Münster, Germany. The earlier work also benefited from presentations at Georgetown, George Washington University, New York University, Washington and Lee University, and Washington University law schools. I thank students in my corporate crime seminars and federal criminal law courses for their comments over the years. I also thank Tim Heaphy, Andy Mao, Jonathan Rusch, Dr. Theo Waigel, Joseph Warin, and many others who have been involved in these fascinating corporate prosecutions for taking the time to speak to me about their work.

Assembling the database of federal corporate prosecution agreements was possible only with invaluable help over the years from Jon Ashley and the University of Virginia Law Library. Jon Ashley has helped not only to collect that material but also to collect data from these prosecution agreements, organize these materials so that they could be made available online as a resource, and collect U.S. Sentencing Commission data, and he has helped throughout with the process of considering what new types of data we could examine. Jon has simply been invaluable to this research since it began in 2006, when I first started to collect federal corporate deferred and non-prosecution agreements. I also thank John Roper and Michelle Morris of the University of Virginia Law Library for their help over the years with this work, and the many prosecutors, defense lawyers, and other practitioners who have brought corporate prosecution agreements to our attention and provided useful feedback over the years on the online resource pages.

Once these materials were collected and scanned, a team of superlative research assistants helped to review and code all of the documents, as well as provide research assistance regarding legal issues raised by such prosecutions: James Cass, Christine Chang, Caitlin Connolley, Amanda Gill, Emily Green, Audrey Golden, Daniel Guarnera, Yaqiong Huang, Mark Johnson, Bryan Jones, Benjamin Lubarsky, Kyle Mathews, Walker McCusik, Tim McLaughlin, Erin Montgomery, Brian Rho, Richard Rothblatt, Georgina Shepard, Louis Shernisky, Melina Shoppa, Elaine Singerman, Elizabeth Studdard, and Stephen Sun. Vahid Gholampour provided invaluable help discussing and conducting the regression analysis presented in the Appendix.

This book would not have been possible without the intellectual contributions of my generous and thoughtful colleagues at the University of Virginia

School of Law. This research was also financially supported by summer research grants from UVA Law.

My most heartfelt appreciation is reserved for my family, who supported this work over many years. My greatest thanks are to my wife, Kerry Abrams, who is a lovely and brilliant partner in all things.

INDEX

ABA. *See* American Bar Association

ABB Ltd., 166–168, 315n81, 335nn99–102, 104–05, 341n26

Abbott Laboratories, 170, 293

Acceptance of responsibility, 60–62, 85, 148, 159, 160–162, 236, 256, 283, 315n74, 333n60

Acquittals, 79, 98, 111, 113, 115, 127, 131, 206, 214–217, 262, 280, 325n170, 341n39, 343nn78,79

Act to Prevent Pollution from Ships (APPS), 230–233, 345n38

AIG, 187

Alschuler, Albert, 268, 269, 352n76

American Bar Association (ABA), 66, 179–180, 279, 320n46

Antitrust, 234–239; Antitrust Division of DOJ, 66, 84, 237–238, 321n69; Bank of America case, 66; BMS, 182–183; corporate leniency program, 76, 84, 237–238; fines, 150, 158, 199, 235; immunity deals, 96–97; price fixing, 234; prosecutions of foreign firms, 215–216, 234–238, 243

Arlen, Jennifer, 56, 155, 160, 278

Arthur Andersen, 12–13, 19–44, 84–87; conviction reversed on appeal, 41–42; sentencing, 147–148

Ashcroft, John, 189–190, 339n66

Attorney-client privilege, 91, 180

AU Optronics, 199, 235–237

BAE, 15, 218–219, 221–225, 246, 293

Banks, 2, 16, 65, 254–255; convictions of, 254–255, 258–259; LIBOR prosecutions, 250–252, 256–258; non-prosecution agreements, 254; prosecutions for Bank Secrecy Act violations, 100–104, 279; prosecutions of employees, 84; Swiss Banks, 228–229, 244–245; "too big to jail" concerns with non-prosecutions, 2, 254–255, 259–261

Bank Secrecy Act, 100–104, 259, 279, 349n16

Barclays, 61, 103, 157, 250–252, 256–257

Bharara, Preet, 219

Bibas, Stephanos, 143

Bierschbach, Richard, 143

Big Pharma, 104–106; settlements, 277

Birkenfeld, Bradley, 225–227

Black, William K., 82, 253, 272

BP, 14, 117–122, 127, 128–146, 181–183

Brady v. Maryland, 204, 206–207

Braithwaite, John, 57

Breach of prosecution agreement, 75–76, 78, 166, 193

Breyer, Justice Stephen, 155, 199

Bribery Act, 15, 248

Bristol-Myers Squibb, 77, 173–174

Brooklyn Plan, 54–56

Buell, Samuel, 168, 321, 325, 334, 335

CEO, 23, 61, 72, 180; acknowledgements of responsibility by, 151; acquittals of, 98, 214, 280; apology by, 256–257; convictions of, 14, 99, 115; denial of knowledge by, 108; failure to prosecute, 255; firing, 15, 73, 173, 183; knowledge of crimes, 21; prosecutions of, 97, 99, 107, 115; resignations by, 11, 21, 27, 111; sentencing of, 87; walk of shame, 84–85, 169

Certification, 280–281

CFO, 107, 108, 280

Chamber of Commerce, 41, 92, 269

Christie, Chris, 189

CITGO, 136–137

Citizens United v. F.E.C., 4, 200–202

Class actions, 137–140

Clawbacks, 72, 103, 280

Clean Air Act, 99, 121

Cohen, Mark, 98

Collateral consequences, 16, 42, 150, 170, 275, 285; as concern of prosecutors, 59, 286; as factor in leniency, 63, 255; prosecuting subsidiaries instead of parent to avoid, 170, 258, 274. *See also* Debarment

Collective knowledge theory, 270

Commodities Futures Trading Commission (CFTC), 256

Community Service, 14, 141–142

Compliance, 55, 71–80, 191–195, 237, 276–278; affirmative defense, 155, 269; assessing compliance, 159, 278–279; credit for compliance, 159–160; in DPAs or NPAs, 48; as factor in decision to prosecute, 56, 148–149, 156; lack of, 190–191; plea agreement terms, 11, 70, 72; supervision by monitors, 11, 13, 70, 145, 163, 175–176, 182–190; terms in deferred prosecution agreements, 74–75, 181

Conspiracy, 111; to commit securities fraud, 174; to defraud the United States, 227; to file false tax returns, 113; to fix prices, 199, 235–236; to violate the FCPA, 107

Cooperation, 31–32, 58–59, 160–161; and amnesty, 66–67, 237; among prosecutors, 272, 298; coerced, 231; factor in decision whether to prosecute, 56, 316n104; factor in fine-reduction, 159, 328n83; global, 223, 225, 229, 238, 244, 246–247; of informants, 88–93; and leniency, 3, 11–12, 19, 62, 63, 103, 113, 148–149, 156, 171, 215, 256, 274, 286; money reward for, 233; non-cooperation, 225, 236, 321n69; terms in agreements requiring, 182

Corporate crime rate, 261–263

Corporate criminal liability, 270; foreign standards for corporate criminal liability, 183, 223–224; and homicide, 130–131; legal establishment of, 4, 33–36; proposals to alter standards, 268–269; purpose of, 217; questioning of concept, 167; undermining of, 171. *See also* Respondeat superior (Master-Servant rule)

Debarment, 42, 67, 150; corporate death sentence, 150, 275; from Medicare or Medicaid, 105

Deepwater Horizon, 143–146, 266

Deferred prosecution agreements, 6, 13, 143, 165, 255; compliance terms, 74–75; criticism, 67, 103; judicial review, 75, 282; origins, 55–56; U.K. adoption, 248; unrelated terms, 76–77, 83

Department of Health and Human Services Office of Inspector General, 105, 106, 110

Department of Justice (DOJ): Asset Forfeiture and Money Laundering Section, 124; Corporate Fraud Task Force, 54–55, 107; Financial Fraud Enforcement Task Force, 55; Office of International Affairs, 229; policy on monitors, 174–175; policy on privilege waivers, 114; policy on prosecution, 55–56; policy on victims, 128; violations of *Brady v. Maryland*, 206–207

Deterrence, 83, 99–100, 149, 155, 275

Deutsche Bank, 50, 79, 245

Dodd-Frank Act, 37, 43, 226, 267, 275, 280

DOJ. *See* Department of Justice

Double jeopardy, 214, 243, 342n75

Drug prosecutions, 264–265

Ebbers, Bernard, 108–109

Employee prosecutions, 12, 82–84; crimes of prosecution, 83; lack of, 13, 96, 115; numbers of officers and employees prosecuted accompanying organizational deferred and non-prosecution agreements, 83–84, 96–97; numbers prosecuted accompanying organizational plea agreements, 84

ENRD. *See* Environment and Natural Resources Division

Enron, 19–33

Environmental crimes, 128–129, 178

Environmental Protection Agency (EPA), 129, 191, 266–267; and BP, 122, 135–136, 145; and Dow Chemical Company, 209

Environment and Natural Resources Division (ENRD), 65–66, 129, 178

Epstein, Richard, 66–67

False Claims Act, 355n119

FBI. *See* Federal Bureau of Investigation

FCPA. *See* Foreign Corrupt Practices Act

Federal Bureau of Investigation (FBI), 205–207, 271–172
Fifth Amendment rights, 92–94, 201, 211–212
Filip, Mark F., 56
Financial Fraud Enforcement Task Force, 6, 54–55
Financial Institutions Reform, Recovery, and Enforcement Act (FIRREA), 260
Fines, 68–68, 157–158; Alternative Fines Act, 133; antitrust fines, 235; average corporate fines, 292; cases involving no fine, 149; civil fines, 241; corporate criminal fines, 5; and DPAs or NPAs, 294; fines against foreign corporations, 220–221; largest corporate criminal fines, 149–150, 293; payment, 295; and restitution paid, 125; total criminal fines for organizations, 5
FIRREA. *See* Financial Institutions Reform, Recovery, and Enforcement Act
Fisse, Brent, 57
Food, Drug, and Cosmetics Act (FDCA), 104, 110
Food and Drug Administration (FDA), 104, 110, 154
Foreign companies, 219–222
Foreign Corrupt Practices Act (FCPA): enactment of the FCPA, 9–10, 36, 239–240; fines, 304; guidance from DOJ and SEC, 241; numbers of FCPA corporate prosecutions, 240; prosecutions of foreign companies, 239; prosecutions of individual employees, 95–96; SEC enforcement, 241–242; types of resolutions, 241
Forfeiture, 124–125, 139
Fortune 500, 62
Fortune Global 500, 62
Fourth Amendment rights, 202, 207–210
Fraud: definition of, 64–65; health care fraud, 65, 104–105; legislation against, 43; mail fraud, 65; mortgage fraud, 271; number of federal fraud convictions, 115; psychology of, 88; securities fraud, 65, 138, 177–178, 267; sentencing, 162; tax fraud, 136, 227; wire fraud, 65

GAO. *See* Government Accountability Office
Garrity v. New Jersey, 93
Germany, 3, 10, 183, 224, 240
GlaxoSmithKline (GSK), 106, 293
Gleeson, Judge John, 265, 283
Global financial crisis, 127, 250, 251

Goldman Sachs, 259–260
Google, 45
Government Accountability Office (GAO), 278, 299
Guidant, 153–154, 293

Hale v. Henkel, 208, 211
HealthSouth, 97–98, 214
HHS-OIG. *See* Department of Health and Human Services Office of Inspector General
Holder, Eric, 252, 253, 265
HSBC, 101–104, 273, 283

Immigration prosecutions, 264
Informants, 12, 84, 89, 234
Internal Revenue Service (IRS), 51, 52–54, 67, 79, 226, 228–229
Ionia Management, S.A., 229–234
IRS. *See* Internal Revenue Service

Jacobs, James, 176
Jaros, David, 140
Jenkins & Gilchrist, 79
JPMorgan, 124, 260
Judicial review, 285; lack of requirement for, 190
Jurisdiction, 242–244; over foreign companies, 219, 221–222, 230
Jury instructions, 37

Kahan, Dan, 168
Kaplan, Judge Lewis, 58, 94, 112
Kennedy, Justice Anthony, 41, 201
Khanna, Vikramaditya, 43
KPMG, 48–53, 54; coercion of, 94–95; confession, 60; as cooperator, 89; deferred prosecution agreement, 13–14; employee prosecutions, 88–90, 93; end of DOJ agreement with, 78; negotiations with prosecutors, 58–60; outcome of cases, 112–114; punishment of, 67–68; senate testimony, 45–46; waiver of privilege, 92

Lacey, Frederick B., 174, 181, 182
Levin, Sen. Carl, 46, 52, 53, 102, 260

LIBOR, 250–252, 257, 259
Lynch, Judge Gerard, 285

Madoff, Bernard, 43, 124, 161–162
Magic pipe, 230–234, 269
Market capitalization, 70, 133, 262n45
Marshall, Chief Justice John, 200
Mass incarceration, 263–266
McNulty, Paul J., 56
Mendelsohn, Mark, 240
Money laundering: Asset Forfeiture and Money
    Laundering Section at DOJ, 124; average fines,
    295; Bank Secrecy Act and related laws and
    regulations, 37, 97, 100, 279; charges in deferred
    prosecution agreements, 64; FBI's Financial
    Intelligence Center, 272; fines, 150; HSBC case,
    101–104, 265, 268; individual prosecution, 84
Monitors, 15; data on use in deferred and
    non-prosecution agreements, 175; cost of, 187,
    189–190; definition of, 174–175; foreign
    corporate, 247; improving effectiveness, 191–192,
    278–279, 228–284, 286; lack of, 190–191;
    monitor appointment, 177–178; revolving-door
    concern, 271; SEC monitors, 267; selection of,
    178–179, 284; work of, 184–186
Morgan Stanley, 98–99

Nader, Ralph, 67
New York Attorney General's Office, 272, 298
New York Central & Hudson River Railroad v.
    United States, 4, 33–36
Non-prosecution agreements, 8, 76, 291; compared
    to declinations, 7–8, 254; criticism, 274, 283;
    numbers of non-prosecution agreements, 76;
    terms of agreements, 74–75; undisclosed
    agreements, 64; victims rights, 140; Wall Street
    banks, 255

Obstruction of justice, 25–27, 43, 86, 209
OCC. See Office of the Comptroller of the
    Currency
Occupational Safety and Health Administration
    (OSHA): 120–121, 132–135
Office of the Comptroller of the Currency
    (OCC), 268

Organizational Sentencing Guidelines: 147–148,
    278, 286; adoption of the guidelines, 155–156;
    corporate death penalty, 156–157; factors
    increasing punishment, 158–159; factors
    reducing fines, 159–161; fines, 157–158
Organization for Economic Cooperation and
    Development (OECD), 71; OECD convention,
    239–240
Ostrich instruction: 82; trial of Bernard Ebbers,
    108–109

Panalpina, 95, 160
Pfizer: 6, 70, 104–105; Pharmacia & Upjohn: 166,
    169–170, 293
Pinto, 130–131
Plea agreements, 162–163
Posner, Judge Richard, 81
Privilege waiver, 92, 114
Probation, 163–165, 169
Public corporations, 13, 22–23, 42, 262–263;
    FCPA prosecutions, 239; fines for those
    prosecuted, 70, 150, 301–303; numbers
    prosecuted, 262–263; prosecutions of
    employees, 84, 96, 107

Rakoff, Judge Jed, 253, 273
Recidivism, 165–168
Respondeat superior (Master-Servant rule), 4,
    35–36, 81; comparison with corporate liability
    standards in other countries, 223–224
Restitution, 69, 122, 123–124, 125–126
Revolving door concern, 271

SAC Capital, 258, 285
Sarbanes-Oxley, 43, 137, 180, 280
Saudi Arabia: HSBC, 102; Al Yamamah, 218
SEC. See Securities and Exchange Commission
Securities and Exchange Commission (SEC),
    22, 137, 267–268; civil enforcement against
    corporations, 267–268; civil settlements
    and admissions, 60–61, 267–268; FCPA
    enforcement, 240–242, 267; Office of the
    Whistleblower, 225–226
Sentencing Guidelines. See Organizational
    Sentencing Guidelines

Serious Fraud Office, 218, 222–223, 224–225, 248

Seton Hall Law School, 77n131, 182

Shareholders, 21, 23, 138–139

Siemens, 1–3, 8–12, 151–153, 173, 183–184, 184–186, 193–195, 246, 293

Sixth Amendment rights, 212–213

Skeel, David, 43

Skilling, Jeffrey, 87, 115

Sotomayor, Justice Sonia, 198–199, 201

Southern Union v. United States, 196–200, 217

Specter, Sen. Arlen, 95–96

Standard & Poor's, 260

Stevens, Justice John Paul, 201

Stora Enso Oyj, 214–216

Structural reform, 176–177, 276–277

Stuntz, William, 43, 207

Subpoena, 53, 202, 207–209, 211

Subsidiaries: convicted rather than the parent, 169–170; corporate culture, 104–107; foreign subsidiaries, 258; recidivist corporations, 166–167

Sutherland, Edwin, 87

Switzerland, 2, 48, 222, 226–227, 228, 244–245

Tax shelters, 46, 49–52, 79–80

Thompson, Larry, 56

Thompson Memorandum, 56, 91; factors, 59, 65; revisions in Filip Memo, 56

Too big to fail, 1, 252–253, 258

Too big to jail: criticism of bank prosecutions, 2, 253; criticisms of corporate prosecutions generally, 1–2, 254–255

UBS, 226–228, 244–245, 258

Uhlmann, David, 73

U.N. Iraq Oil for Food Program, 244

United Kingdom, 218, 223, 225, 248

United States v. Booker, 155

Upjohn v. United States, 91

U.S. Attorney's Manual, 56, 163

U.S. Coast Guard, 229–233

U.S. Postal Inspection Service, 68

U.S. Sentencing Commission: 6, 26; data collection, 63; data, 125

U.S. State Department, 225

UVA Law Library, 7, 291

Victims: role in corporate prosecution, 14, 145–146; Crime Victims' Rights Act, 127, 136; victims and deferred prosecution, 140–141; victims' rights, 122–124; victims' statements, 131–132, 134

Volcker, Paul, 244

Waigel, Theo, 11, 173, 183–186

Wegelin & Company, 245

Whistle-blowers, 104–105, 225–228; Dodd-Frank Wall Street Reform and Consumer Protection Act, 275

White-collar crime: concept of, 87–88; evolving federal law, 36–37; individuals prosecuted, 82–83; recidivism, 165; sentencing, 43

Worldcom, 108–109

Zimmerman, Adam, 140